Moses Mendelssohn and the Enlightenment

SUNY Series in Judaica:
Hermeneutics, Mysticism, and Religion

Michael Fishbane, Robert Goldenberg, and Elliot Wolfson, Editors

Moses Mendelssohn and the Enlightenment

Allan Arkush

STATE UNIVERSITY OF NEW YORK PRESS

Production by Ruth Fisher
Marketing by Fran Keneston

Published by
State University of New York Press, Albany

For information, address the State University of New York Press,
State University Plaza, Albany, NY 12246

Library of Congress Cataloging-in-Publication Data
Arkush, Allan, 1949–
    Moses Mendelssohn and the Enlightenment / Allan Arkush.
        p.   cm. — (SUNY series in Judaica)
    Includes bibliographical references and index.
    ISBN 0-7914-2071-X. — ISBN 0-7914-2072-8 (pbk.)
    1. Mendelssohn, Moses, 1729–1786.   2. Leibniz, Gottfried Wilhelm,
Freiherr von, 1646–1716—Influence.   3. Wolff, Christian, Freiherr
von, 1679–1754—Influence.   4. Enlightenment.   5. Philosophy,
Jewish.   6. Haskalah.   I. Title.   II. Series.
B2693.A75   1994
193—dc20   93-39401
                                                            CIP

10 9 8 7 6 5 4 3 2 1

In memory of my grandfather,

Samuel Squire

Contents

Acknowledgments

A decade and a half ago, when I was a graduate student at Brandeis University and he was already "retired," I made the acquaintance of the late Professor Alexander Altmann. I asked him a question pertaining to one of his articles on Moses Mendelssohn, something having to do with Mendelssohn's views with regard to the immortality of the soul. He gave me a concise, useful answer, and took my phone number. The next day he called and invited me to come to his home. There he treated me to tea, conversation, offprints, and suggestions. He encouraged me very strongly to consider doing a dissertation on Mendelssohn. When I remarked that he himself may have rendered any such study superfluous, he said only one thing: *"yesh od makom le-hitgadder bo"*; that is, there is still room for further work.

I eventually came to agree with him and did write a dissertation on Mendelssohn under the direction of Professor Marvin Fox, to whom I am deeply indebted for his skillful guidance, invaluable instruction, and constant moral support. The book that follows constitutes a revised and expanded version of that dissertation.

I owe an incalculably large debt of gratitude to my undergraduate adviser and lifelong counselor, Professor Werner J. Dannhauser. It is from him, above all, that I have learned how to avoid splitting either my infinitives or, much more important, my loyalties.

I would like to thank Norman and Yedida Stillman, my colleagues and sometime chairpersons at Binghamton University, who did all they could to facilitate the completion of this book (not to mention a host of other things). I wish to express my gratitude, in addition, to the Lynde and Harry Bradley Foundation for granting me a research fellowship during the academic year 1991–92, without which I would never have been able to finish this volume.

Finally, I have to thank Bonnie and Arielle for their help. It was not academic, but it was indispensable.

Introduction

There is no other figure in the history of modern Jewish thought quite like Moses Mendelssohn. He is unique, to begin with, in having been the only important thinker to combine adherence to the rationalist philosophy of the German Enlightenment with loyalty to Judaism. While there have been many Jewish Kantians, Hegelians, existentialists, and so on, Mendelssohn was the only noteworthy Jewish disciple of Leibniz and Wolff.

Mendelssohn is quite unusual, too, in having attained great prominence outside the Jewish world. With the possible exception of Martin Buber, none of the other thinkers commonly reckoned among the most important philosophers of Judaism in modern times has enjoyed a comparably high regard in leading non-Jewish intellectual circles. In the middle of the eighteenth century, Mendelssohn was widely known as "the German Socrates," and even today, at a time when the philosophical school to which he belonged has for the most part ceased to be of interest, there are scholars who stress the significance of his position in the rationalist tradition.[1]

One can say also that Mendelssohn's uniqueness lies in the degree to which his activities as a cultural and political reformer have come to overshadow his significance as a philosopher of Judaism. Even though Jewish historians no longer follow Heinrich Graetz, the nineteenth-century pioneer of Jewish historiography, in according immense importance to Mendelssohn's activities, most still continue to see him as a major participant in the shaping of the modern Jewish world, as a man who contributed greatly to bringing the Jews of Europe "out of the ghetto" and into the mainstream of Western civilization.[2] In the history of Jewish religious thought, on the other hand, Mendelssohn is usually described as the propounder of an "ephemeral solution" to the new problems confronting Judaism, as the blazer of a trail that few subsequently chose to follow.[3]

Nevertheless, in spite of the fact that his interpretation of Judaism constituted something of a "dead end," it has continued to attract a considerable amount of attention. Over the years, there has been a steady, if never especially broad, stream of scholarly treatments of the concept of Judaism elaborated in *Jerusalem* and in some of Mendelssohn's other works. There are, I believe, two main reasons for this. First, Mendelssohn's very prominence has made it virtually inevitable that researchers would continue to reexamine his fundamental principles. Second, his efforts mark the *first* major attempt by a modern thinker to reconcile any branch of the European Enlightenment with Judaism. As the founder of modern Jewish thought, he simply cannot be overlooked.

The purpose of this study is to make one more contribution to the already extensive literature dealing with Mendelssohn's synthesis of the philosophy of Leibniz and Wolff and Judaism. In spite of everything that scholars have written so far, there is, in my opinion, much more to be said on this subject. The true character of Mendelssohn's thought has not yet been sufficiently understood. What Efraim Shmueli has said of his remarks pertaining to messianism could be said with regard to his views on many other matters as well: they "raise more questions than they resolve."[4] And what Alexander Altmann has said of Julius Guttman could be said with equal justification of almost every other student of our subject: He "may have taken too rosy a view of the manner in which Mendelssohn managed to balance the conflicting forces in his soul."

After expressing these reservations about Guttman's admittedly "masterful account of Mendelssohn's philosophy of Judaism," Altmann concluded his last published article on Mendelssohn's concept of Judaism with the pointed observation that "Neither his theory of Judaism nor his personality were as unified as might have appeared on the surface."[5] As is well known, no one has done more to illuminate the surface of Mendelssohn's writings or to probe beneath it than Alexander Altmann. With his massive biography of Mendelssohn as well as numerous other books and articles dealing with specific aspects of his metaphysics, his moral and political philosophy, and his concept of Judaism, he elevated the study of Moses Mendelssohn to a level that it had hitherto never attained.[6] Even Altmann, however, has left certain crucial issues unresolved. Although he sometimes marveled at the degree to which Mendelssohn succeeded in harmonizing his philosophical convictions and his Judaism, he leaves us wondering, in the end, whether the views that he expressed were ultimately "held together less by the force of incontestable logic than by a concatenation of personal convictions and loyalties."[7]

Did Mendelssohn construct a coherent synthesis of rationalist philosophy and Jewish religion, or was his theory of Judaism not only an ephemeral solution but an unstable one as well? This is the question that this book will attempt to answer. In order to address it, we must focus our attention first on Mendelssohn's discussion of matters pertaining to religion in general in his major philosophical writings and then on his treatment in *Jerusalem* and elsewhere of Judaism in particular.

Mendelssohn, as a disciple of Leibniz and Wolff, firmly maintained throughout most of his philosophical career that reason could demonstrate the fundamental truths of natural religion; that is, the existence of God, providence, and immortality. Basing himself chiefly on Leibniz and Wolff, but drawing also on the writings of others, especially other representatives of the German Enlightenment, he wrote a number of important works in which he sought to uphold these principles. Diverse and powerful attacks on the doctrines of the Leibniz-Wolffian school eventually shook his confidence in its viability, but they did not cause him to lose his faith in the powers of reason. He never ceased to reiterate his understanding of the doctrines of natural theology, but he did come to believe that the time had come for his own method of defending them to be supplemented by another, as yet unknown philosophical teaching.

What Mendelssohn absorbed from Leibniz and Wolff in no way threatened his adherence to Judaism. Their philosophical teachings were fully compatible with the acceptance of biblical revelation. Leibniz and Wolff themselves, it is true, had presented them together with affirmations of the suprarational truths taught by Christianity, but they could just as easily be combined, instead, with an affirmation of the truth of the Old Testament alone— which is essentially what Mendelssohn did.

Unlike his principal mentors, Mendelssohn was, in the broad sense of the term, a liberal. His overall political philosophy was, to be sure, thoroughly rooted in a teleological view of the purpose of human existence, but he was also deeply influenced by the newer, more liberal strains of political thought that had emerged during the previous century in Western Europe. While Leibniz and Wolff both voiced their support for a paternalistic state, one that would take a strong interest in directing the spiritual lives of its citizens, Mendelssohn joined Locke and various other thinkers in advocating the protection of liberty of conscience.

It was not his metaphysics but his liberalism that Mendelssohn had to struggle to reconcile with traditional Judaism. Almost immediately after presenting his first defense of the right to liberty of conscience Mendelssohn had to contend with an anonymous critic, the author of the *Searching After Right and Light*, who called upon him to explain how he, as a believer in the revealed character of the Old Testament, could possibly take such a position. Contrary to what many scholars appear to think, this was a perfectly legitimate question, one which confronted Mendelssohn with an intractable theoretical dilemma. It is in large part to respond to it that he wrote the work in which he made his most complete presentation of his concept of Judaism, his *Jerusalem*.

It was not, however, the tension between liberalism and traditional Judaism that presented the greatest challenge to Mendelssohn. On a deeper level, he had to deal with the arguments of Spinoza and a significant number of skeptical thinkers who denied the very possibility of divine revelation and denigrated both the Old and the New Testaments. For an adherent of Judaism, in Mendelssohn's day, who wished to uphold the truth of his religion, there could scarcely be a more urgent task than to refute the attacks of these skeptics (except, of course, insofar as they targeted the New Testament).

On the basis of a superficial reading of Mendelssohn's writings, one would never imagine the magnitude of the challenge with which these thinkers confronted him. For the most part, he does not face them directly. Reading between the lines, however, one is able to discern the extent to which his entire defense of Judaism takes the form of a response to critics he barely deigns to mention. A number of scholars have indeed noticed and analyzed the significance of Mendelssohn's partly concealed confrontation with Spinoza's *Theologico-Political Treatise*. As I shall seek to show, however, they have with regard to this question done little more than scratch the surface. They have failed to appreciate not only the extent to which Mendelssohn attempts to come to terms with Spinoza and other radical critics of revealed religion but also the extent to which he is unsuccessful in doing so.

Many scholars have, to be sure, identified weaknesses and inconsistencies in Mendelssohn's interpretation of Judaism. And virtually all have taken note of his failure to develop a viable and satisfactory philosophy of Judaism that would have a lasting influence. What has not been sufficiently understood is the extent to which he failed to cope with even the most potent contemporary threats to revealed religion in general and Judaism in particular. I would go further and say that Mendelssohn himself was entirely aware of this failure and that much of what he says is aimed at disguising it. In the final analysis, Mendelssohn's defense of Judaism was, I believe, more rhetorical than real.

In part, Mendelssohn's presentation of Judaism was designed to deflect rather than to refute the kinds of arguments being made in his day by critics like Spinoza. His principal motive for adopting such a strategy was, I will argue, his desire to retain his credentials as a faithful Jew, credentials that he needed mainly to have any hope of success in propagating a version of Judaism suitable to modern times. While posing as someone who sought to restore "ancient, original Judaism" he was in reality trying to fashion a Judaism unlike any that had ever been seen before. His basic goal was to cut his ancestral religion to match, more or less, a pattern previously fabricated by some of the leading political philosophers of the modern era. Like them, Mendelssohn strove above all to modify the scriptural religion to which he owed allegiance so that it could serve as a civil religion.

We will begin our examination of Mendelssohn's unique synthesis of the philosophy of Leibniz and Wolff and Judaism with a review of what Mendelssohn thought it was possible to learn through the unassisted use of human reason. In Chapter 1 we will survey the general context in which he operated. We will examine the ways in which Leibniz, Wolff, and their successors attempt to prove the existence of God and present their concepts of divine providence and human immortality. We shall then, in Chapters 2 and 3, review Mendelssohn's own understanding of natural theology and its ramifications, its strengths and its weaknesses. We will begin with an examination of his proofs, derived largely but not entirely from his predecessors, for the existence of God, providence, and immortality and conclude with an examination of his response to the growing opposition to rationalist metaphysics. In Chapter 4 we will explore the foundations of Mendelssohn's liberalism.

After completing our examination of Mendelssohn's approach to rationalist metaphysics and liberal politics, we will turn to his treatment of Judaism. We will begin, in Chapter 5, by examining the contemporary critique of revealed religion with which Mendelssohn was very much preoccupied, a critique rooted in the thought of Spinoza and further elaborated by British, French, and German thinkers in the course of the eighteenth century. We will also consider, in this chapter, the ways in which a number of Gentile critics sought to compel Mendelssohn to explain his adherence to Judaism. In Chapter 5 we will try to show how Mendelssohn dealt with both the critics of revealed religion in general and his own direct adversaries in particular. What we shall see, I believe, is that his response to all of these critics was, by and large, an inadequate one and that he himself was well aware of its deficiencies. In Chapter 6 we shall examine the way in which Mendelssohn endeavored to refashion Judaism in conformity with a preconceived design. We shall see how, taking his cue from other political philosophers, he sought to update his ancient faith, to make it possible to maintain one's loyalty to it and at the same time to participate without reservations in the cultural and political life of an enlightened and well-organized modern state.

Notes

1. See Frederick Beiser, *The Fate of Reason: German Philosophy from Kant to Fichte* (Cambridge and London: Harvard University Press, 1987), pp. 92–93.

2. Heinrich Graetz, *History of the Jews*, ed. Bella Löwy (Philadelphia: Jewish Publication Society, 1895), vol. 5, p. 292. Chapter 8 of Volume 5 bears the subtitle "The Mendelssohn Epoch." Graetz there speaks of the "rejuvenescence or renaissance of the Jewish race, which may be unhesitatingly ascribed to Mendelssohn." *Out of the Ghetto* is the title of Jacob Katz's seminal volume on "the social background of Jewish emancipation (1770–1870)," a study in which Mendelssohn looms very large. For a comparable assessment of Mendelssohn's significance, see Michael Meyer, *The Origins of the Modern Jew* (Detroit: Wayne State University Press, 1967), pp. 29ff.

3. The phrase was coined by Michael Meyer (ibid.), but it reflects a widely held view.

4. Efraim Shmueli, *Seven Jewish Cultures: A Reinterpretation of Jewish History and Thought*, trans. Gila Shmueli (Cambridge: Cambridge University Press, 1990), p. 169.

5. Alexander Altmann, "Moses Mendelssohn's Concept of Judaism Re-examined," in *Von der mittelalterlichen zur modernen Aufklärung; Studien zur jüdischen Geistesgeschichte* (Tübingen: J.C.B. Mohr, 1986), p. 248.

6. Most of Altmann's publications on Mendelssohn are noted in Michael Albrecht's extensive bibliography, "Moses Mendelssohn: Ein Forschungsbericht, 1965–1980," in *Deutsche Vierteljahrs Schrift fur Literaturwissenschaft und Geistesgeschichte* 57 (1983): 64–166. See also Allan Arkush, "The Contribution of Alexander Altmann to the Study of Moses Mendelssohn," in *Leo Baeck Year Book*, 34 (1989): 415–20.

7. Alexander Altmann, *Moses Mendelssohn, A Biographical Study* (University: University of Alabama Press, 1973), p. 518.

1

The Leibniz-Wolffian Background

Moses Mendelssohn was a devoted disciple of the leading lights of the *Aufklärung*, Gottfried Wilhelm Leibniz (1646–1716) and Christian Wolff (1679–1754). From his discovery of their writings as a young man to his composition, near the end of his life, of what Immanuel Kant described as the "most perfect product" of the school to which he belonged, he remained within the Leibniz-Wolffian fold.[1] It is important, therefore, for our purposes, to clarify the extent of his loyalty to this school of thought, to elucidate the manner in which the teachings of Leibniz, Wolff, and their other disciples constituted the basis of his philosophy of religion.

Mendelssohn followed his mentors in placing paramount emphasis on the importance of rational proof for the existence of God, on an account of divine providence, and on demonstrations of the immortality of the human soul. It will accordingly be necessary for us to review, first of all, the manner in which these philosophers elaborated their major proofs for the existence of God. Then, to acquire an understanding of the roots of Mendelssohn's concepts of providence and immortality, it will be necessary for us to examine, above all, the views expressed in Leibniz's *Theodicy* and other related works. We will need to look, in addition, at the way in which Leibniz and Wolff and some of their disciples formulated their arguments in defense of the immortality of the soul, arguments of which Mendelssohn was later to make use.

Leibniz, Wolff, and their disciples all believed in the possibility of articulating a comprehensive natural theology; that is, a theology based on reason alone. They did not all maintain, however, that unassisted human reason was the only means of acquiring religious knowledge, or that it could provide knowledge of everything that human beings needed to know. Leibniz and Wolff both affirmed the truth of Christian revelation. They denied that revelation could include anything that contradicted the teachings

1

of reason, but they maintained at the same time that it could teach things that were "suprarational." As we shall see, not all of their disciples followed them in drawing this distinction. All of them, including Mendelssohn, however, had to come to terms with their mentors' Christian orthodoxy.

As a consequence of their acknowledgment of the truth of Christian revelation, Leibniz and Wolff affirmed, in addition to the tenets of natural theology, various revealed religious doctrines. For our purposes, it will not be necessary to clarify the nature of all of their specifically Christian teachings. To some degree, however, their Christian beliefs influenced their accounts of natural theology, especially their treatments of divine providence and immortality. To understand what they have to say with respect to natural theology, therefore, we will have to devote some attention to various aspects of their discussions of revealed theology. We will also have to consider the important transformation that takes place within the Leibniz-Wolffian school when some of its later representatives begin to present natural theologies free of any Christian coloration.

The Existence of God

According to Leibniz, "Our reasonings are founded on two *great principles*: that of *Contradiction* . . . and that of *Sufficient Reason*."[2] The first principle states that "of two contradictory propositions the one is true, the other false. . . ."[3] It is not, needless to say, Leibniz's discovery nor does it require any explanation. By virtue of the latter principle "we consider that no fact can be real or actual, and no proposition true, without there being a sufficient reason for its being so and not otherwise, although most often these reasons just cannot be known by us."[4] This principle, too, is far from abstruse, but it is not self-explanatory. In elucidating it, we shall see that it leads almost immediately to a proof for the existence of God.

The preceding definition of the principle of sufficient reason, taken from section 32 of the *Monadology*, alludes to two different kinds of truths, which Leibniz designates in the very next section of the same work as "those of *reasoning* and those of *fact*." The former type of truths includes those that are necessary and the opposite of which is impossible; the latter type includes those that are not necessary and the opposite of which is possible. According to Leibniz, both types of truths require, as Nicholas Rescher has put it, "a grounding rationale" for being the way that they are. In the case of truths of reasoning, "this validating sufficient reason is provided by the operation of the principle of contradiction in that the denial of such truths leads to contradiction."[5] The sufficient reason for the existence of contingent truths or truths of fact cannot be sought in their logical necessity but only through an examination of the things that cause them to be the way that they are. "Here," however,

> the resolution into particular reasons can go on into endless detail, because of the immense variety of things in nature and the *ad infinitum* division of bodies. There is an infinity of shapes and motions, present and past, that enter into the efficient cause of my present writing, and there is an infinity of minute inclinations and dispositions of my soul, present and past, that enter into its final cause.

A resolution that can "go on into endless detail" is clearly one that brings us "no further ahead." Consequently, the sufficient reason for the existence of truths of fact "must lie outside of the entire sequence or *series* of this detail of contingencies, however infinite it may be."[6] It can only be "found in a substance which is the cause of this series or which is a necessary being bearing the reason for its existence within itself, otherwise we should not yet have a sufficient reason with which to stop. This final reason for things is called *God*."[7] Thus, the elucidation of the principle of sufficient reason turns quite quickly into a cosmological proof for the existence of God.

Leibniz also propounded his own version, or rather versions, of the ontological proof for God's existence, which was still known in his day as the Cartesian proof. Descartes was of course not the originator of this method of proving God's existence, which had first been developed by St. Anselm in the eleventh century. What Descartes had done was to revive it, following a period during which it had fallen into disrepute.[8] Leibniz himself gratefully acknowledged the service Descartes had thereby performed; nevertheless, he was not entirely satisfied with the Cartesian version of the ontological proof.

The argument of Descartes was that God had to be thought of as being possessed of all the perfections. On the basis of this, and on the basis of the premise that existence is one of the perfections, he reasoned that it was part of God's essence to exist. This argument, according to Leibniz, is not fallacious, but it is an incomplete demonstration which assumes something which should also be proved in order to render the argument mathematically evident. The point is that it is tacitly assumed that this idea of a wholly great or wholly perfect being is possible and does not imply a contradiction.[9]

To complete what Jan Rohls has called his *improved ontological argument*, Leibniz believed that this assumption had to be proven.[10]

Leibniz, as Rohls has observed, "did not believe it to be self-evident that the concept of the most perfect or the absolutely necessary being was free of contradiction." He thought, on the contrary, that it was entirely possible that this concept was just as laden with contradictions as those of the fastest movement or the greatest number (which can never be specified). To prove that the definition of God as the most perfect being was not a mere "nominal definition," that is, a definition to which there is, in the real world, no corresponding object, but a "real definition," it was necessary to show that it was logically possible for a being to be the most perfect of all beings.[11]

The manner in which Leibniz did this, and thereby repaired the defect in Descartes's argument, has been succinctly summarized by Stuart Brown. Leibniz, he writes, defined

a "perfection" as any "simple quality which is positive and absolute", i.e. as a "simple form". He invoked his Platonic atomism further by claiming that all such *simple* forms are compatible with one another in the same subject. Incompatibility can only occur as between complex qualities. Thus, for example, red and green would not be "simple forms" for Leibniz because a definition of them (in terms of primary qualities) would explain why one and the same thing cannot be both red and green (all over at the same time). The simple forms are logically independent of one another and hence can all inhere in one subject.

Thus, "by identifying God's 'perfections' with the 'simple forms' Leibniz is able to claim that the notion of a most perfect being is possible . . ." And because existence itself is a perfection, the possibility of the existence of a most perfect being necessarily implies the real existence of such a being. Leibniz, as Brown puts it, thereby joins Descartes "in holding that it is part of God's *essence* to exist."[12]

As Rohls has noted, Leibniz considered this form of the ontological argument to be needlessly complicated. He therefore gave preference to the version of the argument that proceded not from the concept of the most perfect being but from that of the necessary being.[13] Here, too, his argument begins with a demonstration of the possibility of the being whose existence is to be established. In this case, however, the demonstration takes the form of a proof of the *impossibility* of the negation of the concept in question. "For if the negation of the proposition that God exists is impossible, since it contradicts the definition of God to say that God does not exist, then one can draw from the fact that it is possible that God exists the conclusion that God does exist."[14] Leibniz's concept of possibility belongs, as Dieter Henrich has observed, to a metaphysics that "does not yet distinguish between the logical possibility of a thought and the real possibility of an existent being. A concept whose definition contains no contradiction is thereby already defined as real; the possibility of its object is assured."[15]

In addition to the cosmological proof and these different versions of the ontological proof Leibniz developed a number of other proofs for God's existence. In the *Monadology*, for instance, he includes an argument on the basis of the existence of eternal truths.[16] Elsewhere he presents his own version of the physiotheological proof. He argues that the purposeful direction and pre-established harmony of the world serves as "one of the most effective and palpable proofs for God's existence."[17] The cosmological and the ontological proofs are, however, the only ones that Mendelssohn accepted and further refined and are therefore the only ones of interest to us in the context of this study. Having outlined Leibniz's presentation of these proofs, we must now briefly consider how they were further developed in the writings of Christian Wolff as well as those of one of Wolff's students, Alexander Baumgarten.

In both his Latin and his German writings on metaphysics Wolff reiterated the cosmological proof for God's existence in the form that Leibniz had given it.[18] In general, he left no doubt that he preferred the cosmological argument to all others. The ontological argument, in both of its principal forms, can be found only in his Latin works. He differs somewhat from Leibniz in the way in which he interconnects the cosmological and the ontological proofs, but since Mendelssohn does not follow him in this respect at all, there will be no need for us to look into this difference here.

What we need to note is one of Wolff's important linguistic usages, a term that Mendelssohn adopted from him. In his presentation of the ontological proof based on the idea of God as the most perfect being, Wolff speaks of God as being possessed of all of the mutually compatible "realities" to the highest possible degree. By *realities* he means nothing other than what Leibniz referred to as *perfections*. In his ontological proof, he speaks of existence as a reality that God must possess.[19]

Alexander Gottlieb Baumgarten (1714–1762), an important disciple of Wolff, is a figure whose name is today familiar only to those with a special interest in the German Enlightenment.[20] Among them, Baumgarten is remembered primarily for the originality of his ontology. The only aspect of that ontology of which it is necessary for us to take note has been conveniently summarized by Altmann. According to Baumgarten, he writes,

> all that exists is totally (*omnimode*) determined, and the reverse is equally true: Everything that is totally determined exists. In the case of the most perfect being only essential or inner determinations can apply. Hence it is sufficiently determined by dint of its essence, and it either exists or is altogether indeterminate and impossible. Since it cannot be impossible, as has been shown, it necessarily exists.[21]

In the following chapter we will examine the way in which Mendelssohn made use of this formulation.

Providence and Immortality

From the idea of God as the most perfect or the necessary being Leibniz and Wolff derived knowledge of the divine attributes. In basically similar ways, they sought to show that the most perfect or necessary being must be independent, absolutely infinite, possessed of boundless understanding and infinite power, and so forth. We need not explore in detail the manner in which they proceeded from their fundamental premises to their doctrines of God, since the primary subject of our study, Moses Mendelssohn, neither reiterated what they said nor attempted to improve upon their efforts in this area.

This is not to say, of course, that we have no further interest in Leibniz's and Wolff's teachings with regard to natural theology. What we must investigate, however, is not the way in which they arrived at their understanding of God's nature but the way in which they conceived God, as he was known through reason, to rule the world dependent upon him. In other words, we must examine their views concerning divine providence and the related principle of the immortality of the soul. The natural place to begin such an inquiry would be, it would seem, with Leibniz's *Theodicy*.

"The historical significance of Leibniz's philosophy of religion," as Henry E. Allison has written, "is based largely upon his *Theodicy* (1710)."[22] In this well-known work, he elaborated his concepts of divine providence and grace, "which became generally adopted by the *Aufklärung*."[23] Frequently summarized, famously satirized by Voltaire, many of the main ideas expressed in the *Theodicy* are in all likelihood more familiar to contemporary readers than any other aspect of Leibniz's thought. It is primarily in this work, for instance, that he sets forth his frequently misunderstood and much-maligned theory that this world constitutes "the best of all possible worlds."

Leibniz expounds his concepts of divine providence and immortality not only in the *Theodicy*, however, but also in a number of other writings such as his *Causa Dei* (a "methodical abridgement" of the *Theodicy*) and his *Monadology*. We will have occasion to refer in this section to a number of these works. We should also repeat, at this point, that the *Theodicy* as well as several other of the writings to which we will be referring here combine philosophical reasoning with specifically Christian theological ruminations. While our concern, for the most part, is with the purely philosophical aspects of Leibniz's opus, we will, to a certain extent, have to examine the way in which his philosophical and his Christian convictions are interrelated.

Leibniz's cosmological and ontological proofs are designed to demonstrate God's existence. His account of divine providence, on the other hand, is intended not only to set forth his understanding of the way in which God rules the world but also to win the hearts of his readers. An omnipotent and infinitely good God has created, he seeks to show, the best of all possible worlds. There is, to be sure, much evil in this world—but it is not to be blamed on God himself. There is much less of it than people are accustomed to believe, and there exists a compensatory afterlife. The sight of what God has created, Leibniz says, ought to fill us with love for him.[24] Ultimately, however, he finds it difficult to describe the existing world in a way that will persuade his readers that this is the case. Christian doctrine concerning the afterlife, as we shall see, greatly complicates his task.

As Allison observed, Leibniz's teaching on divine providence was generally adopted by the *Aufklärung*. The later representatives of the German Enlightenment did not, however, adopt unquestioningly the views propounded by Leibniz in the *Theodicy* and in his other writings and subsequently restated by Wolff. They accepted the main points of Leibniz's philosophical understanding of divine providence, but they did not adjust it, as he had, to accomodate traditional Christian doctrines. As we shall see, abandoning these doctrines made it possible for them overcome the difficulties that had beset Leibniz and to propound a view of divine providence better suited than that of Leibniz himself to meet the goals he was seeking to achieve.

In the early sections of the *Causa Dei*, the abridgement of the *Theodicy*, Leibniz outlines what he calls *preparatory knowledge*; that is, the knowledge on which a defense of divine providence is necessarily based. What he does here is, in essence, to elucidate the character of the altogether perfect being whose existence is known to us by virtue of the proofs we examined in the previous section of this study. Two dimensions of God's perfection, he explains, are his greatness and his goodness. The greatness of God has two main elements: his omnipotence and his omniscience. God's omnipotence is displayed by his absolute independence of everything outside of him as well as by the dependence on him of all things—the merely possible no less than the actual. God's omniscience comprehends everything that can ever become an object of the understanding. It therefore encompasses everything in this world, that which already exists as well as that which will come to pass.[25]

"God," according to Leibniz, "is the primary center from which all else that exists emanates." He created the world ex nihilo. And this great creative act marks only the beginning of his activity. He ceaselessly sustains the world. The "created substances depend upon God who preserves them and can produce them continually by a kind of emanation just as we produce our thoughts."[26] For Leibniz, as Nicholas Rescher has put it, "God sustains the world by *thinking* of it in a particular sort of way." In affirming God's continual involvement in sustaining the world, however, Leibniz does not mean to suggest that he is forever tinkering with what he has created. As Rescher says,

> while Leibniz assumes a God who is "on duty" twenty-four hours a day, every day, to assure THAT the world keeps on existing, he precludes an *intervening* God who readjusts WHAT is going on. The course of world history is settled by a once-and-for-all creation-choice and there is no possibility and no need of God's having any "second thoughts" on the matter. In

the correspondence with Samuel Clarke, Leibniz emphatically and scornfully rejects any idea of a "hands-on" God who needs to readjust or rewind the universe on the pattern of an imperfect clockmaker who has made a defective timepiece.[24]

Needless to say, a Christian thinker like Leibniz cannot reject the possibility of direct divine intervention in the world's affairs without explaining how such a theory can be reconciled with the occurrence of the biblical miracles. Leibniz does so in the *Theodicy*, where he urges his readers to "bear in mind that the miracles which happen in this world were also enfolded and represented as possible in this same world considered in the state of mere possibility, and God, who has since performed them, when he chose this world had even then decreed to perform them."[28] Because he views the miracles as events woven into the divine plan from the very outset, Leibniz has no need to modify his overall theory to account for their possibility.

Following his treatment of the power of God, in the *Causa Dei*, Leibniz turns to a discussion of divine goodness. God's goodness, he writes, represents a perfection of his will. Unlike an imperfect will, which may have a merely apparent or a lesser good as its object, the divine will always aims at the *best*. This *best* does not include all the goods that receive the approval of God's *antecedent will*, for it is not possible for all good things to coexist. God therefore selects those goods that make up the greatest possible sum of perfections, and his *consequent will* brings them into existence. This selection is called the *decree* of God.

Leibniz defines *providence* as the combination of God's goodness and greatness, which manifests itself in the creation and preservation of the entire universe. He defines *divine justice* as the combination of God's goodness and greatness "in the special government of substances endowed with reason."[29] Providence leads, he maintains, to the coming into being of what must be considered to be the best of all possible worlds. This is something that, in his opinion, one could ascertain a priori, without even casting a glance at what lies before our eyes. One knows this to be the case "since God has chosen this world as it is."[30] For Leibniz it is, then, possible to arrive at a theoretically unimpeachable vindication of providence without giving any attention at all to its actual operations. *Whatever* exists is by definition the best.

Leibniz does not, however, leave the matter at that. He seeks on a number of occasions to elucidate more precisely what it is that makes this world the best of all those that God could possibly have created. "It follows from the supreme perfection of God," he writes, for instance, in his *Principles of Nature and of Grace, Founded on Reason:*

> that he has chosen the best possible plan in producing the universe, a plan which combines the greatest variety together with the greatest order; with situation, place, and time arranged in the best way possible; with the greatest effect produced by the simplest means; with the most power, the most knowledge, the greatest happiness and goodness in created things which the universe could allow . . ."[31]

Here and in some other passages it almost seems as if "the best of all possible worlds" is tantamount to the world stocked most plentifully and in the most orderly fashion with possible things. But this is not quite the case. We do not really begin to grasp the meaning of Leibniz's most famous phrase until we pose the question that John Hick used as the heading for one of the subsections concerning Leibniz in the chapter entitled "Eighteenth Century Optimism" in his book *Evil and the God of Love*: " 'Best Possible'—For What Purpose?" The short answer to this question, supplied by Hick, is that the best world is "that which best serves the purpose that God is seeking to fulfill by means of it."[32] But, as Hick himself recognizes, this only begs another question: What was that purpose?

According to Leibniz, God brought the world into being for the sake of his own glory. "In designing to create the world," he "purposed solely to manifest and communicate his perfections in the way that was most efficacious and most worthy of his greatness, his wisdom and his goodness."[33] At first glance, this may seem to identify as God's purpose something that far transcends the concerns of the world's inhabitants. Yet if God's self-manifestation is the purpose of creation, it is obvious that those beings who are capable of receiving divine communications and appreciating God's glory will play a central role in the whole divine scheme of things. These beings Leibniz identifies in the *Monadology* as the rational souls or spirits (*esprits*). He describes them as constituting, among other things, "images of divinity itself—of the very Author of nature." In all of creation they are the only beings "capable of knowing the system of the universe, and of imitating it to some extent through constructive samples, each spirit being like a minute divinity within its own sphere."

Not only do these spirits resemble the divinity, but they are "capable of entering into a kind of community with God" that Leib-

niz designates as the City of God. This city "is a moral world within
the natural world, and is the most exalted and the most divine of
the works of God. And it is in it that the glory of God truly consists,
for there would be none at all if his grandeur and goodness were
not known and admired by the spirits."[34] Leibniz's contention, then,
that God created the world for the sake of his own glory is one that
is far from relegating the spirits, a category that includes human
beings, to a secondary place in the entire divine plan. They are in
fact indispensable for the enhancement of God's glory.

What lends the spirits their importance is their rationality,
their ability to know the system of the universe and, as a result, to
love its Creator. This love of God constitutes, in turn, "the greatest
good and interest" of rational souls,

> For it gives us a perfect confidence in the goodness of our Au-
> thor and Master, and this produces a true tranquility of the
> spirit. . . . It is true that the supreme happiness . . . cannot
> ever be full, because God, being infinite, cannot ever be known
> entirely. Thus our happiness will never consist, and ought
> never to consist, in complete happiness, which leaves nothing
> to be desired and which would stupefy our spirit, but in a
> perpetual progress to new pleasures and new perfections.[35]

Because spirits "are of all substances the most capable of perfection," God "who in all things has the greatest perfection will have
the greatest care for spirits and will give not only to all of them in
general, but even to each one in particular the highest perfection
which the universal harmony will permit."[36]

As Leibniz states in the *Theodicy*, "the happiness of intelligent creatures is the principal part of God's design, for they are
most like him." This statement is immediately subjected, however,
to an important qualification. Leibniz does not see how one can
prove the happiness of intelligent creatures to be God's "sole aim."[37]
For

> God has more than one purpose in his projects. The felicity of
> all rational creatures is one of the aims he has in view; but it
> is not his whole aim, nor even his final aim. Therefore it hap-
> pens that the unhappiness of some of these creatures may
> come about by concomitance, and as a result of other greater
> goods.[38]

One cannot help but be puzzled by what Leibniz says here. After
all, what greater good could there be? He never identifies one. He

does tell us that God's *sole* purpose in creating the world was "to manifest and communicate his perfections in the way that was most efficacious and most worthy of his greatness, his wisdom and his goodness." This communication is the cause of the happiness of all of his rational creatures. How, then, can there be a greater good than their happiness, one whose implementation would sometimes result in their experiencing unhappiness or even in the failure of some of them ever to experience happiness?

The key to understanding this passage lies, it seems, in Leibniz's statement that "in the "City of God" God sought to bring about as much "virtue and happiness as is possible."[39] It is not, in fact, for the sake of the accomplishment of some other good that rational creatures must endure unhappiness. Their sufferings are, rather, an unavoidable result of God's creation; even the best of all *possible* worlds is not devoid of such flaws. Why not? Why is it not possible for an omnipotent God to create a world in which there would be no impediments to the complete fulfillment of the principal part of his design? The answer to these questions, Leibniz would say, cannot be known. All we can know is that this world is the best of all those that are possible, for God would otherwise not have chosen to create it. And this world evidently is one in which some rational souls must suffer unhappiness.

In creating the best of all possible worlds, Leibniz acknowledges, God has brought into being a world in which not only unhappiness but also a considerable measure of evil is to be found. He devotes a great deal of effort to accounting for existing evils in a way that both exculpates God of any responsibility for them and minimizes their extent. Leibniz has a dual purpose here: he seeks to defend the principle of God's absolute goodness, and he also attempts to depict the results of the "best possible plan," which God has implemented in a manner that will instill in his readers a love of God.

According to Leibniz, God's will is divided not only into an antecedent will and a consequent will, but also into a productive will and a permissive will. The productive will has reference to God's own actions, the consequent will to the actions of other beings. The permissive will has as its object not the actions themselves but merely the permission to engage in them. In spite of its perfection and its attachment to the best, the divine will is not absolutely opposed to the existence of all things that are less than good. It may permit evils to come into being.[40]

All evils are divided into (1) metaphysical evils, (2) physical evils, and (3) moral evils. Metaphysical evils are the restrictions on metaphysical goods; that is, inanimate, animate, and rational things. Conceiving of these evils causes pain and displeasure. Pain and displeasure are themselves physical evils. Moral evils occur when the will of a rational being is set in motion by something that has the false appearance of a good. Its natural consequence is physical evil.

None of these evils can ever be the object of God's will, that is, his antecedent will, which encompasses the perfections of things in general as well as the happiness and the virtue of all intelligent substances.[41] On the other hand, God's consequent will, or his decree, does not simply prevent all evils from coming into being. For sometimes the avoidance of a particular evil would have the result of obviating the occurrence of a greater good.[42]

Metaphysical and physical evil may serve as means for the attainment of higher goods; this can never be true, however, of moral evil. One may never commit a bad deed in the hope that good will come out of it. Nevertheless, moral evil can sometimes be an indispensable precondition for the attainment of a greater good or the avoidance of a greater evil. God, therefore, while never committing a moral evil, will, when he has reason to do so, permit such evils to take place.[43]

God's productive will is never responsible for the commission of any evil, but God's permissive will may permit evils to occur, including the moral sins of rational beings. But why? To answer this question, Leibniz, resorts to an analogy between God and human beings. Human beings have, under certain circumstances, a moral duty to permit evils to take place. This is the case, namely, when the prevention of a given evil would entail the commission of a still greater evil. Much the same thing can be said of God. If God had chosen to create a world in which he had prevented sin from coming into being, he would have created a world inferior to the existing world and would thereby have acted in a manner unbefitting his own perfection. He would have chosen to bring into existence a world that was not the best of all possible worlds.[44] One might, in short, imagine a world in which there was no sin, but it would not be a better world than the one that exists. Thus, the presence in the world of moral evil in no way impugns the goodness of God.

There are, however, those for whom the abundance of physical evils in this world calls into question the existence of divine providence. Leibniz responds to their complaints by observing that (1) most of these evils are men's own fault and (2) we are insufficiently grateful for the benefactions we receive from God and devote more of our attention to the evils that befall us than we do to the good that we enjoy incessantly. For those who are upset by what they regard as the unjust distribution of goods in this world, he has a different answer. First, he observes that all the afflictions in this world cannot be compared with the glory of the future life. Second, he maintains that the suffering that we undergo here on earth has its useful purposes; it is a necessary precondition for our happiness in this world and the next.

For Leibniz, then, the complete vindication of providence requires reference to the the rewards obtainable in the afterlife. That all rational souls are immortal and proceed, following death, to another life is something that he believes reason to be capable of demonstrating. The precise nature of this afterlife, however, is something he considers to be entirely beyond the purview of reason, something that only revelation can illuminate. In his attempt to reconcile the tendency of his own thought with authoritative, revealed teachings concerning the life after death, Leibniz, as we shall see, runs into some rather serious impediments.

Leibniz's understanding of the immortality of the soul is bound up with his idea of the soul as a *monad*. To grasp what he has to say concerning immortality, however, it is not necessary to enter into any extensive consideration of precisely what it is he means by this term. It should suffice to note that he defines *monads* as "the true atoms of nature and, in a word, the elements of things." Monads, he states, "can neither come into being nor end save all at once; that is, they can begin only by creation and end only by annihilation."[45] All monads have *perceptions* and *appetites* in a sense that Leibniz explains but that for our purposes it will not be necessary to clarify.[46] Souls differ from other monads in that their "perception is more distinct and accompanied by memory."[47]

Simply by virtue of its identity as a monad the soul, "that mirror of an indestructible universe, is indestructible . . ."[48] In addition,

> It follows from the perfection of the supreme Author not only that the order of the entire universe is the most perfect possible, but also that each living mirror which represents the universe according to its own point of view, that is each *monad* or each substantial center, must have its perceptions and its appetites regulated in the best way compatible with all the rest. From this it also follows that souls, that is to say, the most dominant monads, or rather animals themselves, cannot fail to awake from the state of stupor into which death or some other accident may place them.

"Rational souls," Leibniz likewise asserts, "are exempt from everything which might make them lose the quality of citizens of the society of minds, since God has provided so well that no changes in matter can make them lose the moral qualities of their personality."[49]

Rational souls retain their former identities even after their death. They remain forever members of the "City of God." This is the limit, however, of what unassisted human reason can determine. "As far as the particulars of this condition of the human soul after death are concerned and in what way it is exempted from the transformation of things, revelation alone can give us particular instruction; the jurisdiction of the reason does not extend so far."[50]

To complete his teaching on immortality, therefore, Leibniz must have recourse to Christian revelation. This teaches him that some souls will ultimately attain blessedness in the afterlife. Like nearly all of his contemporaries, however, he understood the Christian tradition to teach that "the number of men damned eternally will be incomparably greater than that of the saved."[51] He notes at one point that some of the Fathers of the Church thought otherwise and sought to deny eternal damnation or greatly to reduce the number of those who will suffer it. He himself does not believe, however, that it is possible to take refuge in their "unacceptable opinions."

His adherence to the received Christian doctrine concerning the afterlife creates great problems for Leibniz. In his vindication of divine providence he sought, as we have seen, to eliminate any grounds for doubting God's goodness on account of the evils found in this world. In response to those who would question divine providence on the basis of the injustices prevalent in our world, Leibniz argues, as we have seen, that all the afflictions here below cannot be compared with the glory of the future life. He maintains that the sufferings that we undergo on earth serve as a necessary precondition for our happiness in this world and the next. But, it must be asked, is not the significance of this afterlife vitiated by the fact that so few human beings are destined to enjoy it?

The generally accepted Christian teaching creates another, more profound problem as well. In our examination of Leibniz's understanding of God's purpose in creating the world we saw that the rational souls or spirits were the chief object of God's concern. Because spirits "are of all substances the most capable of perfection," God "who in all things has the greatest perfection will have the greatest care for spirits and will give not only to all of them in general, but even to each one in particular the highest perfection which the universal harmony will permit." He says, furthermore, that "the happiness of intelligent creatures is the principal part of God's design, for they are most like him." Granted, there are limits to the amount of happiness that it is possible for him to extend to intelligent creatures. But can these limits really be so confining? If even "the best possible plan" entails the damnation of most human beings, how can Leibniz really expect his readers to love the being responsible for its implementation?

Leibniz is not oblivious to these difficulties. In view of the dismal posthumous fate of most human beings, he ultimately acknowledges, the next world does not seem to provide much of a remedy for the harshness of this one. For it is possible to object "that there too the evils outnumber the goods, since the elected are very few."[52] In response to this plaint, Leibniz is prepared to suggest that it is possible that the glory of the blessed is great enough in the eyes of God to outweigh the sufferings of all the damned.[53] At greater length, however, and with greater fervor, he proposes another solution:

> Today, whatever bounds are given or not given to the universe, it must be acknowledged that there is an infinite number of globes, as great as and greater than ours, which have as much right as it to hold rational inhabitants, though it follows not at all that they are human. . . . It may be that all suns are peopled only by blessed creatures, and nothing constrains us to think that many are damned. . . . Moreover, since there is no reason for the belief that there are stars everywhere, is it not possible that there may be a great space beyond the region of the stars? Whether it be the Empyrean Heaven, or not, this immense space encircling all this region may in any case be filled with happiness and glory. It can be imagined as like the Ocean, whither flow the rivers of all blessed creatures, when they shall have reached their perfection in the system of the stars.

In comparison to these vast regions, our globe and its inhabitants are "almost lost in nothingness." And "since all the evils that may be raised in objection before us are in this near nothingness, haply it may be that all evils are almost nothingness in comparison with the good things which are in the universe."[54] Any objections to divine providence based on the great number of the damned are, therefore, founded on ignorance.[55]

As we have noted, Leibniz sought to achieve two principal

goals in his discussion of divine providence. He attempted, first of all, to explain God's governance of the universe. But he also sought to do so in a manner that would redound to God's glory, that would fill his readers with a sense of admiration and love for their Creator. After reviewing his overall theory, we can say that it attains the first of Leibniz's goals by providing a comprehensive, consistent account of the way in which God has implemented a plan for accomplishing his own purposes. It describes God as having brought the world into being primarily to promote his own glory through benefactions to its rational inhabitants, by extending to them the greatest possible degree of perfection and happiness. It explains, in addition, why there are of necessity certain limits to the extent of these benefactions, why even the best of all possible worlds must inevitably contain certain evils, perhaps even a surplus of evils. To attain the second of Leibniz's goals, however, it is necessary for his theory to go beyond mere self-consistency. It must portray God in a way that renders him worthy of love.

Leibniz seems to think that he has done so. He claims to have shown "that the world is governed in such a way that a wise person who is well informed will have nothing to find fault with and can find nothing more to desire."[56] He maintains, beyond this, that his account of divine providence provides a basis for loving God, that "it is easy to love him as we ought of we know him as I have said."[57] But he seems also to be aware that this may be difficult for people to accept.

In the end, Leibniz can complete his defense of the goodness of God's overall plan only by referring to the afterlife, where the injustices of this world are supposedly redressed. It appears, however, that his only reliable source of knowledge concerning the afterlife, biblical revelation, tells him of a realm where the evils still seem vastly to outnumber the goods, at least as far as human beings are concerned. If so, how can people regard their Maker with love in their hearts? To deal with this problem, Leibniz is forced to suggest that in God's eyes the eternal damnation of the vast majority of human beings may be of relatively little significance. Alternatively, and, it seems, with more conviction, he has recourse to some rather strange ruminations regarding human beings' hypothetical coinhabitants of the universe who—again, hypothetically—enjoy greater happiness than they do. These peculiar notions may restore the *possibility* of a universe in which goods outnumber evils, but it is difficult to believe that they could suffice to nurture people's love for the God who may have created it.

The principal problem Leibniz faces is, then, one that has its roots not in what reason teaches concerning the nature of God and the world but in the contents of divine revelation. God, our reason teaches, wants all rational souls to be happy, and "puts this purpose into execution as far as the general harmony will permit." Only to a rather limited extent do considerations relating to the general harmony of things on earth stand in the way of the fulfillment of this divine purpose. Metaphysical, physical, and moral evils undeniably abound here below. But there is no *philosophical* reason why these evils could not all be supposed to find their remedies in the afterlife, where all human beings could be allowed, in accordance with God's purposes, to resume their progress toward perfection and happiness—like the denizens of Leibniz's fanciful extraterrestrial realm, of whom "nothing constrains us to think that many are damned." Unfortunately, however, such a supposition is rendered impossible, for Leibniz, by a Christian dogma he apparently feels bound to accept as authoritative.

Whether Leibniz truly believed in the eternality of punishment for any souls at all is open to doubt. In his *New Apology for Socrates, or Investigation of the Doctrine of the Salvation of Heathens* (Berlin, 1772), a work attacking the doctrine of eternality of punishment, Johann August Eberhard maintained that Leibniz privately rejected this doctrine but nevertheless propounded it publicly because he was attempting "to accommodate his views to the teaching of the various religious parties in order to win popularity for his system. Thus, he was forced to find a sense in which the doctrine of the eternality of punishments is reconcilable with the best of all possible worlds."[58] More recently, Leo Strauss, too, has argued that "Leibniz did not really believe in eternal damnation, as it was understood by Christian tradition."[59] Fortunately, it is not necessary for us to attempt to determine here whether Eberhard and Strauss were correct in their assumptions. Our concern is not with what Leibniz may have secretly believed but with what he publicly taught and the impact his teachings had on his disciples, including, above all, Moses Mendelssohn.

Despite the fact that he did not really believe in the Christian doctrine of eternal damnation, Leibniz, according to Strauss, had no real difficulty accommodating himself to it. "For Leibniz," he writes, "the purpose of creation is primarily the beauty and order of the world in its entirety . . ." Consequently he sees all suffering as being "basically justified in the context of the universe . . ."[60] Here, I believe, Strauss has misinterpreted Leibniz's position. For Leibniz, as we have seen, God's primary purpose in creating the world is not the establishment of order and beauty for their own sake but self-glorification through the *communication* of knowledge of himself and his creation to his rational creatures, who themselves derive happiness from this knowledge. It is therefore rather awkward for him to have to deal with the fact, taught by divine revelation, that the preponderant majority of rational creatures known to us, that is, human beings, are destined not to perfection and happiness but to eternal damnation. It is, indeed, because he cannot escape this fact that Leibniz is forced to modify his statement that "the happiness of intelligent creatures is the principal part of God's design" with the qualification that it is not his "sole aim." For if it were, one would evidently have to say that he had sabotaged his own efforts, at least as far as the preponderant majority of the human race is concerned.

Nothing constrains us to believe, Leibniz argues, that damnation will be the lot of any of the rational souls dwelling (perhaps) beyond the stars. And, he must have believed, if it were not for the prevailing interpretation of the New Testament, there would be nothing to constrain us to believe that most inhabitants of the earth face such a fate. Neither would there be, in the absence of this teaching, any need to hypothesize the existence of multitudes of unknown, happy beings in order to be able to credit God with the creation of a world in which the goods outnumber the evils. Were it not for the standard Christian doctrine, nothing indeed would have prevented Leibniz from affirming that God's sole purpose in creating the world was to reveal his glory to his rational creatures and that God, in his infinite goodness, makes sure that all rational creatures, including all human beings, ultimately make their way to an afterlife where they experience "perpetual progress to new pleasures and new perfections." Once they were prepared to discard the old Christian teaching, this is in fact what Leibniz's disciples were, if they wished, free to maintain.

A considerable amount of time had to pass, however, before any of them was prepared to take such a step. Wolff, in his discussion of divine providence and immortality, essentially reiterated the teachings of Leibniz. As Thomas P. Saine has observed,

> there is scarcely any significant difference between the fundamental ideas of Leibniz's *Theodicy* and Wolff's statements concerning God, the world, and the soul in the *German Metaphysics*. What Leibniz dealt with, however, only partly and in the form of answers to various objections of Pierre Bayle against the possibility of justifying the God of revealed religion by means of reason, Wolff brought into the framework of

a comprehensive system and lent the form of an unshakably solid structure of thought.[61]

Nevertheless, as Saine himself has noted, there are some respects in which Wolff's treatment of divine providence and immortality diverges from that of Leibniz. Unlike Leibniz, Wolff confines himself to a consideration of matters that can be learned through reason alone. He distinguishes, we should note, in much the same way as Leibniz between rational truths and suprarational truths. The former, he says, "we know through reason, the latter through Holy Scripture." Rational truths belong to the province of philosophers (*Weltweisen*); suprarational truths are the concern of theologians (*Gottes-Gelehrten*). "Whoever wishes to pass judgment on both at once must be at once a philosopher and a theologian."[62] Wolff does not wish to be such a person and aspires only to be a philosopher. To the extent that he concerns himself with theology it is with natural theology, which, despite its name, constitutes a branch of philosophy and consists only of the knowledge of God obtainable through unassisted reason.

Wolff himself, as Saine puts it, respected the boundaries between philosophy and theology, "and he did not permit himself to criticize the doctrines of the church. On the contrary, he repeatedly affirmed his own orthodoxy, as he understood it—though he never tried to define it."[63] Still, even in the course of discussing purely philosophical matters, Wolff did not refrain from saying things that called into question the degree to which he truly accepted traditional Christian teachings. Unlike Leibniz, but in a manner fully consistent with the basic tenor of Leibniz's thought, he displayed a desire to downplay as far as possible the significance of the occurrence of miraculous, divine interventions in the natural order of things. His evident uneasiness regarding this question as well as some of his statements with respect to revelation brought Wolff into unsought conflict with the orthodox theologians of his day.[64]

For the most part, however, in his treatment of divine providence, Wolff steered clear of such problems. "In general," as Saine puts it, he "faithfully followed the Leibnizian line of thinking: in the doctrine of the best of all possible worlds, in the assertion that God cannot prefer the imperfect to the perfect," and in other, related matters as well. What marks his discussion of divine providence is, to quote Saine one last time, the fact that "For Wolff, theodicy is practically a self-evident matter . . ." Leibniz had settled everything, and "Wolff is not inclined, in so far as theodicy is concerned, to think any further. He is in general very conservative in his attachment to traditional, Christian-moral teachings."[65]

Leibniz and Wolff both attempted to elucidate what could be known of divine providence through reason alone. They simultaneously affirmed the truth of Christian revelation and its suprarational doctrines concerning God's governance of the world, as they were understood by contemporary Protestant theologians. They succeeded in large measure in bequeathing their rational understanding of divine providence to the thinkers of the *Aufklärung*. Increasingly, however, the philosophers who followed in their footsteps, and some like-minded theologians as well, tended to affirm their rational teachings while rejecting traditional Christian teachings.

"The consequences of the Leibniz-Wolffian philosophy" with regard to theological and religious matters, as Konrad Feiereis has put it, "can be further pursued in two different tendencies: in the Protestant neology and in the Enlightenment philosophy of the second half of the eighteenth century . . ."[66] These two currents of thought are both of interest to us. Both of them, however, include the works of numerous, prolific, and original writers, men to whom it would not be possible to do justice within the context of a broad, general review of the Leibniz-Wolffian background of Moses Mendelssohn's thought. Fortunately, for our purposes, it will not be necessary to consider these thinkers one by one. All we need to do is to obtain an overview of the ways in which they proceed on the basis of assumptions drawn from Leibniz and Wolff to conclusions that these earlier philosophers would no doubt have reached themselves had they been free of all theological constraints.

Let us begin with the representatives of Protestant neology, which was, as Henry E. Allison has written in an extremely useful survey of this movement, "the dominant theological tendency in Germany during the latter half of the eighteenth century." What chiefly characterized the neologists was their refusal to accept without question the nonrational teachings of Christianity. They affirmed the historicity of Christian revelation, but they insisted on interpreting its content in the light of what they considered to be rational. "Within the neological camp," writes Allison,

> whose leaders included Sack, Spalding, Jerusalem, and Semler, these considerations took the form of a philosophical, historical, and philological examination of traditional Christian doctrine. Starting with the presupposition of the identity of "true and original Christianity" with the religion of nature, these men rejected the doctrines found to be irreconcilable with this postulate and showed, by means of historical and philological criticism (here Semler is the main figure), either

that these doctrines were not in fact based upon a true interpretation of Scripture, or that they were later, and completely
unjustified accretions.[67]

Wielding their historical, philological and philosophical weapons, the neologists launched systematic attacks on the entire complex of Christian dogmas. "Not only original sin, but also predes-
tination, the damnation of heathens, the vicarious satisfaction, and
the eternality of punishments were seen to be thoroughly at variance with the new humanistic spirit and were thus rejected." To
epitomize the underlying spirit of the movement, Allison quotes
the following rhetorical questions voiced by one of its leading figures, Johann Friedrich Wilhelm Jerusalem:

> Where is it found that men should be damned because of their
> inborn depravity? Where, that men who live outside of the
> Christian religion, where that the heathen, where that un-
> baptized infants should be damned? Where, finally, that most
> terrible of all ideas: that God has determined to damn some
> men for all eternity?

Where Leibniz, then, had struggled to reconcile his own understanding of God's plan for humankind with some rather grue-
some Christian doctrines, and where Wolff had at least voiced no
criticisms of the revealed teachings, the neologists rebelled against
the authority of tradition. And they did so, in large part, on the
basis of principles of natural theology that they imbibed from the
writings of Leibniz and Wolff themselves. This is especially clear,
as Allison shows, in the case of Johann August Eberhard, the author of the *New Apology for Socrates, or Investigation of the Doctrine of the Salvation of Heathens*. In this work, Eberhard's "particular concern was with the doctrines of the damnation of heathens
and the eternality of punishment."[68] Eberhard, as we have already
seen, was convinced that Leibniz did not really accept these doctrines, but only paid lip service to them to accommodate his views
to generally accepted opinions. He himself felt no need to make any
such compromises. Instead, he repudiated "Leibniz's treatment of
Christian dogma, in terms of the general principles of the Leib-
nizean philosophy . . ."[69]

One cannot identify Eberhard, however, or this particular
book as having exercised any influence on the development of Mendelssohn's thought. If anything, the opposite seems to have been
the case. According to Altmann, it was "no doubt under the influ-

ence of Mendelssohn's strenuous rejection of the concept" of eternal punishment that Eberhard composed his *New Apology*.[70] The neologist theologian who did, on the other hand, have a significant influence on Mendelssohn was Johann Joachim Spalding (1714–1804).

A leading Berlin cleric, Spalding "presents a religious teaching, based on the philosophy of Leibniz and Wolff and influenced by the physiotheological literature, which seeks to conciliate the mentality of the partisans of Enlightenment." He avoids all mention of supernatural revelation, and he refuses to engage in theological controversies, which he treats as matters of secondary importance.[71] Spalding "established his literary reputation with his 'Thoughts on the Destiny of Man' (*Gedanken über die Bestimmung des Menschen*, 1748), one of the most beloved books of the age (thirteen editions by 1794)."[72] Mendelssohn was among the innumerable readers of this book who were powerfully affected by it, and for this reason it will be worth our while to pay rather close attention to it.

"Spalding's meditation was," as Altmann has put it, "a faithful mirror of the Leibniz/Wolffian philosophy, which saw in this world the best of all possible worlds and felt justified in declaring what was and what was not compatible with the notion of God."[73] In his reflections on the destiny of man, Spalding does not, to be sure, take as his point of departure the nature of God or God's designs for the universe. He begins, so to speak, from the ground up, with man himself.

A consideration of the human search for satisfaction and meaning in this world brings Spalding fairly quickly to the realization that happiness is to be sought not in sensual pleasure or in material wealth but in virtue and understanding. A life of pure self-seeking or unrestrained self-indulgence leads only to a sense of enervation and futility. In living virtuously, however, "I feel within me sensations which lead me to forget myself, which have as their object something other than myself and my advantage . . .; sensations of the good and of order, which my mere will has not made and which my mere will cannot destroy . . ."[74] It would constitute a betrayal of my own nature to ignore these sensations and to pursue nothing other than my own pleasure. "I will therefore aspire continually to strengthen and in all possible ways to satisfy the inclination to the good implanted in me. The happiness of the human race, which makes such a pleasant impression on me, must unalterably be an object of my most earnest endeavours and must be my own happiness."[75]

Virtuous deeds by themselves suffice to render me happy, whatever my fate may be, says Spalding. Beyond this, however, "all of nature serves to multiply my pleasure." Contemplating it, I see that "All is order; all is proportion; all is consequently a new object of pleasure, love, and joy." And this leads to the further thought of "a prototype of the perfections, of an original beauty, of a first and general source of order."[76] The realization of the existence of such an infinite being inspires inexpressible feelings of admiration, devotion and humility. Compared to this being, the "earth is a speck, a point. And I upon this earth—what am I?" This question does not lead, however, to self-abasement. It is immediately followed by the reflection that I am after all something, since I perceive this order and can contemplate its origins. "I will not stand still until I have pursued this beauty to its first source. Only there shall my soul find rest. There, with all its capacities pleased, all its drives satisfied, full of divine light, and delighted in the worship and adoration of the supreme, universal perfection, shall it forget everything base as well as itself."[77]

For Spalding, all aspects of the natural order reflect the limitless goodness of God. Living naturally, in accordance with the inclinations implanted in us by God, we can be happy, he initially says, even in the face of great adversity. By the end of his essay, however, there is a shift in his outlook. He comes, with considerable reluctance, to the conclusion that living in accordance with his true purpose is not enough to guarantee one happiness in this world. On the contrary, only death brings an end to the oppression of the virtuous and the good fortune of the wicked. "This contradicts all of my expectations, which were based on concepts of order." Observing this state of affairs, Spalding cannot refrain from asking:

> Can the unalterable rules of fairness allow that a soul which is as it should be is forever weakened, embittered, or robbed by an evil power of the natural, happy consequences of its inner righteousness, which would otherwise have been reward enough for it? Is it fitting that an honest nature, which deserves to be happy, be the prey of wickedness, the victim of unjust persecutions? that innocence and justice be condemned? that virtue sigh beneath hunger and nakedness and contempt, and often find its final reward in pain and torture at the hands of a cruel hangman and at the command of a still crueler tyrant? and that, on the other hand, perfidy and murderousness, in seizing the pleasures and advantages of this life, never discover what it means to turn away from the eternally just and to rebel against the laws of universal government?

Spalding's answer to this long string of rhetorical questions is a resounding "No!" It is not possible that the world will continue to be governed in this way. Something better necessarily lies ahead. "There must be a time when everyone receives his due," when the "disharmony" prevailing here below gives way to a just order. "Thus consoled, I await a remote succession of times which will be the full harvest of the present seed, and which will, by means of a universal, appropriate retribution, vindicate the Wisdom that rules over all."

It is only after he has arrived in this manner at the conviction that there must be a compensatory afterlife that Spalding considers the relation between observable human nature and human posthumous destiny. Scrutinizing himself, he sees signs of preparation for the harvest that lies ahead.

> I detect in myself capacities which are capable of infinite development, and which can also manifest themselves equally well outside of any connection with this body. Should my ability to know and to love the truth and the good cease at a time when it has either just become suited through practice to ascend much more quickly to a greater perfection, or when it has hardly begun to unfold and to stir? That would be too much vain endeavor in the arrangments of an infinite wisdom.[78]

It is, consequently, evident that a life after death awaits us. Knowing this, it should be possible for us to bear all of the travails of this life and to face the prospect of death with equanimity. Spalding concludes with the declaration that "I will therefore fill my entire mind ever more with the consolatory idea that I will yet live in another condition in which, by the nature of things and in accordance with the beneficent rule of the supreme wisdom, I ought to expect nothing but good . . ."[79]

Clearly, Spalding is not a metaphysician after the manner of Leibniz and Wolff. But just as clearly, his "Thoughts on the Destiny of Man" reflect, as many scholars have noted, the pervasive influence of the Leibniz-Wolffian philosophy. This philosophy shapes his ideas of God's benevolence, the structure of the world, and the purpose for which God has created rational souls. What is present in Leibniz's teaching and virtually implicit in that of Wolff but absent in that of Spalding, the Protestant cleric, is any recognition of the existence of some tension between this understanding of the overall divine design and traditional Christian dogmas. In typical neological fashion, Spalding has set these dogmas aside, and he has thereby cleared the way for a more unrestrainedly anthropocentric and optimistic version of the Leibniz-Wolffian philosophy.

As the heirs of Leibniz and Wolff, Feireis identifies, in addition to the neologists, the later philosophers of the *Aufklärung*. Unlike neology, he writes, which "still wrapped the cloak of the Christian name around natural religion," even as it simultaneously sacrificed the supernatural truths of revelation, the philosophy of the *Aufklärung* in part went so far as to reject Christianity. Its most radical rationalists denied not only the necessity but the possibility of a supernatural revelation.[80] Among the leading representatives of this tendency Feireis numbers Baumgarten, G. F. Meier, Hermann Samuel Reimarus, C. W. Wieland, and Lessing. Of these thinkers, the only one who appears to have exercised a noticeable influence on Mendelssohn's teaching concerning divine providence and immortality is Reimarus, and it is to his thought that we will now turn.

"There was," as Charles H. Talbert has put it, "a public and a private Reimarus."[81] The public Reimarus was, above all, the author of *The Foremost Truths of Natural Religion*. In the course of the second half of the eighteenth century this highly popular exposition of the basic teachings of natural religion went through six editions in Germany and was translated into Dutch, English, and French.[82] It is with this work alone that we shall concern ourselves here. We will, for the most part, postpone our consideration of "the private Reimarus," the author of the famous "Wolffenbüttel Fragments," to the second part of this study.

What chiefly differentiates *The Foremost Truths* from these posthumously published fragments and the larger work from which they are taken is their divergent assessment of revealed religion in general and Christianity in particular. At bottom, Reimarus believed in the sufficiency of natural religion. As Günter Gawlick has observed, he considered Christianity to be not a divine religion at all but a mere human invention that led people away from natural religion.[83] In writings not intended for publication, Reimarus was, as we shall see, a relentless critic of both the Old and the New Testaments. In *The Foremost Truths*, on the other hand, he adopted a rather different approach.

It is not quite accurate to say, as Talbert did, that in this work he "took pleasure in showing that the demands of natural religion and those of Christianity agreed, or complemented one another."[84] What he did, rather, was simply to assert that they complemented one another, that natural religion was the necessary foundation of Christianity. He sought to leave the impression that his defense of the former was partly motivated by his desire to protect the latter. Reimarus resorted to this "deceptive maneuvre," as Günter Gawlick has characterized it, to avoid exposure to the "social obloquy" that befell not only atheists but even deists or "rational worshippers of God" in his day.[85] At this he was quite successful. His book earned the "undivided applause of the Protestant theologians and was frequently cited in order to refute French atheism."[86]

Reimarus makes no secret of his debt to the Leibniz-Wolffian tradition. He is, to be sure, no more than Spalding a metaphysician of the old school. In the earlier parts of *The Foremost Truths*, where he attempts to demonstrate the existence of God, he avoids any mention of the ontological proof and presents cosmological and physicotheological arguments in a very down-to-earth, commonsensical fashion. The God whose existence he seeks to establish is, however, very recognizably the God of Leibniz's theodicy. He is absolutely omnipotent and possesses complete foreknowledge of everything that is ever to take place. The world he has created is the best of all those that are possible. Reimarus explicitly credits Leibniz with having shown how to explain the existence of evil within this world.[87]

This is not to say, however, that Reimarus's understanding of divine providence is simply identical to that of Leibniz. He parts company with him, most notably, in his explanation of God's purpose in creating the world. Where Leibniz, as we have seen, describes God as having created the world in order to manifest his own glory to his rational creatures, Reimarus sees the purpose of creation as the bringing into being of a world that "encompasses within it all possible living beings, that comprehends all the inner perfection, joy, and happiness that is possible, and all outer perfection and beauty compatible with them." To extend reality to such a world, "to grant life and happiness, according to its kind, to everything that is capable of pleasure is the great aim of the Creator."[88]

Here, of course, Reimarus is restating the age-old idea of the "chain of being," an idea to which Leibniz was by no means a stranger. In fact, as Arthur O. Lovejoy observed in his classic *The Great Chain of Being*, "Among the great philosophic systems of the seventeenth century, it is in that of Leibniz that the conception of the Chain of Being is most conspicuous, most determinative, and most pervasive."[89] Leibniz, however, did not, as did Reimarus, identify the fabrication of such a chain as God's fundamental aim in bringing the world into existence.

This shift in emphasis, in Reimarus's *The Foremost Truths*, implies a diminution of the importance of rational souls in the whole divine scheme of things. From constituting "the principal part of God's design" they are demoted to parts equal in God's eyes to others, including the animals. Reimarus, indeed, makes this explicit. He warns us against our habit of placing ourselves at the center of the universe and seeing ourselves as the purpose of creation. "The world," he emphasizes, "exists for the sake of the living, among whom we are included; all of nature works together to sustain us. But the world exists not for us alone; it exists for the sake of all possible living beings of all kinds and grades."[90]

Rational beings may have lost, in Reimarus's view, their special primacy, but their happiness is still most definitely of a higher order than that of lesser living beings. In the seventh treatise of *The Foremost Truths*, entitled "A Comparison of Man with the Animals," Reimarus explains at great length the precise sense in which this is the case. Unlike many of the animals, he concludes, man is by nature a social being, compelled to join together with his fellows to satisfy his bodily needs. Unlike all of the animals, he desires something more than the satisfaction of these needs. Gifted with reason, he takes pleasure in knowledge of the truth. By nature he seeks to raise himself to an understanding of the source of all truth and perfection. Possessing foresight, he concerns himself not only, as do the animals, with the pleasures of the moment, but with possible and future goods. He has an infinite desire to attain ever greater perfection and felicity.

Our use of reason for the attainment of an ever greater perfection of our minds, and the pleasure we receive from doing so, is what most distinguishes us: "this is human, this is natural, or in accordance with the intention of the creator with regard to our nature."[91] But, Reimarus asks, if a man acts in accordance with his nature, and "chiefly seeks his pleasure in the inner perfection of his understanding and his will," can he be fully content and happy in this world?[92] He faces, after all, innumerable obstacles. Many of these obstacles can certainly be overcome through industry, wisdom, and virtue, Reimarus is prepared to insist. In the end, however, he acknowledges that "a perfection and felicity that would be equal to our desires is not to be hoped for . . ." in this life. For no matter how successfully and happily one conducts oneself, the prospect of impending death is enough to turn everything sour.[93] This is a point which Reimarus endeavors to drive home through a lengthy and impassioned description of the desperate state of mind of the man who believes that his physical death will mark the end of his existence.[94]

We long for a more lasting and better life. This longing "springs from the powers and rules of our understanding, and is in conformity with the essence of our soul and its capacity for greater perfection and felicity." It cannot therefore be dismissed as "an unnatural whim and a sweet dream."[95] The nature of things must correspond to our wishes. We have implanted in us the ability to conceive of something beyond this life and to imagine our future condition as a life of immeasurable duration where we will enjoy much greater felicity than we do in this troubled world. Such a life must exist, for how could God "have roused his rational creatures, through their nature, to an idea of a longer and better life, and to a desire for it, if that were not what he had allotted to us?"[96]

"The hope that our soul is destined to enjoy an infinitely long and happy life after this life is based chiefly on the divine purpose in creation and on God's particular providence with regard to man."[97] It is not on this basis alone, however, that we conclude that an afterlife must exist. We would offend divine justice, Reimarus maintains, if we did not believe that God rewarded those virtuous and pious men who suffer in this world with a better life. It is likewise necessary to believe that sinners who caused great suffering in this world but nevertheless lived prosperous lives will be punished in the future according to their deserts. If the "disharmony" existing on earth were not in this way resolved, not only would divine justice be undermined, but there would be no motive left for virtue and piety or for the observance of divine commandments. In the next life, the pious will attain their proper perfection. The wicked will have to pay for their bad deeds—though whether they will have to do so eternally or whether there will be an end to their punishment is a question Reimarus does not address.[98]

Much of what we said about Spalding could be said, with as much justice, about Reimarus. His work, too, represents a continuation of the main themes of the Leibniz-Wolffian philosophy concerning divine providence and immortality. Like Spalding, he addresses the question of human destiny without basing himself in any way on revelation. Having set aside Christian dogma (without attacking it), Reimarus, like Spalding, is free to develop a more optimistic version of the Leibniz-Wolffian philosophy. If, according to his view, rational creatures have lost their centrality in the divine scheme of things, they have nonetheless gained a more secure hold on happiness. Reimarus emphatically and repeatedly states that God's aim is the happiness of living beings, without ever adding, as does Leibniz, "that the unhappiness of some of these creatures may come about by concomitance, and as a result of other greater goods." He recognizes, to be sure, the limitations on human happiness on earth, but he is firmly convinced that the righteous, at least, are headed for a better life, which will more than compensate for whatever they have suffered here below. And he does not rule out the possibility that even the evil will ultimately enjoy their share of felicity.

As we have seen, the rational teachings of Leibniz with regard to divine providence and immortality set the stage for subsequent treatments of these questions within the world of the German Enlightenment. Leibniz's understanding of God's greatness and goodness, his will and his wisdom, as well as his concepts of the best of all possible worlds, God's promotion of the perfection and felicity of rational beings, and the afterlife all become the common heritage of Wolff, the neologists, and rationalists like Reimarus. What Leibniz does not pass along to all of his successors is a willingness to accomodate his philosophical understanding of divine providence to received Christian teachings.

Christian doctrines concerning the eternal punishment of the overwhelming majority of human beings cast a dark shadow over Leibniz's essentially optimistic teaching. Constrained to accept such doctrines, Leibniz had no choice but to admit that the best of all possible worlds was in the end, for all but the small number of the elect, a dismal and forbidding place. It was with this inescapable reality in mind (whether he truly accepted it or not) that Leibniz formulated his explanation of God's purpose in creating the world. He could not very well say that God created it for the sake of his rational creatures if most of the rational creatures known to his readers were destined to face eternal punishment in the afterlife. To accommodate his teaching to received Christian doctrines, therefore, he emphasized that "the felicity of all rational creatures is one of the aims he has in view; but it is not his whole aim, nor even his final aim." This makes it possible to understand why, in the best of all possible worlds, most human beings will still be unhappy—forever. But whatever Leibniz says, knowledge of this fact undeniably makes it difficult for people to love God wholeheartedly here below.

In abandoning the received Christian doctrine, the later Leibnizians freed themselves of the constraint under which Leibniz himself felt forced to operate. Nothing prevented them from portraying the ultimate destiny of most or all human beings in a favorable light. Nothing, therefore, prevented them from declaring the perfection and happiness of human beings to be part of God's final aim.

Notes

1. Quoted in Alexander Altmann, *Moses Mendelssohn*, p. 684.

2. *G. W. Leibniz's Monadology*, ed. Nicholas Rescher (Pittsburgh: University of Pittsburgh Press, 1991), p. 21, sec. 31. This "student edition" of the *Monadology* includes the most readily available compendium of English translations of lengthy citations from Leibniz's other works. We will cite it, when possible.

3. Ibid., p. 114.

4. Ibid., p. 21, sec. 32.

5. Ibid., p. 118.

6. Ibid., pp. 21–22, sec. 37.

7. Ibid., p. 135.

8. See Dieter Henrich, *Der ontologische Gottesbeweis*, (Tübingen: J.C.B. Mohr, 1967), pp. 10–22.

9. Nicholas Rescher, ed., *G.W. Leibniz's Monadology*, pp. 141–42.

10. Jan Rohls, *Theologie und Metaphysik, Der ontologische Gottbeweis und seine Kritiker*, (Gütersloh: Gutersloher Verlaghaus G. Mohn, 1987), p. 243.

11. Ibid., p. 249.

12. Stuart Brown, *Leibniz* (Minneapolis: University of Minnesota Press, 1984), p. 62.

13. Rohls, *Theologie und Metaphysik*, p. 250.

14. Ibid., p. 251.

15. Henrich, *Der ontologische Gottesbeweis*, p. 47.

16. Rescher, *G. W. Leibniz's Monadology*, p. 22, secs. 43–44.

17. G. W. Leibniz, *Principles of Nature and of Grace, Founded on Reason* (1714) in *Leibniz: Philosophical Writings*, trans. Mary Morris (London, 1934), p. 27, no. 11.

18. Henrich, *Der ontologische Gottesbeweis*, pp. 55–57.

19. Ibid., pp. 58–59.

20. For a brief sketch of Baumgarten's thought, see Lewis White Beck, *Early German Philosophy* (Cambridge, Mass.: Harvard University Press, 1969), pp. 283–86.

21. Alexander Altmann, *Essays in Jewish Intellectual History* (Hanover, N.H. and London: University Press of New England, 1981), p. 130.

22. Henry E. Allison, *Lessing and the Enlightenment: His Philosophy of Religion and Its Relation to Eighteenth-Century Thought* (Ann Arbor: University of Michigan Press, 1966), p. 25.

23. Ibid., p. 27.

24. See G. W. Leibniz, *Theodicy*, trans. E. M. Huggard (London: Routledge & Keegan Paul, 1951), pp. 51–52.

25. Quoted from the French translation of the *Causa Dei* in G. W. Leibniz, *Essais de Théodicée*, ed. J. Brunschwig (Paris: Garnier-Flammarion, 1969), pp. 425–27, secs. 1–13.

26. Nicholas Rescher, ed., *G. W. Leibniz's Monadology*, pp. 163–64.

27. Ibid., p. 165.

28. G. W. Leibniz, *Theodicy*, p. 152.

29. Leibniz, *Causa Dei*, p. 432, sec. 40.

30. Leibniz, *Theodicy*, p. 129.

31. Quoted in Rescher, *G. W. Leibniz's Monadology*, p. 195.

32. John Hick, *Evil and the God of Love*, rev. ed., (San Fransisco: Harper and Row, 1978), p. 167.

33. Leibniz, *Theodicy*, p. 164.

34. Rescher, *G. W. Leibniz's Monadology*, p. 28.

35. Ibid., p. 300.

36. Ibid., p. 279.

37. Leibniz, *Theodicy*, p. 188.

38. Ibid., *Theodicy*, p. 189.

39. G. W. Leibniz, *Principles of Nature and of Grace, Founded on Reason* [1714] in *Leibniz, Philosophical Writings*, trans. Mary Morris, p. 28, sec. 15. See Gaston Grua, *Jurisprudence Universelle et Théodicée selon Leibniz* (Paris: Presses Universitaire de France, 1953), pp. 376ff. for additional, similar statements by Leibniz.

40. Leibniz, *Essais de Théodicée*, pp. 428–30, secs. 18–28.

41. Ibid, p. 431, sec. 33.

42. Ibid., sec. 34.

43. Ibid., sec. 36.

44. Ibid., p. 437, secs. 66–68.

45. Rescher, *G. W. Leibniz's Monadology*, p. 17, secs. 3–6.

46. Ibid., pp. 18–19.

47. Ibid., p. 19, sec. 19.

48. Ibid., p. 27, sec. 77.

49. Ibid., p. 251.

50. G. W. Leibniz, *Discourse on Metaphysics, Correspondence with Arnauld and Monadology*, trans. George R. Montgomery (La Salle, Ill.: Open Court, 1962), p. 233.

51. *Theodicy*, I, 19. See D. P. Walker, *The Decline of Hell: Seventeenth-Century Discussions of Eternal Torment* (Chicago: University of Chicago Press, 1964), p. 35ff, for a review of the scriptural basis of this doctrine as well as the way in which, in the seventeenth century, "this enormous majority of the number of the damned" came to be "felt to be a nuisance."

52. Leibniz, *Essais de Théodicée*, p. 435, sec. 56.

53. Ibid., sec. 57.

54. Leibniz, *Theodicy*, p. 135.

55. Leibniz, *Essais de Théodicée*, p. 436, sec. 59.

56. Rescher, *G. W. Leibniz's Monadology*, p. 302.

57. Ibid., p. 300.

58. Allison, *Lessing and the Enlightenment*, p. 42. Lessing understood Leibniz differently, see pp. 86–90.

59. *Moses Mendelssohn Gesammelte Schriften Jubiläumsausgabe* (henceforth: *JubA*) vol. 3, 2 (Berlin and Stuttgart-Bad Cannstatt: Friedrich Frommann Verlag, 1972), p. civ. Strauss refers the reader to section 272 of the *Theodicy*, which does not, as far as I can see, substantiate his claim.

60. *JubA*, vol. 3, 2, p. ciii.

61. Thomas P. Saine, *Von der Kopernikanischen bis zur Französischen Revolution, Die Auseinandersetzung der deutschen Frühaufklärung mit der neuen Zeit* (Berlin: Erich Schmidt, 1987), p. 135.

62. Ibid., p. 129. In the following discussion of Wolff I rely heavily on Saine.

63. Ibid., p. 130.

64. Ibid., pp. 145–60.

65. Ibid., p. 87.

66. Konrad Feiereis, *Die Umprägung der Natürlichen Theologie in Religionsphilosophie* (Leipzig: St. Benno-Verlag, 1965), p. 32.

67. Allison, *Lessing and the Enlightenment*, p. 38.

68. Ibid., p. 40.

69. Ibid., p. 42.

70. Altmann, *Moses Mendelssohn*, p. 553.

71. Feiereis, *Die Umprägung der Natürlichen Theologie in Religionsphilosophie*, p. 39.

72. Emanuel Hirsch, *Geschichte der Neuern Evangelischen Theologie*, vol. 4 (Munster: Antiquariat T. Stenderhoff, 1964), p. 15.

73. Altmann, *Moses Mendelssohn*, p. 132.

74. Johann Joachim Spalding, *Bestimmung des Menschen* in *Studien zur Geschichte des neueren Protestantismus*, ed. Heinrich Hoffman and Leopold Zscharnack (Giessen: A. Topelmann, 1908), p. 20.

75. Ibid., pp. 21–22.

76. Ibid., p. 24.

77. Ibid., p. 25.

78. Ibid., pp. 27–28.

79. Ibid., p. 30.

80. Feiereis, *Die Umprägung der Natürlichen Theologie in Religionsphilosophie*, p. 68.

81. Charles H. Talbert, *Reimarus: Fragments*, trans. Ralph S. Fraser (Philadelphia: Fortress Press, 1970), p. 6.

82. Ibid., p. 6. For additional information concerning the book's lasting popularity, see Hermann Samuel Reimarus, *Die vornehmste Wahrheiten der natürlichen Religion*, ed. Günter Gawlick (Göttingen: Vandenhoeck and Ruprecht, 1985), p.33.

83. Ibid., pp. 11–13.

84. Talbert, *Reimarus: Fragments*, p. 6.

85. Reimarus, *Die vornehmste Wahrheiten der natürlichen Religion*, p. 13. Until "it pleases God to pave a way to unfettered, public freedom" for such a faith, he argued in the preface to the *Apologie*, its champions ought to guard it "like a secret treasure, in conscientious silence."

86. Feiereis, *Die Umprägung der Natürlichen Theologie in Religionsphilosophie*, p. 77.

87. Reimarus, *Die vornehmste Wahrheiten der natürlichen Religion*, p. 612.

88. Ibid., pp. 615–16.

89. Arthur O. Lovejoy, *The Great Chain of Being* (Cambridge, Mass.: Harvard University Press, 1976), p. 144.

90. Reimarus, *Die vornehmste Wahrheiten der natürlichen Religion*, pp. 430–31.

91. Ibid., pp. 566–67.

92. Ibid., p. 571.

93. Ibid., p. 573.

94. Ibid., pp. 723ff.

95. Ibid., p. 706.

96. Ibid., pp. 708–9.

97. Ibid., p. 691.

98. Ibid., pp. 719–21.

2
Mendelssohn's Natural Theology

Moses Mendelssohn was the last great representative of the Leibniz-Wolffian school. From Leibniz and Wolff, above all, he derived the substance of his metaphysics or natural theology. He reiterated and refined these philosophers' major proofs for the existence of God. His concept of divine providence was essentially Leibnizian, as was his demonstration of the immortality of the human soul. Even where Mendelssohn differed significantly from his mentors, it was not because he departed from Leibnizian principles but because he applied them more thoroughly and consistently than did Leibniz himself.

In this chapter we will review Mendelssohn's natural theology, concentrating on his dependency on the metaphysical writings of his predecessors as well as on the extent to which he introduced new and original arguments in defense of the fundamental principles of God, providence, and immortality. We will also consider the extent to which he sought, in his presentation of his arguments, to respond to some of the specific objections made by the contemporary critics of traditional metaphysics.

The Existence of God

As we have just noted, Mendelssohn's proofs for the existence of God were not original arguments but were based on the major proofs that had been presented by the Leibniz-Wolffian school, the cosmological and the ontological arguments. Mendelssohn, to be sure, did not simply borrow these proofs, but, as Alexander Altmann has pointed out, he refined and reformulated them in a number of different ways. Often he did so to respond to the arguments of critics of the proofs for God's existence, particularly Immanuel Kant. Altmann has described Mendelssohn's procedure in exhaustive, detailed analyses of each of his proofs at each stage of its development. In reviewing these proofs it will, accordingly, be necessary to pay particularly close attention to Altmann's studies.[1]

The Cosmological Proof

As we have seen, the proof from the contingency of the world in its Leibniz-Wolffian form rests on Leibniz's well-known principle of sufficient reason. In virtue of that principle, according to Leibniz, "no fact can be real or actual, and no proposition true, without there being a sufficient reason for its being so and not otherwise, although most often these reasons just cannot be known by us." There are in the world real facts, truths of fact, which are contingent, which might not have come into being. There must be a sufficient reason for their existence, one that lies outside of the whole series of contingencies. "And so the ultimate reason of things must be in a necessary substance, in which the detail of the changes is present only eminently, as in its source. It is this that we call *God*."[2] Wolff adopted this Leibnizian proof from contingency, and Mendelssohn followed Wolff's exposition of it in the *Treatise on Evidence*.

It is only in *Morning Hours* that Mendelssohn departs, as Altmann has observed, from Wolff's exposition of the proof from the contingency of the world. He does so not by giving it an original twist but by laying a particular stress "on a certain aspect of Leibniz's doctrine that Wolff does not seem to have utilized in his presentation of the proof," that is, "Leibniz's view that contingent truths depend on the principle of fitness or choice of the best in contrast to eternal truths, which follow from God's understanding."[3] Mendelssohn, as Altmann puts it, "links this metaphysical distinction with his own epistemological theory of the difference between thinking, willing, and approving, a tripartite division of the faculties of the soul" that played a significant part in his aesthetics.[4] God brought into being the existing contingent things, says Mendelssohn, because they were the best, and in choosing the best he was exercising his faculty of approval. In connecting this aspect of Leibniz's thought with the proof from the contingency of the world, Mendelssohn in no way alters that proof; he merely clarifies the inner-divine motivation for bringing into being the world of which God, as the necessary being, is otherwise known to be the sufficient reason.

In the *Treatise on Evidence*, Mendelssohn's presentation of the cosmological proof does not lead to any further complications.

In *Morning Hours*, however, his exposition of that proof is immediately followed by a question: "As for this necessary being itself, where does the reason for its own existence lie?" Mendelssohn's answer is a reference to the ontological argument: the reason for the existence of the necessary being lies "in its inner essence, in its inner possibility; i.e., it exists because it is thinkable (*denkbar*); its nonexistence cannot be thought and is therefore an untruth (*Unwahrheit*)."[5] "It would seem," as Altmann has observed, that Mendelssohn "thereby indicated the need for the cosmological argument to fall back upon the ontological . . ."[6]

In Chapter XVI of *Morning Hours*, just before the presentation of the ontological proof with which the book concludes, Mendelssohn presents a version of the cosmological proof that he characterizes as "an attempt at a new proof for the existence of God from the incompleteness of self-knowledge."[7] This attempt proceeds along a path that, Mendelssohn says, as far as he knows, has been followed by no other philosopher.[8] Instead of seeking to prove that contingent things could not have come into being unless they had been *caused* to exist by a necessary being, Mendelssohn here sought to show that they could not have come into existence unless they had been *thought* by a being whose intellect was capable of thinking them.

The basis of Mendelssohn's argument is, as Altmann put it, "the assumption that the possible cannot be considered possible unless actually thought to be so; and that the real too, apart from also being possible and on this score alone requiring to be an object of thought, cannot be said to have objective reality unless recognized as such by some subjective mind."[9] I know that I exist, Mendelssohn argues, and I can also see that my own subjective mind is not equipped to grasp all aspects of my existence. Yet, if everything real, including me, must have an ideal existence in thought, "there must be in existence a being which represents to itself in the clearest, purest and most detailed manner everything that pertains to my existence." But this is far beyond the capacity of any contingent being, indeed of all contingent beings taken together.

> In a word, no truth can be thought, as being possible, with the highest degree of knowledge, and no reality can be thought, as being real, in the most perfect manner by a contingent being. There must therefore exist a thinking being, an understanding, which thinks in the most perfect manner the sum of all possibilities, as being possible, and the sum of all realities, as being real. . . . *There exists an infinite understanding, etc.*

The *et cetera* leads, presumably, to the existence of a being that possesses infinite understanding, that is, God.

The most vulnerable point of this argument, and the one that Mendelssohn made the most strenuous effort to defend, is its premise, the notion that nothing possible or real can have objective reality unless it exists in thought. Immediately after completing his argument Mendelssohn takes note of the following possible objection to that premise: "I understand very well, many people may say, that everything real can be nothing other than thinkable. But how does it follow from this that some being must in fact think it? Is this not a case of concluding from a possibility to a reality, from *can* to *occurs* (*von Können auf Geschehen schliessen*)?"[10] Mendelssohn responds to this objection with a long excursus on the nature of possibility. When we say that something *can* exist or that it is possible, he explains, we are referring to something that is not yet actual. "At bottom, everything possible, in so far as it is merely possible, is not an objective predicate of a thing."[11] When we attribute a possibility to something, we are not referring to anything that is actually present but to a quality that that thing might take on, under other circumstances. That is to say,

> . . . from the present state, from the real condition of a thing, the thought can arise in a thinking subject that under other circumstances that thing can exist in a different condition, and that therefore this other condition is thinkable. All possibilities therefore have their ideal existence in the thinking subject and it ascribes them to objects as thinkable. An unthought possibility is a true absurdity (*ein wahres Unding*).

Thus far, in answer to the objection he himself had raised, Mendelssohn has sought to show that everything possible must be thought in order to exist as a mere possibility. The objection, however, had focused not on the possible but on the real. Why *must* the real be thought in order to exist? Mendelssohn does not address this question directly. He seems to be supposing that what applies to the merely possible must also apply to the real, because everything real was merely possible before it came into existence. In any case, on the basis of the argument we have examined, he arrives at the conclusion that "everything real must not only be *thinkable*, but must also be *thought* by some being. To every real existence there corresponds in some subject an ideal existence; to every thing an idea."[12]

The most potent objections to this "attempt" at a new proof for the existence of God were made by Ludwig Heinrich Jakob in his Kantian critique of Mendelssohn's *Morning Hours.* Jakob refused to accept Mendelssohn's basic premise. "One can," he wrote, "still distinguish the *possible* from the *thinkable.*" The possible can be defined much as Mendelssohn defined it, as expressing an objective condition that is not an objective predicate; it merely refers to that which may come into being in accordance with certain logical laws. *Thinkable*, on the other hand, expresses the relationship between certain signs or characteristics (*Merkmale*) and the knowing subject itself. "The idea of the thinkable is therefore a mere postulate in the human mind, without which the real cannot be known. It is a general concept, which must necessarily be found in all objects. But that is why many things can be objectively real whose objective possibility and reality are not known by any thinking being."[13] Jakob proceeds to give examples of what he means. A clock, he says, can tell time without anyone ever observing it to do so. An artist needs only to fashion his work in accordance with the proper rules. Even if he subsequently dies, his work may persist forever. What is to prevent us, Jakob asks, from regarding the world as such a work of art, "which a wise architect put in order," and which he then abandoned forever?[14] There would, in that case, be no reason why it could not contain innumerable possibilities and realities unknown to any thinking subject.

Jakob acknowledges, a little later, that if the "possible" means merely that which is subjectively possible, then it has to be thought in order to be possible, for "thoughts cannot hover around outside thinking beings." But if "possible" means the objectively possible, "there is no reason why these things have to be thought." Likewise, argued Jakob, there is no reason why "the real" has to be represented by a thinking being to attain reality. He rejected, in short, both Mendelssohn's original argument and his defense of his basic premise against a possible objection. According to Altmann, Jakob's arguments seem to have "failed to live up to the point made by Mendelssohn." He does not explain, however, why he believes this to be the case.[15]

The Ontological Proof

In the *Treatise on Evidence* Mendelssohn presents the ontological proof just as he there presents the cosmological proof; that is, forthrightly, without any apologies, and with evident confidence that it is irrefutable. He is well aware, however, of the uniqueness and the difficulty of the ontological proof, a difficulty that, he suggests, lies more in the way it has been expounded in the past than in the proof itself. He decides, for that reason, to give it "a lighter twist."

"Since the existence of a thing is in general so difficult to explain," he writes, "let us begin with non-existence." There are two different ways in which a thing can be nonexistent: it must be either impossible or merely possible. An impossible being is one to which contradictory attributes are ascribed. This cannot be true of the most perfect being, which is characterized only by "realities" (*Realitäten*) and not by negations or limitations. Because with respect to the most perfect being all realities are affirmed and all negations are denied, there can be no contradiction in the conception of it. Whoever says that the most perfect being contains a contradiction contradicts himself. If the most perfect being is not impossible, the only other reason for regarding it as nonexistent would be that it is merely possible. But this cannot be the case, for the existence of a merely possible being is only a mode, "whose reality can only be explained through another reality." Such a being is dependent on some other being for its existence. "Now the most perfect being cannot exist in this manner, for this would contradict its essence, for everyone can see that an independent existence is a greater perfection than a dependent one . . ." Because, then, the most perfect being cannot be impossible and it cannot be merely possible, it cannot be nonexistent; it must exist.[16]

Following the exposition of this proof, Mendelssohn seeks to show the same truth in a different way. This time, as Altmann has observed, he simply spells out "the implications of the concept of existence according to Alexander Gottlieb Baumgarten's ontology . . ." According to that ontology, as Altmann puts it,

> all that exists is totally (*omnimode*) determined, and the reverse is equally true: Everything that is totally determined exists. In the case of the most perfect being only essential or inner determinations can apply. Hence it is sufficiently determined by dint of its essence, and it either exists or is altogether indeterminate and impossible. Since it cannot be impossible, as has been shown, it necessarily exists.[17]

These, then, are the ways in which Mendelssohn expounded the ontological proof in his *Treatise on Evidence*. Not until 1778, a decade and a half after the composition of the treatise, did he write anything further concerning this kind of proof for the existence of God. At that time, for reasons Altmann has explained, Mendels-

sohn wrote a very brief essay in defense of the ontological proof
that he circulated privately among certain of his philosophical
friends, critics of that proof.[18] In this essay Mendelssohn presented
certain new versions of the ontological proof. Their novelty lay, as
Altmann put it, "in the distinction between objective being and
subjective thinking, and in the endeavor to show that what is objectively untrue cannot be subjectively thought and, vice versa,
what is subjectively unthinkable cannot be objectively true."[19]
Seven years later, however, when Mendelssohn presented in *Morning Hours* what he "believed to be true in the matter" of proofs for
God's existence, he did not restate these unpublished proofs. Yet he
did take up and amplify something else that first appeared in the
1778 document; that is, a response to Kant's critique of the ontological argument.

In his treatise of 1763, *On the Only Possible Proof for the Existence of God*, Immanuel Kant propounded a conception of existence that, in his opinion, effectively undercut the ontological argument. Existence, he maintained, is not a real predicate or a
determination. It is merely the positing of a thing. Existence,
therefore, is not a reality or a perfection. The actual contains no
more than the merely possible. The most perfect being does not,
therefore, necessarily exist.[20]

In his 1778 essay Mendelssohn made the following observations with regard to his new versions of the ontological proof: "By
the way, I made no assumption to the effect that existence was
either a reality or a perfection. I take it no one will deny that it is a
positive determination (*determinatio positiva*), or since words are
irrelevant, that it can be transformed into a positing predicate
(*predicatum ponens*)." According to Altmann, this was obviously
"an attempt at invalidating Kant's objection to the ontological argument. By equating existence with a positive determination and
reducing the latter to a positing predicate, Mendelssohn sought to
dissolve the criticism into a mere verbal quibble (*Wortstreit*), a
method of which he was extremely fond."[21]

In *Morning Hours* Mendelssohn dealt with this matter more
fully. After first reviewing the ontological proof, he paraphrased
Kant's objection to it, and then made the following statement:

> I can admit this. Actual existence may be not a quality
> (*Eigenschaft*) but the position of all qualities of a thing, or it
> may be something else inexplicable, that is well known to all
> of us; it is enough that I can think the contingent without this
> position. I can omit existence from the idea of the contingent

without cancelling the idea. It remains a concept without an object. But this is not the case with respect to the necessary being. I cannot separate existence from the idea of it without annihilating the idea itself. I must think the concept and the object, or give up the concept itself. Everything rests on this important distinction, and this distinction by no means rests on an arbitrary definition; it follows from the concept itself, and the most stiffnecked opponent cannot cast doubt upon it.[22]

Mendelssohn, then, as we can see, made no attempt to defend the idea that existence was a predicate or a reality. He was prepared to grant the validity of Kant's views concerning the nature of existence. But it is not completely clear that it was necessary for him to do so. Kant's views on existence were, as Allen W. Wood has argued, far from unassailable. In his book *Kant's Rational Theology*, Wood engages in an extensive analysis of the argument presented by Kant in *The Only Possible Proof* and repeated in the *Critique of Pure Reason*. In the end, he concludes that

> Kant does succeed in setting forth a view about existence and predication which, if it is correct, does rid us once and for all of the concept of logically necessary existence, and with it the ontological argument. But he provides us with no good reasons for thinking his view to be the correct one. Kant's view has been, and still is, widely accepted and is even (owing to its adoption by Gottlob Frege and Bertrand Russell) incorporated into the standard systems of formal logic, via the existence quantifier. Yet no one as far as I can tell has ever presented a really persuasive argument for it.[23]

Rather than dispute Kant's conception of existence, however, Mendelssohn granted that it might be valid. He therefore sought to uphold the ontological argument without making any further reference to existence as being a reality or a perfection that the most perfect being must possess. Instead, he shifted his ground. He resorted to what Dieter Henrich has designated as the second ontological argument, the argument not from the idea of the most perfect being but from the idea of the necessary being.[24] The necessary being, Mendelssohn maintained, cannot be conceived otherwise than as existing and must therefore exist.

Nevertheless, even this argument is not presented as if it were absolutely decisive. Mendelssohn raises the following objection against it, placing it in the mouth of a hypothetical opponent:

But do you not in the end draw conclusions . . . from your thoughts with regard to reality, from your capacity or incapacity to form concepts to the nature of things? The necessary being must actually be present because man cannot think it otherwise? . . . Who guarantees that *what we must think of as real must also really exist (würklich vorhanden sey, was wir uns als würklich denken müssen)*?[25]

Mendelssohn responds to this objection not, as one might expect, with a ringing assertion that whatever rational creatures regard as necessarily existing must necessarily exist but with the following statement:

Happy are we if so much is granted to us for the time being; if our opponents concede that man *must* think a Divine being as existing in reality. This [admission] would be a step of great importance. Everything would be gained thereby for the entire system of human insights, mental attitudes, and actions. For is a man capable of more than the pursuit of convictions and actions according to human powers?[26]

"Thus," as Altmann has written, "Mendelssohn was quite content to leave the debate at this point. The admission that man was inevitably led toward forming a concept of a necessary and most perfect being seemed to him a momentous step in the right direction and almost as beneficial to mankind as the acknowledgement of the validity of the proofs for the existence of God."[27]

Providence and Immortality

Nowhere is the Leibnizian basis of Mendelssohn's understanding of divine providence and immortality more evident than in his *Sache Gottes*, a work he composed toward the end of his life for the use of his son Joseph and some of his Jewish acquaintances and that he apparently did not intend to publish. This brief work constitutes to some extent a paraphrase and to some extent a revision of Leibniz's *Causa Dei*, his "methodical abridgement" of the basic teachings of the *Theodicy*. But while the *Sache Gottes* very plainly has its roots in Leibniz's thought, it is also, as Leo Strauss has observed, the only one of his writings in which Mendelssohn explicitly takes issue with the man who was for him the highest philosophical authority. To be sure, his disagreements with Leibniz are not, as Strauss puts it, "unique to this individual . . . rather, they are characteristic of the later German Enlightenment. The difference between the *Causa Dei* and the *Sache Gottes* gives palpable expression to the progress which the Enlightenment had made in Germany since Leibniz."[28]

Of Mendelssohn's earlier, published writings, those that deal most comprehensively with the questions with which we are here concerned are his correspondence on "the destiny of man" with his friend Thomas Abbt (and his later comments on that correspondence) and his *Phaedon*. In these writings, too, Mendelssohn's standpoint is basically Leibnizian, although both the manner in which he expresses his views and the overall direction of his thinking reflect the influence of Spalding, Reimarus, and other disciples of Leibniz and Wolff.[29]

In this section, we shall review Mendelssohn's discussion of providence and immortality in his philosophical writings. We shall seek to identify both its Leibnizian elements and the ways in which it adopts and modifies the treatment of these subjects in the writings of other, later representatives of the Leibniz-Wolffian school. In addition, we shall consider those aspects of Mendelssohn's account of divine providence and his proofs for the immortality of the soul that are, in fact, original. What we shall see, in the end, is that Mendelssohn's treatment of these matters is fully in accord with the spirit of the later *Aufklärung*.

Large parts of the *Sache Gottes* consist of nearly verbatim translations of passages from Leibniz's *Causa Dei* or of paraphrases of them. Mendelssohn repeats all the details of Leibniz's delineation in that work of God's attributes, his omniscience, omnipotence, etc. He adopts his definition of providence as the combination of God's goodness and greatness which manifests itself in the creation and preservation of the entire universe. He follows Leibniz in regarding God's original plan for the universe as one which encompasses, down to the last detail, everything that will ever happen.

For Mendelssohn, as for Leibniz, it is necessary at some point to come to terms with the question of miracles. In a world in which everything has from the beginning been wisely arranged by God, what need is there for miracles to take place? Yet Mendelssohn, like Leibniz, adhered to a religious tradition which affirmed the historicity of innumerable miracles. How was it possible for him to account for them?

There exists only one thorough study of Mendelssohn's understanding of miracles, Alexander Altmann's article entitled "Moses

Mendelssohn on Miracles." Reviewing all of Mendelssohn's scattered references to the subject, Altmann observes "a certain ambivalence and ambiguity." "At times," he writes, Mendelssohn "stresses the admissability of miracles as Divine acts that infringe upon the natural order. On other occasions he almost downgrades the miracle as inferior to the operations of Divine providence enacted through natural causality."[30]

In the *Treatise on Evidence*, Mendelssohn, as Altmann puts it, "breaks a lance for miracles." "Every natural event," he writes,

> has a threefold cause: First, it can be understood from the Divine power that produces it from nothing, and without this cause it is altogether impossible. It has, secondly, its cause also in the system of Divine purposes, and this too is indispensable for its existence; for God would not will its production unless He approved of it. Finally, its existence can also be understood from the efficient cause in nature, and this cause can be dispensed with if necessary. For God can produce whatever conforms to his purposes by a miracle the existence of which cannot be explained through secondary causes.[31]

Elsewhere, however, most notably in *Morning Hours*, Mendelssohn speaks, as Altmann has noted, rather disparagingly of "the mentality that always looks for miracles in order to discover the finger of the Godhead."[32] He contrasts that mentality unfavorably with the philosophical view, represented by Leibniz and Shaftsbury, which recognizes "that every effect in nature agrees with the Divine purpose and, at the same time, flows from his power." "Not to ignore God's governance and providence in the very minutest events," Mendelssohn writes, "and not to ignore them precisely because these things happen in the ordinary course of nature; thus to revere God in natural events rather than in miracles; this, it seems to me, is the highest enoblement of human concepts, the most sublime manner of thinking about God, His governance and providence."[33]

Both of these types of statements—those admitting the possibility of miracles as well as those that appear, as Altmann puts it, to reduce the role of miracles to a superfluity—can be found, as Altmann has shown, in Mendelssohn's early writings as well as in his later works. Consequently, in his opinion, "These alterations cannot be construed to follow a pattern of development but are indicative of a dialectic pervading the entire span of his life." It is, as Altmann states, a dialectic, and not a contradiction, for, although

Mendelssohn occasionally downplays the significance of miracles and disparages the faith that depends on them, he never openly denies their possibility.[34] To the extent that Mendelssohn does affirm the possibility of miracles, however, it is evidently not because his philosophical system requires him to do so but because his faith in the validity of the Bible prohibits him from doing otherwise.

Following Leibniz, Mendelssohn defines divine justice or divine rule as the combination of God's goodness and greatness "in so far as they extend to those substances which are gifted with reason and capable of felicity."[35] And, employing Leibniz's terminology, he maintains that the combination of divine goodness and divine greatness known as providence results in the coming into being of what one can describe with absolute certainty as the best of all possible worlds. It is the best, for Mendelssohn as for Leibniz, not only because it is the product of a God who, by his very nature, cannot act otherwise, but also in the sense that it best fulfills God's overall purpose.

Mendelssohn, however, does not share Leibniz's understanding of this purpose. For Leibniz, as we have seen, the best of all possible worlds is the one most suited to the display of God's own glory. God's concern with the communication of his perfections has led him, it is true, to make "the happiness of intelligent creatures" a central part of his plans. He promotes it "as far as the general harmony will permit." That is to say, the advancement of "other, greater goods" necessarily results in the "unhappiness of some of these creatures." In the case of the only intelligent creatures known to us, that is, human beings, a certain measure of unhappiness is necessarily the lot of all in this world and an immense measure is the lot of the overwhelming majority throughout all eternity. As we have already seen, it is not any imperative of his philosophical thought that leads Leibniz to conclude that God had set such drastically restrictive limits to the happiness of human beings but rather the contents of Christian theology, which stipulate the eternal damnation of most men. And it is this theological teaching that impels him to attribute to rational beings something less than absolute importance in the entire divine scheme of things.

In the writings of the neologists and the later *Aufklärung* rationalist philosophers, there is, as we have seen, a more pronounced emphasis on the central place of God's creatures in his overall plan for the world. Having abandoned the traditional Christian dogma concerning the eternal punishment of most human souls, these writers felt free to carry Leibniz's thought in the direction of what appears to be its logical conclusion and to treat the happiness of human beings as a fundamental divine goal. This happiness represents for them, at the very least, one dimension of God's final purpose. As Reimarus put it, "to grant life and happiness, according to its kind, to everything that is capable of pleasure is the great aim of the Creator."[36]

In this respect, Mendelssohn clearly follows Reimarus, and even takes things somewhat further. Unlike Reimarus, who refuses to attribute to God a greater regard for rational creatures than for the rest of the living beings, he affirms without qualification that God created the world for the sake of the happiness of its rational inhabitants. Mendelssohn argues, furthermore, that divine justice requires that all rational creatures be treated equally as ends in themselves. From these premises it follows that *every rational creature without exception* is allotted as much and as great an amount of felicity as is possible without prejudice to the supreme wisdom.

Mendelssohn does not, like Leibniz, deduce God's purpose directly from a consideration of his attributes. Instead, through contemplation of the world's contents, in a manner reminiscent of Spalding and Reimarus, he arrives at the idea that the happiness of his rational creatures is God's final aim. His inquiry into the purpose of creation begins with an examination of the results of creation, an examination based on the assumption that the world exists for the sake of something contained within it. The existing world is, he believes, the proper place to begin an inquiry into God's purposes since it unquestionably reflects them. "The immeasurable universe fulfills the purposes of God. Nature in its entirety signifies the thoughts of the Omnipotent, but through signs, which are the things themselves. Every new form which they assume is a thought of the Infinite which is fulfilled."[37] That this is the case is obvious from the simple fact that the world exists. Providence, as Mendelssohn often remarks, never misses its mark. Since the world exists, God must have intended to create it precisely as it is. But what is its overall purpose? Answering this question is the goal of the fictional Socrates, Mendelssohn's spokesman in his *Phaedon*, a revision of the Platonic dialogue of the same name.[38]

At the beginning of the third dialogue of the *Phaedon* Socrates divides all the substances in the world into two categories, the lifeless and the living. That the lifeless substances were not created for their own sake is, he says, self-evident, for they are neither conscious of their own existence nor capable of attaining any degree of perfection. The purpose of their existence is rather to be sought in the living and perceiving part of creation.

The living and perceiving part of creation is itself divided into two classes, the sensing and feeling natures and the thinking ones. The sensing and feeling natures include all the animals who walk the face of the earth, with the exception of human beings. It is for their sake, in part, that the lifeless things exist, so that they may be provided with sustenance, enjoyment, and comfort. But they are also capable of more than the mere attainment of pleasure. All of their feelings and natural drives are properties of the simple, incorporeal essences within them that are conscious of themselves as well as other things. Hence these animals possess a true perfection. As beings capable of becoming more or less perfect the animals already belong to the category of ends; that is, things that exist for their own sake. On the other hand, we see in them, as long as they are with us on earth, no continuing progress toward a higher degree of perfection. They remain instead creatures whose lives are determined almost entirely by unchanging instincts implanted within them.

> Now this immobility, this stupid satisfaction with what has been attained . . . is a sign that they are not the final goal of the great plan of creation, but are simply lesser ends which are at the same time means and which are meant to be useful to things with worthier and more elevated destinies in the fulfillment of God's final purposes.[39]

These worthier things are the rational natures, the "underlords" (*Unterherrn*) of creation.

The rational creature is a being whose life is governed not by innate instincts but by an incessant striving toward higher degrees of perfection. From the moment he appears on earth he is engaged in sharpening his senses, his powers of imagination, his memory, his reason, and his other mental powers. The beauty of nature forms his taste and refines his sensibility. As soon as he enters into society he find more ways of perfecting himself. He acquires duties and rights, privileges and obligations; he develops concepts of justice, fairness, honor, etc. Social intercourse and sociability nourish in him all the moral virtues. They kindle his heart to friendship and love, his breast to bravery. Ultimately, the rational creature acquires true concepts of God and his attributes. "Oh! What a bold step to higher perfection!" He learns to understand the relationship between the Creator and all of nature, including himself. Every-

thing he possesses he comes to see as "the gifts of their good father." All the goodness and wisdom in the world he regards as "the
thoughts of the Omniscient," which He allowed people to read in
the "book of Creation" in order to educate him to attain higher perfection.[40]

Mendelssohn's Socrates admits that the portrait he has
drawn of a man advancing toward perfection corresponds not to the
generality of humankind but only to a few noble souls who are the
ornaments of humanity. Might it not be the case, then, that God's
purpose in creating the world was to bring into existence this select
group of rational beings, and that all other rational beings exist
primarily for their sake? This is a possibility which Mendelssohn's
Socrates cannot accept. All rational beings, he insists

> belong to the same class, and the difference between them is
> only a matter of more or less. From the most ignorant man to
> the most perfect among the created spirits, all have the des-
> tiny, so appropriate to the wisdom of God and so suitable to
> their own powers and abilities, of making themselves and
> others more perfect.[41]

Socrates implicitly rejects the idea that the human race exists for
the sake of its most talented members. Similarly, in his notes to his
correspondence with Thomas Abbt, Mendelssohn, in his own name,
rejects Abbt's suggestion that, as Mendelssohn puts it, "our earth
could perhaps be subordinate to another planet and everything
that happens on it." If that were the case, man would be "merely a
means of which Providence made use to attain higher purposes"
elsewhere. But, Mendelssohn maintains,

> Providence either has no final purpose, or it has as its object
> the world of spirits, the knowing part of creation, which is
> capable of [using] reason and [attaining] felicity. These all be-
> long to one class, and therefore have a similar vocation, dedi-
> cation, and calling in their existence. Either they are all
> merely means to higher ends, or every individual one of them
> has a part in the last and highest purpose of wisdom and
> goodness. Providence would therefore not be unjust to any one
> of them on this or any other planet.[42]

It would have been unjust, according to Mendelssohn, for providence to have made some rational creatures mere means and
others ends in themselves. Since providence can never be unjust,

all rational creatures must have the same status in the divine scheme of things; they must all be part of the final and supreme purpose of creation.

Nevertheless, in spite of the fact that the world exists for the sake of the perfection and felicity of its rational inhabitants, the lives of these "underlords" of creation have their unpleasant sides. In sections 52 and 53 of the *Sache Gottes*, which repeat almost word for word the contents of the identically numbered sections of Leibniz's *Causa Dei*, Mendelssohn takes note of the grievances of those who are dissatisfied by life on earth, who complain of the physical evils they have to suffer and what they perceive to be an unjust fate. "Physical goods and physical evils, they say, are not apportioned in this life according to people's deserts, according to the measure of moral good and evil. Here below things often go poorly for the good and well for the evil."[43]

Up to a point, Mendelssohn's response to these complaints is the same as that of Leibniz. He reiterates Leibniz's statements to the effect that (1) most of the physical evils from which people suffer are their own fault and (2) we are insufficiently grateful for the benefactions we receive from God and devote more of our attention to the evils that befall us than we do to the goods that we enjoy incessantly. In his response to complaints regarding the seemingly unjust distribution of goods among good and evil people, however, Mendelssohn appears to part company with Leibniz.

To this kind of complaint, he observes, Leibniz offers a twofold answer. He maintains (1) that all the afflictions in this world cannot be compared with the glory of the future life and (2) that the suffering people undergo here on earth is a necessary precondition for their happiness in this world and the next. As far as Mendelssohn is concerned, all of this smacks too much of the "common, popular moral teaching" (*der allgemeinen populären Sittenlehre*) in which "every virtue aims at compensation, and in which moral good is held to be desirable simply on account of the accidental reward one expects in return for it."[44] He contrasts this orientation unfavorably with the more elevated moral teaching of the wise, according to which virtue is not simply a means of attaining felicity but is itself felicity. Nevertheless, in spite of his critique of Leibniz, Mendelssohn too is ultimately capable of dealing with the problem of undeserved suffering and unmerited prosperity only by resorting to the notion of a compensatory afterlife. "No system of morality," he admits, "can exist without the expectation of an infinite future. The structure of the doctrine of virtue and vice is on all sides full of holes that cannot be filled, if man's soul is not immortal."[45]

Where Mendelssohn truly parts company with Leibniz is in his understanding of the nature of the afterlife. Leibniz, as we have seen, affirmed the traditional Christian teaching that in the next world "the number of men damned eternally will be incomparably greater than that of the saved." He struggled manfully, but rather awkwardly, to present this undeniable fact in a manner that would still permit belief in a world in which there was more good than evil. The best he could do was to suggest that the members of the human race constituted only an infinitesimal portion of the rational creatures in God's universe and that "nothing constrains us to think that many [of the others] are damned . . ." In comparison to the vast regions inhabited by these hypothetical creatures, our globe and its inhabitants are "almost lost in nothingness." And "since all the evils that may be raised in objection before us are in this near nothingness, haply it may be that all evils are almost nothingness in comparison with the good things which are in the universe."[46]

Leibniz's solution to the problem posed by Christian doctrine provides Mendelssohn with an easy target for gentle mockery. To have recourse to it, he says, "would be as good as to give up on providence, insofar as we ourselves are concerned."[47] It would offer "pitiful consolation for us poor earthlings, who should be destined to nothing but suffering."[48] Far from being consoled, in fact, by knowledge of the existence of countless creatures happier than ourselves, it might very well render us even more miserable to learn of those enviable beings who would have such an advantage over us.

Fortunately, however, "neither our religion nor our reason knows anything of this fantastic hypothesis." We can be assured, on the contrary, that "not a single individual who is capable of felicity, is destined for damnation, not a single citizen in the city of God [is destined] to eternal misery."[49] In reality, every single individual is ultimately destined to attain a certain measure of happiness. To understand how Mendelssohn arrives at these conclusions, we must go beyond an examination of the *Sache Gottes* and consider what he says elsewhere concerning the posthumous lives of human souls. We must focus our attention, in particular, on his treatment of this subject in his *Phaedon*.

At bottom, Mendelssohn's belief in immortality rests on Leibniz's monadology. This is something he chose to make completely clear only in letters to his philosophically minded friends.[50] Even to the reader unfamiliar with this correspondence, however, his debt to Leibniz is evident. His entire argumentation in defense of immortality takes its bearings from a distinction derived from Leibniz; that is, the distinction between the indestructability of the soul and its immortality.[51] Both in what he says regarding the soul's indestructability and in his presentation of his proofs for its immortality he repeatedly relies on the arguments of Leibniz and his disciples.

In his *Phaedon*, Mendelssohn seeks first to demonstrate that the soul is an imperishable substance. He then seeks to prove that the soul, in its life after death, remains conscious of its own identity and in possession of its faculties, that is, that it is immortal. His case for the indestructibility of the soul in the *Phaedon* consists, as Leo Strauss has observed, of two parts, both of which can be traced back to the work's Platonic model: (1) the argument that only composite things are perishable, whereas those things that are not composite are imperishable and (2) the argument that the soul is not a composite but a simple thing. Elsewhere, in his *Treatise on the Incorporeality of the Human Soul* and in his Hebrew *Book of the Soul*, Mendelssohn makes the same basic arguments, albeit in a somewhat different fashion. In the *Phaedon*, Mendelssohn's Socrates contends in the first dialogue that "*all changeable things cannot remain unchanged for a moment (alles Veranderliche konne keinen Augenblick unverandert bleiben)*."[52] He then observes that such changes as occur necessarily take place gradually. Nothing is ever suddenly destroyed. With the death of an animal, for instance, its body does not cease to exist but breaks up into parts, which then become the constituent parts of other composite things. Socrates then maintains that

> When we say . . . that the soul dies, then we must mean one of two things: Either all of its powers and capacities, its actions and its affections suddenly cease, vanish, as it were, in a trice; or it undergoes, like the body, gradual metamorphoses, innumerable transformations, which proceed in a continual series. And in this series there is a point when there is no longer a human soul. Something else has come into being, just as the body, after countless transformations, ceases to be a body, and becomes dust, air, a plant or even a part of another animal.[53]

The first alternative, sudden disappearance, is ruled impossible for, as Socrates has already shown, such annihilation is contrary to the laws of nature. "Between being and non-being there is a terrible gap, which the gradually operating nature of things cannot leap over."[54] And neither need one fear any supernatural, divine annihilation of the soul by means of a miracle. God would never do such an evil thing. All that remains, then, is the second alternative, the gradual deterioration of the soul until it ceases to be a soul. But this too, says Socrates, is impossible, for no matter how slow the process would be, its last step would always represent a transition from being to nothingness. Following the death of the body, therefore, the soul "will persist, will be eternally present. If it is present, then it must act and suffer; if it must act and be affected, it must have concepts, for perceiving, thinking and willing are the only ways in which a soul can act and be affected." The chief obstacle to admitting this, Socrates acknowledges, is the fact that it is difficult to conceive of the soul persisting in this way without a body. "Is it not our experience that here in this world we can never think without sense-impressions?" Nevertheless, he says, it is wrong to draw any conclusions concerning the nature of the next life on our experience in this one. In ways that we are unable to understand, the human soul leaves its corpse behind and continues to live.[55]

Up to this point Mendelssohn's Socrates has sought to show that the soul, as a simple, non-composite being, is not subject to decay and will never disappear. He has not, however, shown that the soul is indeed such a being. That is the task which his interlocutors demand that he undertake in the second dialogue of the *Phaedon*. "Perhaps," suggests one of them, "sense perception in the animals and even man's reason are nothing but qualities of a composite, just as life, health, harmony, etc. which according to their nature and character can last no longer than the combinations from which they are inseparable?"[56] In response to this objection, Socrates seeks to show that reason cannot be a quality of a composite and must therefore be a quality of a simple, imperishable being—the soul. He does so, ultimately, by arguing that all composition of simple things necessarily reflects the activity of reason. Without such activity, without the comparison and juxtaposition of disparate parts, the most perfectly constructed building is nothing but a heap of sand and the voice of the nightingale is no more harmonious than the croaking of an owl. Indeed, without the activity of reason, "there exists in nature no whole composed of many separate parts; for these parts each have their own existence, and they must be placed alongside one another, compared, and considered as parts of a combination if they are to constitute a whole."[57] These are things that the thinking faculty, and nothing else in all of nature, is capable of doing. But if this is granted, then it must be acknowledged that this thinking faculty itself cannot possibly consist of a whole composed of disparate parts. It cannot be the cause of itself.[58] Or, as Alexander Altmann has put it, in his summary of the argument of the second dialogue, "the soul cannot be regarded as the result of a composition of material elements because its activity has to be presupposed in order to explain that a composite "appears" different from its parts."[59] Altmann, in agreement with Leo Strauss as well as Mendelssohn's contemporary, Christian Garve, regards this argument as an incomparably precise formulation of the argument for the immateriality of the soul.[60]

The third dialogue of the *Phaedon* contains Mendelssohn's most elaborate defense of the doctrine of the soul's immortality. Mendelssohn's Socrates there makes three separate arguments. Two of them are, by Mendelssohn's own admission, borrowed from earlier thinkers, while the third is completely original. Here we will consider first the arguments Mendelssohn inherited from his predecessors. After that, we will turn to his original argument for the immortality of the soul.

It is a question posed by Cebes, one of Socrates' intelocutors, at the beginning of the second dialogue, that sets the third dialogue in motion. Cebes had asked Socrates to go beyond a demonstration of the imperishability of the soul and to clarify the nature of the afterlife. If it were to consist of anything less than a conscious, rational life, according to Cebes, it would be a fate worse than that of the animals. Acknowledging that he is correct, Socrates sets about proving that the soul's posthumous existence indeed meets the stipulated conditions.

Socrates begins his argument with the survey of the world's contents, which we examined earlier in this section and which leads, as we have seen, to the conclusion that this world exists so that its rational inhabitants might continue their progress toward perfection and felicity. From this he deduces that it cannot be the wish of the Supreme Being to allow the progress of these rational creatures to come to a standstill or, worse, to have these creatures lose all the fruits of their efforts. "Is it consistent," Socrates asks,

> with the Supreme Wisdom to produce a world in order to make the felicity of the creatures which inhabit it arise from the contemplation of its wonders and a moment later deprive them of the capacity for contemplation and felicity? Is it consistent with Wisdom to have made such a phantom of felicity, which always comes and goes, the final aim of its wondrous deeds? No, my friends! Nature has not instilled us with the desire for eternal felicity in vain. It can and will be satisifed.

The design of the creation will subsist as long as the things created; the admirers as long as the work in which those perfections are visible.

In the next life, Socrates continues, rational creatures will continue to traverse the path they pursue on earth and will never cease to grow more perfect and virtuous. For them to stand still anywhere on this path would obviously conflict with the divine wisdom, goodness or omnipotence, and could not be part of God's plan.[61]

This argument alone suffices to demonstrate the immortality of the human soul. But Mendelssohn's Socrates does not rest content with it. He strengthens his case by emphasizing the extent to which human beings have need of a faith in the existence of an afterlife. "How pitiable," he says

is the lot of a mortal whose comforting expectation of a future life has been upset by unfortunate sophistries! He must not reflect on his condition, and must live in something like a state of insensibility, or fall into despair. What is more frightening to a human soul than annihilation? And what is sadder than a man who sees it coming toward him with powerful steps and who, in the inconsolable fear with which he awaits it, already believes he feels it?[62]

There is, in addition, "another unhappy consequence" of the opinion that the soul is mortal. Those who adhere to this belief are ultimately compelled to deny the existence of divine providence. For they can see clearly enough that "there is much in the affairs of this world that does not agree with the concepts we must form of God's attributes." Many things are impossible to reconcile with the idea of his goodness or his justice. This is not to say, of course, that this world is as bad as its accusers claim it is. Still, it is not possible to vindicate providence without reference to a future life.[63]

Now that we have examined the arguments in the third dialogue that were derived, by Mendelssohn's own admission, from other thinkers, it is time to consider his original argument for the immortality of the soul, the one he later designated as the proof from the harmony of our duties and rights or the proof from the collision of duties.[64] Rather unusually, Mendelssohn attempts with this proof to demonstrate the immortality of the soul by means of a political-philosophical argument. He seeks to show that certain well-established doctrines of political philosophy can only be maintained if one assumes that the human soul is immortal and that it must therefore be immortal.

According to Mendelssohn, the law of nature dictates that men seek the perfection of their condition, which he defines as consisting of their "preservation and improvement" of themselves and others. In the next chapter, we will explore more fully his understanding of this natural law and its implications. For now, we need only take note of Mendelssohn's observation that there exists a certain tension between these different demands. Sometimes one's self-preservation will stand in the way of one's self-improvement or the improvement of others; sometimes, for instance the performance of a moral duty will require self-sacrifice, even what is called by patriots the *supreme sacrifice*.

For the man who believes in the existence of an afterlife, such a sacrifice, even if it involves the loss of his life, is a choice he can will himself to make. When he gives up his life, he is not, after all, terminating his existence but only bringing to an end its earthly— and less important—stage. He can look forward to his own preservation and the continuation of his own progress toward perfection in the next life. But if there is no afterlife, if man's soul is ultimately destined to perish along with his body, then the preservation of corporeal life becomes the indispensable precondition for any further progress toward perfection. The man who rejects belief in an afterlife will therefore feel impelled to seek to protect his life at all costs. "As soon as loss of our life entails the loss of all existence, life ceases to be a means; then its preservation becomes the object, the only aim of our wishes." The denier of immortality would let all of creation collapse "if only he could preserve himself."[65]

According to Mendelssohn, there can, however, be no doubt that the state has the right to call upon every citizen to sacrifice his life for the sake of of the common good. The undeniable right of the state to the devotion of its citizens directly contradicts, therefore, what the denier of immortality sees as his right to do whatever is necessary to preserve his own existence. A person who believes he possesses such a right may consequently face a "collison of duties."

At this point Mendelssohn draws an analogy between the "realm of truth" and the "realm of justice." In the realm of truth, he maintains, there can be no room for doubt; everything within it is either definitely true or definitely false. The realm of justice is of the same nature: "Before its throne all quarrels and disputes about right and the absence of right are settled on the basis of eternal and immutable rules." There can never be an occasion, therefore, when two moral entities have a similar right to one and the same thing. In the mind of God, "all the duties and rights of a moral entity, just like all truths, are in the most perfect harmony." The implications of this analogy are obvious. The collision between the undeniable right of the state to the devotion of its citizens and the denier of immortality's supposed right to deprive the state of his service clearly indicates that the latter right is a spurious one. Because it does not exist, its presupposition, that is, the mortal nature of the human soul, must be false.[66]

One of Mendelssohn's critics, Christian Garve, contended that this was a circular argument. According to Garve, one can conclude that one has a duty to give up one's life only on the basis of a conviction of the existence of higher ends than life itself. If one determines that there are no such ends, one immediately loses any reason to believe that one has a duty to sacrifice one's life for anyone or anything else. In actuality, therefore, the collision of duties to which Mendelssohn pointed, the conflict between the unbeliever's narrow concern with his own self-preservation and his admitted duty to the state, can never occur.[67]

Mendelssohn subsequently noted Garve's objection, but he did not regard it as a refutation of what he had written. The proof of one's duty to die for the state, he argued, in response to Garve, is compelling even to the man who believes in the existence of no end higher than life itself. It "can take many paths, which lead to the goal without going in a circle. One can take as one's point of departure the obligatory character of social life. This can be proved independently of the immortality of the soul, and is therefore based, like all moral truths, on metaphysical propositions." Mendelssohn did not take the time to show in detail how this could be done, since, he said, it would take him too far afield, and, in addition, these things had already been sufficiently worked out by others. He did go on to reaffirm, though, that

> no human society can exist if the whole does not in certain circumstances have the right to sacrifice the life of one of its members for the common good. Epicurus, Spinoza, and Hobbes could not deny this proposition, although they did not wish to recognize any higher end than life itself. They probably saw that no social life can take place among men if the whole is not granted this right. But since the concepts of right and duty were not sufficiently developed, they did not perceive that this right also presupposes the duty on the part of the citizen to sacrifice himself for the benefit of the whole, and

that this duty is not in accordance with nature if the soul is not immortal.[68]

This, then, is Mendelssohn's original and rather peculiar argument for the immortality of the soul. It is designed to prove the existence of immortality indirectly, by showing that the assumption of its opposite, the mortality of the soul, leads to results that are incompatible with something already known quite apart from any considerations related to the immortality of the soul; that is, that the state has the right to demand of its citizens the "supreme sacrifice." Unfortunately, however, this new argument does not withstand close scrutiny.

If it is indeed true that a man's duty to die for the state can be established, as Mendelssohn claims, entirely on the basis of "metaphysical propositions" and without any reference to the immortality of the soul, such a duty would simply *override* any duty of self-preservation, regardless of whatever one thought of one's soul's posthumous prospects. The demonstration of the existence of such a right on the part of the state would automatically prove the existence of certain limits to what one is entitled to do to preserve oneself. The denier of immortality would face therefore not a collision but a clear hierarchy of duties. Anyone who concluded that his duty of self-preservation permitted him to defy the state's orders would be reasoning incorrectly.

What is truly peculiar about Mendelssohn's argument, however, is his admission, in the end, that the state's right to demand self-sacrifice *cannot* be established without reference to the immortality of the soul. Such a right, he observes, "presupposes the duty on the part of the citizen to sacrifice himself for the benefit of the whole," and this "duty is not in accordance with nature if the soul is not immortal." But if this is the case, the immortality of the soul is *in effect* a *premise* of the argument in defense of the state's right to demand self-sacrifice. How, then, can it be possible to declare that the state's possession of such a right makes it necessary to admit the existence of immortality? The immortality of the soul cannot at the same time be the premise of the argument for the state's right to demand self-sacrifice and a conclusion that follows from it. Garve was, after all, basically right: Mendelssohn's original proof of the immortality of the soul is a circular argument.

Mendelssohn employs, as we have seen, a number of different arguments in defense of the idea of the immortality of the human soul. Clearly, however, the argument that occupies the most important place in his presentation is the argument that the wise fulfillment of God's very aims in creating the world requires the existence of an afterlife in which rational creatures can continue to perfect themselves and thus render themselves more fit to accomplish their creator's designs. And since Mendelssohn, as we have seen, maintains that all rational creatures are to an equal degree ends in themselves and not subordinate to others, this argument has further implications, which are most fully spelled out in the *Sache Gottes*: "Not a single individual capable of felicity is destined for damnation, no citizen in the state of God is destined for eternal misery. Each one goes his own way, each one passes through his series of determinations [*Bestimmungen*], and moves from stage to stage to the degree of felicity appropriate for him."[69]

Unlike Leibniz, Mendelssohn was free to disregard the stern Christian dogma according to which most men faced eternal damnation in the afterlife. Nothing prevented him from maintaining that God, in his goodness, ultimately extended a certain degree of felicity to all men in their lives after death. And this, indeed, is what he held to be the case. In doing so, he was, like his predecessors among the neologists and the later Leibnizians, carrying Leibniz's thought to its logical conclusion, where he himself might have carried it had he not been prevented from doing so by the prevailing dogma of his day.

In the life after death, Mendelssohn contends, every rational creature ultimately attains felicity. This does not mean, however, that death marks a transition to a life utterly unlike what has preceded it and that all rational creatures are immediately elevated to a level of existence beyond punishment and unhappiness. On the contrary, it is in the afterlife, according to Mendelssohn, that God inflicts punishments on those who deserve them.

Mendelssohn was always reluctant to enter into any detailed discussions of the life after death. Basically, he said, the afterlife is a place where we will carry on what we have begun on earth. Reason cannot tell us "in what form we will continue to exist, in what region, with what ethereal body, with what senses and organs."[70] Even revelation cannot instruct us any further on these matters, for it would have to speak in a language incomprehensible to us and to presuppose basic ideas we do not possess. It is possible that we will develop new senses in the next life, or we may simply make more effective use of the senses we have now. We may gain access to new sources of pleasure and new powers, or we may simply bring those we now possess to a higher degree of perfection. In this life, however, we are as incapable of understanding such matters as those born deaf are incapable of appreciating the pleasures of music and those born blind are incapable of understanding the beauty of painting.[71]

Nevertheless, whatever form things take in the afterlife, it is clear that there will be punishments for the wicked. These punishments will not be inflicted for the sake of retribution; they will be exclusively corrective. "In my opinion, there is no punishment other than that which is for the benefit of the sinner, for his education."[72] The punishments imposed in the afterlife are intended to be educative; and because they are the work of God, they cannot be without effect. Once they have brought about the repentance of the sinner, they will be rescinded.[73] Ultimately, then, even the worst of sinners will be induced to repent, in ways we cannot imagine, by educative punishments. He will no longer be misled by his false understanding to do evil. The afterlife is not an instant panacea. It is, in essence, a place where the process of perfection, begun on earth, will be carried on. For sinners, it is initially a place of suffering. Eventually, however, their suffering comes to an end, and even the worst of men resumes his progress toward perfection and felicity.

As we noted at the beginning of this section, Mendelssohn's views on providence and immortality are deeply rooted in the philosophy of Leibniz. Yet they are not identical to those that find expression in the *Theodicy* and in Leibniz's other works. Mendelssohn, along with many other representatives of the later stages of the *Aufklärung*, significantly modifies and softens Leibniz's account of the divine governance of this world. Like Spalding and Reimarus and other neologists and rationalists, he describes our world as one in which the perfection and happiness of rational beings is not a divine aim decidedly subordinate to other divine aims and, in practice, largely unfulfilled, but an aim that is part and parcel of God's final purpose.

This world, according to Mendelssohn, constitutes the beneficently furnished setting in which human beings commence their progress toward the goals set for them by God. But it is also, inevitably, a place fraught with difficulties and filled with evil and suffering. Happily, it is not the only world people will live to experience. Of this Mendelssohn is convinced by the arguments of Leibniz. In his own proofs for the immortality of the soul he tends, however, to employ the kind of argumentation found in the writings of Spalding and Reimarus. Like them, he first presents an emotionally evocative description of life on earth, one that highlights this planet's inability to serve as the location for human beings' complete attainment of perfection and felicity. He then proceeds to the conclusion that God, in his goodness, *must* therefore have included a sequel to it in his overall plan.

Mendelssohn does not, however, place the primary emphasis on the very same aspects of life on earth that Spalding and Reimarus choose to highlight. Spalding depicts in grim colors and indicates by means of a long series of rhetorical questions the disturbingly inappropriate fates of the righteous and the wicked on this earth. Convinced that this cannot constitute the entire divine design, he concludes that there must be a life after death. Reimarus focuses mainly on the great discrepancy between men's wishes and the shortness of their earthly lives. An afterlife must exist, he reasons, for how could God "have roused his rational creatures, through their nature, to an idea of a longer and better life, and to a desire for it, if that were not what he had allotted to us?"[74] Mendelssohn is as convinced as Spalding (and Reimarus, too, for that matter) of the necessity of a rectification of the "disharmony" prevailing on earth in the afterlife, and he is no less convinced than Reimarus of people's desperate need to be consoled by the knowledge of their own immortality. What is of primary importance for him, however, is people's evident inability to reach the goal set for them by God within the confines of earthly existence. It is this, above all, that leads his Socrates to ask whether it is "consistent with the Supreme Wisdom to produce a world in order to make the felicity of the creatures inhabiting it arise from the contemplation of its wonders and a moment later deprive them of the capacity for contemplation and felicity?" The answer to this question can only be a negative one.

Spalding and Reimarus, among others, refused to follow Leibniz and to accommodate their teachings to the Christian dogma of the eternal punishment of most human souls. Mendelssohn not only discards this doctrine but attacks it (if only in the *Sache Gottes*, a work he had no intention of seeing published). In his discussion of the *Sache Gottes*, Leo Strauss compares Leibniz's teaching with that of Mendelssohn. "For Leibniz," he writes,

> the purpose of creation is primarily the beauty and order of the world in its entirety; for Mendelssohn, on the other hand, it is primarily the felicity of man, every man. . . . From this it follows that for Leibniz all suffering is basically justified in the context of the universe . . . while for Mendelssohn the suffering of any man whatsoever, in so far as this suffering is not of use to that very individual, is a decisive objection against the perfection of the universe.[75]

Strauss's characterization of the differing views of Leibniz and Mendelssohn is undoubtedly accurate, as is his presentation of their implications. Yet he confuses cause and effect. What was true, as we saw in Chapter I, of such figures as Spalding and Reimarus was true of Mendelssohn as well. That is to say, it was not Mendelssohn's different understanding of God's purpose in creating the world that led him to differ with Leibniz with regard to man's ultimate destiny, but, on the contrary, it was his repudiation of Leibniz's view of the fate of most men in the afterlife that made it possible, indeed inevitable that he would provide a differing description of God's purpose in creating the world.

What Mendelssohn was doing in relation to Leibniz was, in other words, comparable to what he described in an appendix to the third edition of *Phaedon* as what a Socrates would have done had he sought to demonstrate, "in our day," the immortality of the soul.

A friend of reason, such as he was, would certainly have gratefully accepted from other philosophers that part of their doctrine which was based on reason, no matter what country or religious party they otherwise belonged to. Where rational truths are concerned, one can agree with anyone, and nevertheless find many things untrustworthy which he accepts on faith (*das er auf Glauben annimmt*).[76]

Upholding the part of Leibniz's doctrine based on reason and discarding what was based on another religion's revelation, or an interpretation of that revelation, Mendelssohn could portray a world that was not only the best of all possible worlds but one that human beings could have no difficulty regarding as one that was fully hospitable to all creatures like themselves. Far from casting a shadow over their lives on earth, their knowledge of divine providence would supply them with a profound sense of consolation and enable them to love God unreservedly.

Notes

1. See especially "Moses Mendelssohn's Proofs for the Existence of God," in *Essays in Jewish Intellectual History*, pp. 119–41, and *Moses Mendelssohn*, pp. 123–25, 322–27 and 678–86.

2. See earlier, p. 3.

3. See Alexander Altmann, *Essays in Jewish Intellectual History*, p. 125.

4. Ibid., pp. 125–26.

5. *JubA*, vol. 3, 2, p. 97. Altmann, *Essays in Jewish Intellectual History*, pp. 126–27.

6. "Mendelssohn did," as Altmann goes on to note (*Essays in Jewish Intellectual History*, p. 127), "make an attempt to render the cosmological argument self-sufficient." This attempt was, however, as he himself demonstrates, unsuccessful. "In a recapitulation of the proof in Chapter XVI of *Morning Hours*, he drew a distinction between the independent and the necessary being of God. Both aspects, he said, followed from the premise that contingent beings exist. For contingency has two aspects. It meant (a) that the thinkability or possibility of the contingent did not entail existence; and (b) that contingent beings depended on things other than themselves. Hence their sufficient reason had to be a cause that was both independent and necessary: independent in the sense that its reality was thinkable without a cause; and necessary in the sense that its thinkability was sufficient to explain its existence. It was real because it was thinkable or possible, and its nonexistence was unthinkable. The novelty of this deduction lies in the fact that it tries to prove God's necessary being from the very concept of contingency as a cosmological datum. The nerve of the argument is the definition of the contingent as that whose existence is not implied in its thinkability. By starting out from this meaning of contingency, we are led to the concept of God as *causa sui* in the very sense in which the ontological argument understands it, yet without actually employing the ontological proof. Here the cosmological argument appears to yield the existence of an absolutely necessary being. Yet on closer inspection one has to admit that the necessary being arrived at is still tied to the world of contingent beings and not necessary in an absolute sense. Kant's objection stands."

7. *JubA*, vol. 3, 2, p. 138.

8. According to Leo Strauss (*JubA*, 3, 2, p. 308), "Mendelssohn was led to his 'new proof' by his critique of the traditional proof which deduces the existence of God from the existence of eternal truths."

9. Altmann, *Essays in Jewish Intellectual History*, p. 128.

10. *JubA*, vol. 3, 2, pp. 142–43.

11. Ibid., p. 144.

12. Ibid., p. 145.

13. Ludwig Heinrich, Jakob, *Prüfung der Mendelssohnschen Morgenstunden oder aller spekulativen Beweise für das Daseyn Gottes* (Leipzig: J. S. Heinsius, 1786), p. 238.

14. Ibid., p. 239.

15. Quoted in Altmann, *Essays in Jewish Intellectual History*, p. 128.

16. *JubA*, vol. 2 (Berlin, 1931; reprint Stuttgart, 1972), p. 300.

17. Altmann, *Essays in Jewish Intellectual History*, p. 130.

18. Altmann, *Moses Mendelssohn*, pp. 322–27.

19. Altmann, *Essays in Jewish Intellectual History*, p. 132. See *JubA*, vol. 12, 2, pp. 117–19 for the proofs themselves.

20. *Immanuel Kants Werke*, ed. Ernst Cassirer, vol. 2 (Berlin: B. Cassirer 1922), pp. 164–72.

21. Quoted in Altmann, *Essays in Jewish Intellectual History*, p. 133.

22. *JubA*, vol. 3, 2, pp. 152–53.

23. Allen W. Wood, *Kant's Rational Theology* (Ithaca, N.Y.: Cornell University Press, 1978), p. 110.

24. Henrich, *Der ontologische Gottesbeweis*, p. 4.

25. *JubA*, vol. 3, 2, p. 154.

26. Ibid., translated in Altmann, *Essays in Jewish Intellectual History*, p. 136.

27. Altmann, ibid., pp. 136–37. "There can be little doubt," Altmann continues, "that in paying tribute to this admission he was not thinking of something merely hypothetical and desirable but had in mind Kant's notion of the "transcendental ideal" (A576ff.). Although Kant recognized the archetypal *ens realissimum* only as a "regulative idea," he left no doubt that on such grounds we not only *may* but *must* assume a wise and omnipotent Author of the world (A725). Mendelssohn seems to have guessed, and rightly so, that there was solid common ground between him and Kant as far as ultimate beliefs were concerned."

28. *JubA*, vol. 3, 2, p. ci.

29. In the preface to the *Phaedon* and again in an appendix to the third edition of that work, Mendelssohn acknowledges that the arguments he has placed in Socrates' mouth in this dialogue are mostly derived from other thinkers. He identifies his sources as Baumgarten's *Metaphysics* and Reimarus' *Essays on the Chief Truths of Natural Religion* (*JubA*, vol. 3, 1, p. 139). Scholars have agreed that the reference to Baumgarten "must be a mistake" (ibid., p. 418, where Leo Strauss surveys the literature). Reimarus, on the other hand, was unmistakably one of Mendelssohn's sources for the arguments found in the third dialogue. And, as Strauss has noted, there are "considerable correspondences" between the third dialogue and Spalding's *The Vocation of Man* as well as Crusius' *An Outline of Necessary Rational Truths*.

30. Altmann, *Essays in Jewish Intellectual History*, p. 142.

31. Ibid., p. 143, for the translation quoted previously. See. *JubA*, vol. 2, p. 307, for the original.

32. Altmann, *Essays in Jewish Intellectual History*, p. 149.

33. Quoted in ibid., p. 150. See *JubA*, vol. 3, 2, p. 128, for the original.

34. Altmann, ibid., p. 142.

35. *JubA*, vol. 3, 2, p. 221, sec. 1.

36. See earlier, p. 27.

37. *JubA*, vol. 6, 1, p. 19.

38. In a dialogue, as Leo Strauss has shown, "one cannot identify without further consideration the author's views with those of one of his characters," see *On Tyranny* (Ithaca, N.Y.: Cornell University Press, 1963), p. 29. In this case, however, there is no reason to believe that Socrates is anything other than Mendelssohn's mouthpiece. In his subsequent defense of the arguments made in the dialogue (see especially *JubA*, vol. 3, 1, pp. 143–69), Mendelssohn never suggests that his Socrates espouses any views he himself does not hold.

39. *JubA*, vol. 3, 1, p. 109.

40. Ibid., pp. 111–12.

41. Ibid., p. 113.

42. *JubA*, vol. 6, 1, p. 46.

43. *JubA*, vol. 3, 2, p. 235, sec. 53.

44. Ibid., pp. 235–36, sec. 55. Leo Strauss (vol. 3, 2, p. ciii) rightly questions whether Mendelssohn has adequate reason to attribute to Leibniz support for "the popular moral teaching."

45. Ibid., vol 3, 2, p. 237.

46. See earlier, p. 16.

47. *JubA*, vol. 3, 2, p. 240.

48. Ibid., p. 250.

49. Ibid., p. 240.

50. See Altmann, *Moses Mendelssohn*, pp. 165, 172, and also the remarks of Leo Strauss in *JubA*, vol. 3, 1, p. xxv.

51. See *JubA*, vol. 3, 1, pp. xxv–xxvi.

52. *JubA*, vol. 3, 1, p. 63. Criticized later for basing his entire argument in this way on a teaching derived from Wolff and Baumgarten, Mendelssohn retorted that far from being unique to those thinkers this principle goes back as far as Heraclitus and Pythagoras (*JubA*, vol. 3, 1, pp. 132–33).

53. Ibid., p. 69. Here, as he notes in the appendix to the *Phaedon* (*JubA*, vol. 3, 1, p. 135), Mendelssohn is relying on Ruggiero Giuseppe Boscovich's "law of continuity."

54. *JubA*, vol. 3, 1, p. 70.

55. Ibid., p. 73.

56. Ibid., p. 82.

57. Ibid., p. 92.

58. Ibid., p. 93.

59. Altmann, *Moses Mendelssohn*, p. 155.

60. Ibid., p. 155, and *JubA*, vol. 3, 1, p. xxviii.

61. *JubA*, vol. 3, 1, pp. 114–15.

62. Ibid., vol. 3, 1, p. 115. See also *JubA*, vol. 3, 2, p. 68 (*Morning Hours*), for a less impassioned statement: "Without God, providence, and immortality, all the goods of this life have in my eyes a contemptible value, and life here below seems to me, to make use of a well-known and often misused saying, like wandering in the wind and bad weather without the consolation of finding protection and shelter in an inn in the evening."

63. Ibid., pp. 120–22.

64. Ibid., pp. 155–56.

65. Ibid., vol. 3, 1, p. 116–17.

66. Ibid., pp. 117–18.

67. Ibid., pp. 156.

68. Ibid., pp. 156–57.

69. Ibid., vol. 3, 2, p. 240, sec. 60.

70. In a letter to Herder (*JubA*, vol. 12, 1, p. 182), who had thought that the *Phaedon* indicated otherwise, Mendelssohn affirmed his conviction that the human soul would, in its posthumous life, continue to possess some kind of a body. "Streichen Sie zuförderst in meinen *Phädon* alle die Stellen durch, wo ausdrücklich gesagt wird, dass unsere Seele künftighin ganz ohne Körper seyn wird. So viel erinnere ich mich noch, das meine Absicht war, die Sache unentschieden zu lassen, um die sehr verwickelte Frage von der Unsterblichkeit nicht durch zu viele Nebenknoten zu verwirren. Aber im Herzen war ich, bin ich noch jetzo, völlig überzeugt, dass *kein eingeschränkter Geist ganz ohne Körper seyn köne.*"

71. *JubA*, vol. 6, 1, pp. 42–43.

72. Ibid., vol. 3, 1, p. 231.

73. *Jerusalem*, p. 124.

74. See earlier, p. 29.

75. *JubA*, vol. 3, 2, p. ciii.

76. Ibid., vol. 3, 1, p. 151.

3
The Crisis of Reason

For decades, Mendelssohn energetically defended the principles of natural theology. While he himself continued to adhere to the basic teachings of the Leibniz-Wolffian school, however, the intellectual climate in Germany underwent momentous changes. "The reputation of this school," as he himself put it in *Morning Hours* (1785), "has since [the first half of the eighteenth century] greatly declined and, in the course of its demise, has brought the reputation of speculative philosophy in general down with it." Partly responsible for the current, dismal situation were the most recent philosophical anatagonists of traditional metaphysics, especially "the all-crushing Kant."[1] But there were other culprits, too. The best minds in Germany, Mendelssohn complained, were concerned with nothing but empirical investigations of the natural world. At the same time, a penchant for irrationalism and fanaticism was becoming all too prevalent.

In 1761, in his *Treatise on Evidence*, Mendelssohn had unhesitatingly offered a positive answer to the question posed by the Royal Academy in Berlin: "Whether metaphysical truths in general, and the first principles of natural theology and morality in particular, are susceptible of the same evidence as mathematical truths . . ."[2] A quarter of a century later, when he wrote *Morning Hours*, he could no longer speak so unequivocally. He felt that all he could do was to bequeath to his friends and to posterity a report of what he had always held to be true. In the aftermath of the collapse of speculative philosophy, it was too late to "give the wheel a shove" and restore to its former glory the kind of philosophy that had, in "the cyclical course of things" (*Zirkellauf der Dinge*), fallen under foot. He himself, at any rate, in his weakened condition, could not even conceive of making an attempt to turn things around again. This was a task for a stronger mind, for a profound thinker like Kant, who would apply the same intelligence, one could hope, to the reconstruction of metaphysics that he had once dedicated to demolishing it.

In the meantime, for as long as metaphysics lay in the dust, Mendelssohn could advise little besides reliance on "common sense." This recommendation has led some of his contemporaries as well as some recent scholars to contend that he was a defector from the camp of reason and had joined up, however tentatively, with its opponents. The matter, however, is not so simple. Although Mendelssohn admitted the inadequacy of his own philosophy, he by no means lost faith in reason as the final arbiter of the most important disputes. Common sense, to which he ascribed for the time being such a vital role, was itself, according to his own description of it, but a form of reason. And metaphysics, he clearly believed, may have been in disarray but it was nevertheless far from obsolete. Its time would come once again.

Kant and Jacobi

By the third quarter of the eighteenth century, the metaphysical tradition to which Mendelssohn adhered was under attack from a variety of fronts. Many of these critiques he considered to be of little consequence. The threats he perceived to be most dangerous, however, and he made it his purpose to meet were those emanating from Immanuel Kant and F. H. Jacobi. We have already observed Mendelssohn's attempt to grapple, in his final presentation of the ontological proof for God's existence, with certain of Kant's arguments. As he was well aware, however, Kant was not merely a critic of the ontological argument but someone who sought utterly to destroy traditional metaphysics, which he considered to be the product of the misuse of human reason. The indispensable truths of natural religion, according to Kant, were accessible not through the use of theoretical reason but only through the use of what he called *practical reason*. Jacobi, even more than Kant, was an opponent of the entire rationalist tradition. For him, however, the error of previous philosophers lay not in the inappropriate use of reason but in the very fact that they resorted to it at all. Reason, he believed, even if it were correctly employed, led ineluctably in the wrong direction, to Spinozism, that is, to atheism, and ought therefore to be abandoned in favor of Christian faith.

To Mendelssohn, as Frederick Beiser has written, "Kant and Jacobi each represent the two horns of a dilemma: dogmatism versus skepticism, or mysticism versus nihilism. Jacobi is a dog-matist or mystic since his *salto mortale* evades the demands of criticism; Kant is the skeptic or nihilist since he destroys the meta-physics necessary to justify moral and religious belief." To vindi-cate his own rationalist metaphysics, Mendelssohn had to "settle his accounts with Kant as well as Jacobi." Settling accounts did not, however, necessarily entail forthright confrontation.

By the time he had to face Kant's new, critical thinking and Jacobi's irrationalism Mendelssohn was, in Beiser's words, "too old and frail to risk a contest" with such formidable opponents.[3] His response to both of his major adversaries was indirect and often oblique. He did not seek to refute them so much as to undercut them. It will therefore not be necessary, for the purposes of our study, to review in any great detail the precise nature of the chal-lenge each of these thinkers posed to Mendelssohn's most cher-ished convictions. We need only outline their overall positions as broadly as possible.

Mendelssohn's acquaintance with Kant and his writings dates back to the early 1760s. Although he had his differences with the earlier, "precritical" Kant, it was only the author of the *Critique of Pure Reason* (1781) who presented him with severe problems. Kant's goal in this epoch-making work was to undertake, as Rich-ard L. Velkley has trenchantly stated, "an investigation of the limits of past approaches to metaphysical inquiry and a determina-tion of the possible context, defined by human reason itself, for all such inquiry." According to Kant, "What all earlier approaches in metaphysics had lacked was a prior critique or 'propaedeutic' to metaphysical inquiry which would determine the total context of possible knowledge."

In the *Critique of Pure Reason* Kant sought to remedy this deficiency. He endeavored to show, among other things, that the categories implicit in all logical thought "both are necessary for de-fining the context of possible knowledge for minds such as ours ('discursive') and have no application beyond that context—they are limited to the very same realm they help make possible." Our metaphysical striving, therefore, "cannot be satisfied theoretically." This does not mean, however, that it cannot be satisfied at all. Kant's propaedeutic seeks to "ground a new culture in which hu-man reason will truly satisfy that striving, nondialectically."[4] The form of human reason capable of accomplishing this task is "practi-cal reason."

No less than Wolff, Kant maintains that unassisted reason provides us with complete knowledge of our moral duties. But we require more than that. We need to be able to hope that moral action on our part will ultimately bring into being a moral world. As Velkley puts it, "Such a world embodies the ideal convergence of the 'ought' of freedom and the 'is' of nature. Only for the purpose of conceiving that convergence does reason postulate God and a future life. Thus moral reason's need to postulate that ideal convergence is the ground of the inquiries that constitute metaphysics."[5] These postulates of practical reason "are the successors to the discredited speculative 'ideas' of reason's dialectic (God, soul, and world)."[6]

Mendelssohn no doubt appreciated the magnitude of the Kantian threat to traditional metaphysics and understood that Kant was seeking a nontheoretical yet rational basis for affirming the truth of the fundamental principles of natural religion. He could not help but be aware, too, of Kant's hopes that he himself would prove receptive to his new, critical philosophy. Shortly after completing the *Critique of Pure Reason*, Kant dispatched a copy to Mendelssohn. In a letter (or draft of a letter) to Marcus Herz, he referred to Mendelssohn as "the most important . . . among all those who could explain its point to the world." To Kant's dismay, however, Mendelssohn not only failed to explain his philosophy to the world but "for reasons of health and on account of other preoccupations, declined to study and review his 'system.'"[7]

Mendelssohn's other major adversary, F. H. Jacobi, is today infinitely less well-known than Kant. His name is familiar, for the most part, only to specialists in the thought of late eighteenth-century Germany. Jacobi was, however, a figure of considerable importance in his own day and one who exerted a great, if infrequently recognized, influence on the subsequent history of philosophy. He composed his most significant writings in the course of a bitter controversy, now known as the *Pantheismusstreit*, in which he and Mendelssohn became embroiled.

The fascinating and complex story of this controversy has been told at great length and with immense skill by Alexander Altmann and Leo Strauss. Altmann, Strauss, Hermann Timm, Frederick Beiser, and other scholars have all analyzed its philosophical ramifications from a variety of different perspectives.[8] For our purposes, it will not be necessary to review all of the ground these scholars have covered or to undertake a fresh analysis of the entire controversy. It will suffice for us to identify at this point the general nature of the antirationalist position taken by Jacobi during his dispute with Mendelssohn. A little later, we shall examine the roles played by some other figures, including Kant, in the *Pantheismusstreit*.

Initially, the controversy concerned the question of the recently deceased Lessing's secret beliefs. Jacobi claimed to have been informed directly—and, of course, privately—by Lessing himself that he was a disciple of Spinoza and was indeed convinced that "There is no philosophy other than Spinoza's." What Jacobi wished to do, however, was not so much to expose Lessing's clandestine heresy as to point to Lessing's intellectual evolution as evidence supporting his own "general thesis that reason of necessity leads to atheism and fatalism." Jacobi himself believed "that all metaphysical systems are ultimately identical (if they are only consistent), and that they all have damaging consequences for morality and religion."[9] They all lead to "nihilism" (a term originally coined by none other than Jacobi).[10]

Precisely why Jacobi believes this to be the case is a matter that it will not be necessary for us to explore, because Mendelssohn himself never ventured to make Jacobi's indictment of reason a target of philosophical criticism. What is of importance for us to understand, however, is the alternative that, in his opinion, this situation forces us to confront. Beiser has put it most succinctly: "either we follow our reason and become atheists and fatalists; or we renounce our reason and make a leap of faith in God and freedom. In more general terms, we have to choose either a rational skepticism or an irrational faith. There is simply no comforting middle path between these options, no way to justify morality and religion through reason."[11]

Mendelssohn's Response

Mendelssohn's response to the disparate challenges of Kant and Jacobi was in part to restate, in a tentative fashion, the arguments which he had repeatedly reaffirmed but now had to acknowledge to be insufficiently convincing. Yet he did not remain entirely on the defensive. As we saw in Chapter 2, he made an effort to deal with Kant's objections to the ontological proof for God's existence. More significant, he engaged in a two-pronged counterattack against some of his opponents' fundamental assumptions. In response to Jacobi, he attempted to show that in fact dogmatism of the type Jacobi represented posed the greatest threat to morality, whereas reason could provide it with solid support. In response to Kant's skepticism, to which he apparently felt he had no adequate philosophical answers, Mendelssohn emphasized the necessity for reliance in times of philosophical uncertainty on "common sense."

The best way to begin a consideration of Mendelssohn's counterattack against Jacobi and Kant would be to turn to the eighth lecture of *Morning Hours*, where he focuses on the dangers inherent in the views of a figure whom we have not yet mentioned, the prominent German educational theorist Johann Bernhard Basedow. It is evident, as several scholars have observed, that Basedow is not for him an individual of philosophical significance in his own right but a mere stand-in for his more menacing adversaries.[12] Mendelssohn criticizes Basedow for introducing "into philosophy a new principle of knowledge, which he calls the duty to believe." According to Basedow, people have a duty to believe in the truth of any proposition upon which their felicity depends. Having established to his own satisfaction that men could not be happy in the absence of God, providence, and immortality, he maintained that he had thereby placed these comforting doctrines beyond all doubt.

Despite his agreement with Basedow's basic premise, Mendelssohn firmly rejects this line of reasoning. If we wish to obtain the truth with regard to matters of such fundamental importance, he states, we must not let our wishes interfere with our convictions. We must proceed dispassionately, imitating the method of the mathematicians. It is true, according to Mendelssohn, that in metaphysical investigations, unlike in mathematics, our entire happiness rests on the results at which we arrive. "We tremble before the truth itself, if it is not in accord with our welfare. With every doubt our peace of mind threatens to disappear, our whole system of happiness to collapse."

Contemplating the hazards of philosophical inquiry, Mendelssohn expresses his gratitude to Providence for occasionally arranging for the existence of "friends of truth" who have the strength of mind to examine the propositions on which their own happiness depends. "They exert their powers to arouse doubts that cost them their own peace of mind; they strive to bring to light objections against accepted teachings, which may very well embitter their entire existence here below." The price these individuals pay for their exertions is, however, one that brings benefits to all. "Without these sacrifices for the sake of truth, all knowledge of the truth would degenerate into prejudice and blind faith." Unrestricted inquiry sometimes has a frightful influence on human morality, but prejudice and blind faith "lead to superstition and fanaticism

(*Schwärmerey*), which are no less dangerous." We must therefore pay heed to any doubt anyone expresses, "even if it threatens to ruin our entire system."[13] Such doubts are designed by Providence to serve as a kind of antidote to the most dangerous maladies. They lead people, in the end, past the rejection of all basic principles back to the truth.[14]

In his earlier work, Mendelssohn had spoken rather coolly of sowers of doubt like Epicurus and Hume and described only the people who confuted their arguments as the gifts of Providence to humankind.[15] In *Morning Hours*, however, he sees the hand of God even in the most unlikely quarters, in the ranks of those who pose the greatest threat to religion. Mendelssohn's enthusiasm for free inquiry is indeed great; it is not, however, marked by a lack of concern with regard to where it will lead. It is not quite accurate to say, as Beiser does, that in arguing against Basedow Mendelssohn steadfastly maintained "the necessity of pursuing an investigation despite the moral and religious consequences."[16] In fact, Mendelssohn shows complete confidence that, whatever hazards they may have to deal with along the way, those who engage in rational inquiry will in the end lead people to the truth.

The extent to which Mendelssohn's treatment of Basedow serves as an indirect response to Jacobi is readily apparent. Mendelssohn, in effect, turns the tables on Jacobi. He is prepared to concede that there is some merit to his claim that certain perils are attached to philosophical investigations, but he is by no means ready to grant that the results of such inquiries are as completely harmful as Jacobi insists they must be. Rather, the failure to engage in philosophical investigations has the most dangerous consequences. The stultification of free inquiry ineluctably leads, according to Mendelssohn, to the rise of superstition and fanaticism, whose evil effects are worse and more lasting than those of philosophical doubts. The leap of faith is a leap into the dark. If indeed Mendelssohn also intended Basedow to serve as a stand-in for Kant, it was because he saw Kant's moral philosophy, too, as one that abandoned the attempt to prove the truth of the religious principles with which human morality is inextricably intertwined and instead treated them as true simply because it was necessary for people to believe in them.

Mendelssohn had already laid the groundwork for his treatment of "common sense" in the third lecture of *Morning Hours* by drawing a distinction between rational knowledge (*Vernunfterkentniss*) and sound understanding (*gesunde Menschenverstand*). He defines the former as knowledge of the thinkable and the unthinkable, or judgments and inferences that are drawn from our sense-impressions by the proper use of our understanding.[17] Sound understanding and reason, he says, are "basically one and the same." The only difference between them is the speed with which they go to work. Whereas reason investigates the path before it very cautiously and proceeds fearfully, watching every step, sound understanding, operating without self-consciousness, moves ahead swiftly and fearlessly.[18]

The significance of this distinction becomes clear only in the tenth lecture of *Morning Hours*. If in the eighth lecture, in his answer to Basedow, Mendelssohn appears to be a fervent champion of philosophical inquiry, by the time he reaches the tenth lecture his confidence in its capabilities seems to some extent to have dissipated. Here he relates an "allegorical dream" that reflects his notion of the inherent inability of what he labels *speculation* to achieve its goals on its own and in its need to resort to the guidance of "common sense." In this dream Mendelssohn finds himself in a group that is being led through the Swiss Alps by two guides, "a young, sturdy Swiss, strong of limb but not endowed with the finest understanding," and a tall and gaunt woman, "serious-looking, with an introspective mien, possessing a fanatical physiognomy and fantastically garbed" (*ernsthaft, mit in sich gesenkten Blicken, von schwärmerischer Physiognomie und phantastisch bekleidet*) and having something resembling wings attached to her head. After following these guides for a certain time, the group arrives at a crossroads. Here the guides appear to part. "He hurries with quick steps to the right, she flutters with her wing-like being to the left," and the group remains at the crossroads, uncertain whom it ought to follow. At this point a rather elderly matron calmly approaches the group. She reasssures its members that they will not be left without leaders for very long and then makes the following speech:

> The persons given to you as leaders are called Common Sense (*sensus communis*) and Contemplation (*contemplatio*). They sometimes part for a short time, not infrequently on trifling grounds. If the travelers are patient enough to wait for them at the crossroads, and not to follow either of them, they come back in order to let me resolve their dispute. In most cases, the right tends to be on his side, and she, contrary to what one might expect, listens to reason. On the other hand, when the right is sometimes on her side, he, the headstrong fellow, cannot be made to yield. To the most persuasive arguments

that I put before him he responds with a rustic laugh and a dimwitted jest, and obstinately goes his own way. Nevertheless, the travelers, who trust me, know what to do when this happens.

One of the travelers then asks the matron to identify herself. She has only enough time to declare that on earth she is known as Reason (*Vernunft*) before she is suddenly interrupted by a dreadful noise. Somehow, unaccountably, Common Sense and Contemplation are on the scene once again (this is a dream, after all). They are presumably attempting to rejoin Reason, who will iron out their current dispute. But before they can do so, an unidentified, menacing crowd intervenes, surrounds Contemplation, and seems bent on overrunning Common Sense and Reason, too. It is at this point that Mendelssohn awakens.[19]

Altmann has cogently explained what this part of the dream is meant to symbolize. It reflects, he writes, Mendelssohn's feeling that the "gains of the Enlightenment, which were based on reason, and the simple truths of universal religion, which were anchored in common sense and not in the extravagencies of mystical faith, were both under attack by a clamorous crowd personified, in his mind, by Jacobi."[20] What is the result of this attack? Can Reason, the ultimate arbiter, succeed in fending it off? Apparently, fear of its inability to do so frightens Mendelssohn into wakefulness.

The earlier part of this dream corresponds, Mendelssohn immediately informs us, to the views he holds during his waking hours.

> As soon as my speculations lead me too far away from the highway of common sense, I stand still and try to orientate myself. I look back to the point from which we have departed and I try to compare my two guides. Experience has taught me that in most cases the right is on the side of common sense and that reason has to favor speculation decisively if I should leave common sense and follow speculation. Indeed, in order to convince me that the steadfastness of common sense is only ignorant stubborness, reason has to show me how common sense could possibly have taken leave of the truth and gone astray.[21]

Asleep or awake, then, Mendelssohn generally has more confidence in common sense than in speculation. On the basis of experience, he is prepared to follow common sense when it is in disagreement with speculation, even if reason has not spoken decisively in its favor. And although he is aware that speculation is sometimes more reliable than common sense, he will follow the former rather than the latter only when reason clearly authorizes him to do so.

In a later work, *To Lessing's Friends*, Mendelssohn reiterates even more forcefully his high estimation of common sense or, as he denotes it here, "plain, sound understanding (*eines schlichten gesunden Menschenverstandes*)." He identifies himself, in the passage in question, as a great admirer of demonstrations in metaphysics, as someone who is firmly convinced that the fundamental truths of natural religion are as capable of being proved as any mathematical proposition. Yet, he says, "my certitude of religious truths does not depend so absolutely on metaphysical arguments that it stands or falls with them. One can raise doubts against my arguments, show me mistakes in my reasoning, and my certitude nevertheless remains unshakeable." This certitude rests ultimately on evidence that is as indubitably clear and certain to "the uncorrupted, unbefuddled human understanding" as any proposition in geometry.[22]

Mendelssohn proceeds from this point to assert, as he did in *Jerusalem* and elsewhere, that the fundamental truths of rational religion are readily accessible to all men at all times, in all places, at all levels of civilization. He provides two examples of the way in which representatives of very disparate climes are able, in a commonsensical fashion, to latch onto the truth of God's existence. The first is a simple Greenlander, wandering across the ice, one beautiful morning, in the company of a meddlesome missionary. Upon seeing the first rays of dawn shine forth among the icebergs, he says to the missionary: "Look, brother, the new day! How beautiful must be he who made this!" This argument is fully sufficient for the Greenlander before the missionary has led him astray, and says Mendelssohn, "it is still so for me." It has just as much force, he continues, as "the plain, artless argument of the Psalmist:

> He that planted the ear,
> Shall he not hear?
> He that formed the eye,
> Shall he not see?
> He that teaches men knowledge,
> The Eternal, knows the thoughts of man.[23]

This simple conclusion has, as far as Mendelssohn is concerned, all the power of an irrefutable demonstration. "To my speculation I assign only the task of correcting the utterances of sound understanding (*die Aussprüche des gesunden Menschenverstandes*), and, as far as possible, transforming them into rational knowledge." This statement is followed by Mendelssohn's final restatement of what we have already come to know as his "method of orientation."[24]

Wizenmann and Kant

Mendelssohn's "method of orientation" has been the subject of much discussion, both among his contemporaries and among later generations of scholars. Some have seen it as signifying an abandonment of his previously firm commitment to reason; others have maintained, on the contrary, that it reflects his continued readiness to reaffirm the sovereignty of reason. Still others have regarded his entire discussion of the demonstrability of religious truths as evidence of muddled and inconsistent thinking. It is, indeed, not at all surprising that such a division of opinion should exist. Mendelssohn's treatment of this whole matter is far from unambiguous.

In the immediate aftermath of the appearance of *Morning Hours*, one of Jacobi's friends, Thomas Wizenmann, wrote a volume entitled *Critical Investigation of the Results of Jacobi's and Mendelssohn's Philosophy by a Volunteer (Die Resultate der Jacobischer und Mendelssohnischer Philosophie von einem Freywilligen)*.[25] Like Jacobi, Wizenmann believed it to be impossible to develop rational proofs of the fundamental truths of natural religion. In his opinion, the historical experience of revelation was the only possible source of sure knowledge of God and his relationship to man.[26] Wizenmann would therefore have been at odds with Mendelssohn even if he had never developed his "method of orientation." Only Mendelssohn's description of this method, however, prompted Wizenmann to launch an attack on him. He accused Mendelssohn of inconsistency for proclaiming his belief in the sovereignty and sufficiency of reason while at the same time subjecting it to the guidance of another, nonrational authority: common sense. If one probed beneath the surface of this inconsistency, he believed, one would recognize that Mendelssohn, at bottom, was not really the rationalist that he pretended to be.

In the course of his lengthy and rather diffuse critique, Wizenmann cites a number of passages in which Mendelssohn reiterates unequivocally his belief in reason's capacity to prove the fundamental truths of natural religion. He juxtaposes them with the passage from *To Lessing's Friends*, which we have just examined, where Mendelssohn describes sound understanding as the indubitable source of religious knowledge, which speculation should merely endeavor to refine. Precisely what, Wizenmann then asks, does Mendelssohn mean by *sound understanding*? And on what basis does he regard it as an unfailing source of religious truths?

"If Mendelssohn felt it to be his duty," writes Wizenmann, "to defend reason against the claims of revelation and faith, one should have expected that he would at least have sought to elucidate the sources of human knowledge in such a manner that it would be possible to form a distinct concept of their character." But he did not do so. He did not even define what he meant by *common sense*, claims Wizenmann, dismissing as entirely insufficient the passage from the third lecture of *Morning Hours*, which we have already examined. "If he had not given us a few examples, one would never have been able to guess what he meant by the utterances of sound understanding."[27] The examples to which Wizenmann here refers are those Mendelssohn presents in *To Lessing's Friends*, the commonsensical Greenlander and the Psalmist.

It is on the Greenlander alone that Wizenmann focuses his attention. He analyzes this hypothetical character's mode of reasoning in the light of what Beiser has termed his "essentially Kantian-style epistemology."[28] Before turning to his discussion of the Greenlander's mode of reasoning, therefore, we must briefly review the basis of this epistemology.

In Wizenmann's eyes, all of our convictions concerning our own existence and that of things outside of ourselves are dependent upon "a simply inexplicable deception (*einer schlechterdings unerklärlichen Täuschung*)." By deception he does not mean to imply that our senses supply us with evidence of things that have no real existence but only that the reality of the objects of which they inform us *"cannot be proven."*[29] One's conviction of one's own existence and of that of the surrounding world "rests on experience and on faith in this experience (*auf Erfahrung beruhet und auf Glauben an diese Erfahrung*). The impression on one's senses is so strong that no further justification is necessary.[30]

From this knowledge derived from experience and accepted on faith one can deduce many things, but only with regard to the world that one is capable of perceiving directly. When one leaves the "ground of experience" and begins to reason about realms beyond the reach of human perception, one engages in a kind of speculation that can never lead to sure knowledge.[31] And this, according to Wizenmann, is precisely what Mendelssohn's Greenlander does.

The Greenlander is gifted by nature with a will and an understanding and consequently also with the concept of a will an understanding. "It is impossible," he thinks,

> for him to arrange or produce anything without purpose and reflection; and it is therefore just as impossible for him to imagine order, proportion, beauty and existence in general, without will and understanding. Sometimes the uncivilized man goes still further, and completely transfers his manner of being to the objects outside of himself. Not only does he see a will and an understanding in action in every relationship, in every ordered effect of nature, but he even regards everything that is in motion as being alive. It is the same deception of nature. Every activity, every movement, which he himself produces, comes from or has as its cause a living impetus and impulse; and therefore everything that is in motion and in operation seems to him to be living. From this source, from this dearth of separation or abstraction, from this beautiful and maternal deception of nature emerge everywhere crude pantheism and the belief in one God. Man transfers to nature his own manner of being, sees everywhere beings like himself, and fashions a deity from and like himself (*aus und nach sich selbst*).[32]

What the Greenlander does, in a nutshell, as Wizenmann observes elsewhere, is to draw, however crudely, the following inference: "Wherever there is order, a thought has taken effect, since I can produce no order without thought." And this leads him to God. The Greenlander's inference is, indeed "the guide and the *ne plus ultra* of all systems of God."[33] It represents a way of thinking for which much can be said, but it is not immune to criticism. "If the Greenlander's inference is examined, the question arises: wherein lies the evidence (the real evidence) for that childishly simple (*kinderleichten*) inference, considered apart from any speculative propositions?"

Wizenmann immediately answers this question with some more questions of his own: "Does it lie in the natural deception, that he confuses his own manner of being with the relations between things outside of himself? This evidence may suffice for the Greenlander, who in most cases does not distinguish between deception and reality. But for the philosopher?"[34] Elsewhere, a similar question evokes from Wizenmann a succinct answer: "Are they therefore rational grounds that give to man in every circumstance of life the firm conviction of the existence of a deity? As far as we can see, it is an ineluctable deception of nature, it is a spark, that springs from the actual relationship of man to the world, it is *faith in a revelation of nature (Glaube an eine Offenbarung der Natur).*"[35]

Closely examined, the "sound understanding" eulogized by Mendelssohn turns out to be, in Wizenmann's opinion, not a form of reason but a kind of faith. The very fact that Mendelssohn has recourse to it as a necessary guide for speculation proves, he argues, that he was not at bottom a true partisan of reason. Despite his "zealous defense of demonstrations," Mendelssohn himself evidently had very little confidence in their absolute value.[36] "I at least" writes Wizenmann, "do not know with what right a demonstration that must orient itself, a demonstration that requires a foreign guide, a demonstration that in no way bears within it its own evidence, can ever be called a *demonstration.*"[37] Mendelssohn's admission of the need for reliance on sound understanding in order to guarantee the fundamental truths of natural religion was therefore tantamount to a recognition that "a pure, completely demonstrative, apodictic proof for the existence of God" was not really feasible. In reality, the most for which Mendelssohn believed one could hope, according to Wizenmann, was a chain of inferences that would provide a solution to the problem of God's existence until a still cleverer person showed up and put an end to the game.[38]

In this manner Wizenmann dismisses Mendelssohn's expressed hopes for the advent of a stronger mind, for a profound thinker like Kant, who would restore metaphysics to its former glory. He takes note of Mendelssohn's anticipation of the appearance of such a person, but he also alludes to his suggestion that there is a "cyclical course of things," one in which advances in metaphysics are always followed by the emergence of new skeptics with new challenges. Instead of focusing his attention, as Mendelssohn does, on the high points of this cycle, Wizenmann concentrates on the low points. Their recurrence indicates to him that, even in Mendelssohn's opinion, reason can never finally accomplish the task of constructing an irrefutable natural theology.

Wizenmann does more than claim that Mendelssohn implicitly admitted the inadequacy of reason as a means of attaining certain knowledge of the existence of God. He attributes to him a clear awareness of the incompatibility of his frequently reiterated absolute commitment to reason with his ultimate reliance on common sense. He is unable, he writes, "to entertain the thought that Mendelssohn himself did not perceive this contradiction." But, if he perceived it, why did he not make an attempt to eliminate it? Why did he continue to reiterate his confidence in the power of demonstrations? At one point Wizenmann expresses a certain reluctance to probe Mendelssohn's motives to get to the bottom of this riddle.[39] Elsewhere, however, he speculates that his wavering between two incompatible positions, his failure to present in an unequivocal manner his true, irrationalist position, may have been due to a desire on his part to avoid suffering the fate of Jacobi. Mendelssohn, suspects Wizenmann, did not want to be exposed to the "witch-hunting (*Kezzergerichte*) of his intended audience, which automatically condemned anything that smacked of faith."[40]

Wizenmann, however, rips away the veil. The true, underlying situation is entirely clear to him: "In spite of the terminological difference between faith and the utterances of a sound understanding, Jacobi and Mendelssohn were in perfect agreement that conviction of the fundamental truths of religion is possible and real even without demonstration and without what one usually and more properly calls rational grounds."[41] Despite appearances, then, Mendelssohn was really "not so far removed" from Jacobi.[42]

In October 1786, five months after the appearance of Wizenmann's *Critical Investigation*, Immanuel Kant made his own contribution to the *Pantheismusstreit* in a short essay entitled "What Does It Mean: To Orient Oneself in Thinking?" As Frederick Beiser has observed, the *Critical Investigation* "was the starting point for Kant's reflections on the pantheism controversy." Beiser is only partly correct, however, in maintaining that "It was indeed Wizenmann who convinced Kant that Jacobi and Mendelssohn were both heading in the dangerous direction of irrationalism . . ."[43] Kant certainly agreed with Wizenmann that Jacobi was an enemy of reason, but he saw Mendelssohn in a very different light. He did believe that Mendelssohn had not fully realized the significance of what he was doing when he made certain concessions to common sense. But this did not prevent Kant from regarding him as a complete rationalist, as someone who "steadfastly and with righteous zeal" maintained that only genuine, pure reason (*bloss der eigentliche reine Menschenvernunft*) ought to serve as the means by which people oriented themselves.[44]

Kant's disagreement with Wizenmann on this point stems in part from his very different evaluation of Mendelssohn's notion of common sense. Unlike Wizenmann, he does not comment on Mendelssohn's failure to define this term nor does he try to elucidate his usage of it by examining the contexts in which he employs it. All he does, at first, is to note that Mendelssohn, in referring to the faculty that ought to serve as a guide to speculation, designates it sometimes as common sense (*Gemeinsinn*), sometimes as sound reason (*gesunde Vernunft*), and sometimes as plain human understanding (*schlichten Menschenverstand*). Kant himself, however, when he has occasion in the course of his essay to discuss this faculty, consistently refers to it as sound reason (*gesunde Vernunft*), the designation that connects the faculty in question most closely with reason pure and simple.

Kant strives to clarify not what Mendelssohn may have intended to say when he referred to sound reason but what it is he was actually describing. When human reason seeks, he explains, to understand things beyond the bounds of experience, and which cannot therefore become the object of human knowledge, it is acting in response to a "feeling of its own *requirements* (*das Gefühl des der Vernunft eigenen Bedürfnisses*).[45] Our reason feels a requirement to lay the foundation for the concept of all conditioned things with the concept of something unconditioned. It feels a need likewise to presuppose the existence of such an unconditioned being, without which it can scarcely arrive at a satisfactory explanation for the existence and evident purposefulness of the things contained in the world. Reason requires the existence of something that it cannot demonstrate; that is, an intelligent originator of the world.[46]

Not only in its "theoretical" but also in its "practical" use does reason require, according to Kant, the existence of God. Kant proceeds to elaborate, at this point, his well-known explanation of the existence of God as a postulate of practical reason. The pure practical use of reason consists, he says, in the prescribing of the moral law. Not to enforce this law but to guarantee the objective reality of the highest good, practical reason has need of the idea of a supreme being.

"It is not, therefore, *knowledge*," Kant concludes, but a felt *requirement* of reason by which Mendelssohn (without knowing it) orients himself in speculative thinking."[47] Kant thus claims to understand Mendelssohn better than Mendelssohn understood himself. In relying on sound reason, he says, Mendelssohn did not really comprehend what he was doing, but he was doing the right thing. He was not taking a dangerous step toward irrationalism but utilizing reason, appropriately, in a manner he could not adequately describe. The "source of judgment" (*Quelle der Beurtheilung*) he labels common sense or sound reason really ought to be given a different name, "and none is more fitting than that of a *rational faith* (*Vernunftglaubens*)." Such a faith is rational in that "it rests on no other data than those that are contained in *pure reason*." Nevertheless, even though it is entirely rational, it always remains a form of belief and not of knowledge.[48]

What ultimately guarantees Mendelssohn's status as a rationalist, in Kant's eyes, is not the essential rationality of *gesunde Vernunft*. It is rather Mendelssohn's insistence that the results attained by the employment of sound reason must be placed before a higher, more indubitably rational court. Basing himself, no doubt, on the allegorical dream presented in the tenth chapter of *Morning Hours*, Kant notes that Mendelssohn continues to seek "the final touchstone of the admissability of any judgment (*den letzten Probirstein der Zulässigkeit eines Urtheils*)" "*only in reason*," even if he sees it as being "guided in the selection of its propositions by insight or a bare requirement and the maxims of its own usefulness (*durch Einsicht oder bloss es Bedürfniss und die Maxime ihrer eigenen Zuträglichkeit in der Wahl ihrer Sätze geleitet*)."

Kant does not then, criticize Mendelssohn for, as Beiser puts it, seeing "common sense as a special faculty of knowledge that has the power to correct reason."[49] He faults him, not for relying on common sense, but only for misunderstanding the true nature of the rational faculty it represents and for failing to devise an appropriate name for it. Far from regarding Mendelssohn as a traitor to reason, Kant commends him for continuing to treat reason as the ultimate authority. The only thing that really disturbs Kant is Mendelssohn's tendency to credit speculation with too much power. He upbraids him for continuing to believe that it could "straighten everything out by means of demonstrations."[50] As Altmann correctly summed things up, Kant praises "Mendelssohn's resolve to check the flights of speculation by sound common sense," and criticizes him for allowing "too much to the speculative faculty."[51]

This is, in effect, Kant's answer to Mendelssohn's appeal to him in the Preface to *Morning Hours*. Mendelssohn, it will be recalled, spoke there, rather ruefully, of the "all-crushing Kant," the destroyer of traditional metaphysics. But he also expressed what we might call a pious hope that Kant would one day rebuild what he had destroyed. Kant responded to this plea, after its author's death, by criticizing him for continuing to the end to place too much confidence in metaphysics. It would really have been necessary for Mendelssohn to rely on *gesunde Vernunft*, he observes, only if he (like Kant himself) had been fully convinced of the insufficiency of speculative reason. And this is a realization "to which his sagacity would ultimately have brought him if, together with a longer lifespan, he had been favored with the kind of mental agility

more characteristic of one's early years, which facilitates the modification of old, familiar ways of thinking in the aftermath of a
change in the state of knowledge."[52] Although this statement may
have the appearance of a compliment, one is entitled to suspect
that it is at bottom Kant's rather condescending way of saying that
Mendelssohn was probably too hidebound in his thinking to have
appreciated the latest advances in the sciences (that is, Kant's own
philosophy) even if he had been fortunate enough to live a longer
life.

Both Wizenmann and Kant were themselves participants in
the *Pantheismusstreit* and not mere scholarly observers of it. Here,
it will not be necessary for us to engage in a full-scale examination
of their contributions to this controversy, an examination that
would take us far beyond the scope of this book. We should note,
however, that each of them had aims of his own to advance and
that their different goals may have colored their reading of Mendelssohn. Wizenmann, as a supporter of Jacobi and an opponent of
rationalism, may have wished to characterize Mendelssohn, as far
as possible, as a de facto renegade from the camp of philosophy and
and to claim him as someone who recognized, however reluctant he
may have been to admit it, the paramouncy of faith. Kant, on the
other hand, in his desire to retain Mendelssohn as an ally in his
combat against what he saw as Jacobi's fanaticism, may have been
prepared to place some of what he perhaps saw as his missteps in
the best possible light. Nevertheless, it does seem as if both of
them based their assessment of Mendelssohn's real views solely on
the interpretation of his writings.[53]

Contemporary Scholarship Concerning the Pantheismusstreit

Subsequent students of the *Pantheismusstreit* have not analyzed Mendelssohn's contribution to it with anything resembling
the sense of urgency we find in the writings of Wizenmann and
Kant. Nevertheless, there is among them a division of opinion that
corresponds in many respects to the one that arose, as we have
seen, in the immediate aftermath of the exchanges between Mendelssohn and Jacobi. Following a brief examination of some of the
more recent scholarship dealing with the position Mendelssohn
took in the course of the controversy, we shall attempt to shed
some additional light on this question.

To some extent, Leo Strauss, in his important discussion of
Morning Hours and *To Lessing's Friends*, can be seen as having
taken a position similar to that of Wizenmann. Strauss depicts

Mendelssohn as someone who slowly lost his confidence, during the decades between his prize essay of 1763 and his composition of *Morning Hours*, in the Leibniz-Wolff philosophy and increasingly "took refuge on the neutral isle of common sense." Unlike Wizenmann, however, Strauss regards the shift in Mendelssohn's position as a consequence not primarily of his disappointment with earlier metaphysics but as a result of his having taken a public position in defense of Judaism.

Strauss begins by noting that at first, in the *Treatise on Evidence*, Mendelssohn placed no limits on the power of reason. Nevertheless, even in this early work he acknowledged the degree to which moral truths were more readily accessible to common sense than to reason. The decisive turnabout came, according to Strauss, only when Mendelssohn was engaged in his controversy with Lavater and Bonnet and, above all, when he was writing *Jerusalem*.[54] Compelled to undertake a simultaneous defense of his Judaism and his rationalism, Mendelssohn had to defend Judaism as a purely rational religion. Yet the Bible's teaching is not set forth in the form of demonstrations. And Mendelssohn could not, on account of his modern presuppositions, follow in the footsteps of Maimonides and attribute to the prophets an understanding that transcended that which was acquired through demonstrations. He could therefore come to the aid of Judaism only by greatly restricting the significance of demonstrative knowledge.

In *Jerusalem* Mendelssohn states, as Strauss notes, that it is not always necessary or useful for men to have a sophisticated understanding of the principles of natural theology. "Very often," he writes, "as the Psalmist says, *the babbling of children and infants will suffice to confound the enemy*." That is to say, a simple man, who is as yet unacquainted with rational concepts of nature and causality but who hears and sees "the all-vivifying power of the Deity everywhere" has acquired an adequate grasp of what he needs to know.[55] In Mendelssohn's last work, *To Lessing's Friends*, the connection between his growing affinity with the philosophy of common sense and his defense of Judaism becomes, according to Strauss, perfectly clear. There Mendelssohn speaks of Judaism as consisting solely of a revealed legislation that, in his own words, "presupposes natural and rational conviction of religious truths." And when he refers to rational (*vernünftmassige*) convictions, "it is not a question of metaphysical argumentation, as we are accustomed to engage in it in books, or of pedantic demonstrations, but of the statements and judgments of plain human understanding, which looks things straight in the eye and calmly considers them."[56]

The last stage of this development is, according to Strauss, the teaching of *Morning Hours* and *To Lessing's Friends* on the relationship between speculation and common sense. In these works, as we have seen, Mendelssohn displays a greatly reduced confidence in the ability of speculative reason to arrive on its own at correct results with regard to matters of the greatest importance. Strauss sees such statements as indications of the moment when theistic metaphysics lost faith in the sufficiency of reason and was forced to seek refuge on "the neutral isle of common sense."[57]

Strauss, then, as Alexander Altmann has put it, attributes Mendelssohn's turn from "the demonstrative type of philosophical argument" to "a philosophy of common sense" to "an increasing concern with the defense of Judaism, a task which Mendelssohn could not hope to accomplish successfully by rigorous demonstration." Altmann himself was "not at all sure that this is correct."[58] He did not elaborate at all on his reasons for questioning the validity of Strauss's reasoning, but his doubts were certainly well-founded. One can see why Mendelssohn would have been unable to follow the example of medieval Jewish philosophers and to attribute the most sophisticated philosophical knowledge to the biblical prophets. And, in view of this, it is obvious that Mendelssohn could not insist on the *indispensability* for salvation of a philosophical understanding of the proofs for God's existence without implying the inferiority, in a crucial respect, of what he sometimes describes as the "old, original Judaism." But at no point in his philosophical career, not before and not after he commenced his public defense of Judaism, did Mendelssohn place such an absolute value on philosophical knowledge. From his point of view, it did not detract from the status of Moses or Isaiah that Leibniz possessed greater metaphysical knowledge than they did. Contrary to what Strauss says, therefore, he could have defended Judaism without downplaying the importance or denying the possibility of philosophical knowledge of religious truths.

As we have just observed, Altmann was unwilling to accept Strauss's explanation of Mendelssohn's reasons for having recourse to a philosophy of common sense. He does not, however, dispute the fact that Mendelssohn did, in the end, turn to common sense nor does he explicitly take issue with any other aspect of Strauss's treatment of this matter. At the conclusion of his article on Mendelssohn's proofs for the existence of God, Altmann comments that "What Mendelssohn's affirmation of common sense meant in terms of his religious beliefs cannot be discussed here" and refers the reader to Strauss's treatment of this question. He then observes that "It is clear, however, that the proofs for the existence of God that he so strenuously upheld were not the raison d'etre of his faith. Both Mendelssohn and Kant were convinced of ultimate metaphysical truths on grounds other than purely theoretical."[59]

Elsewhere, Altmann acknowledges that it is true that "Mendelssohn became increasingly disenchanted with philosophy *more geometrico* . . ." He immediately adds, however, that "he never abandoned his conviction that the demonstrative method alone was qualified to defend the truths of natural religion (which were the truths of Judaism) against skepticism, atheism and superstition."[60] This may seem, at first glance, to contradict the statements cited in the previous paragraph. How, after all, can one assert that Mendelssohn both retained his faith in the unrivaled power of the demonstrative method and "was at the same time convinced of ultimate metaphysical truths on grounds other than purely theoretical?" This was, of course, the problem that provoked Wizenmann into asserting that Mendelssohn could not possibly have believed what he said about the necessity of demonstrations. Altmann, however, apparently did not take Wizenmann's objections very seriously. He clearly believed that Kant was correct in concluding that, as he put it, "Mendelssohn's idea of common sense was firmly anchored in reason."[61] His reliance on grounds that were not purely theoretical need not, therefore, have amounted to a repudiation of the feasibility of theoretical demonstrations of the fundamental truths of natural religion.

Manfred Kuehn deals briefly with Mendelssohn in his recent book on the influence in Germany during the last third of the eighteenth century of the Scottish commonsense philosophers, Thomas Reid, James Oswald, and James Beattie. As Kuehn amply demonstrates, these thinkers were opponents of the epistemological skepticism of David Hume, which they perceived as a threat to morality and religion. Among other things, they argued, in Reid's words, that "there are certain principles . . . which the constitution of our nature leads us to believe, and which we are under a necessity to take for granted in the common concerns of life . . . these are what we call the principles of common sense; and what is manifestly contrary to them, is what we call absurd." What Reid is saying, according to Kuehn, is that the principles of common sense have "the characteristics of natural necessity and indispensability. They are at the root of our ability to reason and can thus not be themselves rationally explained."[62]

Mendelssohn, Kuehn maintains, acquired his understanding of common sense from Reid. His dependency on him should not, however, "mislead us into thinking that Mendelssohn is simply copying the Scots." Unlike them, he "does not take common sense to be absolute or infallible," and unlike them, he "is far from wanting to give up all the rights of pure reason." "Common sense and reason," Kuehn quotes Mendelssohn as saying, "are basically one and the same." They "flow from the same source."[63] For Kuehn, then, Mendelssohn's explanation of common sense in the third lecture of *Morning Hours* is entirely satisfactory, as it clearly was not for Wizenmann but apparently was for Kant (and, for that matter, Altmann).

Not all recent scholars have, like Strauss, Altmann, and Kuehn, conclusively located the real basis of Mendelssohn's convictions either in his use of his rational faculties or in his acceptance of a faculty other than reason as an ultimate authority. Frederick Beiser, the author of the most careful recent study of this issue, argues that Mendelssohn, in the end, "offers us only the most confusing advice. He cannot decide which faculty deserves priority," common sense or speculation.

> Sometimes he says that we must trust our common sense and silence our reason until it returns to the fold of our ordinary beliefs. The truths of natural religion remain unshakable to him, he confesses in his *An die Freunde Lessings*, even though all the demonstrations of the existence of God should fail. . . . But is not this faith in common sense, and this mistrust in the demonstrations of reason, a betrayal of Mendelssohn's credo? At other times Mendelssohn says that the task of reason is "to correct" common sense, and he recognizes the possibility that common sense can err by not sufficiently investigating the reasons for its beliefs. Indeed, in arguing against Basedow, Mendelssohn unequivocally takes his stand with speculation, steadfastly maintaining the necessity of pursuing an investigation despite the moral and religious consequences.

Mendelssohn's views, according to Beiser, bear the stamp of his ambivalence. They reflect a fear on his part of the consequences of giving priority to either faculty. "If he follows his speculation alone, then he could arrive at skepticism, rejecting some of the essential beliefs of common sense, morality, and religion; but if he follows his common sense alone, then he might lapse into dogmatism, dismissing all inquiry and criticism as sophistry. In the case of a persistent conflict between speculation and common sense, Mendelssohn's method of orientation leaves us with no means of steering between these two dangerous extremes."[64]

Mendelssohn's allegorical dream leaves this task, it would seem to reason. But, Beiser asks,

> what is this figure of reason that so blithely settles the conflicts between speculation and common sense? If it is a faculty of criticism, a faculty that demands to know the reasons for our beliefs, then it amounts to nothing more than speculation. If, however, it is an intuitive faculty, a faculty that judges all issues according to "a natural light," then it is little more than common sense. We therefore do not seem to have any criterion for the identity of this mysterious faculty, a criterion that does not boil down to either of the very faculties whose disputes are to be settled.[65]

Unable to identify a counterpart in the real world to the figure of reason appearing in the allegorical dream, Beiser refuses to regard it as having any genuine meaning and dismisses it from further consideration.

Not since Wizenmann composed his *Critical Investigation* has anyone argued as vigorously as Beiser that Mendelssohn's position on these matters was marked by a deep inconsistency. Beiser does not contend, however, as did Wizenmann, that Mendelssohn's contradictory statements cloaked an unacknowledged abandonment of reason in favor of something that could best be described as faith. He believes him to have been sincere in maintaining that common sense and speculation are merely different forms of the faculty of reason. What he holds against him is his failure to explain which of these two forms of reason must serve as the ultimate arbiter of our judgments. In saying that we ought sometimes to follow common sense and at other times to follow speculation, Mendelssohn has failed, he claims, to give us a hard and fast rule. For that reason, his method of orientation may prove useless precisely when we need it most. The figure of reason that resolves, in Mendelssohn's allegorical dream, all disputes between common sense and speculation Beiser regards as a mere chimera.

Conclusion

We see, then, that over the years there has been, to say the least, a considerable amount of disagreement concerning Mendelssohn's final position on the question of what ought to constitute the ultimate authority for our judgments. In the eyes of some, his continued affirmations of the sovereignty of reason are not to be taken at face value. Whatever he may have said, they maintain, he evidently deserted the camp of the rationalist philosophers and took refuge on "the neutral isle of common sense" or in a kind of faith, which he unconvincingly disguised as reason. In the eyes of others, he clearly persisted in his allegiance to theoretical reason as the ultimate arbiter of all disputes. To still others, Mendelssohn appears to have been unable to decide whether final authority ought to rest with common sense or with speculative reason.

All in all, this is not an easy dispute to resolve, but we must make an attempt to do so. What we can say, to begin with, is that Wizenmann is no doubt correct in maintaining that Mendelssohn fails to define clearly the nature of common sense or to elucidate its relationship to reason. He goes too far, however, when he maintains that Mendelssohn believed common sense to be nothing more than a kind of faith. In doing so, he is unwarrantedly attributing his own views to a philosopher who gives no evidence of sharing his "Kantian-style epistemology."

Whatever status Mendelssohn might have accorded to common sense, he is, as Kant recognized, entirely candid when he expresses his full confidence in the power of reason to demonstrate the fundamental truths of natural religion. He has, to be sure, evidently lost his faith in the metaphysics of the Leibniz-Wolff school, but not in the possibility of a theistic metaphysics that would arrive at the same happy conclusions regarding God's relationship to the world and its inhabitants. As he makes quite clear, he is awaiting the advent of a strong-minded reasoner who will be able to "give the wheel a shove" and to restore metaphysics to its former glory. Mendelssohn intends his "method of orientation" to be of use only during the current interim period, when common sense and speculation are unfortunately at odds with regard to what can be said with certainty about the most important matters. It is all that he expects to have at his disposal until the wheel turns, until, in "the cyclical course of things," the skeptics and the fanatics are once again defeated by those who both possess the truth and can provide an irrefutable, rational defense of it.[66] Mendelssohn looks forward, if only rather forlornly, to such a time.

Mendelssohn's longing for the arrival of that day finds expression in the allegorical dream in *Morning Hours*. The figure of Reason, in this dream, must not be seen as a mere chimera. It is rather the embodiment of what Mendelssohn believes is sorely lacking in the contemporary world, an individual capable of satisfactorily adjudicating the disputes between common sense, which affirms the validity of the fundamental truths of natural religion, and speculation, which has ceased to do so. What gives Reason this power is her *knowledge* of the truth. She can size up the claims of common sense and speculation and determine authoritatively which of the two is correct. But she exists only in a dream. What Mendelssohn learns from his conversation with her is only that common sense is on the whole more reliable than contemplation. This corresponds, he tells us, to what his own experience has taught him. Out of prudence, therefore, and not, like the matronly figure, on the basis of omniscience, Mendelssohn himself usually chooses, when the two diverge, to follow common sense rather than his own speculations. He is disposed to follow it, in short, not because it is a sure guide but merely because it is a better guide, for the time being.

Wizenmann was wrong to believe that Mendelssohn had altogether ceased to anticipate "a pure, completely demonstrative, apodictic proof for the existence of God" and had sought the source of eternal verities instead in common sense, which was in essence a form of faith. It is true that he accepted the guidance of common sense on faith, but what he had faith in was, in the end, the reasonableness of doing so. He also continued to retain faith in reason's demonstrative powers. From where, we may ask, did this latter faith come? All we can say, I believe, is that it was the product of his own intense yearning for total certainty of the truth of God's existence and beneficent providence.

Notes

1. *JubA*, vol. 3, 2, pp. 3–4.

2. Quoted in Altmann, *Mendelssohn*, p. 112. See also *JubA*, vol. 2, p. xlv.

3. Beiser, *The Fate of Reason*, p. 105.

4. Richard L. Velkley, *Freedom and the End of Reason*, (Chicago and London: University of Chicago Press, 1989), pp. 23–24.

5. Ibid., p. 141.

6. Ibid., p. 138.

7. Quoted in Altmann, *Moses Mendelssohn*, p. 348.

8. See Altmann, *Moses Mendelssohn*, pp. 638ff; Beiser, *The Fate of Reason*, pp. 44ff; Hermann Timm, *Gott und die Freiheit* (Frankfurt am Main, 1974), pp. 135ff; Leo Strauss in *JubA*, vol. 3, 2, pp. xiiff.

9. Beiser, *The Fate of Reason*, p. 80.

10. Ibid., p. 4.

11. Ibid., p. 80.

12. See, for example, Altmann, *Moses Mendelssohn*, p. 679; Beiser, *The Fate of Reason*, p. 97.

13. *JubA*, vol. 3, 2, p. 72.

14. Ibid., pp. 71–72.

15. *Jerusalem*, p. 95.

16. Beiser, *The Fate of Reason*, p. 101.

17. *JubA*, vol. 3, 2, p. 28.

18. *JubA*, vol. 3, 2, pp. 33–34. Beiser (*The Fate of Reason*, p. 98) mistakenly maintains that Mendelssohn sees the conflict between philosophy and ordinary belief as a conflict between common sense and speculation, "and does not use the terms 'faith' (*Glaube*) or 'reason' (*Vernunft*)." In his subsequent discussion of the third lecture of *Morning Hours* he speaks, accordingly, of the contrast Mendelssohn draws between common sense and speculation. In fact, however, Mendelssohn makes no mention here of common sense (*Gemeinsinn*) or speculation. He distinguishes repeatedly between reason (*Vernunft*) and sound understanding (*gesunde Menschenverstand*).

19. *JubA*, vol. 3, 2, pp. 81–82.

20. Altmann, *Moses Mendelssohn*, p. 680.

21. *JubA*, vol. 3, 2, p. 82.

22. *JubA*, vol. 3, 2, pp. 197–98.

23. Psalm 94, 9–11. As Leo Strauss has observed (*JubA*, vol. 3, 2, p. 327), Mendelssohn omits a part of the second verse, where the psalmist speaks of God as a chastiser of nations. Strauss describes this as a characteristic omission.

24. *JubA*, vol. 3, 2, pp. 198–99.

25. As Hermann Timm has observed (*Gott und die Freiheit*, p. 243), Wizenmann is today a forgotten figure. Timm's own brief biography of him (pp. 245ff) is the best of which I am aware.

26. Ibid., pp. 253ff.

27. Thomas Wizenmann, *Die Resultate der Jacobischer und Mendelssohnischer Philosophie von einem Freywilligen*, (Leipzig: Göschen, 1786) pp. 62–63.

28. Beiser, *The Fate of Reason*, p. 112.

29. Wizenmann, *Die Resultate*, p. 31.

30. Ibid., pp. 64–65.

31. Ibid., pp. 64–67.

32. Ibid., pp. 52–53.

33. Ibid., p. 67.

34. Ibid., pp. 68–69.

35. Ibid., p. 54.

36. Ibid., pp. 70–71.

37. Ibid., p. 80.

38. Ibid., p. 74.

39. Ibid., p. 80.

40. Ibid., p. 63.

41. Ibid., p. 47.

42. Ibid., p. 36.

43. Beiser, *The Fate of Reason*, p. 110. On this point, Beiser's assessment falls surprisingly wide of the mark. Perhaps he was misled by the manner in which Kant opened his essay. After briefly describing how Mendelssohn had subjected reason to the guidance of common sense, he made the following comments: "Who would have thought that this confession would be so ruinous (as in fact, it inevitably was) not only to his own beneficial opinion of the power of the speculative use of reason in matters of theology, but that even common, sound reason, on account of the ambiguity with which he contrasted the exercise of this faculty with speculation, would be in danger of becoming the foundation of fanaticism and furthering the complete dethronement of reason?" With this statement, however, Kant does not wish to impugn Mendelssohn's intentions or to imply that he himself was headed in the direction of irrationalism. What he is suggesting is that Mendelssohn, through his use of ambiguous terminology, had unwittingly supplied the enemies of reason with ammunition. The dangers to which Kant refers materialized not in Mendelssohn's own writings but, as we learn in the very next sentence of his essay, "above all in the not insignificant conclusions of the penetrating author of the *Critical Investigation*," that is, Wizenmann. See *Immanuel Kant's gesammelte Schriften*, ed. Royal Prussian Academy of Sciences (Berlin: Geroge Reimer, 1912) vol. 8, p. 134.

44. *Immanuel Kant's gesammelte Schriften*, vol. 8, p. 134.

45. Ibid., p. 136.

46. Ibid., p. 138.

47. Ibid., p. 139.

48. Ibid., p. 140–41.

49. Beiser, *The Fate of Reason*, p. 117.

50. *Immanuel Kant's gesammelte Schriften*, vol. 8, p. 140; also p. 151.

51. Altmann, *Moses Mendelssohn*, p. 680. See also *Die trostvolle Aufklärung, Studien zur Metaphysik und politischen Theorie Moses Mendelssohn* (Stuttgart-Bad Connstatt: Friedrich Frohmann Verlag, 1982), p. 151.

52. *Immanuel Kant's gesammelte Schriften*, vol. 8, p. 140.

53. As Timm (*Gott und die Freiheit*, pp. 443–44) has observed, Wizenmann, with good reason, considered himself to be the addressee of Kant's essay on orientation. Already on the verge of death, he was able to respond to it only in a fragmentary fashion. He rejected Kant's attempt to portray Mendelssohn as a complete rationalist. Kant may have been correct, he said, in identifying Mendelssohn as someone who orientated himself on the basis of a perceived requirement of reason, while mistakenly regarding it as knowledge. But this still left him among those who, unlike Kant himself, "only set up a blind and uncomprehending cry for reason (*nur ein blindes und verstandloses Geschrei für die Vernunft erheben*)."

54. See *JubA*, vol. 3, 2, p. lxvi.

55. *Jerusalem*, p. 95.

56. *JubA*, vol. 3, 2, pp. lxvii and 197.

57. Ibid., pp. lxix–lxx.

58. Altmann, "Mendelssohn's Concept of Judaism Reexamined," in *Von der mittelalterlichen zur modernen Aufklärung*, p. 242.

59. Altmann, *Essays in Jewish Intellectual History*, p. 137.

60. Altmann, "Mendelssohn's Concept of Judaism Reexamined," pp. 242–43.

61. Altmann, *Essays in Jewish Intellectual History*, p. 137.

62. Manfred Kuehn, *Scottish Common Sense in Germany, 1768–1800: A Contribution to the History of Critical Philosophy*, (Kingston and Montreal: McGill-Queen's University Press, 1987), p. 29.

63. Ibid., pp. 115–17.

64. Beiser, *The Fate of Reason*, p. 102.

65. Ibid., p. 101.

66. In both of the passages in which Mendelssohn discusses his "method of orientation" he speaks, we should note, in a very personal vein. The original statement, in *Morning Hours* (*JubA* vol. 3, 2, p. 82) reads as

follows: "As soon as my speculations lead me too far away from the high-way of common sense, I stand still and try to orientate myself. I look back to the point from which we have departed and I try to compare my two guides. Experience has taught me that in most cases the right is on the side of common sense and that reason has to favor speculation decisively if I should leave common sense and follow speculation. Indeed, in order to convince me that the steadfastness of common sense is only ignorant stub-borness, reason has to show me how common sense could possibly have taken leave of the truth and gone astray." In *To Lessing's Friends* (ibid., p. 198), he writes that "As long as both of them, sound understanding and speculation, are still in accord, I follow them wherever they lead me. As soon as they diverge, I seek to orient myself . . . " In describing his method of orientation, Mendelssohn never claims to be outlining anything more than the path he himself considers it advisable to follow. He no doubt re-garded his own conduct as exemplary, but there is no reason to assume that he believed it ought to be adopted universally. Philosophers of the future are not bound to employ it.

4
Religion, Morality, and Politics

Securing the foundations of natural theology was Mendelssohn's primary concern in his writings on religion, but it was not his sole preoccupation. He sought, in addition, to explain the vital necessity of religion for both the individual and society as a whole. During the final decade of his life he devoted his attention also to more practical questions pertaining to the proper constitution of religious organizations and the appropriate relationship between such organizations and the states in which they carried on their activities.

Mendelssohn dealt with all of these matters within the context of his overall philosophic understanding of morality and and the purpose of the state, which was of Leibniz-Wolffian provenance. Here, indeed, he owed more to Wolff than to Leibniz. For although Leibniz wrote rather extensively on moral and political matters, only in the writings of Wolff did Mendelssohn find a full-blown moral and political philosophy on which he could draw. Accordingly, we must begin our present inquiry with an examination of Wolff.

It will not be necessary, for our purposes, to undertake a comprehensive investigation of Wolff's moral and political philosophy. Our concern is entirely with the way in which his philosophical position relates to his treatment of religion. Following our consideration of the pertinent aspects of Wolff's thought, we will consider the connection between moral and political philosophy and religion in Mendelssohn's own writings. On the whole, as we shall see, Mendelssohn works within the general framework of Wolff's thought. He disagrees with him, however, on a matter of central importance, and as a consequence arrives at significantly different practical conclusions.

The Wolffian Background

Human beings proceed toward perfection, Wolff explains in his *German Ethics*, by rendering their condition (*Zustand*) more perfect; that is, more in harmony with its own earlier and later state and, altogether, with the essence and nature of man (*dem Wesen und der Natur des Menschen*).[1] Wolff does not proceed from this point, as one might expect, to delineate precisely what constitutes the essence and nature of man and then to specify the elements of human perfection. His point of departure is the assertion that men by nature seek what is good for themselves and their fellow men, that which leads to their perfection, and avoid what is bad, that which hinders their perfection (though in their ignorance they may confuse the two and pursue what only appears to be good and avoid what only appears to be bad).[2] From this observable fact he deduces a rule that should govern all our voluntary actions: "*Do that which renders you and your or another's condition more perfect; avoid that which renders it more imperfect.*"[3] He then derives a natural law from this rule: "Since nature obligates us to do that which renders us and our condition more perfect, and to avoid that which makes us and our condition less perfect, the rule: *Do that which makes you and your condition more perfect and avoid that which makes you and your condition less perfect* is a law of nature."[4] For Wolff, it appears, the transition from *is* to *ought* is utterly unproblematic. "Seinsgesetze," as Anton Bissinger has untranslatably remarked, "sind für ihn fraglos auch Sollensgesetze."[5] Because men are bound by the law of nature to pursue their own perfection, the pursuit of perfection is a duty incumbent upon all of them. In the course of breaking this general duty down into specific duties Wolff ultimately reveals more of what he means by human perfection.

Wolff divides the human condition into an inner condition, that of the soul and the body, and an outer condition, the circumstances under which the individual lives. Because the law of nature demands that a man do that which renders him and his condition more perfect and that he avoid that which renders him less perfect, he must take care of his soul as well as his body and his outer condition. "Therefore we have to undertake three kinds of actions for our own sake, the first being those that further the perfection of our soul, the second those that further the perfection of the body, and the third those which further the perfection of our outer condition."[6] To each form of perfection there correspond specific types of goods. Those through which the condition of our soul is rendered more perfect are the goods of the mind; those that further the perfection of our bodies are goods of the body; those that further the perfection of our outer condition are the goods of fortune.[7] Because we are duty-bound to perfect our inner and outer condition, we are obligated to seek these different kinds of goods.[8]

Our duty to perfect our souls is divided into a duty to perfect our understanding and a duty to perfect our will.[9] Understanding, Wolff explains, is a faculty of the soul by means of which it clearly conceives of the possible. Because the perfection of the soul grows in proportion with its increased ability to conceive of things clearly, "we are with respect to our understanding obligated to do everything that advances the number and clarity of its ideas, and conversely to avoid anything that hinders it."[10] Because we are obligated to strive ever to increase the number of things of which we can form ideas, "we must neglect no opportunity to obtain a concept of something or to learn something." We must seek to obtain as much knowledge as possible.[11]

The perfection of the will consists of never willing anything other than the good, and indeed "of that which is good" willing "the better."[12] This perfection obviously depends on the perfection of understanding, because one can will the good only if one knows what it is.[13] Through willing the good one prepares oneself to order all of his actions in accordance with the law of nature, "and therefore one must improve the will if one wishes to partake of true felicity."[14]

The goods of the body are, put simply, health and moderation.[15] The body is not to be overindulged, but neither is it good to neglect it. Those who concern themselves exclusively with their souls are acting in contravention of the law of nature no less than those who devote their attention solely to the well-being of their bodies. One's outward condition is also to receive due attention, but never at the expense of the well-being of one's mind or body.[16]

Only after he has clarified the nature of one's duties toward oneself does Wolff turn to a discussion of one's duties to others. At the beginning of Part IV of his *German Ethics*, basing himself on the rule derived in Part I from observation of human behavior, Wolff asserts that one is obligated to strive to perfect not only one's own condition but that of others as well, in so far as possible.[17] Our duties toward others are identical with our duties toward ourselves, though they do not take precedence over them.[18]

Clearly, it is not within one's power to respond to all of the calls of duty. And to a certain extent those demands to which one can respond are mutually exclusive. When one faces the necessity of choosing among several goods, what is one to do? Wolff has only the vaguest counsel for people who find themselves in such straits. The individual must decide what to do for himself, taking into consideration all aspects of his personal situation and limitations.[19] In any case, complete perfection is beyond one's reach. "Since," Wolff wrote,

> the greatest perfection belongs to God, and cannot be allotted to any creature, it is not possible for a man ever to attain it, even if he daily devotes all of his strength to doing so. He can therefore do nothing more than progress from one perfection to another, and avoid imperfection more and more. And this is the highest good that he can attain. The *highest good of man or his blessedness (Seeligkeit)* can be correctly explained as an unhindered progress toward greater perfections.[20]

Progress toward perfection and avoidance of imperfection bring men pleasure; "the highest good or the blessedness of man is accompanied by a constant sense of enjoyment."[21] This condition of lasting happiness constitutes felicity *(Glückseligkeit)*.[22] Thus, pursuit of perfection in obedience to the law of nature leads men to felicity.[23] Not felicity, however, but perfection is the goal of human endeavor. Felicity is, as Hans-Martin Bachmann has put it in his review of Wolff's ethics, "only a side-effect of blessedness."[24]

Now that we have examined the basic outlines of Wolff's understanding of perfection and felicity it is necessary to consider his view of the relation between these concepts and the fundamental principles of religion. Wolff's derivation of the natural law that orders one to pursue perfection is, as we have seen, independent of any reference to the will of God. At the same time, however, he identifies it as being not only a law of nature but the law of God as well.[25] It is particularly useful, Wolff emphasizes, for one to be aware of this congruence between own's natural obligations and one's duties to the Deity. Such knowledge strengthens one's motivation to pursue the good and shun evil; it makes it easier for one to practice virtue and endure hardships.[26]

Religious knowledge, according to Wolff, is related to natural law not only insofar as it provides an additional incentive to the performance of one's duties; knowledge of God is itself something commanded by the law of nature. Because man is obligated to strive for as much knowledge as it is possible for him to attain, and since God is the most perfect of all things known to us, "man is obligated to know God."[27]

Nevertheless, in spite of the usefulness as well as the inherent importance of obtaining knowledge of God, it is not indispensably necessary for men to possess such knowledge to pursue the correct path in life. In Wolff's opinion, the obligatory character of the law of nature is firmly fixed; it would persist "even if man had no superior who could bind him to it; indeed, it would persist even if there were no God."[28] One need not have knowledge of its divine character to acknowledge one's obligation to obey it and to live virtuously.[29] This is not to say, of course, that the believer has no advantage over the atheist. To the man who pursues perfection in conscious obedience to the divine law, a higher degree of virtue is accessible—*Gottseligkeit*.[30] Still, according to Wolff, the atheist has access to everything he needs to know to live correctly.

Wolff maintains, as we have just seen, that people are at all times bound to live in accordance with the law of nature, which obligates them to fulfill certain duties toward themselves, their fellow human beings, and God. It is extremely difficult for them to perform these duties, he claims unless they join forces to create a civil society where they can be secure and comfortable.[31] Security and comfort are therefore means to an end. One enters into society not simply in order to attain these means, but so that one "can fulfill more easily one's natural duties, unhindered by others, and thereby reach the felicity of which one is capable."[32]

In society, a person ought not to be hindered by others, but this does not mean that one ought to be left simply to one's own devices. Upon entry into social relations people surrender their natural liberty to the state authorities, who are thereby empowered to establish institutions and promulgate laws aimed at accomplishing the purpose of society; that is, people's fulfillment of their duties and their attainment of perfection and felicity.[33] These authorities, Wolff maintains, stand in a quasi-paternal relationship to the rest of the state's members. "Ruling persons are related to subjects as are fathers to children" and have an unlimited right to demand their obedience.[34] They have the right to order them to do whatever serves the general welfare and security of the state and brings their inner and outer condition closer to perfection.[35] The powers Wolff grants to the authorities are thus quite broad. For our purposes, however, it is not necessary to survey them. Our concern is solely with the way in which this general theory shaped Wolff's understanding of the correct role of the state in matters pertaining to religion.

At first glance, it might not appear as if Wolff would regard religion as a matter of major concern to the state authorities. In his *German Ethics*, as we have seen, he maintained quite emphatically that people do not require knowledge of religious truths to fulfill their duties to themselves and others. Even atheists, he stated, can be brought to understand that they should live in a morally correct manner. It might therefore seem that the state, the guardian of people's general welfare and security, would have little reason to care whether or not its citizens were religious. Yet Wolff's confidence in the moral potential of enlightened atheists did not diminish his sense of the social necessity of religion. In his *German Politics* he argued that religion is a necessary supplement to civil obligations, which cannot by themselves restrain people from committing crimes in secret, out of sight of their neighbors. Only a childlike fear of God can accomplish that purpose. The same fear also serves as an indispensable guarantee of people's adherence to their oaths, an adherence that is, in Wolff's view, of vital importance to society. He therefore sees no place in society for those who deny the existence of God. They are not to be tolerated.[36]

Wolff was aware that his refusal in the *German Politics* to extend toleration to atheists appeared to conflict with what he had written in the *Ethics* concerning their moral mettle. He resolved this apparent contradiction by pointing to the fact that in society, "only the smallest minority of men are rational; most are uncomprehending and do not properly understand the nature of voluntary actions. And thus, in the case of most men, atheism would lead to an evil way of life." The teachers of atheism may themselves be moral men, but their teachings will, in general, have no other effect than to uproot the fear of God, which is what makes the strongest impression on most people. "And thus one cannot tolerate atheists in public life, for they are dangerous seducers."[37]

Wolff's understanding of the vital importance of religious faith led him to assert that the state should not only suppress atheism, but that it should also take active measures on behalf of religion. He called for the appointment of public instructors who possessed basic theological knowledge and were capable of imparting it to others.[38] In addition, he maintained that people are obligated to worship God and that the state ought therefore to pass laws fixing the time and place of obligatory public services.[39]

Ideally, the rulers of the state are "good fathers," whose actions are conducive to the welfare of their subjects. Wolff recognized, however, that reality sometimes falls short of the ideal and those charged with authority act in ways contrary to their subjects' best interests. But that did not alter the subjects' duties to their rulers.[40] Under no circumstances, in his opinion, should religion serve as anything other than a source of support for the state's authority.

Mendelssohn on Morality and Religion

The Royal Academy in Berlin in 1761 asked, among other things, whether the first principles of morality are as demonstrably certain as mathematical truths.[41] In his prize-winning *Treatise on Evidence*, Mendelssohn argues that they are. Following Wolff, he states that all of men's appetites aim only at the *"real or apparent perfection* (maintenance and improvement) *of the inner or outer condition of themselves or their fellow men."* From this he derives a "universal practical maxim" that constitutes "the first law of nature": *"Make your own and your fellow man's inner and outward condition, in due proportion, as perfect as you can."*[42] For Mendelssohn as for Wolff, to repeat the words of Anton Bissinger, "Seinsgesetze" are also "Sollensgesetze."[43]

Mendelssohn proceeds to outline other ways in which it is possible to establish by means of reason alone the validity of this law of nature. He then adds, as does Wolff, that the law of nature is not only a law of reason but a divine law as well. For "As soon as one assumes that a God, who cannot act without the wisest intentions, created the world, then no proposition in Euclid can be more rigorously demonstrated than this, that the natural law just mentioned must be the will of God."[44]

The limited purposes of the *Treatise on Evidence* do not require Mendelssohn to expand on this definition of perfection or to delineate the specific obligations entailed by natural law. Elsewhere, however, we find a more complete definition of what he means by *preservation* and *improvement*, one whose Wolffian provenance is similarly evident: "The perfection of man consists . . . apart from the well-being of the body, in a purified understanding, an honest heart and a fine and tender feeling for true beauty, or in the harmony between the lower and the higher powers of the soul."[45] Mendelssohn's best elucidation of this definition is found in his description in the *Phaedon*, which we examined in Chapter 2, of a man fulfilling his human destiny (*Bestimmung*).[46] This is not, of course, a complete depiction of a man who has reached perfection. For Mendelssohn as for Wolff, human perfection is not an attainable goal; it is a never-ending process.[47] But the man—and such a man is admittedly rare—who has reached the level described in the *Phaedon* has traveled quite far down the road to perfection.

For Mendelssohn, it should be clear, human perfection is not the same thing as intellectual perfection. He does maintain, it is true, that the development of the understanding brings the greatest pleasure. "Anyone," he writes, "who is acquainted with true reason, and who walks in its ways, can have no doubt concerning either the utility or the fullness of the pleasure which flow from its sources."[48] But even though rational knowledge is "the peak of that which is worthy of being sought," "Mendelssohn is far from entrusting the business of the perfection of man to reason alone. . . . What he advocates is the harmonious development of the whole man."[49] To begin with, he does not ignore the importance of physical well-being. There is in his writings no trace of asceticism.[50] The body's needs are to be met so that the soul's higher powers can be developed. Then, as a constituent element of human perfection Mendelssohn lists "an honest heart." Perfection depends on more than the performance of one's moral duties; it requires a heart filled with a "wholesome enthusiasm for virtue."[51] The presence on Mendelssohn's list of the next element of perfection—a sense of beauty—is most probably due to the role played by an aesthetic sensibility in promoting morality.[52]

Mendelssohn, as we have seen, follows Wolff in affirming the existence of a natural law obligating men to pursue perfection. Although he does not, like Wolff, elucidate the nature of human perfection in the context of an extensive elaboration of that natural law, it is clear from what he does say about perfection that he sees it in essentially the same terms as Wolff. For Mendelssohn, too, perfection is a process that can never be completed but that can be continually advanced by progress toward perfecting the whole man, physically, morally, and intellectually. Like Wolff, he sees increasing perfection as something which is accompanied by an increase in felicity.

Nevertheless, it cannot be said that Mendelssohn adopts Wolff's understanding of perfection and felicity without modification. Included in his own account of these matters is an important constituent of felicity altogether absent from Wolff's presentation: men's natural liberty. Unfortunately, despite the significance of this concept for his entire moral philosophy, Mendelssohn never offers a full definition of what he means by liberty. In an early writing on Rousseau, he defines it as "a condition in which no external compulsion prevents us from satisfying our true needs in an innocent way." "By the satisfaction of our true needs," as Altmann has observed, Mendelssohn here "understood the fulfillment of our duties."[53] But this is only half the story. From his observations elsewhere, it is clear that liberty, for Mendelssohn, also encompasses to some extent the condition in which no external force compels us to satisfy our true needs. According to Mendelssohn, this natural liberty "makes up a great portion of men's felicity."[54]

In placing such great emphasis on men's possession of liberty Mendelssohn deviates significantly from Wolff. Wolff, as we have seen, viewed men's natural liberty as a right that, in Altmann's words, "could be surrendered and was actually surrendered by the social contract." Mendelssohn conceived of no such total surrender. For him liberty had, as Altmann has written, "a moral, even a metaphysical, quality that resisted annihilation through the social contract."[55] He saw liberty as an indispensable precondition of both moral and intellectual perfection. It is not enough for a man to perform benevolent deeds. The practice of benevolence renders a man happier than selfishness, but only if it proceeds "from his own will and his own free impulse."[56] Only a free man can achieve moral perfection, for moral virtue is the result of struggle, self-overcoming, and sacrifice, and it cannot come into being without them.[57] Similarly, intellectual perfection can take place only where one is free—though not necessarily, as we shall see, entirely free—to fall into error.

The liberty that Mendelssohn is most concerned to see people retain is liberty of conscience or, to put it in other terms, freedom of religion. It is his firm conviction that religion must be voluntary, that a person's religious convictions are his own private concern and that "religious actions, by their very nature, permit neither coercion nor bribery. They either flow from the free impulse of the soul or they are an empty show and contrary to the true spirit of religion."[58] It is primarily for this reason that he concludes that churches, that is, all religious organizations, ought to operate on a completely voluntary basis. He also argues, however, that churches can acquire no *right* to compel their members to believe or act in any particular fashion. His denial of the existence of such a right is bound up with his political theory, which we shall discuss in the next section.

The maintenance of people's freedom of religion is clearly a matter of the greatest importance to Mendelssohn. It is not equally clear, at first, that he considers religion itself to be of indispensable importance in people's lives. It would seem that for Mendelssohn, as for Wolff, reason alone should suffice to establish solid foundations for morality and that he should be as prepared as Wolff to state that even an atheist—if he possesses sufficient intelligence—ought to acknowledge the binding character of the first law of nature and all that follows from it. In his later works, however, there are clear indications that he believed that knowledge of the law of nature must be supplemented by the knowledge of religious truths. In a well-known passage in *Jerusalem*, for instance, he states that,

"Without God, providence and a future life, love of our fellow man is little more than a foppery into which we seek to lure one another so that the simpleton will toil while the clever man enjoys himself and has a good laugh at the other's expense."[59]

This and other, similar statements have not always been accepted at face value. The discrepancy between such remarks and Mendelssohn's apparent acceptance elsewhere of the self-sufficiency of natural law has led Leo Strauss to suspect that Mendelssohn sometimes tailored his views to fit what he himself condescendingly characterized as "the popular moral teaching."[60] "The popular moral teaching" is, as we saw in Chapter 2, Mendelssohn's designation for the doctrine in which "every virtue aims for a reward, and the morally good is held to be desirable solely for the sake of the accidental reward one expects in return for it."[61] Mendelssohn, it is true, disparages this system, contrasting it unfavorably with the more elevated morality according to which "the good in and of itself not only furthers felicity but is felicity." Yet he was in no great hurry to uproot the popular misconceptions. As long as the common man is incapable of understanding a better teaching, he believed, it would be inexcusable to attempt to do so. And he betrayed little hope that the "common heap" would ever be capable of comprehending a better teaching. According to Strauss, Mendelssohn's occasional emphasis on the indispensability of the afterlife for moral virtue represents a concession to the popular teaching, one made, presumably, with the intention of contributing in some way to the fortification of the morality of the multitude.

It is very doubtful, however, that Mendelssohn's remarks regarding the indispensability of religious knowledge for the support of virtue can be so easily dismissed as purely exoteric statements. In the *Sache Gottes*, the very same work in which he makes the previously quoted remarks concerning the popular moral teaching and the need to preserve it, he also observes that the popular system contains much that is true. Its concepts have to be refined but not discarded. "We have seen on another occasion," he there remarks, "that no system of morality can exist without the expectation of an infinite future. The structure of the doctrine of virtue and vice is on all sides full of holes that cannot be filled, if man's soul is not immortal."[62]

The other occasion to which Mendelssohn is referring is the third dialogue of the *Phaedon*. There his spokesman, Socrates, sketches at some length what he believes to be the contrasting moral horizons of the man who believes in the existence of an afterlife and the man who does not. Though life, he says, is a contemptibly paltry thing, for the man who has no hope that it will be followed by something better, it is all there is. "According to his doctrine, his present existence must be for him the highest good, the most painful and tormented life must for him be infinitely preferable to death, the complete annihilation of his being. His love of life must be simply indomitable." For such a man the concepts of honor and fame will have no meaning. He will care not at all for the welfare of his children, his friends, and his country. His least significant pleasure will be of infinitely greater importance to him than the welfare of the rest of the human race.[63]

The man who believes in the existence of an afterlife sees things differently. "He who hopes for a future life and posits progress toward perfection as the purpose of his existence can say to himself: Look! You were sent here to make yourself more perfect through the furtherance of the good. You must therefore further the good, even at the cost of your own life, if it cannot be otherwise preserved." Should tyranny threaten his country, should justice be in danger of being overthrown, should religion and truth be persecuted, such a man will tell himself to use his life for the purpose for which it was given to him, to die, if necessary, to preserve for the human race these "precious means to felicity." For in certain circumstances it is necessary to see life itself as nothing but a means of furthering happiness.[64]

Are these portrayals themselves merely another concession to the popular moral teaching, or are they something that Mendelssohn genuinely believed to be accurate? And if he really took them seriously, how can what he says here be reconciled with his apparent belief in the autonomy of moral law? To answer these questions we must take another look at Mendelssohn's understanding of human perfection and the law of nature.

Mendelssohn, we recall, defined the perfection of one's condition as its preservation and improvement.[65] The law of nature, he stated, commands men to seek both of these goods. But the two, it is clear, are not always compatible. Sometimes one's self-preservation will preclude one's pursuit of self-improvement or the improvement of others; sometimes the performance of a moral duty will require self-sacrifice. For the man who believes in the existence of an afterlife, such a sacrifice, even if it entails the loss of his life, is a possible choice. When he sacrifices his life, he is not, after all, giving up his existence but only bringing to an end its earthly stage. He can look forward to his own preservation and the continuation of his own progress toward perfection in the next life. But if there is no afterlife, if man's soul is ultimately destined to perish along with his body, then the preservation of corporeal life becomes the indispensable precondition for any further progress toward perfection. Therefore, the man who rejects belief in an afterlife, if he acts consistently with his own beliefs, will seek to protect his life at all costs. "As soon as loss of our life entails the loss of all existence, life ceases to be a means; then its preservation becomes the object, the only aim of our wishes." The denier of immortality would see all of creation go under "if only he could preserve himself."[66] He, too, follows the natural law of seeking his own perfection, but it leads him astray. Without the knowledge of immortality, the imperative to seek perfection is perverted into the unprincipled striving for self-preservation. Hence the law of nature must be supplemented by knowledge of the truths of religion. This, it seems, is what Mendelssohn genuinely believed; it is not necessary to regard it as something meant simply for the consumption of the "common heap."

To be sure, the religious knowledge indispensable for morality is rather minimal. It need not consist of a clear and distinct comprehension of natural theology as it is expounded by philosophers like Mendelssohn. A rudimentary understanding of the fundamental principles of God, providence, and immortality will suffice to direct man along the proper path. Knowledge of this kind, Mendelssohn repeatedly asserts, is readily accessible to all. In the *Counterreflections*, he writes that God, in fulfillment of his purposes, has made sure that even the wildest and the crudest of peoples obtain "concepts and moral certainty of the truths of natural religion which are indispensable to their felicity."[67] Similarly, he says in *To the Friends of Lessing* that "In every condition of life in which man finds himself, at every level of enlightenment he has reached, he has sufficient data and capacity, opportunity and powers to be convinced of the truths of rational religion."[68]

Knowledge of the principles of natural religion is, for Mendelssohn, indispensable in more ways than one. Not only is it of crucial importance for the support of morality, it is something without which one would be unable to attain any peace of mind. The man who possesses true concepts of God and his attributes not only derives great pleasure from a contemplation of God's works; he has been freed of a great burden, one that deprives the atheist of any lasting happiness. "Without God, providence, and immortality," Mendelssohn wrote in *Morning Hours*, "all the goods of this life have in my eyes a contemptible value, and life here below seems to me, to make use of a well-known and often misused saying, like wandering in the wind and bad weather without the consolation of finding protection and shelter in an inn in the evening."[69] The relation between knowledge of religious truths and felicity is even more forcefully indicated in the *Phaedon*:

> How pitiable is the lot of a mortal whose comforting expectation of a future life has been upset by unfortunate sophistries! He must not reflect on his condition, and must live in something like a state of insensibility, or fall into despair. What is more frightening to a human soul than annihilation? And what is sadder than a man who sees it coming toward him with powerful steps and who, in the inconsolable fear with which he awaits it, already believes he feels it?[70]

Mendelssohn does admit, in effect, that those who have been misled in this way by sophistries do not always wallow in despair. If they are fortunate, they may succeed in repressing their dismal thoughts. Nevertheless, they cannot prevent them from slinking around in their minds, "like a snake among flowers," and poisoning all their pleasures. Their happiness can never be permanent.

Mendelssohn on Religion and State

As we have seen, Wolff's teleological understanding of human nature leads him to conceive of the state in teleological terms. The state's ultimate purpose, he maintains, is to enable people to proceed toward the attainment of their own perfection and that of others. On the whole, according to Wolff, religion plays an indispensable part in directing most people toward the pursuit of these goals, and for this reason the state ought actively to lend its support to it and regulate it. Religion, as he understands it, should always assist and never hinder the state's exercise of its authority.

Mendelssohn likewise adheres to a teleological understanding of human nature. He maintains that people enter into civil society not simply to enhance their security but to fulfill their natural duties more effectively, and he regards the state as an entity properly concerned with men's eternal as well as their temporal welfare.[71] Far more than Wolff, as we have seen, he is convinced that people need to be familiar with the fundamental truths of natural religion if they are to recognize these duties and act accordingly. Like Wolff, he conceives of religion as a source of support for the state. Nevertheless, he does not agree with him that the state ought to do its best to foster the growth of religion within its boundaries. He argues, instead, that people's religious beliefs should remain entirely, or at any rate almost entirely, beyond the purview of public authorities.

Mendelssohn's divergence from Wolff on this important question is due primarily to his different understanding of the nature of human perfection and felicity. Unlike Wolff, he maintains that liberty makes up an important part of a man's happiness in this world. He also emphasizes, as we have seen, the absolute necessity of liberty for the practice of true religion. Coerced religion, in his eyes, is not religion at all.

Mendelssohn's fundamental interest in protecting religious liberty is compounded by his concern for the welfare of the Jewish people, who in his day were still, virtually everywhere, the victims of religious discrimination or persecution. It is, indeed, his concern for the welfare of the Jews that is mostly responsible for his decision publicly to voice his support for liberty of conscience. He articulates his position on this matter for the first time in an apologetical work, his Preface to the German edition of Manasseh ben Israel's *Vindiciae Judaeorum*, but his fullest treatment of the question can be found in *Jerusalem*.

In the first part of *Jerusalem* Mendelssohn outlines a contractarian theory of the origin and legitimate powers of the state. He describes the state of nature, men's emergence from it through the transfer of some of their natural rights to the government they agree to establish, and the manner in which that government can legitimately exercise its authority. He does not do so, however, in great detail. With this theory, it is clear, he is not trying to resolve all of the fundamental political questions human beings face but only to provide a justification for something he knows to be worthy of protection even without the aid of any social contract theory: the liberty of conscience.

In this section we will examine Mendelssohn's understanding of the proper relationship between religion and the state. We will consider, to begin with, his attempt to ground the right to liberty of conscience in a social contract theory. It is, as we shall see, a less than fully successful effort. He does not make a convincing argument for the existence of such a right, nor does he uphold it unreservedly. In spite of his support for untrammeled liberty of conscience, Mendelssohn still tries to preserve, in a manner inconsistent with the principles he is espousing, something of the paternalistic state advocated by Wolff. We will next examine the manner in which Mendelssohn seeks to combine a teleological understanding of the state with support for the existence of religious institutions that operate completely outside of the state's jurisdiction. We will take note of some of the problems to which this leads but to which Mendelssohn devotes little attention and discusses only very circumspectly.

Liberty of Conscience

In Section 1 of *Jerusalem*, Mendelssohn provides a detailed account of "the origin of the rights of coercion" belonging to the state. He describes the situation prevailing in the state of nature, where individuals have exclusive rights to their "natural property"; that is, their own capacities, the products of their industry, and the goods of nature that they have appropriated for themselves. In the state of nature, people may do whatever they want to do with their own property, provided they do not injure others. They may, if they wish, cede to other people, through contracts, their rights to any particular part of their natural property. When such contracts are made, they must be kept. If I (as a denizen of the state of nature) enter into one of them, the right to decide what to do with one of my possessions, "which previously formed a part of my goods, that is, which was my own, has become, through this cession, the good of my neighbor, his property, and I cannot take it away from him again without committing an offense."

The state of nature is destined not to last. Impelled by their own nature to leave it, people enter into "the state of social relations," where they can transform their "fluctuating rights and duties into something definite." They do so by means of contracts indistinguishable from those by which individuals transfer any of their goods to others. These contracts effect the transfer of some of their "movable," "immovable," or even "spiritual" goods to the proprietorship of the state. It is not necessary, for our purposes, to examine the character of this transfer in any greater detail, because Mendelssohn's primary aim in his treatment of this subject is not so much to elucidate the origins of the state's coercive rights as to explain why it lacks any such rights in the realm of convictions.[72]

"In general, men's convictions," Mendelssohn observes, "are not amenable to any coercion." Therefore,

> I cannot renounce any of my convictions, as a conviction, out of love for my neighbor; nor can I cede and relinquish to him, out of benevolence, any part of my own power of judgment. I

am likewise in no position to arrogate to myself or in any way acquire a right over my neighbor's convictions. The right to our own convictions is inalienable, and cannot pass from person to person; for it neither gives nor takes away any claim to property, goods and liberty.[73]

In underlining the inviolability of men's convictions, Mendelssohn is not saying anything that had not already been maintained by earlier thinkers. What is unprecedented is the way in which he proceeds directly from this premise to the following conclusion: "neither church nor state has a right to subject men's principles and convictions to any coercion whatsoever."[74] Even "the smallest privilege which you publicly grant to those who share your religion and convictions is to be called an *indirect bribe*, and the smallest liberty you withhold from dissidents an *indirect punishment*."[75]

This argument for the right to liberty of conscience is, as Alexander Altmann has pointed out, twofold. The state may not coerce men's beliefs because, in Altmann's words, "1) the social contract does not include the yielding of a coercive right with respect to convictions, and 2) convictions are by their very nature noncoercible." Altmann also observes that "Reason 1) is not elaborated by Mendelssohn." Furthermore, it is problematic. It

is based on the assumption that the state is established solely for the sake of security. From this it follows that the social contract has no concern with religion or opinions. Hence these matters cannot be subjected to state authority. Mendelssohn, who assigns to the state also the care for the citizens' happiness in this world and the next and who, thereby, includes right convictions among the concerns of the magistrate, needs the second reason to ensure liberty of conscience and of expression.[76]

Reason 1 is, according to Altmann, an insufficient foundation for liberty of conscience, because it is based on the assumption that the state exists only for the sake of security, an assumption in conflict with Mendelssohn's expressed views on the nature and purpose of the state. I would argue, however, that reason 1 is not based on any such premise, but only on the assumption that matters pertaining to its citizens' "right convictions" are beyond the sphere in which the state can legitimately exercise *coercion*. This assumption is perfectly in accord with his belief that the state may indeed seek to influence its citizens' convictions, but only through *persuasion*.

The real problem with reason 1 is its apparent arbitrariness. Ultimately it rests on nothing more than Mendelssohn's assertion concerning the types of transfers of rights that take place when the social contract is established. It does not firmly rule out the possibility that in some cases the social contract might include the renunciation of the right to one's own convictions. Reason 2 does just that. But it does so, as we shall see, in a questionable way.

Mendelssohn was, of course, by no means the first to argue that convictions are by nature noncoercible and that men therefore have an inalienable right to believe whatever they wish. Spinoza, for instance, had stated that, "Inward worship of God and piety in itself are within the sphere of everyone's private rights, and cannot be alienated."[77] But he did not maintain that this right necessarily provided the basis for any further rights. Religious coercion, he believed, violated no one's right to maintain his own convictions, since individuals were always free to continue believing whatever they wished, no matter what they were compelled to say or do. The state, he contended, retained the right to establish or forbid the espousal of particular religious doctrines or the practice of particular religions.[78] This is not to say, however, that the state ought to exercise this right. Unlike Hobbes, who thought that it ought to do so, Spinoza believed that religious toleration was a policy more conducive to the establishment of civil peace. It was, he believed, a good thing, even if people did not have a "right" to enjoy it.[79]

Like Spinoza, Mendelssohn believed that any attempt to coerce beliefs ignored the fact that they were by nature noncoercible. Unlike Spinoza, however, Mendelssohn maintained that the individual's inalienable right to his own convictions rendered every attempt to coerce his convictions illegitimate. The state therefore had no right to command or prohibit, or even to aid or impede in any way, the practice of any particular religion.

This argument may have been, as Altmann has put it, "a masterful stroke," but it is difficult to see the logic behind it.[80] A right can be said to yield another right only when the possession of the former is impossible without the possession of the latter. The right to self-preservation, for instance, necessarily yields the right to secure the means necessary for self-preservation, for without that additional right it would not take effect. Men's right to their own convictions, however, remains intact even if they are not permitted to espouse them, and no amount of coercion can uproot them if they are determined to hold on to them. There is, therefore, no sound basis for Mendelssohn's assertion that men's inalienable right to their own convictions necessarily bars the government from rightfully attempting to interfere with them.

It is, in addition, questionable whether Mendelssohn was fully consistent in his application of the principle of men's right to liberty of conscience. It would seem according to this line of reasoning, that the state should not make any attempt at all to suppress the expression of any conviction whatsoever. Yet Mendelssohn, who, like Wolff, perceived atheists to be a danger to the public welfare, was likewise prepared to countenance state action limiting their right to express their views freely. He did not, it is true, call forthrightly for their suppression, as Wolff did, but instead said that "the state, to be sure, is to see to it from afar that no doctrines are propagated which are inconsistent with the public welfare, doctrines which, like atheism and Epicureanism, undermine the foundations on which the felicity of social life is based."[81] But even if the state is only supervising these matters "from afar," does not that constitute a violation of Mendelssohn's principles? Altmann does not believes that it does. This objection, in his opinion,

> ignores the fact that Mendelssohn did not vindicate to the state any right of *coercion* in respect of atheists; that he included atheists among the beneficiaries of toleration; and that he considered vigilance of the kind described not as a right but as a duty flowing from the very purpose of the state as guardian of the public good. The same consideration that prompted him to integrate religion into the sphere of the state's interests also caused him to limit tolerance insofar as atheism was concerned.[82]

According to Altmann, Mendelssohn does not call for coercion to be directed against atheists. By "seeing to it from afar" Mendelssohn means that the state should act "in the most general way, without entering into philosophical or theological minutiae; in other words, without exercising coercive power and assuming the mantle of authority in the intellectual realm."[83] If this is the purport of Mendelssohn's remarks, we are still left wondering exactly what sort of action he believed the state would be entitled to take. Any action at all, however, even if it did not constitute *coercion*, strictly speaking, might still involve withholding at least "the smallest liberty" from dissidents—a practice that, as we have seen, Mendelssohn explicitly declared to be inadmissable.

Altmann also notes that Mendelssohn includes atheists

among the beneficiaries of toleration. Yet according to Mendelssohn's principles, religious dissidents are entitled to receive more than mere toleration; they have a right to nothing less than full and untrammeled liberty. Mendelssohn's restrictions—no matter how weak they are—deny that to them. As for Altmann's third point, that vigilance is not the right but the duty of the state— what is the difference? Can a state have a duty to engage in actions that it has no right to perform? A duty necessarily implies a right. In this case the duty in question implies a right for which Mendelssohn supplies no source. The fact that this vigilance is being exercised for the sake of the public good does not remove but rather compounds the difficulty. If that becomes the criterion, what is left of liberty of conscience? Why should not the state then be entitled to exercise vigilance not only against antireligious doctrines but also against religious doctrines it deems harmful?

Altmann's arguments do not, then, succeed in erasing the contradiction in Mendelssohn's thought. It must be admitted, however, that that contradiction does not appear to be a very large one. Mendelssohn's rather nebulous reminder of the need for the state to be vigilant against atheists seems to call for only a very slight circumscription of their rights. It is, in fact, quite striking how free he allows atheists to remain, in view of his frequently restated opinion concerning their great potential to do harm. It is possible, however, that appearances are deceiving, and that Mendelssohn believed that the state in fact ought to exercise coercive power to prevent atheists from expressing their pernicious views in public; that is, that it ought to censor their writings.

Determining Mendelssohn's attitude toward censorship is not an easy thing to do. It is a matter he never discussed in his published works. His only references to censorship are found in writings that not only were not made public but that were most definitely intended to be kept private, his contributions to the secret deliberations of the Berlin Wednesday Society.[84] In his *vota* or comments on proposals initiated or lectures delivered by other members of that society Mendelssohn twice addressed the question of censorship. On the first occasion he expressed a considerable amount of skepticism regarding its likely utility. On the second occasion he offered a rationale for maintaining it.

Mendelssohn's earlier remarks on censorship are found in a *votum* written in response to a lecture by Carl Wilhelm Möhsen on the subject of "enlightenment."[85] In that *votum* Mendelssohn suggests certain guidelines for future debate of the issues raised by Möhsen. He begins by expressing the wish that historical examples could be found of instances in which enlightenment in general and *"unrestricted freedom"* of expression in particular *"really"* did any harm to the felicity of the public. Later he remarks that

> Even if it be true (as I really take for granted) that certain prejudices shared by a whole nation must be spared by all honest people in view of the circumstances, the question still remains: are their limits to be determined by laws and censors or are they, like the limits of prosperity, gratitude and sincerity, to be left to the discretion of every individual? Since they are variable by their very nature, their limit cannot be fixed by permanent laws, and to leave the decision to the whim of censors seems to me altogether more harmful than the most unrestricted liberty.[86]

What he says here, as Altmann has noted, unmistakably indicates where Mendelssohn stood in regard to liberty.[87] His remarks represent, however, something less than an absolute denunciation of the evils of censorship. He does not deny that unrestricted liberty of expression can ever harm the public weal; he simply asks for actual evidence of such harm having taken place in the past. He is as alert as any twentieth century civil libertarian to the risks inherent in the enactment of legislation providing for censorship or in the establishment of boards of censors who would be able to prohibit certain writings on the basis of their own preferences. To raise questions concerning the means of implementing censorship is not, however, the same thing as to deny its legitimacy altogether. For all of his evident suspicion of censorship, Mendelssohn stops short of doing the latter. He does not say what one might expect the author of the only recently completed *Jerusalem* to say; namely, that the state possesses no right to tamper with its citizens' liberty to express their own convictions. Instead, he discusses censorship entirely in terms of what is good for the public, without making any reference whatsoever to the way in which questions of human rights might pertain to the matter at hand.

Not long after writing this *votum* Mendelssohn composed another one in which he dealt with the question of censorship, this time in a very different fashion. Here, instead of calling for historical examples of the harm caused by unrestricted freedom of expression, Mendelssohn simply acknowledged that the propagation of certain ideas may have deleterious effects. "Whoever publicly propounds a harmful opinion," he wrote, "immediately and directly injures others." Censorship, then, has its obvious uses. The problem with censorship laws, however, is that they are all too likely to have the opposite effect from the one intended. Although it does no harm to let it be known to the public that censorship exists, clear governmental prohibition of particular ideas is liable to bring too much attention to the very thing the government wishes to suppress. Consequently Mendelssohn recommends that "censorship laws which concern the *content* of a writing and which seek to restrict the freedom to express one's opinion on a certain subject must be kept as secret as possible."[88]

On the question of censorship, then, there is a certain lack of consistency in Mendelssohn's position. On the one hand, he seems very suspicious of censorship, and on the other hand, he acknowledges its utility and makes recommendations concerning the way in which it should be carried out. Before charging Mendelssohn with self-contradiction, we should remember, however, the special character of his pronouncements on this subject, i.e., their having been composed as contributions to the deliberations of the Wednesday Society. "Since it is a question of a secret society," as Michael Albrecht points out, "things could be discussed here very differently than in essays which were from the outset destined for publication."[89] It is difficult, therefore, to be certain that anything he says in this context represents his carefully considered and deeply held view on the matter at hand. One can never be sure that he is not, say, playing devil's advocate and making the best possible defense of a position concerning which he still has his doubts. Perhaps this is what he was doing in the first *votum*, when he seemed so hostile to the practice of censorship. On the other hand, it is conceivable that in the second *votum* he is merely "thinking aloud."

We have been investigating Mendelssohn's writings on the question of censorship solely with a view to determining whether he might not have been hinting in *Jerusalem* at the advisability of state censorship of the writings of atheists and Epicureans. Mendelssohn's vague remarks in *Jerusalem* about the state exercising a distant sort of vigilance over such people are, to be sure, far from constituting a clear call for any such censorship. In evaluating their significance we must, however, bear in mind what Mendelssohn said in his second votum concerning the dangers of open discussion of the content of censorship laws. When such laws are enacted, he maintained, the precise nature of the materials being censored should be kept as far as possible from public view. But if Mendelssohn believed that governments ought to be cautious in dealing with these matters, perhaps he thought that the same applied to political philosophers as well. If so, it may be the case that his cryptic statements in *Jerusalem*, his recommendation that the state "see to it from afar" that atheists and Epicureans not be allowed to disseminate their views, represents an oblique, veiled approval of state censorship of them.

Whether this is indeed the case, or whether Mendelssohn had in mind less direct state action against atheists, as Altmann suggests, it is in any event clear that in his contributions to the deliberations of the Berlin Wednesday Society he stopped short of insisting that the state do nothing to violate the inalienable rights of atheists to express their convictions. And even if he did not in fact call for the censorship of atheists, it is significant that he was at least at one point prepared to endorse censorship of any ideas whatsoever. Censorship of any kind is not compatible with the contention that the government has no right to interfere with its citizens' profession of their convictions.

At the end of his *votum* on the freedom to express one's opinions Mendelssohn briefly explains, as we have seen, why the laws must sometimes step in and prevent people from expressing their views. "But whoever publicly propounds a harmful opinion immediately and directly injures others." In saying this, however, he concedes the validity of a principle that tends to undermine his main argument for the absolute right to liberty of conscience. He acknowledges that words are in effect deeds and that the right to one's own convictions therefore does not automatically imply a right to perform the deed of giving expression to them. And if the espousal of harmful opinions can be considered to be a dangerous kind of action that government has the right to prevent, does not the government also have the right to take measures to suppress the public espousal of religious doctrines it deems harmful? Once Mendelssohn grants the legitimacy of censorship, one cannot help but wonder what remains of his argument for the *right* to liberty of conscience.

Unlike Wolff, Mendelssohn attempts to demonstrate the existence of a human right to liberty of conscience. He does so, as we have seen, by means of patently faulty argumentation. In addition, some of his remarks in *Jerusalem* and in other contexts raise serious questions with regard to the degree to which he remained a consistent defender of the exercise of that right. To be fully consistent, Mendelssohn would have had to assert, as did his contemporary, Thomas Jefferson, that a man had every right to profess belief in "twenty gods, or no god."[90] He would have had to oppose unswervingly any limitation of religious freedom, even with respect to atheists. Mendelssohn did neither of these things. Instead, he evinced a willingness to curtail, at least to some extent, the exercise of a right whose absolute character he himself had sought to demonstrate.

What Mendelssohn really wanted, it seems, was to have the best of both worlds. He wanted to maximize the extent to which human beings enjoyed the freedom of religion, but he also wanted to take some measures to avoid the worst excesses to which such freedom could lead, excesses that, in his opinion, might threaten the stability of the state as well as its ability to further its citizens' eternal well-being. Fearing these same dangers, Wolff could advocate strong opposition to them, without violating his principles. Mendelssohn could not do so without violating his own more libertarian principles. But neither could he bring himself to ignore such dangers altogether. At the very least, he equivocated. But it seems as if he may also have been prepared to indicate—however obliquely—his support for a certain amount of suppression of free speech on the part of some dangerous individuals.

State and Church

Prior to Mendelssohn's time, the most influential philosophical proponent of liberty of conscience was unquestionably John Locke. At the very beginning of *Jerusalem*, Mendelssohn indicates his sympathy with Locke's overall goal but disapproves, at the same time, of the manner in which he sought to reach it. The central premise of Locke's argument, as Mendelssohn understands it, is his definition of the state as a society of men who have united collectively to promote their temporal welfare, not their eternal welfare. Mendelssohn finds fault with this definition. What reason is there, he asks, "to restrict the purpose of society solely to the *temporal?*" If the state has the power to contribute to the advancement of people's eternal felicity, then it must have the duty to do so. And if it lacks such a power, then it is clearly an institution essentially subordinate to the church, one that must give way whenever there is a collision between its interests and those of religion. Apparently, Mendelssohn greatly fears that denial of the state's right to involve itself in the promotion of its citizens' eternal felicity will lead to the reassertion of the unqualified supremacy of the church and all that that entails.

Mendelssohn has, in addition, a more general complaint against Locke and other, unnamed thinkers. It is a mistake, he believes, to endeavor to draw, as they do, a very sharp distinction between people's temporal well-being and their eternal well-being.

How people conduct themselves here below has, he insists, a direct bearing on their posthumous fate.[91]

This characterization of Locke's position does not begin to do justice to his argument. Locke clearly justified his exclusion of the state from any involvement in the spiritual lives of its citizens by explaining why it is ill-equipped to engage in such activities.[92] In fact, his views on this matter are, to a large extent, as we shall see, similar to those of Mendelssohn. Furthermore, his treatment of the Christian religion in *The Reasonableness of Christianity* amply demonstrates his recognition of the relationship between one's conduct in this world and one's fate in the next.[93] It is not our purpose here, however, to defend Locke against Mendelssohn's criticism but to attempt to grasp, in the light of this criticism, what it is that Mendelssohn is seeking to achieve. What we see is that he wishes to construct a theory that establishes the basis for liberty of conscience but that at the same time clearly accords recognition to the importance of the state as an agent charged in some sense with promoting its citizens' eternal welfare.

Following his critique of Locke, Mendelssohn draws a distinction between the ways in which the state may advance the perfection and felicity of its citizens and the ways in which religion may do the same. Ideally, they both seek to exert a beneficial influence by means of persuasion alone, through moral education and through the inculcation of sound beliefs. Public institutions base their teachings on "the relations of men to each other"; religious institutions base theirs on "the relations between man and God."[94] Both sorts of institutions seek to shape people's convictions and their actions. Under ideal circumstances, they work together in perfect harmony. "[R]eligion should come to the aid of the state, and the church should become a pillar of civil felicity." The church ought to teach, among other things, "that serving the state is true service of God."[95]

Under less than ideal circumstances, the state may have to resort to coercion to attain its legitimate ends. This is not to the liking of religion. It "withdraws its support," Mendelssohn asserts, "from civil actions, insofar as they are not produced by conviction but by force. Nor can the state expect any further help from religion, once it can act only by means of rewards and punishments; for insofar as this is the case, man's duties toward God no longer enter into consideration, and the relations between man and God are without effect."[96] Whenever *any* state acts coercively, it seems, religion should stand aside. If a state can act *only* coercively, religion should offer it no support whatsoever.

Here Mendelssohn is apparently endeavoring to remedy what he sees as one of the deficiencies of Locke's argument. Unlike Locke in his *Letter Concerning Toleration*, he depicts the state as an institution concerned, in its own way, with the advancement of people's eternal welfare. He seeks to show that state and church should aim at the same goals, follow different but parallel paths, and walk hand in hand. However, when the state ceases to perform its function in an optimum fashion, it forfeits the right to religion's support.

This general division of the roles of state and church is not without its problems. First of all, one must ask, how does Mendelssohn think the state can contribute usefully to the moral education of its citizens? As we have already seen, he repeatedly maintains that no nontheistic system of ethics can be considered viable. If this is the case, the state's nonreligious educational efforts, its teachings based on "the relations of men to each other," are doomed to be inadequate. Why, then, should not the state at least be entitled to invoke the vital principles of natural religion in defense of the morality it seeks to propound?

With regard to the attitude of the churches toward the state's use of coercion, it is far from clear why Mendelssohn should feel compelled to take such an extreme position. Does he really mean to suggest that religious authorities should never offer any religious sanction for the state's employment of force, even if it is used against the worst sort of malefactors? A regime entirely dependent upon force must qualify to be designated as a despotism. Yet, as Mendelssohn acknowledged more than once, even despotism, the worst form of government, will under some circumstances the best possible regime.[97] If such a state finds itself in the unfortunate position of being able to attain its ends only by the use of force or threats, why should not the church nevertheless continue to remind people that the service of the state is still service of God?

An even more significant problem that arises from Mendelssohn's division of the responsibilities of church and state pertains to the possibility of conflict between state and religion. It is the business of the church, under the best of circumstances, to teach "that serving the state is true service of God." But there are, as we have seen, times when the church must end its support for the state. Are there also times when it is obligated to turn against the state? How ought it to behave if, say, a nondespotic state, one that governs its people largely through education and persuasion, embarks upon an evidently unjust course of action? What if, for instance, the state launches an unjust war? This happens, as Mendelssohn's Socrates observes in the *Phaedon*, as often as anything else.[98] And in war, Mendelssohn believed, it is obviously the case that only one of the combatant nations "has right on its side."[99] What, then, are the churches of the country that is clearly in the wrong supposed to do? Do they have an obligation to speak out, to denounce the immoral conduct of their state's leaders? Or should they simply keep quiet?

Mendelssohn never addressed these questions directly in *Jerusalem* or any of his other published writings. In one of his contributions to the discussions of the Berlin Wednesday Society, however, he did touch on a related matter, the question of a possible conflict not between the demands of religion and those of the state, but between the demands of the state and the conditions under which man can best fulfill his vocation as a human being. A consideration of the way in which Mendelssohn dealt with this issue may shed some light on his reasons for neglecting to treat the subject of possible conflicts between church and state.

In the essay entitled "What Is Enlightenment?" Mendelssohn draws a distinction between "1) the vocation of man as *man*, and 2) the vocation of man as *citizen*."[100] By virtue of the fact that he is a man, a man requires enlightenment, but there are different kinds of enlightenment. "The enlightenment that interests man as man is *general*, without any class distinctions; the enlightenment of a man considered as a citizen is modified according to *class* and *occupation*." Consequently, "human enlightenment (*Menschenaufklärung*) can come into conflict with civic enlightenment (*Bürgeraufklärung*). Certain truths which are useful to man as man can sometimes injure him as a citizen." In this connection a fourfold distinction has to be drawn. "Collisions can occur between 1) essential or 2) accidental vocations of man, and 3) essential or 4) inessential, accidental vocations of the citizen." Of all these possible collisions the one that is of most importance from our point of view is the one between the essential vocation of man as man and his essential vocation as a citizen.

If a man does not fulfill his essential vocation as a man, Mendelssohn says, he sinks to the level of the beasts. On the other hand, without men's fulfillment of their essential vocations as citizens, the constitution of the state ceases to exist. There is no problem if men's duties as men and their duties as citizens happen to be perfectly compatible with one another. But, "Unhappy is the state which must confess that within it the essential vocation of a man is not in harmony with the essential vocation of the citizen, that the enlightenment which is indispensable to mankind cannot be spread over all the classes of the realm without the constitution being in danger of collapsing." If this proves to be the case, what is to be done? "Here philosophy places its hand on its mouth! Necessity may here prescribe laws, or rather forge the bonds which are imposed on mankind in order to bring it low and keep it continually oppressed!"[101]

Obviously, it is only in a badly organized polity that a conflict can arise between the state's own needs and man's fulfillment of his vocation. Nevertheless, when such a conflict arises, the needs of the state take precedence. The state may legitimately enact laws that may have the effect of reducing men to the level of animals.

This statement has provoked some indignation. According to Werner Schneiders, "Mendelssohn obviously shrinks from adopting the political critique that follows from the Enlightenment's philosophical insights into the nature of the state." Even in theory "he capitulates before the naked power of the state organization," though he does, admittedly, denounce it at the same time.[102] In the opinion of Norbert Hinske, however, this judgment is too severe. Schneiders, he maintains, fails to take into consideration the context in which Mendelssohn's essay was originally written. Its immediate addressees were the members of the Wednesday Society, a society that consisted almost exclusively of leading officials of the Prussian state. With all their readiness for reform, loyalty to this particular state was a fundamental component of their activities. Mendelssohn bears this in mind, according to Hinske, when he warns these "friends of Enlightenment" against any attempt on their part to seek in the purported or even the actual interest of the political order something like a philosophical justification for a violation of the essential vocation of man. It is only necessity that "may here prescribe laws, or rather forge the bonds." Mendelssohn's *votum* is therefore anything but a capitulation. "It is a warning against complicity."[103]

Hinske's observations seem far closer to the mark. Mendelssohn was anything but servile. His acknowledgement of the state's right to act contrary to man's best interest is clearly only a grudging one, and it is difficult to imagine how, under the circumstances, he could have spoken differently. If, however, as Hinske argues, Mendelssohn had to operate under certain constraints when he discussed the relation between man's vocation and the interests of the state with like-minded, enlightened thinkers, it is obvious that a frank discussion of possible conflicts between religion and state in his published writings would have posed even greater difficulties.

Mendelssohn, after all, was not in the position of, say, a rabbi in the United States today, free to weigh the issues of morality and politics in obedience to his conscience alone and to pronounce his decisions more or less uninhibitedly. He belonged to a despised religion, he was not a citizen of any land, and he did not reside in a free state. Even to write as much as he did in *Jerusalem* about the relations between church and state required a considerable degree of audacity. To go further and to engage in a discussion of such delicate moral questions as those involving possible conflicts between the requirements of religion and those of the state would not only have taken him far afield from his main purpose; it might have been highly imprudent as well.

Conclusion

Mendelssohn clearly derived his basic understanding of human perfection from the philosophy of Leibniz and Wolff. Contrary to Wolff, however, he insisted that religious belief is simply indispensable for the pursuit of true perfection. Without belief in God, providence, and immortality, he believed, an individual is bound to misconstrue the purpose of his existence and conduct his life in an improper fashion.

Wolff had, indeed, thought that this was the case as far as the majority of mankind was concerned and had formulated his political philosophy accordingly. He assigned the state an important role in the governance of people's religious lives. Mendelssohn did not, as one might have expected, share his opinion on this matter. Imbued with a greater love of liberty and eager to gain a measure of freedom for the Jews, he developed a very different, much more liberal sort of political-philosophical position.

As we have sought to demonstrate, Mendelssohn's liberal political philosophy is to some extent based on incomplete and unsound argumentation. For one thing, he does not really deal adequately with the question of church-state relations at times when the state is failing to fulfill its proper function. And, as we have seen, his argument for the existence of a *right* to liberty of conscience is seriously flawed and less than fully consistent with some of his expressed—or half-expressed—views.

It is not difficult to understand why, in his desire to promote liberty of conscience, Mendelssohn would have striven to upgrade it from a mere desideratum to an inalienable human right. Such an argument might, if successful, contribute greatly to the advancement of religious freedom and the welfare of the Jews. The fact that he did not really prove what he set out to prove does not detract from the seriousness of his intentions. Nor should we be unduly surprised to see him recoil somewhat from accepting all of the consequences that follow from his absolutist, libertarian principles. Knowing what harm atheists could do, Mendelssohn was apparently prepared to bend his principles a little to prevent them from running wild.

Given Mendelssohn's very limited aims, it is not surprising, either, that he should fail to answer every question pertaining to his view of church-state relations. It is easy enough, in addition, to explain why, as a Jew and a very marginal subject of the king of Prussia, he would prefer not to enter into a discussion of all of the ramifications of his position. Prudence dictated that he avoid certain aspects of this subject, particularly those relating to possible limitations on the churches' loyalty to the state.

Notes

1. Christian Wolff, *Vernünfftige Gedancken von der Menschen Thun und Lassen zu Beförderung ihrer Glückseligkeit* (henceforth, *German Ethics*) (New York, 1976), vol. I, p. 2.

2. Ibid., vol. I, pp. 3–11.

3. Ibid., vol. I, p. 12.

4. Ibid., vol. I, p. 19.

5. Anton Bissinger, "Zur metaphysischen Begründung der Wolff-schen Ethik" in *Ch. Wolff, 1679–1754, Interpretationen zu seiner Philosophie und deren Wirkung* (Hamburg, 1983), p. 151. Observing that for Wolff perfection lies in what is according to nature, Hans-Martin Bachmann has remarked on the similarity of his position to that of the Stoics, "who ordain that man should freely live in harmony with nature," *Die naturrechtliche Staatslehre Christian Wolffs* (Berlin, 1977), p. 81.

6. Wolff, *German Ethics*, vol. II, p. 224.

7. Ibid., vol. II, p. 242.

8. Ibid., vol. II, p. 243.

9. Ibid., vol. II, p. 253.

10. Ibid., vol. II, p. 254.

11. Ibid., vol. II, p. 255.

12. Ibid., vol. II, p. 372.

13. Ibid., vol. II, pp. 373–74.

14. Ibid., vol. II, p. 433.

15. Ibid., vol. II, pp. 437ff.

16. Ibid., vol. II, p. 225.

17. Wolff's treatment of the relationship between one's duties toward oneself and one's duties toward others is problematic and has generated much disagreement. For an overview of the discussion, see Bachmann, *Die naturrechtliche Staatslehre Christian Wolffs*, pp. 84–89.

18. Ibid., pp. 88–89.

19. Wolff, *German Ethics*, vol. II, p. 226.

20. Ibid., vol. I, p. 44.

21. Ibid., vol. I, p. 49.

22. Ibid., vol. I, p. 52.

23. Ibid., vol. I, p. 57.

24. Bachmann, *Die naturrechtliche Staatslehre Christian Wolffs*, p. 89.

25. Wolff, *German Ethics*, vol. I, p. 30; vol. III, p. 654.

26. Ibid., vol. III, p. 656.

27. Ibid., vol. III, p. 657.

28. Ibid., vol. I, p. 20.

29. Ibid., vol. I, p. 21.

30. Ibid., vol. I, p. 45.

31. Wolff, *Vernünftige Gedanken von dem Gesellschaftlichen Leben der Menschen und Insonderheit dem Gemeinen Wesen*, Leipzig, 1736 (henceforth *German Politics*), vol. I, p. 213.

32. Ibid., vol. I, p. 227.

33. Ibid., vol. II, p. 459; Diethelm Klippel, *Politische Freiheit und Freiheitsrechte im deutschen Naturrecht des 18. Jahrhunderts* (Paderborn, 1976), pp. 48–50. See also Altmann, "The Quest for Liberty in Moses Mendelssohn's Political Philosophy," in *Humanität und Dialog: Lessing und Mendelssohn in neuer Sicht*, Beiheft zum Lessing Yearbook, ed. Ehrhard Bahr, Edward P. Harris, and Laurence G. Lyon (New York, 1976), p. 42.

34. *German Politics*, vol. II, p. 230.

35. Ibid., vol. V, p. 435.

36. Ibid., vol. III, pp. 368, 369.

37. Ibid., vol. III, p. 369.

38. Ibid., vol. III, p. 319.

39. Ibid., vol. IV, p. 421.

40. Ibid., vol. V, p. 434.

41. See Altmann, Moses Mendelssohn, p. 113.

42. *JubA*, vol. 2, p. 317.

43. See earlier, p. 100.

44. *JubA*, vol. 2, p. 318.

45. Ibid., p. 166.

46. See earlier, p. 50.

47. *JubA*, vol. 2, p. 113.

48. *JubA*, vol. 1, 1, p. 62.

49. Altmann, *Die trostvolle Aufklärung*, p. 25.

50. See Strauss, *JubA*, vol. 3, 2, p. lxi.

51. *JubA*, vol. 1, p. 421. The very "exercise of moral powers is genuine felicity of the spirit." (*JubA*, vol. 6, 1, p. 43). As Mendelssohn put it in *Jerusalem* (p. 47), "Man cannot be happy without beneficence, not without passive, but also not without active, beneficence." Precisely why this is the case is not a question of decisive importance. "Whether this benevolence toward others is a basic drive in the human soul, and leads to one's own improvement only as a consequence, as the adherents of the benevolent system maintain, or whether benevolence itself is an aspect of the drive to one's own perfection, as Mr. Abbt maintains here in the name of the so-called selfish philosophers, nothing is changed in the conduct of man with respect to virtue and felicity. If he wishes to be happy, a man must promote felicity; it is admitted by one side, and it is not denied by the other, that whoever furthers the felicity of his fellow creatures thereby improves his own inner condition, becomes a better man, in a word, increases his own felicity. With these reciprocal admissions the moral philosopher can be satisfied" (*JubA*, vol. 6, 1, p. 38).

52. See Hans Joachim Schneider, *Moses Mendelssohns Anthropologie und Ästhetik* (Berlin, 1970), p. 283.

53. *JubA* vol. 2, p. 100. "Die Freyheit ist ein Zustand, darinn wir von keinem äusserlichen Zwange abgehalten werden, unsern wahren Bedürfnissen auf einer unschuldigen Weise ein Genüge zu leisten." Translated by Altmann in his "The Quest for Liberty in Moses Mendelssohn's Political Philosophy," p. 44.

54. *Jerusalem*, p. 52.

55. Altmann, "The Quest for Liberty in Moses Mendelssohn's Political Philosophy," p. 44. "We meet here," Altmann observes, "the first of a series of modifications which Mendelssohn was to apply to the Wolffian system."

56. Ibid., p. 53.

57. *JubA*, vol. 6, 1, pp. 433–34.

58. *Jerusalem*, p. 60.

59. Ibid., p. 63.

60. *JubA*, vol. 3, 2, p. ciii.

61. See earlier, p. 52.

62. *JubA*, vol. 3, 2, p. 237.

63. *JubA*, vol. 3, 1, pp. 115–16. Mendelssohn does not insist that this will always be the case. Among the deniers of immortality there have been heroic spirits, men prepared to give their lives for freedom and virtue. But they have acted under the influence of their passions, not on the basis of their principles. They are acting similarly if they commit suicide to escape the miseries of this life (cf. *JubA*, vol. 1, pp. 293ff).

64. Ibid., pp. 116–17.

65. See earlier, p. 105.

66. *JubA*, vol. 3, 1, pp. 116–17.

67. *JubA*, vol. 7, p. 74.

68. *JubA*, vol. 3, 2, p. 198.

69. Ibid., p. 68.

70. *JubA*, vol. 3, 1, p. 115.

71. *Jerusalem*, pp. 37–40.

72. See Nathan Rotenstreich, *Jews and German Philosophy* (New York: Schocken Books, 1984), p. 20.

73. *Jerusalem*, p. 61.

74. Ibid., p. 70.

75. Ibid., p. 61.

76. Ibid., pp. 187–88.

77. Benedict Spinoza, *Theologico-Political Treatise*, trans. R. H. M. Elwes (New York: Dover Publications, 1951), p. 245.

78. Ibid., p. 258.

79. Ibid., Chapter 19; see also Hilail Gildin, "Spinoza and the Political Problem," in *Spinoza, A Collection of Critical Essays*, ed. Marjorie Grene (New York: Anchor Books, 1973), pp. 384–87.

80. Altmann, *Die trostvolle Aufklärung*, p. 223.

81. *Jerusalem*, pp. 62–63.

82. Altmann, *Moses Mendelssohn*, p. 223.

83. Altmann, *Die trostvolle Aufklärung*, p. 223.

84. For a description of this society, see Alexander Altmann, *Moses Mendelssohn*, pp. 654–55.

85. See *JubA*, vol. 6, 1, p. xxvi.

86. Ibid., p. 111. A full translation of the *votum* appears in Altmann, *Moses Mendelssohn*, p. 661.

87. Altmann, "The Quest for Liberty in Moses Mendelssohn's Political Philosophy," p. 50.

88. *JubA*, vol. 6, 1, p. 124.

89. Michael Albrecht, "Moses Mendelssohn: Ein Forschungsbericht, 1965–1980," p. 72. Albrecht, to be sure, concludes from this only that Mendelssohn could speak more concisely in such a setting, because he could presume a certain high level of discussion among his addressees.

90. Thomas Jefferson, *Notes on the State of Virginia*, ed. William Peden (Chapel Hill: University of North Carolina Press, 1955), p. 159.

91. *Jerusalem*, p. 39.

92. John Locke, *The Works of Locke* (London: Thomas Tegg, 1823) vol. 6, pp. 11ff.

93. See later, p. 251.

94. *Jerusalem*, p. 41.

95. Ibid., p. 43.

96. Ibid., pp. 44–45.

97. Ibid., p. 42; *JubA*, vol. 6, 1, p. 134. See also Altmann, "The Quest for Liberty," p. 52.

98. *JubA*, vol. 3, 1, p. 120.

99. *Jerusalem*, p. 46n. See also *JubA*, vol. 3, 1, p. 119: "Ein Krieg der auf beiden Seiten gerecht ist, ein allgemeiner Krieg aller moralischen Wesen, wo jedes in Wahrheit das Recht auf seiner Seite hat; ein Streit, der an und für sich selbst, auch von dem allergerechtesten Richter der Welt, nicht nach Recht und Billigkeit entschieden werden kann: was kann ungereimter seyn?"

100. *JubA*, vol. 6, 1, p. 116.

101. Ibid., p. 117.

102. Werner Schneiders, *Die wahre Aufklärung, Zum Selbstverständnis der deutschen Aufklärung* (Freiburg, 1974), p. 49.

103. Norbert Hinske, "Mendelssohns Beantwortung der Frage: Was ist Aufklärung? oder über die Aktualität Mendelssohns," in N. Hinske, ed., *"Ich Handle mit Vernunft . . ." Moses Mendelssohn und die europäische Aufklärung* (Hamburg: Meiner, 1981), p. 110.

5
Spinoza and Other Adversaries

The teachings of his principal mentors, Leibniz and Wolff, clearly placed no obstacle in the way of Mendelssohn's continued adherence to Judaism. Both of these philosophers acknowledged the possibility and, indeed, the reality of divine revelation. They did not, needless to say, accept unquestioningly the actual historicity of every purported revelation. To be recognized as genuine, they maintained, a revelation had to fulfill certain criteria. Its occurrence had to be adequately authenticated and, most important, its contents had to be—at least in a limited sense—rational. Although they were prepared to acknowledge that a genuine revelation could disclose certain truths unattainable by unassisted human reason (*suprarational* truths), they insisted that such a revelation could not contain anything that ran *contrary* to reason.[1]

Biblical revelation, according to Leibniz and Wolff, met these conditions. This meant, of course, that they considered both the Old and the New Testaments to be of divine origin. But this Christian orientation posed no serious difficulties for Mendelssohn. Although agreeing with Leibniz and Wolff that the Old Testament revelation was demonstrably valid, he argued (primarily in writings not meant for publication) that the New Testament was both insufficiently authenticated and replete with irrational teachings.

Mendelssohn, in short, did not face the kind of problem that beset many medieval and modern Jewish philosophers. He did not have to struggle to bring his general philosophy and his Jewish faith into accord. There is, in fact, only one area where the relationship between the two can be said to be problematic. Traditional Judaism offers only limited support for Mendelssohn's philosophical understanding of human immortality and in some respects conflicts with it. As we shall see, this issue did pose certain difficulties for him, but none of them proved to be insurmountable.

Still, one cannot say that Mendelssohn was able to affirm the reasonableness of his religion without confronting any major impediments. There is, to begin with, a very real tension between the liberal teachings we examined in Chapter 4 and the theocratic tendencies inherent in traditional Judaism. Unmistakably present in the Old Testament, the principle of theocratic government is enlarged upon in subsequent Jewish writings.[2] This discrepancy between his rational principles and the tenets of his religion creates a sizable problem for Mendelssohn, one that his critics forcibly called to his attention almost immediately after he issued his first public plea in favor of liberty of conscience.

On a still deeper level, Mendelssohn had to deal with a number of important critics of revealed religion in general and Judaism in particular. By the latter half of the eighteenth century, such thinkers abounded. Many of them, including people for whom Mendelssohn had the greatest respect, had written works aimed at undermining the common foundation of Judaism and Christianity, the Old Testament. These men were not, of course, combating Judaism alone, but were engaged, above all, in a more or less open campaign against the Christian religion. Fritz Bamberger is therefore very much mistaken when he writes that Mendelssohn lived "in a milieu dominated by the ideals he, his friends, and the 'enlightened age' itself proclaimed," and therefore felt, at first, no need "to declare and justify his religious commitment."[3] On the contrary, much of what Mendelssohn's contemporaries, and even his friends, were saying was bound to be particularly troublesome to any contemporary rationalist who also wished to uphold the truth of Judaism.

Mendelssohn formulated his earliest apologetic arguments in the course of his dispute with Johann Caspar Lavater (1741–1801), a faithful Christian. He composed most of what he wrote in defense of Judaism, however, with less pious adversaries in mind. In his principal Jewish work, his *Jerusalem*, he focused his attention chiefly on the demands of two direct antagonists, who challenged him to reconcile his Judaism and his liberalism, and on the more fundamental and broader critique of revealed religion that had been gaining strength in the course of the eighteenth century.

The general outlines of the defense of Judaism formulated by Mendelssohn are well known. Judaism, he argues, is based on an historically authenticated divine revelation. It is not, however, a revealed religion but a revealed legislation. It presupposes the principles of natural religion, adding to them only a set of laws whose chief purpose, it seems, is to assist its recipients (and, indirectly, the rest of humankind) in maintaining their grasp of these principles. Whatever it may have been in the past, adherence to Judaism is now completely voluntary and conflicts in no way with the espousal of the individual's right to liberty of conscience.

Because Mendelssohn developed this concept of Judaism in the course of responding to his various opponents, it will be useful for us to review the different types of challenges he faced before we examine what he himself has to say. We will begin accordingly, by reviewing in this chapter the more general contemporary critique of revealed religion. From there we will proceed to a consideration of the arguments made by the critics who confronted Mendelssohn directly.

The most important of the critics of revealed religion with whom Mendelssohn had to deal was undoubtedly Baruch Spinoza. Spinoza's *Theologico-Political Treatise* (1670) was, in the words of Leo Strauss, "*the* classic document of the 'rationalist' or 'secularist' attack on the belief in revelation."[4] This notorious work quickly became something of an underground classic, a book that played a great, if incalculable, part in nurturing religious skepticism across Europe. It is impossible to measure the precise extent of its influence, since the very disreputable character of the book often made it imprudent for its students to cite it, even when they leaned heavily upon it. But signs of its impact can be perceived very widely.

Spinoza certainly exercised some influence on the English Deists, a group of thinkers who constituted a crucial link in the history of unbelief. Paul Hazard, for one, has argued that he "provided weapons for the German school of unbelief, Mathias Knutsen and his band of *Conscienciari*, F. W. Stosch and the rest of them, as well as for the English Deists, Shaftesbury, Collins, Tindal, and most blatant and conspicuous of them all, John Toland."[5] The leading Continental disciple of these Deists was of course Voltaire. One of the foremost spokesmen of the Enlightenment, he repeatedly made use of Spinozist and Deist arguments to undermine the credibility of the ancient Israelites and their prophets as well as the veracity of the Old Testament.[6]

Even more closely linked to Spinoza were two German thinkers whose critiques of revealed religion were of particularly great importance for Mendelssohn: Hermann Samuel Reimarus and Gotthold Ephraim Lessing. In his published works, as we saw in Chapter 1 of this study, Reimarus presented himself as a defender of natural religion who was deeply concerned also with the preservation of Christianity.[7] In a huge compendium entitled "Apology for Rational Worshippers of God" (*Apologie oder Schutzschrift für die vernünftigen Verehrer Gottes*), however, which he intended only for his trusted friends and never planned to see published, he launched a multifaceted attack on biblical revelation. In view of his overall aims, "It should come as no surprise," as Frederick Beiser has written, "that Reimarus was an avid student of Spinoza's *Tractatus* and that much in his *Apologie* breathes a Spinozist spirit."[8] Others have described it, with no less justice and without, in effect, disagreeing with Beiser, as a lucid and comprehensive restatement of the radical Deist argument against the truth of both the Old and the New Testaments.[9]

While employed in the ducal library at Wolfenbüttel, Lessing gained access to a manuscript copy of the *Apologie*. From 1774 to 1778 he published excerpts from it. For the sake of Reimarus's posthumous reputation and to protect the privacy of his surviving children, he concealed the name of their author. Lessing accompanied these so-called *Fragmenten aus der Ungenannten (Fragments of an Unnamed)* with his own rather extensive "counterassertions," ostensibly intended to show, among other things, that Reimarus's critique left the true core of Christianity untouched. Whatever he may have said in defense of the essential principles of Christianity, however, "[i]n publishing Reimarus's work, Lessing was," as Beiser has noted, "airing Spinoza's views."[10] And, indeed, Lessing himself was "part and parcel of the Spinozist tradition in Germany . . ." It is clear from his "counterassertions" that he was "in the direct line of succession from the early Spinozists." Like them, he "believed in the value of biblical criticism, natural religion, tolerance, and equality. He too was deeply indebted to the *Tractatus*, which probably first fired his interest in Spinoza."[11]

This century-long, "Spinozist" critique of revealed religion, extending from Spinoza himself to Lessing, will be our chief concern in this chapter. Although Mendelssohn made few explicit references to the writings that constitute this heretical tradition, he clearly knew them well and was fully cognizant of their significance. He was manifestly familiar with Spinoza's *Theologico-Political Treatise* and the writings of the English Deists.[12] Living in Berlin in the middle of the eighteenth century, he could not help but know of Voltaire's campaign against revealed religion. He was surely familiar with the writings of Reimarus. Indeed, he wrote to Lessing that he considered the full text from which the "Fragments" were taken (and that he had been one of the few people to see) to be "very important in every respect . . ."[13] And, above all, he lived through the *Fragmentenstreit*, the epoch-making controversy generated during the 1770s by Lessing's publication of what came to be known as the "Wolffenbüttel Fragments."[14]

Despite his thorough acquaintance with these theoretical attacks on the foundations of Judaism, Mendelssohn did not exactly leap to meet the challenge they presented. When he first took note of Spinoza, at an early point in his philosophical career, it was not to answer what he had to say against revealed religion but to write what Frederick Beiser has called "the first attempt at an objective philosophical treatment" of his thought.[15] Although respectfully reevaluating Spinoza's metaphysical doctrines, he neglected entirely to deal with his critique of revealed religion. In direct response to the Deists' harsh characterizations of Judaism, Mendelssohn wrote nothing, nor did he ever seek to formulate any kind of response to Voltaire's antibiblical campaign. During the *Fragmentenstreit* he remained a silent bystander.

Eventually, however, in *Jerusalem*, a book he wrote primarily to deal with other challenges, Mendelssohn cautiously took up the gauntlet. He referred there to Spinoza only once by name, but, as Julius Guttman and others have observed, the book is in many respects a kind of counter-*Theologico-Political Treatise*.[16] Virtually every scholar who has ever discussed *Jerusalem* has noted the extent to which it also reflects the influence of various Deist writings. And although he made no mention of Voltaire or Reimarus, Mendelssohn explicitly took issue, in the second part of the book, with some of the views expressed by Lessing in the course of the *Fragmentenstreit*. As we shall see, there is good reason to believe that he was particularly preoccupied, at the time he wrote *Jerusalem*, with this vital controversy, which had taken place only a few years prior to its publication.

To understand this Spinozist critique of revealed religion, which was of such great significance to Mendelssohn, it will be necessary for us to examine the broad outlines of the theological sections of the work that gave rise to it, Spinoza's *Theologico-Political Treatise*. We will need to take note, also, of some of the arguments made by the English Deists and Voltaire, particularly insofar as they not only repeat but also enlarge upon the Spinozist critique. Finally, we will need to take a very close look at certain aspects of the Reimarus fragments brought to publication by Lessing and Lessing's own accompanying "Counterassertions."

Spinoza and his disciples may have posed, in Mendelssohn's day, the greatest theoretical threat to biblical religion, but no prominent representative of this camp ever "picked a fight," in public, with Mendelssohn himself or sought to coerce him into explaining his continued adherence to Judaism. The first adversary to make such a demand of him was anything but an enemy of revealed religion. Johann Caspar Lavater, a Swiss theologian, sought to goad Mendelssohn into explaining publicly why he remained a Jew and did not follow a more rational course of action; that is, convert to Christianity. A decade later, two new critics sought to induce Mendelssohn to deal with what they maintained were inconsistencies between certain of his previously expressed principles and the teachings of reason. In direct response to these three critics Mendelssohn composed most of his apologetic writings on Judaism. It is therefore important, for our purposes, to understand precisely what they were trying to obtain from him.

Spinoza

In the *Theologico-Political Treatise*, Spinoza launched an unprecedentedly bold attack on biblical revelation. He did not, however, throw all caution to the winds. As Leo Strauss has shown, he developed his critique of revelation within an extremely complex and self-contradictory web of argumentation, one that partially conceals the radical character of his thought. In many passages of the treatise he takes care to base himself on the Bible. "Arguing from the conceded premise that the Bible is the only document of revelation, Spinoza demands that the pure word of God be not corrupted by any human additions, inventions, or innovations, and that nothing be considered a revealed doctrine that is not borne out by explicit and clear statements in the Bible." [17] We will consider, in Chapter 7, Spinoza's reasons for sometimes acknowledging biblical authority and basing his arguments upon it. For now, however, we must focus on those passages in which he comes close to abandoning any pretense of piety and turns against the Bible, making it "the target of philosophical criticism." [18]

Spinoza's rejection of biblical revelation is rooted, ultimately, in his denial of the existence of an extramundane divine entity capable of bestowing a revelation and in his belief in the inviolability of the natural order. He begins his assault on biblical revelation in the *Treatise*, however, not with a clarification of the basis of his thought but by seeking to discredit the human beings who have claimed to be the recipients of God's revelations. Drawing on the Bible itself for most of his evidence, he attempts to show that the ancient Hebrews, including their most revered prophets, were an ignorant and superstitious people who mistook figments of their own imagination for divine utterances and wrongly attributed to God what was really due to natural causes.

In the first two chapters of the *Treatise* Spinoza takes aim at the biblical prophets. Ostensibly acknowledging that they were in fact God's chosen emissaries, he seeks to show that they were nevertheless rather limited men. They were not, as many traditionalists had maintained, especially wise. The Bible repeatedly illustrates their ignorance of nature. "Nothing," for instance, is clearer than that Joshua, and perhaps also the author who wrote his history, thought that the sun revolves round the earth, and that the earth is fixed, and further that the sun for a certain period remained still." Isaiah apparently believed the same thing.[19] Other prophets betrayed their ignorance of nature in other ways. Furthermore, Spinoza asserts, it is not "only in matters of this kind, but in others more important" that "the prophets could be, and in fact were, ignorant." For "they taught nothing special about the Divine attributes, but held quite ordinary notions about God, and to these notions their revelations were adapted . . ."[20]

Some of these ordinary notions were, according to Spinoza, quite mistaken. Moses, for instance, believed that God was in some sense a corporeal being and that men could not behold Him "not so much from inherent impossibility as from human infirmity."[21] He failed to understand that corporeality would involve "a contradiction of the Divine nature." Moses also believed that God resided in the heavens, and for that reason He "was revealed to him as coming down from heaven on to a mountain." To speak with Him, Spinoza mockingly observes, "Moses went up the mountain, which he certainly need not have done if he could have conceived of God as omnipresent."[22]

The biblical prophets held, in fact, a variety of ordinary notions about God, differing among themselves with regard to such questions as whether or not He ever changed his mind. Their prophecies varied, moreover, in accordance with their individual dispositions. If

> a prophet was cheerful, victories, peace, and events which make men glad, were revealed to him; in that he was naturally more likely to imagine such things. If, on the contrary, he was melancholy, wars, massacres, and calamities were revealed; and so, according as a prophet was merciful, gentle, quick to anger or severe, he was more fitted for one kind of revelation than another.[23]

All in all, Spinoza believed, these observations more than sufficiently proved "that God adapted revelations to the understanding and opinions of the prophets, and that in matters of theory without bearing on charity or morality the prophets could be, and, in fact, were ignorant, and held conflicting opinions." From this he concludes that "we must by no means go to the prophets for knowledge, either of natural or of spiritual phenomena."[24] This seems, at first glance, to amount merely to a demotion of the prophets from the status of wise men, previously attributed to them, to a lower status, to little more than unwitting tools in the hands of God, who used them, despite their limitations, to communicate moral knowledge to the people at large. And, indeed, Spinoza no doubt wished to leave this impression. To conceal, to some degree, the radical nature of his thought and to accomplish his overall political purposes (which we will discuss in Chapter 7), he needed to allow the prophets to retain some vestiges of their authority.

Upon further reflection, however, we can see that Spinoza's characterization of the prophets casts grave doubts on their claim to be in any sense messengers of God. In view of their ignorance of natural and divine science, it would be senseless to take at face value their assertions that they have been in communication with the Deity. How could they possibly *know* such a thing? How could they distinguish—reliably—between the word of God and the products of their own lively imaginations? Their own "moral certainty" of their having been addressed by God is clearly not sufficient. The prophets, as Spinoza depicts them, are not the sort of men to whom one can reasonably extend credibility, even if one believes, as Spinoza himself clearly did not, in the possibility of God speaking directly to individual human beings.

The weaknesses of the prophets were, for the most part, only those of the nation to which they belonged. The ancient Israelites, Spinoza repeatedly stressed, were an ignorant and superstitious people. For this reason, the biblical narratives are highly untrustworthy, particularly where they recount events that appear to have contravened the laws of nature.

In the sixth chapter of the *Treatise*, Spinoza describes the Israelites' propensity to misreport what they had witnessed. It is "absolutely certain," he writes, "that every event which is truly described in Scripture necessarily happened, like everything else, according to natural laws." How, then, can one account for those events described in the Bible which appear to be incompatible with the known order of nature?

> It is very rare for men to relate an event simply as it happened, without adding any element of their own judgment. When they see or hear anything new, they are, unless strictly

on their guard, so occupied with their own preconceived opinions that they perceive something quite different from the plain facts seen or heard, especially if such facts surpass the comprehension of the beholder or hearer, and, most of all, if he is interested in their happening in a given way.[25]

Spinoza proceeds to illustrate this general principle by referring to the biblical report of how Joshua made the sun stand still.

In the time of Joshua the Hebrews held the ordinary opinion that the sun moves with a daily motion, and that the earth remains at rest; to this preconceived opinion they adopted the miracle which occurred during their battle with the five kings. They did not simply relate that that day was longer than usual, but asserted that the sun and moon stood still, or ceased from their motion—a statement which would be of great service to them at that time in convincing and proving by experience to the Gentiles, who worshipped the sun, that the sun was under the control of another deity who could compel it to change its daily course. Thus, partly through religious motives, partly through preconceived opinions, they conceived of and related the occurrence as something quite different from what really happened.

This is only one of a host of possible examples. For, in Spinoza's opinion, "many things are narrated in Scripture as real, which were in fact only symbolic and imaginary."[26] Among such things he surely included, it is important for us to note, the divine voice heard by the Israelites at Mount Sinai.[27]

If the prophets were men of little discernment, and the people to whom they brought their message, including the historians among them, were largely devoid of rational understanding and incapable of accurate observation, it would clearly be a mistake to accept their testimony as proof of the occurrence of any divine revelation. This would be the case, according to Spinoza, even if the biblical narratives, as we now have them, were known to be fully contemporaneous with the events they purport to describe. An examination of the texts containing these narratives reveals, however, that they attained their current form only at the very end of the biblical period.

According to Spinoza, the Pentateuch, which contains the accounts of the most important revelations, clearly betrays its late origin in a number of ways. It refers to Moses in the third person and prolongs its narrative after his death. It contains obvious anachronisms and parenthetical remarks stemming from a period subsequent to the one it depicts. On the basis of these facts and other internal evidence Spinoza concludes that "it is clearer than the sun at noonday that the Pentateuch was not written by Moses but by someone who lived long after Moses."[28]

The other historical books of the Bible likewise constitute compilations completed "many generations after the events they relate had taken place." The Pentateuch and these books all give evidence of having been put together "by one man, writing with a definite aim." The intention of this editor, whom Spinoza suspects to have been Ezra the Scribe, was to set forth "the words and laws of Moses" and prove them "by subsequent events."[29]

Spinoza speaks most disparagingly of Ezra's editorial work. He complains that the material in the biblical books is heaped together "promiscuously and without order."[30] In addition to everything else, it must be noted, "these books were not guarded by posterity with such care that no faults crept in."[31] The texts are, in other words, corrupt. Spinoza concludes his effort to discredit those responsible for the transmission of the books of the Bible with a detailed discussion of the evidence for this corruption, a discussion it is not necessary for us to review in detail.

This multifaceted attack on the authority of the Old Testament (and, to some extent, the New Testament as well, although this is not our concern here) is, Spinoza rather implausibly maintains, of only limited significance. Toward the conclusion of the *Treatise*'s chapters on biblical interpretation, he argues that the Bible is essentially a reliable document, one in which "the whole Divine law" has "come down to us uncorrupted" and in which "the main facts of Hebrew history" have been "transmitted in good faith." "Whatever, therefore, is spurious or faulty can only have reference to details," and can have "little to do with salvation."[32] These assertions do not begin to indicate the extent of the transformation of biblical religion that Spinoza intended to effect through textual and historical analysis. Needless to say, they did not clutter the vision of subsequent radical thinkers, who understood the full implications of his study of the Bible.

We have seen how Spinoza sought to weaken the Bible's authority by exposing its faulty underpinnings. It is now time to consider what he has to say regarding its doctrinal content. Spinoza's views on this subject constitute, in the words of Julius Guttman, "an undervaluation of the religious significance of the Old Testament," one that he was to bequeath to "the radical wing of the Enlightenment."[33]

True knowledge of God is accessible, according to Spinoza, only through the use of one's reason. He denies repeatedly that the voice heard at Mount Sinai could have provided the Jews with rational knowledge, with "philosophical or mathematical certitude regarding God's existence" or instruction regarding "the absolute attributes of His essence."[34] He does acknowledge, however, that the Old Testament contains some religious doctrines, albeit "very few and very simple ones." Like the New Testament, it demands from men "nothing but obedience," and it teaches nothing but "that which is necessary for enabling all men to obey God" through loving their neighbors "and without which they would become rebellious, or without the discipline of obedience."[35]

What is necessary for this purpose, Spinoza writes in Chapter XIII of the *Treatise*, "is simply a knowledge of His divine justice and charity."[36] In the following chapter he provides a more detailed breakdown of "the fundamental doctrines of the whole of Scripture" (which are identical with "the dogmas of universal faith"). They include the existence of God, His unity, omnipresence, and absolute sovereignty. They specify that true "worship of God consists only in justice and charity, or love toward one's neighbor" and that living in this manner constitutes the only route to salvation. Deviating from this path does not, however, doom a man, for "God forgives the sins of those who repent."[37]

Spinoza does not really consider all of these dogmas to be true, but he nevertheless regards them as quite useful.[38] He obviously intends to propagate them, not to disparage them. It is not on account of its reiteration of these dogmas, which it shares with the New Testament, that he "undervalues" the religious significance of the Old Testament, but on account of what it adds to them: the Mosaic law. For Spinoza, as Guttman has observed, this law "is a purely political phenomenon."[39]

In the third and fifth chapters of the *Treatise*, Spinoza analyzes the underlying intent of the law propounded in the Pentateuch, scarcely concealing his belief that Moses, not God, was its author. Moses' principal aim, he writes, was to rule single-handedly a recently liberated people, a mass of ex-slaves incapable, on account of its lack of cultivation and its obstinate nature, of governing itself. To fortify his rule, "he left nothing to the free choice of individuals." The Jews "could do nothing but remember the law, and follow the ordinances laid down at the good pleasure of their ruler." Moses realized, furthermore, that it was necessary to inspire the people to obey his law willingly. He "therefore, by his virtue and the Divine command, introduced a religion, so that the people might do their duty from devotion rather than fear. Further, he bound them over by benefits, and prophesied many advantages in the future . . ." The "burdensome" ceremonies Moses prescribed, Spinoza concludes, evidently had "nothing to do with a state of blessedness," and indeed, the entire Mosaic law "had reference merely to the government of the Jews, and merely temporal advantages."[40]

Spinoza states that Moses introduced a religion among the Jews to achieve certain political purposes. He does not hold this against him, however, and is himself, as we shall see, by no means averse to utilizing religion in such a fashion. If he undervalues the religious significance of the Old Testament it is not on account of the fact that Moses was a manipulative leader but because of the limited nature of the rewards he promised. As Guttman has put it, the "principal and decisive argument for his claim that Israel's election was a purely political act is the fact, which he mentions time and again, that the Bible offers only terrestrial rewards or punishments (for instance, the destruction of the Jewish nation) for obedience or disobedience to the Law, but never mentions immortality as a reward for its fulfillment." Here, Guttman notes, Spinoza borrowed and further developed an older Christian argument against Judaism. However, he gave "this familiar criticism an entirely new turn by using it to insist that the Mosaic legislation possesses no religious character whatsoever. His thesis and his arguments recur constantly among his successors in Enlightenment philosophy up to Kant."[41]

Guttman was no doubt correct to identify Spinoza as the man who inspired this new form of anti-Jewish argumentation. Unfortunately, his familiarity with subsequent developments led him to view his writings in a somewhat anachronistic and mistaken light. What is, in fact, particularly striking about Spinoza's treatment of this matter is precisely the extent to which he downplays the whole question of immortality. Unlike many later thinkers, including Mendelssohn, he does not stress the indispensability of a belief in immortality for the maintenance of human morality. His list of the fundamental dogmas of Scripture and, simultaneously, universal religion, refers only to the reward of obedience by "salvation," not eternal life. Even in the passages to which Guttman refers, Spinoza says nothing about the Old Testament's failure to make any mention of the reward of immortality. He focuses on its promises of exclusively temporal rewards, and contrasts these either with "virtue and the true life" or "other matters, wherein man's true happiness consists," spheres in which the Jews merely remained "on a par with the rest of the nations."[42] Only once, in a footnote, does he comment that "a keeping of the commandments of the Old Testament is not sufficient for eternal life, appears from Mark x. 21."[43]

What Spinoza means by the true life and true happiness is outlined in the fourth chapter of the *Treatise*. He there contrasts "human law," which is "a plan of living which serves only to render life and the state secure," and "Divine law," which has to do only with "the highest good, in other words, the true knowledge and love of God." Divine law, as he immediately makes clear, is not a law, strictly speaking, but a way of life. It consists in the pursuit of intellectual perfection, which can be obtained only through the knowledge of nature. It "is evident," Spinoza writes, "that all natural phenomena involve and express the conception of God as far as their essence and perfection extend, so that we have greater and more perfectly knowledge of God in proportion to our knowledge of natural phenomena . . ." The man who prizes such knowledge above all else is "the most perfect and the chief sharer in the highest blessedness."[44]

Spinoza's repeated statements that the Mosaic law aimed only at temporal and not at true happiness were, then, simply another way of saying that it constituted a human and not a divine law, one that regulated the temporal affairs of the Jewish people but in no way directed them toward the "highest blessedness." His intention here is not so much to compare Judaism unfavorably with religions that hold out the promise of an afterlife as to refute the claims of Maimonides and other medieval Jewish philosophers that the law of Moses both regulated the mundane aspects of the Jewish people's life *and* pointed the way, at least for the philosophical few, toward intellectual perfection and the greatest happiness.

The dogmas of the universal faith are one thing, divine law is another. The Old Testament contains the former, which include the principle of divine reward and punishment, but the law of Moses is not tantamount to the latter, because it fails to direct anyone to the study of philosophy. When Spinoza undervalues biblical Judaism as a religion dealing only with temporal matters, he is dissociating it from the highest human pursuits, but he is not at the same time emphasizing that it is devoid of one of the fundamental, indispensable tenets of natural religion, the doctrine of immortality, and that it is therefore an inferior religion. Some of his successors, however, influenced by what he himself said, will, as we shall see, take that next step.

As far as Spinoza is concerned, "if a man is absolutely ignorant of the Scriptures, and none the less has right opinions and a true plan of life," he may attain the most blessed state. In a famous passage at the end of Chapter V of the *Treatise*, he criticizes the Jews for being "of a directly contrary way of thinking," for holding "that true opinions and a true plan of life are of no service in attaining blessedness, if their possessors have arrived at them by the light of reason only, and not like the documents prophetically revealed to Moses." To support this charge he quotes Maimonides's well-known statement, in the *Mishneh Torah*, concerning the "pious among the nations." Gentiles can achieve this status and obtain a place in the world to come, according to Maimonides (as quoted by Spinoza), only if they adhere to the precepts pertaining to the sons of Noah "because God ordained them in the law, and revealed them to us by Moses." If they follow the commandments of the sons of Noah solely because it seems reasonable to do so, they are not to be counted among the "pious among the nations."[45]

Spinoza briefly deplores this teaching, which he does not deem worthy of refutation. He evidently finds it to be both unjustifiable and morally unsound, inasmuch as it leads to the condemnation of people of unimpeachably good ethics. It is not, of course, primarily Maimonides or even the Jews alone with whom Spinoza is here contending. No doubt his real, albeit unacknowledged, target is the Christian teaching that there is no salvation outside the church. Nevertheless, this is an issue that defenders of Judaism against Spinoza (and his successors) will have to confront. Interestingly enough, this is virtually the only *moral* objection Spinoza ventures to make against biblical religion in the *Theologico-Political Treatise*. The book does accuse the Jews, in passing, of nurturing a hatred of the rest of humankind, but it contains nothing resembling the hostile depictions of the moral conduct of the Bible's heroes that pervade the writings of many Deists.

In theory, at any rate, if not in practice, the government of ancient Israel was, according to Spinoza, a theocracy. God was acknowledged to be the sovereign, and "the laws of the state were called the laws and commandments of God. Thus in the Hebrew state the civil and religious authority, each consisting solely of obedience to God, were one and the same." Consequently, "between civil and religious law and right there was no distinction whatever."[46] From Spinoza's point of view, this is clearly not a desirable state of affairs. As Hillel Fradkin has put it, the *Theologico-Political Treatise* "announces by its very title "its concern with the relationship of religion and politics and is in fact extensively if not exclusively concerned with the development and acceptance of political teachings which would subordinate religious authority and activity to political authority, and thereby remove religion as a disturbing factor from public life."[47] The example of the biblical theocracy constituted something of an obstacle to the development and acceptance of such teachings. Spinoza had to explain, accordingly, why it was not a suitable precedent for his contemporaries to follow.

He accomplishes this goal, in some measure, through the characterization of the Mosaic law as a purely political law, one that was intended for the Jews alone and has now, in any case, been rendered completely obsolete by the demise of the Jewish state.[48] Although this argument constitutes only one aspect of his broader campaign against the proponents of theocracy, it has the effect of presenting a serious challenge to the defenders of Judaism. It is one to which Mendelssohn, as we shall see, felt compelled to respond.

We have already taken note, in Chapter 4, of Spinoza's more fundamental, political-philosophical argument for the subordination of religion to political authority. We need not concern ourselves here with the details of this argument, because it was, in the end, not Spinoza's views on this question but his own, even more liberal approach to it that created difficulties for Mendelssohn, in his capacity as Jewish apologist. As we shall see at the end of this chapter, the contradiction between his own expressed position with regard to the relationship between religion and state and that reflected in the Bible was one that one of Mendelssohn's critics virtually forced him to try to resolve.

The English Deists and Voltaire

Defining Deism and enumerating the thinkers who ought to be classified as Deists is a singularly difficult task, one that continues to occupy scholars of English intellectual history.[49] The controversy relating to this matter is, however, of no particular interest to us here, because, as Robert E. Sullivan has ironically observed, "The inability of both Augustans and historians to agree about the meaning of deism does not eliminate the late seventeenth- and early eighteenth-century writers who identified themselves as deists."[50] The writers with whom we are concerned fall into this category. What they had in common was, above all, a certain "coolness toward revelation."[51]

They were not completely candid about this. Many of the English Deists employed what David Berman has called "the art of theological lying." As Berman notes, "if we take Collins, Toland,

Tindal, and Blount at their word, they were really Christian fide-
ists, at least concerning the afterlife . . ."[52] But they should evidently not be taken at their word. Beneath their almost transparent disguises, which Berman easily unravels, these Deists were
deniers of Christianity, and perhaps even covert atheists.[53]

As Paul Hazard has observed, the English Deists readily employed the weaponry of antibiblical argumentation provided by Spinoza in the *Theologico-Political Treatise*.[54] The Deists cut the
prophets down to size, repeatedly emphasizing their intellectual
limitations, their lack of qualifications to serve as intermediaries
between God and humankind. They sought to undermine the authority of the biblical texts, especially their accounts of miraculous
events. They emphasized the primitiveness of the Israelite concept
of God and the purely political character of the Mosaic law. They
stressed, too, the degree to which the Jews demonstrated intol-
erance to those who did not practice their religion.[55]

It will not be necessary, for our purposes, to attempt to determine the exact degree to which the Deists had recourse to Spinoza's writings. What we need to consider, briefly, are those aspects of their critique of the Old Testament that both expand upon
the arguments presented by Spinoza and are of importance for an
understanding of Mendelssohn's Jewish writings. The two matters
of particular concern to us are (1) the way in which some of the
Deists emphasized the significance of the Old Testament's lack of a
doctrine of immortality and (2) their assaults on the moral character of the prophets and other biblical heroes and the biblical Israelites in general. We must also take note of the way in which the
arguments of the English Deists were adopted by their most cele-
brated French disciple, Voltaire.

As we have already observed, Spinoza himself stressed the
fact that the Old Testament promised nothing other than terrestrial rewards for adherence to the Mosaic law. As far as he was
concerned, this only indicated that the law of Moses was not truly
a "Divine law"; that is, it had nothing to do with "the highest good,
in other words, the true knowledge and love of God." Spinoza never
suggested that the Old Testament's lack of a doctrine of immortality branded Judaism as a religion devoid of one of the fundamental, indispensable tenets of natural religion and that it is
therefore a woefully deficient religion. Several of the Deists, on the
other hand, did just that. Thomas Morgan, for instance, argued
that, because the Mosaic law was "barely Civil, Political or National, so all its sanctions were merely Temporal, relating only to
Mens outward Practice and Behaviour in Society, none of its Re-

wards or Punishments relating to any future State, or extending themselves beyond this life . . ."[56]

Whereas Spinoza had relatively little to say in condemnation of the moral character of the biblical heroes, the Deists are very outspoken on this subject. This represented a major departure from the practice of Christian thinkers and theologians of all denominations, for whom the prophets and heroes of the Old Testament were revered figures. They were in large part inspired by Pierre Bayle, a Huguenot exile living in Holland, who undertook, in the seventeenth century, the first significant attempt to subject the character and the conduct of leading biblical figures to critical scrutiny. Bayle, it appears, did not do this to discredit them. In his *Dictionnaire Historique et Critique* he "vigorously criticized Abraham and above all David, but with the opposite intention of leaving room only for God's grace as opposed to the universal sinfulness of mankind."[57] Whatever Bayle's intentions, he supplied later very different kinds of writers with an example they were only too eager to follow.

Among the writers influenced by Bayle was the third Earl of Shaftesbury, whom Mendelssohn held in particularly high esteem.[58] As Reventlow has shown, Shaftesbury, who was personally acquainted with Bayle following his stay in Holland in 1698–99, composed critiques of Joseph, Moses, and other biblical figures strongly reminiscent of those of the Huguenot thinker.[59] Moral criticism of the Old Testament abounds in other Deist writings, too, such as Tindal's *Christianity as Old as the Creation*.[60] In *The Moral Philosopher*, Morgan

> subjects not only the Mosaic law but also the most significant figures of the Old Testament to vigorous moral criticism. Thus for example the character of David is depicted in the blackest colours: "he had been the most bloody Persecutor that ever had been known, and his whole Life had been one continued Scene of Dissimulation, Falsehood, Lust and Cruelty." Several times he goes right through the course of Israelite history from the Exodus to the monarchy, showing other people, like Samuel, Elishah, and the kings of Israel in an unfavorable light . . ."[61]

All of the strictures against the Old Testament found in the writings of the Deists can be found, again and again, in the works of Voltaire. He repeats, more vociferously and in a more artful manner, all of the Deists' arguments against the credibility of the prophets and the authors of the Old Testament narrative. He ridicules and assails the moral standards of the Israelites, focusing most angrily on their unconscionable mistreatment of the Canaanites. He mocks King David and many other biblical heroes for their ignorance and immorality. And he deplores the Jewish religion on account of its primitive conception of God and its lack of a doctrine of immortality.[62] Voltaire says nothing new or distinctive with regard to the matters of interest to us here. He deserves special mention only because of his signal importance as a spokesman of the Enlightenment and because of the way in which he appears to have influenced at least one of Mendelssohn's correspondents.

During the final decades of the eighteenth century, the antireligious writings of Voltaire exerted a strong influence on many thinkers throughout Europe. They attained wide currency in Germany, where they repeatedly evoked a significant reaction. We cannot survey here the full extent of this response, but we must briefly take note of one of its rather minor manifestations; that is, the way in which Voltaire's views are apparently reflected in a letter addressed to Mendelssohn by one of his young, philosophically minded friends, August Hennings.[63]

Hennings, who frequently corresponded with Mendelssohn, wrote to him in April 1782, following the publication of his edition of Manasseh ben Israel's *Vindiciae Judaeorum*. Although fully in agreement with Mendelssohn's plea, in the Preface to this work, for freedom of conscience, he nevertheless objected to the way in which Manasseh had portrayed the Jews as an exceptionally tolerant people. "The history of the Old Testament is full of proofs," he contended, "of how little tolerant the Jews were." His own understanding of natural theology and natural law made it impossible for him "to see the annihilation of so many races and peoples, which the Jews were commanded to undertake, as exceptions, specially commanded by God, to the general rule of tolerance." He could only see the Jews' conduct as proof of how deeply inclined they were to persecution, whenever they themselves had the upper hand. Although the Jews, during their postbiblical history, may rarely have held the upper hand, there is ample evidence that they have still managed to preserve intact their former zeal.[64]

A letter in which Mendelssohn may have responded directly to Hennings's arguments has, unfortunately, disappeared.[65] It is not unreasonable to assume, however, that Hennings's sharp objections were on his mind when he wrote *Jerusalem*, only a short time later. Although Mendelssohn was no doubt familiar with such arguments from his reading of the works of various Deists, including perhaps Voltaire, they must have acquired additional force, for him, when he confronted them in his personal correspondence.

Lessing and The Wolffenbüttel Fragments

Significant as it is for the study of Mendelssohn's views, Hennings's letter cannot begin to compare, however, with the commotion that took place in the German lands, in the 1770s, as a result of Lessing's publication of excerpts from the work of the recently deceased covert disciple of Spinoza and Deist (and, incidentally, the father-in-law of August Hennings), Hermann Samuel Reimarus. Reimarus's *Apologie*, from which Lessing took the famous "fragments," was a large and variegated composition. Mendelssohn, as we have already noted, was one of the few people who had an opportunity, at the end of the eighteenth century, to peruse it thoroughly. In view of the fact that it remained a work unknown to the general public, it will not be necessary for us to include a detailed examination of its text in our general survey of the contemporary critique of revealed religion. With respect to those parts of the manuscript that remained unpublished, we need only note one thing: they were replete with criticisms, reminiscent of the Deists and Voltaire, of the moral character of the Israelite prophets and heroes.[66]

It will not be necessary either, for our purposes, to examine the specifically Christian aspects of the fragments brought to publication by Lessing (which, we ought to note, played an important part in the rise of modern New Testament criticism).[67] We need to consider only the second, third, and fourth of the five excerpts he published in the course of the 1770s. After doing so, we will turn to Lessing's own observations pertaining to these so-called "Fragments of an Unnamed."

The second fragment, we should begin by noting, consists of an extended demonstration of the "impossibility of a revelation in which all men would have good reason to believe." It is evidently designed primarily to undercut Christianity's universal claims by demonstrating how inconceivable it is that a wise and good God would ever have sought to transmit indispensable religious knowledge to everyone on earth through a single, direct revelation. Nevertheless, this fragment contains many arguments with important ramifications even for those who acknowledge the validity of the Old Testament alone. They are to be found principally in the context of Reimarus's discussion of the ways in which people who are not the direct recipients of a given revelation can seek to determine whether they ought to recognize it as genuine. Here he says a great deal concerning the criteria that *any* revelation ought to meet to be acknowledged by *anyone* to be of divine origin.

If everyone were to receive his own direct revelation, Reimarus observes, and therefore be completely certain of its truth, there would never be any need to develop such standards. These criteria are necessary, however, to know how to respond in the event that "only some members of a people receive a revelation directly, and they notify other men of what has been revealed to them . . ." Since on such occasions these "other men only receive this report from men," what they obtain is therefore "not a divine revelation, but a human testimony of a divine revelation." And this testimony is open to doubt. It must always be carefully and critically scrutinized. No one can give it credence without examining the character and the understanding of the witnesses who have provided it. The problem is further compounded "if the revelation took place only at a certain time and was subsequently transmitted" from generation to generation. "It loses more and more of its credibility in being passed from hand to hand, from mouth to mouth." Now it is not only the original recipients who must be proved trustworthy but all of the transmitters of the tradition as well.[68]

Reimarus has much more to say about how one judges, without blindly trusting others, whether "something is or is not a genuine revelation." To pass such a test, a book recounting the occurrence of a revelation must, at the very least, "contain no internal contradiction nor contradict any other clearly known truth." If it propounds even "a single untruth, which conflicts with clear experience, with history, with common sense, with irrefutable principles, or with the precepts of morality," one would have sufficient reason to reject its claim to divine authority. But even if it does not do so, it "is still not divine." To deserve to be recognized as such, it must also contain "prophecies and miracles."[69]

Needless to say, these prophecies and miracles must be demonstrably genuine. The prophecies must be shown, for instance, to have foretold the future in a clear and distinct manner. They must have been transcribed and disseminated prior to the predicted events and must be shown to have met a number of other criteria as well. With respect to the miracles, one must ask whether all of those who witnessed them indeed believed in their miraculous character. If so, were these observers "capable of distinguishing natural and artificial from supernatural effects?" Did the miracles in question constitute a truly purposeful display of God's power? "Whoever has read the history of other peoples knows that all of these investigations of prophetic utterances and miracles are necessary if one does not wish to be deceived."[70]

It is evidently quite difficult, as far as Reimarus is concerned, for a book to earn the right to be recognized as a divine revelation. To do so, it must survive a sustained and multifaceted examination, the kind of examination that by far the largest part of the human race is incapable of undertaking.[71] Most people who accept the validity of a given revelation do so, in fact, without sufficient justification. They simply adhere, out of filial piety, to the religion of their forefathers.[72]

In Reimarus's opinion, the Old Testament clearly cannot withstand this kind of examination. Only people who approach it imbued with loyalty to the faith of their forebears can believe it to contain divine revelations. One could not regard the ancient Israelites as reliable, authoritative witnesses of true prophecies and genuine miracles, even if they had unanimously acknowledged their validity (as they evidently did not). Moreover, most of the books of the Old Testament clearly betray the fact that they are not as old as they are generally believed to be nor were they written by the people usually considered to be their authors. Moses, in particular, can no longer be regarded as the author of the Bible's first five books. And, Reimarus asks rhetorically, "How did the other books come into the hands of the Jews? Who composed them? Who collected them? Who declared them to be canonical?" The fact that these and other questions cannot be answered satisfactorily further undercuts the authority of the Old Testament.[73]

As we noted earlier, Reimarus flatly rejects the possibility of the divine origin of any text that propounds even "a single untruth, which conflicts with clear experience, with history, with common sense, with irrefutable principles, or with the precepts of morality." In his unpublished *Apologie* he repeatedly seeks to demonstrate how the Old Testament fails all of these tests. Of the abundant material at his disposal, Lessing chose to include in the third fragment only Reimarus's review of one particular biblical episode, the passage of the Israelites through the Red Sea.

In a painstaking and, for that matter, rather tiresome retelling of the story of the Israelites' escape from Egypt, Reimarus endeavors to show the great variety of ways in which the details of this story conflict with what we otherwise know of reality. It will not be necessary, for our purposes, to enter into all the nuances of his lengthy treatment of this subject. What he attempts to show, basically, is the sheer impossibility of a huge horde of millions of

Israelites, together with all of their baggage as well as hundreds of thousands of oxen, cattle, and sheep, marching several miles across a muddy river bed, in the dead of night, in the course of a few hours. "Since anyone can readily perceive," he concludes, "that these miracles bear within themselves an internal contradiction and a true impossibility (*einen inneren Widerspruch und wahre Unmöglichkeit in sich halten*), they cannot really have taken place." They are, he believes, unmistakable and very crude fabrications, the work of a writer who neither witnessed the events he purported to describe nor possessed the ability to concoct a remotely plausible description of them.[74] The preposterous account of the exodus alone, it is clear, would suffice to vitiate, as far as Reimarus is concerned, the Old Testament's claim to constitute a divine revelation.

The fourth "Fragment of an Unnamed" is concerned not with an exposition of the details of the biblical narrative but with showing, in the words of its subtitle, "that the books of the Old Testament were not written in order to reveal a religion." What Reimarus actually means to say is, more precisely, that these books do not embody a "supernatural, salvific religion" (*eine übernatürliche seligmachende Religion*), but rather a "mean and base religion" (*eine schlechte und niederträchtige Religion*). A religion of the highest order would have to speak of the "reward and punishment for our actions in a future, eternal life, of the union of pious souls with God in ever greater glory and felicity." The Old Testament, according to Reimarus, does not mention any of these things. He seeks to demonstrate in great detail, through the exegesis of one biblical passage after another, that the five books of Moses, the books of the prophets, the books of Job, Psalms, and Proverbs all know only of earthly rewards and punishments for obedience or disobedience to the God of Israel. On occasion, he argues, they even go so far as to repudiate, in effect, the idea of immortality and to insist that men are on the contrary merely transitory beings.[75] Ancient Judaism therefore possesses "scarcely anything more than the appearance of a religion."[76] Due to the inadequate nature of their religion, Moses and the priests and prophets who succeeded him were unable to wean the Jews away from idolatry. Nor could they, without the promise of immortality, provide their people with sufficient motivation to live virtuously. In view, therefore, of the pressing need for a belief in posthumous reward and punishment, it is obvious that the writers of the Old Testament would have based their teachings upon such a belief, had they only known it to be true. From their failure to make reference to it, one can conclude only that they themselves were unacquainted with it. And from this it follows that their books cannot constitute the divine revelation of a salvific religion.[77]

Only at a rather late stage in their history, according to Reimarus, did the Jews finally acquire some understanding of these matters. It is clear, he argues, that they "knew nothing of the immortality of the soul prior to their captivity [in Babylonia] and their dispersion, nor could they have known anything from their writings, but rather they had cause, from these very writings, to believe the opposite." After having been scattered, however, among peoples who did believe in the immortality of the soul, the Jews began to do the same. "It is thus apparent that they learned this opinion from foreign nations and their philosophers, and adopted it all the more willingly to the extent that they became familiar with it in connection with a rational religion and the natural inclination of men . . ." Their readiness to accept it grew, too, as they learned to abandon any scruples about adding distinctive new ideas, which departed from the literal meaning of the biblical texts, to the teachings of the authors of Scripture.[78]

It was not, of course, all Jews who began at this time to uphold the idea of immortality but the Pharisees alone. This would have entitled them to claim credit for making Judaism into a real religion, Reimarus writes, had they not corrupted their faith with all sorts of foolish innovations which transformed it instead into a sanctimonious, hypocritical system of belief.[79] The Pharisees had two methods of uniting their new ideas with the biblical texts. On the one hand, they claimed that much of what Moses and the prophets originally taught had not been written down but had been transmitted orally, through the generations, to themselves. "On the other hand, they invented a kind of allegorical, mystical, symbolic, indeed kabbalistic interpretation of Scripture." This constituted an art of turning anything at all into anything at all, "of proving from Scripture whatever one wished."[80] Although these methods enabled the Pharisees to incorporate the idea of immortality, along with many other things, into Judaism, they were unable to induce the majority of their fellow Jews, in antiquity, to follow in their footsteps. The way in which a belief in immortality ultimately became the shared belief of all Jews is not a subject Reimarus has reason to discuss.

It would be difficult to discuss Lessing's reasons for seeing these and other excerpts from Reimarus's *Apologie* published without delving into a lengthy discussion of Lessing's own philosophy of religion, a discussion that would take us much too far afield. Because our aim in examining the *Fragmentenstreit* is only to complete our picture of the background against which Mendelssohn composed his defense of Judaism, it is not necessary, in any case, for us to probe too deeply into the underlying motives of any of the controversy's major protagonists. For our purposes, it will suffice to note that Lessing's publication and commentary upon the fragments of Reimarus were part of an effort, as Henry E. Allison has put it, "to find a standpoint in terms of which the positive significance of Christian thought may be appreciated without at the same time vitiating the truth in the deistic and Spinozistic critique of the traditional concept of revelation."[81] What we need to do here is to focus on only one aspect of this dual effort; that is, the way in which Lessing's own "counterassertions" and other observations in the course of the *Fragmentenstreit* echoed and reinforced the critical, Spinozist arguments he found in the work of Reimarus. It will not be necessary for us to elucidate what Lessing considered to be "the positive significance of Christian thought."

There are many matters on which Lessing is in accord with the "Fragmentist." He is prepared to acknowledge that Reimarus has all the facts right and has succeeded in showing that the biblical text is far from infallible.[82] He is even prepared to admit that his critique of the texts of the gospels (which we need not discuss here) is well-founded. He is also ready to acknowledge that Reimarus has shown that the Old Testament does not contain any doctrine of immortality.[83] Indeed, as Allison states, "he even goes a step further and points out that until the time of the captivity, the Hebrews, except for certain enlightened individuals, did not even possess the true concept of the unity of God. Rather than a Supreme Being and Lord of the universe, they merely worshipped Jehovah as a national deity."[84]

Lessing departs from Reimarus, however, in his evaluation of the significance of the imperfection of the biblical text and the deficient character of the religion of the Old Testament. Unlike Reimarus, he does not believe that the Bible must be shown to be flawless if the truth of the Christian religion is to be admitted. In his pithy and oft-quoted words, "The letter is not the spirit, and the Bible is not religion. Hence, objections to the letter and to the Bible are not likewise objections to the spirit and to religion."[85] Again, precisely what Lessing means by *spirit* and *religion* is not our concern here. It is enough for us to note that he accepts, at bottom, Reimarus's critique of the historical reliability of the biblical narrative, while expressing at the same time a *belief* in the truth of the religion it is designed to support.

Similarly, Lessing's acceptance of everything Reimarus has to say about the doctrinal weaknesses of the Old Testament and his identification of additional deficiencies do not prevent him from acknowledging that the biblical text is divinely inspired. He is able to do so on the basis of an innovative and highly influential understanding of biblical religion, one in which God "is viewed as the divine educator," who "orders his revelations in accordance with the developing intellectual capacities of the race."[86] The early Israelites, according to Lessing, had only very limited intellectual capacities, and therefore received revelations of a rather simple kind. They acquired only a rudimentary concept of God and received a moral education suitable for the very young. "They knew of no immortality of the soul; they yearned after no life to come. But now to reveal these things, when their reason was so little prepared for them, what would it have been but the same fault in the divine rule as is committed by the vain schoolmaster who chooses to hurry his pupil too rapidly and boast of his progress, rather than thoroughly to ground him?"[87]

Eventually, however, the Jews matured. From the Greeks and the Persians they learned the more sophisticated principles of genuine monotheism. They then proceeded to read these higher religious conceptions back into their original Scriptures, which proved quite susceptible to being understood in this new light.[88] Like many of the other thinkers we have examined in this chapter, including Reimarus, Lessing also maintained that it was from the Greeks and the Persians that some of the Jews first learned of the immortality of the soul. Here, too, he says, they made an attempt to read new insights back into the Hebrew Scriptures. In this case, however, as Lessing explains in some detail, a rather formidable problem arose. The Old Testament did not really lend itself to reinterpretation in this direction. It did indeed include one or another verse that could be considered to supply a hint (*Anspielung*) or an allusion (*Fingerzeig*) indicating the immortality of the soul. But these verses "naturally" could not serve as the basis for the entire people's belief in a hitherto unknown principle. Immortality thus became and remained the belief only of a certain sect, the Pharisees.[89]

In Lessing's overall scheme of things, this is a highly significant development. It marks the moment at which the Jews finally outgrew the Old Testament. It had been, up until then, an excellent primer, perfectly suited to the needs of a childish people. But now, if they were all to be given an opportunity to rise to a higher stage of religious understanding, the Jews required something else.

"A better instructor must come and tear the exhausted primer from the child's hand—Christ came." The superiority of Christ's teaching lay in the fact that he was "the first *reliable, practical* teacher of the immortality of the soul." His arrival, according to Lessing, rendered Judaism completely obsolete.[90]

Direct Challenges

Mendelssohn's first open adversary, the Swiss theologian Johann Caspar Lavater, was a man quite remote in his thinking from the figures whose ideas we have just reviewed. As far as Lavater was concerned, what Mendelssohn was obliged to explain was not his acceptance of the Old Testament but his refusal to acknowledge that the New Testament had superceded it. In 1769 he provided a German translation of what he regarded as Charles Bonnet's incontrovertible proofs of the truth of Christianity, which had originally appeared in his treatise *La Palingenesie philosophique ou Idees sur l'etat passe et sur l'etat futur des etres vivans*. In a dedicatory epistle Lavater challenged Mendelssohn either to refute Bonnet's arguments publicly or, if he found them to be correct, "to do what prudence, love and truth, and honesty bid you do;—what *Socrates* would have done, had he read this treatise and found it irrefutable"; that is, presumably, to convert to Christianity. Mendelssohn met this challenge and in his correspondence with Lavater and Bonnet as well as in his unpublished *Counterreflections on Bonnet's Palingenesie* outlined for the first time a general theory concerning the nature of Judaism.[91]

More than a decade after the Lavater controversy, Mendelssohn once again found himself compelled to present a public justification of his adherence to Judaism. Responding to what Mendelssohn had said in favor of religious freedom in the Preface to his German edition of Manasseh ben Israel's *Vindiciae Judaeorum*, August Friedrich Cranz composed and anonymously published a pamphlet entitled *The Searching After Light and Right*.[92] According to Cranz, Mendelssohn's arguments for liberty of conscience could indeed be considered to be true and reasonable, but they are not compatible with the religion of the Old Testament. They "directly contradict the faith" of Mendelssohn's fathers.[93]

Cranz agrees with Mendelssohn's statement that worship without conviction, especially if coerced, is meaningless, and therefore something that God could never desire. "Yet," he continues, "it is true that Moses connects coercion and positive punishment with the non-observance of duties related to the worship of God. His statutory ecclesiastical law decrees the punishment of stoning and death for the sabbath-breaker, the blasphemer of the divine name, and others who depart from his laws."[94] If Judaism clearly teaches such things, *The Searching* concludes, it is irreconcilable with Mendelssohn's rational principles. How, then, can he continue to adhere to such a faith?

Up to this point we have been restating Cranz's position as Mendelssohn summarized it at the beginning of Section II of *Jerusalem*. To grasp fully the nature of the challenge he posed, however, it is necessary to examine an additional aspect of *The Searching After Light and Right*, one that Mendelssohn himself neglects to discuss. While pointing to the contradiction between Mendelssohn's liberalism and biblical theocracy, Cranz had acknowledged that the regime depicted in the Bible no longer existed. Theocratic rule, he admitted, "could be carried into practice only so long as the Jews had an empire of their own. . . . But it had to cease, as did the sacrifices, when the Jews lost territory and power, and, dependent on foreign laws, found their jurisdiction circumscribed by very narrow limits." But this, Cranz insisted, was not of any fundamental importance. This

> circumscription is merely the consequence of external and altered political relations, whereby the value of laws and rights that have been laid to rest cannot be diminished. The ecclesiastical law is still there, even if it must no longer be put into practice. Your lawgiver, Moses, is still the drover, with the cudgel, who leads his people with a rod of iron, and would be sharp after anyone who had the least opinion of his own, and dared to express it by word or deed.[95]

In this passage, Cranz sharpens his already harsh characterization of Mosaic law. Not only, he maintains, does it stipulate the punishment of religious wrongdoing, but it also outlaws the free expression of any divergent religious opinions. His principal intention here, however, is to warn Mendelssohn that it will do no good to respond to his challenge by asserting that the conflict between his rational principles and Judaism existed only in the remote past. If such a conflict has in reality been overcome, that is merely the result of accidentally altered circumstances. The contradiction *in principle* between the original aims of Judaism and "purified concepts" would still remain. How, Cranz asks, can a religion "that purports to be founded on divine revelation" be so much at odds with what is reasonable?[96]

In the end, Cranz concluded that the views Mendelssohn had expressed in the Preface marked a definite step away from Judaism. He suggested that Mendelssohn was actually drawing closer to Christianity, because he had apparently torn himself loose from "the servitude of iron churchly bonds" and, "commenced teaching the liberal system of a more rational worship of God, which constitutes the true character of the Christian religion . . ."[97] Another writer, who appended his reflections to *The Searching*, came to a somewhat different conclusion. Mr. Mörschel, a virtually unknown military chaplain, deduced from Mendelssohn's argument that toleration ought to be extended to naturalists that he himself was in reality nothing more than a naturalist and no longer a believing Jew.[98] In *Jerusalem*, as we shall see, Mendelssohn identifies Cranz as by far the more important of these two adversaries, and seeks to respond to him. In the same work, he seeks to answer Mörschel as well.

Conclusion

If the fundamental teachings of Leibniz and Wolff were, on the whole, entirely compatible with faith in Judaism, the same evidently cannot be said with regard to the thought of Spinoza and the later figures who were, to varying degrees, his disciples. Their formidable attacks on the authenticity and contents of biblical revelation placed immense difficulties in the path of a Jewish rationalist, like Mendelssohn, who might wish to defend the truth of his religion against all reasonable opponents. Trenchantly and vigorously, they called into question the very basis of Judaism, its claim to be founded on direct communication between God and man. They demoted the Israelite recipients of revelation from the status of unimpeachable witnesses to that of a superstitious and primitive people, on whose testimony it would not be reasonable to rely. They raised doubts concerning the transmission of the extant biblical narratives. They exposed the Old Testament as a repository of insufficiently developed religious ideas, a set of books in which some of the fundamental truths of natural religion appeared either in inadequate form or not at all. They argued that the Mosaic law was purely political and no longer posssessed any religious value. And, finally, they sought to demonstrate the inferiority of the Old Testament's moral teachings and the depravity of its heroes.

In comparison to the destructive implications of this wide-ranging attack on the foundations of Judaism, the problems posed by a figure like Lavater were relatively minor ones. Lavater understood well enough, and was fully in accord with, Mendelssohn's belief in the revealed character of the Old Testament. He wanted him only to acknowledge that it had been superceded by a subsequent revelation, one of no less indubitable historicity. To answer Lavater, therefore, Mendelssohn did not really have to account for what he *did* believe, but only to explain why he did not believe something else as well.

Despite appearances, the author of *The Searching After Light and Right* was not really trying to persuade Mendelssohn to acknowledge the truth of Christianity. The main thrust of his argument was to underline the contradiction between Mendelssohn's unimpeachable rational principles and his acceptance of the revealed character of the Old Testament. The Searcher's evident, though unexpressed, skepticism with regard to the truth of biblical revelation makes it possible for us to identify him, in the end, as a critic who had more in common with "the Spinozists" than with Lavater.[99] The same seems to be true of Mörschel as well.

Mendelssohn replied directly to the challenges and objections raised by Lavater, Cranz, and Mörschel. He authored no such response, however, to Spinoza's *Theologico-Political Treatise* nor to any of the other critiques of biblical revelation discussed previously. Nevertheless, it will be our contention here that he was, in formulating his defense of Judaism, and especially in *Jerusalem*, equally concerned with dealing with what we have identified as the "Spinozist" critique of revealed religion and with responding to his own outspoken opponents.

Notes

1. Leibniz, *Theodicy*, Preface; on Wolff, see Thomas P. Saine, *Von der Kopernikanischen bis zur Französishen Revolution, Die Auseinandersetzung der deutschen Frühaufklärung mit der neuen Zeit*, pp. 145ff.

2. See Stuart A. Cohen, *The Three Crowns: Structures of Communal Politics in Early Rabbinic Jewry* (Cambridge: Cambridge University Press, 1990), pp. 7–12.

3. Fritz Bamberger, "Mendelssohn's Concept of Judaism," in Alfred Jospe, ed., *Studies in Jewish Thought* (Detroit: Wayne State University Press, 1981), p. 346.

4. Leo Strauss, *Persecution and the Art of Writing* (Glencoe, Ill.: The Free Press, 1952), p. 142.

5. Paul Hazard, *The European Mind (1680–1715)*, trans. J. Lewis May (New York: New American Library, 1963), p. 147.

6. See Norman L. Torrey, *Voltaire and the English Deists* (New Haven, Conn.: Yale University Press, 1963).

7. See earlier, pp. 26–27.

8. Beiser, *The Fate of Reason*, p. 57; see also Allison, *Lessing and the Enlightenment*, p. 47.

9. See Saine, *Von der Kopernikanischen bis zur Französishen Revolution*, p. 219; Feiereis, *Die Umprägung der Natürlichen Theologie in Religionsphilosophie*, pp. 83–84.

10. Beiser, *The Fate of Reason*, p. 57.

11. Ibid., p. 56.

12. See Altmann's comments in his introduction to *Jerusalem*, pp. 16ff.

13. Quoted in Altmann, *Moses Mendelssohn*, p. 255.

14. See Beiser, *The Fate of Reason*, pp. 57–59; Allison, *Lessing and the Enlightenment*, pp. 95ff.

15. Beiser, *The Fate of Reason*, p. 52.

16. See Julius Guttman, "Mendelssohn's *Jerusalem* and Spinoza's *Theologico-Political Treatise*," in Alfred Jospe, ed., *Studies in Jewish Thought* (Detroit: Wayne State University Press, 1981), pp. 361–87; Eliezer Schweid, *Toldot he-Hagut HaYehudit be-Et haHadashah* (Jerusalem: Hakibbutz Hameuchad and Keter, 1977), pp. 129ff.

17. Strauss, *Persecution and the Art of Writing*, p. 193.

18. Ibid., p. 194.

19. Spinoza, *Theologico-Political Treatise*, pp. 33–34.

20. Ibid., p. 35.

21. Ibid., p. 36.

22. Ibid., p. 38.

23. Ibid., p. 30.

24. Ibid., p. 40.

25. Ibid., p. 92.

26. Ibid., p. 93.

27. Ibid., p. 17.

28. Ibid., p. 124.

29. Ibid., p. 129.

30. Ibid., p. 135.

31. Ibid., p. 139.

32. Ibid., pp. 173–74.

33. Guttman, "Mendelssohn's *Jerusalem* and Spinoza's *Theologico-Political Treatise*," p. 364.

34. Spinoza, *Theologico-Political Treatise*, pp. 188–89.

35. Ibid., p. 176.

36. Ibid., p. 177.

37. Ibid., pp. 186–87.

38. Cf. later, Chapter 7.

39. Spinoza, *Theologico-Political Treatise*, p. 364.

40. Ibid., pp. 75–76.

41. Ibid., pp. 364–65.

42. Ibid., pp. 47–48.

43. Ibid., p. 270.

44. Ibid., pp. 59–60.

45. Spinoza, *Theologico-Political Treatise*, p. 80. See *The Code of Maimonides*, Book Fourteen, trans. Abraham. M. Hershman (New Haven, Conn.: Yale University Press, 1949), p. 230.

46. Spinoza, *Theologico-Political Treatise*, p. 220.

47. Hillel Fradkin, "The 'Separation' of Religion and Politics: The Paradoxes of Spinoza," *The Review of Politics* (Fall 1988): 605.

48. Spinoza, *Theologico-Political Treatise*, pp. 72, 247–48.

49. There is a useful survey of scholarly opinion on this subject in Chapter 7 ("The Elusiveness of Deism") of Robert E. Sullivan's *John Toland and the Deist Controversy* (Cambridge, Mass. and London: Harvard University Press, 1981), pp. 205ff.

50. Ibid., p. 215.

51. Ibid., p. 207.

52. David Berman, "Deism, Immortality, and the Art of Theological Lying," in *Deism, Masonry, and the Enlightenment, Essays Honoring Alfred Owen Aldridge*, ed. J. A. Leo Lemay (Newark, N.J.: Associated University Presses, 1987), p. 62.

53. Ibid., p. 77.

54. See Paul Hazard, *The European Mind* (1680–1715), trans. J. Lewis May (New York: New American Libaray, 1963) p. 139ff.

55. Henning Graf Reventlow, *The Authority of the Bible and the Rise of the Modern World*, trans. John Bowden, (Philadelphia: Fortress Press, 1984), pp. 354–410. See also Torrey, *Voltaire and the English Deists*, pp. 117–22.

56. Quoted in Reventlow, *The Authority of the Bible and the Rise of the Modern World*, p. 397.

57. Ibid., p. 401.

58. Altmann, *Moses Mendelssohn*, pp. 109–12.

59. Reventlow, *The Authority of the Bible and the Rise of the Modern World*, pp. 313f.

60. Ibid., pp. 374f.

61. Ibid., p. 400.

62. See above all, Hanna Emmrich, *Das Judentum bei Voltaire*, (Berlin, 1930). See also my article, "Voltaire on Judaism and Christianity," *AJS Review*. vol. XVIII, no. 2, 1993 pp. 223–43.

63. On Mendelssohn's relationship with Hennings, see Altmann, *Moses Mendelssohn*, especially pp. 329–45. Altmann underscores the significance of Voltaire's influence on Hennings.

64. *JubA*, vol. 13, pp. 36–37.

65. Ibid., p. 38.

66. See Hermann Samuel Reimarus, *Apologie oder Schutzschrift für die Vernünftigen Verehrer Gottes* (Hamburg: Insel Verlag, 1972), pp. 220–679, for innumerable examples.

67. See Albert Schweitzer, *The Quest of the Historical Jesus*, (New York: Macmillan, 1948), pp. 13–26.

68. *G. E. Lessings Werke*, ed. Leopold Zscharnack (New York: Hildsheim, 1970), vol. 18, p. 68.

69. Ibid., p. 106.

70. Ibid., p. 107.

71. Ibid., p. 108.

72. Ibid., p. 110.

73. Ibid., pp. 101–2.

74. Ibid., p. 120.

75. Ibid., p. 129.

76. Ibid., p. 121.

77. Ibid., p. 129.

78. Ibid., p. 148.

79. Ibid., p. 149.

80. Ibid., p. 150.

81. Allison, *Lessing and the Enlightenment*, p. 83.

82. *Lessings Werke*, vol. 18, pp. 196ff.

83. Ibid., p. 199.

84. Allison, *Lessing and the Enlightenment*, p. 98.

85. *Lessings Werke*, vol. 18, pp. 186–87, translated in Allison, ibid., p. 95.

86. Allison, ibid., p. 151.

87. Gotthold Ephraim Lessing, *Nathan the Wise, Minna von Barnhelm and Other Plays and Writings*, ed. Peter Denetz (New York: Continuum, 1991), p. 321.

88. Ibid., p. 321.

89. Ibid., pp. 326–27.

90. Ibid., pp. 328–29.

91. See Altmann, *Moses Mendelssohn*, pp. 201ff.

92. Jacob Katz succeeded in identifying Cranz as the author of *The Search*, see "To Whom Was Mendelssohn Replying in his *Jerusalem*," *Zion* 36, nos. 1–2 (1971): 116f [Hebrew].

93. *Jerusalem*. p. 84.

94. Ibid., p. 85.

95. Paul Mendes-Flohr and Jehuda Reinharz, *The Jew in the Modern World* (Oxford and New York: Oxford University Press, 1980), p. 82.

96. *Jerusalem*, p. 85.

97. Ibid., p. 86.

98. Concerning Mörschel, see Altmann, *Moses Mendelssohn*, pp. 510–11.

99. He was asking him, in the words of Ze'ev Levy, "to abandon Judaism and to convert to Christianity not to reinforce the latter creed but to strengthen the folowers of Deism." See Ze'ev Levy, "Johann Georg Hamann's Concept of Judaism and Controversy with Mendelssohn's 'Jerusalem'," *Leo Baeck Institute Year Book* 29 (1984): 297.

6
Mendelssohn's Defense of Judaism

As we noted in the Introduction, Mendelssohn resolved to expound his concept of the Jewish religion only when his adversaries virtually forced him to do so. He was not an eager defender of his faith but a reluctant apologist. His principal goal was not to elucidate all aspects of Judaism but to extricate himself from further controversy.

Mendelssohn's response to the various critics of Judaism was not all of a piece. To some extent, he answered them directly and forthrightly, confronting their hostile ideas regarding Judaism with an authoritative and attractive picture of a religion very different from the one they had imagined. To some extent, however, Mendelssohn found himself unable to develop a satisfactory response to the contentions of his adversaries. They had the more powerful arguments. Rather than admit this, he resorted, on occasion, to some less than straightforward rhetorical strategies, all designed to make his own position seem more cogent than it actually was.

In this chapter we will analyze Mendelssohn's concept of Judaism, paying careful attention to the ways in which it deals—or fails to deal—with the attacks of both the Spinozist critics of his day and the individual critics who attacked him directly, Lavater, Cranz, and Mörschel. We shall begin with an examination of Mendelssohn's account of revelation. After that we will turn to his treatment of the doctrinal content of the Jewish religion, his response to the various attacks on Judaism as an immoral religion, his discussion of Jewish law, and, finally, his way of dealing with the charge that his advocacy of liberty of conscience was manifestly incompatible with his adherence to Judaism.

Revelation

Mendelssohn had little to say about the nature of revelation in general. He devoted considerably greater attention to the question of how a given revelation could be determined to be genuine by those who were not present when it was supposed to have been received. Nowhere in his writings, it is true, did he discuss this question in a thorough, comprehensive fashion. He never set forth what he considered to be all the criteria by which an authentic revelation could be distinguished from one whose truth was insufficiently proven. But he did attempt, on two different occasions, to demonstrate the authenticity of the reports of the Sinaitic revelation. He dealt with this question first in the course of the Lavater controversy and then, in a rather different fashion, in *Jerusalem*.

It was not to the writings of Wolff or any other Gentile thinker that Mendelssohn turned, when searching for criteria warranting the acceptance of Judaism's basic revelation, but to Jewish sources. In Alexander Altmann's words, he "based his acceptance of revelation on the facticity of the event as witnessed by the entire nation," thereby abiding by "the well-known medieval type of historical argumentation."[1] It will consequently be our main task here—after we briefly examine Mendelssohn's overall view of revelation—to examine certain key dimensions of this medieval argumentation, to identify those aspects of it adopted by Mendelssohn in his successive discussions of the Sinaitic revelation, and to consider the extent to which he employed these medieval arguments to refute the Spinozistic position outlined in the previous chapter.

The Miracle of Revelation

One of the major concerns of the medieval Jewish philosophers had been to elucidate the nature of divine revelation. By what means, they asked, did God communicate to Moses, to the other prophets, to ordinary people? To the extensive reflections of Maimonides and others on these and related questions Mendelssohn did not take recourse. Nor does he appear, at first glance, to have taken a different, readily available route and to have followed Wolff in treating revelation as being essentially a miraculous event. On the contrary, he took pains to distinguish between miracles, which have no probative value, and the Sinaitic revelation, a unique—and uniquely authoritative—manifestation of the divine. On closer inspection, however, it becomes clear that Mendelssohn does indeed see things more or less the way Wolff does, even if he expresses his views on this matter in a somewhat understated fashion.

In a letter to Charles Bonnet, the Genevan scientist and philosopher whose work, as we have already noted, had so greatly inspired Johann Caspar Lavater, Mendelssohn strove to underline the difference between miracles and revelation, or rather, between miracles and the revelation that was of greatest significance to Judaism, the one that had taken place at Mt. Sinai.[2] The problem with miracles, he wrote to Bonnet, is that they can be deceptive. But,

> The mission of Moses is another matter. It is based not only on miracles, for, I repeat, miracles are deceptive and are admitted to be so by Moses himself. Rather, it rests on much more secure ground. The whole nation itself, to which this mission was directed, saw the great divine manifestation with their own eyes and heard with their own ears how God made Moses his emissary and spokesman. The Israelites were therefore all together eye- and ear-witnesses of the divine calling of this prophet, and they required neither further testimony nor further proof.[3]

In this letter, Mendelssohn is clearly seeking to demonstrate the superiority of the evidence for the historicity of the Sinaitic revelation. We will consider this aspect of his argument more closely in the next section. For the moment, however, our chief concern is with what he has to say here about the nature of the revelation-event itself. It is, he implies, somehow different from a miracle, more indubitably evident to the senses. But in what does it consist? What is it the Israelites saw and heard with their own eyes and ears? It was surely not God himself, who is, according to Mendelssohn, utterly incorporeal. But if they did not see and hear that which cannot be seen and heard and if they did not experience anything that partook of the miraculous, what could they have witnessed other than events that were entirely natural? If so, how could "the great divine manifestation" at Sinai have supplied "much more secure ground" than that provided by miracles for believing in the truth of Moses's mission?

Ultimately, Mendelssohn dealt with this difficulty by acknowledging, not in his letter to Bonnet but in *Jerusalem*, that the voice heard at Sinai was in fact "a miraculous voice."[4] Precisely what he meant by this is, as Altmann has observed, something that he never explained.[5] At the very least, however, the statement in *Jerusalem* served to undercut the distinction he had earlier sought to maintain between miracles and the events at Sinai. This is still clearer elsewhere in *Jerusalem*, where Mendelssohn refers to the laws revealed to the Israelites through "Moses in a miraculous and supernatural manner."[6]

The Medieval Argument

For the medieval Jewish philosophers, the truthfulness of the biblical narrative was a self-evident assumption. They sought, nevertheless, to *demonstrate* that the Bible accurately documented God's revelation to the ancient Israelites. The best-known arguments on behalf of the Bible's veracity and those that had the greatest influence on Mendelssohn's treatment of this question are those developed by Saadia Gaon, Yehudah Halevi, and Maimonides.

In the introduction to *The Book of Beliefs and Opinions,* Saadia identifies three basic sources of knowledge: "The first onsists of the knowledge gained by [direct] observation. The second is composed of the intuition of the intellect. The third consists of that knowledge which is inferred by logical necessity."[7] In addition to these three sources, the "community of monotheists" possesses another: "authentic tradition." The community accepts this source "by reason of the fact that it is based on the knowledge of the senses as well as that of reason, as we shall explain in the third treatise of this book."[8]

The explanation Saadia provides in the third treatise is a brief one. Jewish tradition is based on knowledge of the senses inasmuch as it rests on the direct observations made not by ourselves but by our early ancestors. But how do we know that their senses did not lie to them? Reason teaches that, "It is only the individual who is subject to and fooled by false impression or deliberate deception. In the case of a large community of men, however, it is not likely that all its constituents should have been subject to the same wrong impressions." Yet, as Saadia acknowledges, a report can also be subject to deliberate misrepresentation. How do we, who were not eyewitnesses of the events reported in the Bible, know that no such misrepresentation has taken place? "Had there been a deliberate conspiracy to create a fictitious tradition, that fact could not have remained a secret to the masses, but wherever the tradition had been published, the report of the conspiracy would have been published along with it."

It is unlikely, according to Saadia, that all the members of a large community of men could have been deceived by the same wrong impressions, so unlikely, it seems, as to be virtually impossible. What is clearly impossible is that a spurious tradition could gain the credence of later generations. A false tradition must either fail to take root at all or, if it does gain credence, it will be shadowed by a report of the conspiracy to distort the truth. If, then, a tradition stems from a large community of men and it remains uncontradicted, "there is no third means of invalidating it." And, "if the traditions transmitted to us by our ancestors are viewed in the light of these [three] principles, they will be found to be proof against these arguments, correct and unshakable."[9]

This, then, is Saadia's argument in defense of the veracity of the Torah and, therewith, of the historicity of the Sinaitic revelation. It is based on the fact that the multitude of ancient Israelites witnessed extraordinary events. But it is not their witnessing of the events described in the Torah that directly certifies their historicity; it is, rather, their witnessing of those events that guarantees that the Torah's description of them is faithful to the facts. It would have been impossible, according to Saadia, to foist the Torah on them and their descendants if its account were not true. At the very least, a conflicting account would have survived alongside the Torah, throwing its narrative into doubt. Because no such anti-Torah exists, the truth of the Torah is unquestionable.

Yehudah Halevi's argument is, to a certain extent, based on Saadia's, but it also contains new elements. In Halevi's *Kuzari*, the rabbi tells the King of the Khazars the story of the Israelites' deliverance from Egypt. "This is," observes the king, "in truth, divine power, and the commandments connected with it must be accepted. No one could imagine for a moment that this was the result of necromancy, calculation or phantasy."[10] When the rabbi describes to the king the way in which God fed the Israelites in the desert the king responds that "this also is irrefutable, viz. a thing which occurred to 600,000 people for forty years."[11] Yet, the rabbi continues, even after these miracles the people retained, "some doubt as to whether God really spoke to mortals." To remove this doubt God arranged for them "to hear publicly the words of God," at Sinai. "Before such an impressive scene," says the rabbi, "all ideals of jugglery vanished."[12]

At Sinai the Israelites abandoned all suspicion that they were being deceived. But were they correct in doing so? Perhaps "jugglery" was somehow involved in what they had witnessed. The king of the Khazars clearly does not suspect that it was, and the rabbi therefore has no cause to argue that it was not. The king likewise shares the rabbi's faith in the authenticity of the documents containing the Jewish tradition. Even before he had met the rabbi, he had learned from the Christian scholastic that the Torah and the records of the children of Israel "are undisputed, because they are generally known as lasting, and have been revealed before a vast multitude."[13] The Moslem doctor had corroborated this.[14] As a result, the king had been convinced that the Jews "constitute in themselves the evidence for the divine law on earth," and he therefore required of the rabbi no additional evidence of the authenticity of the Jewish tradition.[15]

Like Saadia, Halevi bases his argument on the fact that the Israelite multitude witnessed extraordinary things. His king and rabbi do not specifically repeat Saadia's claim that a large community of men cannot fall victim to false impressions, but they do seem tacitly to accept it. They both dismiss the possibility that the people's senses were deceiving them. Unlike Saadia, however, Halevi places special emphasis on the people's experience at Sinai itself. He does not, to be sure, say that the revelation at Sinai was necessary to persuade the people that God was redeeming them and that Moses was his emissary. They already knew that. Their experience at Sinai was necessary only to convince them that God could indeed communicate verbally with man.

For Halevi, as for Saadia, the historicity of the Sinaitic revelation ultimately depends not on the accuracy of the ancient Israelites' senses of sight and hearing but on the authority of the text reporting their experiences. Unlike Saadia, however, he makes no circumstantial argument for the Torah's veracity. Instead, he allows non-Jewish figures, representatives of Christianity and Islam, to make his case for him. They do not make Saadia's argument either; they refer only to the Torah's durability, its having been revealed before a multitude, and its fame. However, in having such spokesmen uphold the truth of the Torah, Halevi is, in effect, making an additional, implicit argument in its defense. Unlike the sacred books of the other religions, the Torah is acknowledged to be true by a general consensus of the most important sectors of humankind.

Unlike Saadia and Yehudah Halevi, Maimonides omitted arguments for the historicity of revelation from his main philosophical work, the *Guide of the Perplexed*. However, in his massive legal compendium, the *Mishneh Torah*, he made an observation that was to have a great influence on Mendelssohn's treatment of that subject.

Moses our master was not trusted by Israel solely because of the signs which he did, for whoever believes on account of signs retains a doubt in his heart that perhaps they were performed by magic and witchcraft. . . . Why was he trusted? Because on Mount Sinai they saw with their own eyes and heard through their own ears—not through a stranger's ears—the fire and the thunder and lightning as he approached the cloud and they heard the voice saying "Moses, Moses, go and tell them such and such things." [16]

Here Maimonides attributes an even greater effect to the events at Sinai than had Halevi. The revelation was necessary to convince the Israelites not only that God spoke to man but even to convince them that Moses was truly a divine emissary. For that purpose it was unquestionably sufficient.

These, then, are the elements of the medieval argumentation in favor of the historicity of revelation that are of importance for an understanding of what Mendelssohn has to say with regard to this overall question. Needless to say, the medieval Jewish philosophers did not deal with the kinds of doubts expressed by Spinoza and his followers. Given the nature of the problems these modern thinkers posed for Mendelssohn, the arguments of Saadia, Halevi, and Maimonides would seem to be rather unpromising material out of which to construct a case in favor of the truth of revelation. Nevertheless, everything Mendelssohn has to say on this subject is drawn from these sources.

Mendelssohn's Adaptation of the Medieval Argument

In the course of his dealings with Lavater and Bonnet Mendelssohn elaborated his first defense of the historicity of revelation, and in the course of responding to Cranz and Mörschel, in *Jerusalem*, he next addressed this question in a comprehensive manner. On both occasions he appears to have formulated his arguments with his opponents in mind, even those arguments he chose, ultimately, to refrain from seeing published. In his dispute with Lavater and Bonnet, he defended the greater credibility of the Old Testament revelation in terms calculated to appeal to people who already acknowledged its truth. In *Jerusalem*, he made an argument that seems, at first glance, to have been designed to appeal even to those utterly lacking in faith.

Initially, Mendelssohn, like Saadia, Halevi, and Maimonides, placed considerable emphasis on the fact that the revelation at Sinai occurred in the presence of a vast multitude. "The whole nation," he noted in a letter to Bonnet, "saw the great divine manifestation with their own eyes and heard with their own ears how God made Moses his emissary and spokesman."[17] The unique circumstances under which this revelation took place, it seems, differentiated it from miracles that had occurred in less public settings and ruled out the need for any further evidence of its divine origin. But why is this the case? Mendelssohn does not assert, as did Saadia, that a large community of men is nearly immune to false impressions, but he seems tacitly to have relied on such an assumption.

For Mendelssohn, however, as for the medievals, it is not the testimony of the ancient Israelites that directly certifies the historicity of the events they witnessed. Everything depends not on 600,000 separate reports but on the authority of one book, the Torah. What evidence does he present that the Torah's account is accurate? Neither in his *Counterreflections on Bonnet's Palingenesis* nor in his letter to Bonnet does Mendelssohn address this question directly. He does not repeat Saadia's argument that the eyewitnesses to the events narrated in the Torah would have thwarted any conspiracy to describe them in an untruthful manner, either by preventing it from gaining credence or by circulating a contradictory account. One can, to be sure, hear an echo of Saadia's argument in Mendelssohn's observation that the Torah's account of events is not contradicted by "a known testimony of any validity."[18] But his main contention in the *Counterreflections* is one derived not from Saadia but from Yehudah Halevi.

In the *Kuzari*, we recall, Yehudah Halevi made an implicit argument in defense of the authority of the Pentateuch by demonstrating the universality of the consensus with regard to its accuracy. In the *Counterreflections*, Mendelssohn makes a similar argument. After pointing to the general absence of consensus with regard to the occurrence of the miracles on which other faiths are based, he notes that there is no such disagreement with regard to the historicity of the revelation which lies at the basis of Judaism. "But however much the testimonies contradict each other, they agree that a certain Moses received directly from God the task of freeing a certain people from slavery . . . [and] that the lawgiver of nature appeared publicly in all his majesty before this entire people, assembled in one place, and gave them laws." This agreement can exist only because the sacred text reporting these events is accepted by Jews, Christians, and Muslims alike. In view, then, of the multitude of witnesses of the original events, and in the light of the universal acceptance of the reports concerning them, Mendelssohn is able to conclude that, "Here, therefore, I have a matter of history to which I can hold fast. This can be my point of departure." Anything that contradicts this fact is by definition false.[19]

At first glance, what Mendelssohn says in *Jerusalem* appears to be simply a more complete version of his earlier argument. While in the *Counterreflections* he had characterized the revelation at Sinai as an historical fact, in *Jerusalem* he provides a more detailed explanation of the nature of historical truths and then proceeds to apply the general principles adduced in that explanation to the revelation at Sinai. He appears to be attempting to demonstrate once again the historicity of that revelation, this time, however, without making any reference to the existing consensus among Jews, Christians, and Muslims regarding its historicity. In fact, his argument, when examined carefully, proves to be highly problematic.

Mendelssohn, as is well-known, distinguishes in Section II of *Jerusalem* between two kinds of truths: eternal truths and historical truths. The latter are not accessible to unassisted human reason but "can only be perceived, by means of the senses, by those who were present at the time and place of their occurrence in nature." Everyone who is not an eyewitness of the event in question must accept it on the basis of the testimony of others who actually observed it.

> Furthermore, those who live at another time must rely altogether on the credibility of the testimony, for the thing attested no longer exists. . . . In historical matters, the authority and credibility of the narrator constitute the only evidence. Without testimony, we cannot be convinced of any historical truth. Without authority, the truth of history vanishes along with the event itself.

Thus, we obtain historical truths only when we have in our hands the testimony of narrators whose credibility is unimpeachable. Fortunately, when God deems it necessary that we possess a truth of this kind, his wisdom "confirms its historical certainty and places the narrator's credibility beyond all doubt."[20] If necessary, this is done by means of miracles.

This brief discussion of historical truths in general is intended to serve as a preface to the treatment of a particular historical occurrence, the revelation at Sinai. After dealing with some other matters, Mendelssohn briefly describes that event. He relates how the people, properly prepared, approach Mount Sinai, where the miraculous voice declares: "I am the Eternal, your God, who brought you out of the land of Mizrayim, who delivered you from bondage,etc." This, Mendelssohn states, is a historical truth. He then continues to paraphrase the message delivered at Sinai:

> I am the Eternal, your God, who made a covenant with your forefathers, Abraham, Isaac, and Jacob, and swore to make of their seed a nation of my own. The time for the fulfillment of this promise has finally come. To this end, I redeemed you from Egyptian slavery with unheard-of miracles and signs. I am your Redeemer, your Sovereign and King; I also make a covenant with you, and give you laws by which you are to live and become a happy nation in the land that I shall give to you.

"All these," Mendelssohn concludes, "are historical truths which, by their very nature, rest on historical evidence, *must* be verified by authority, and *can* be confirmed by miracles."[21]

This is a difficult passage to unravel. According to Altmann, "What Mendelssohn probably meant to convey was that the miracles accompanying the exodus and the heavenly voice at Sinai served to invest the series of events that led up to the giving of the Law with a more than ordinary significance, endowing them with the aura of the divine."[22] We cannot, however, accept Altmann's hypothesis without subjecting this passage to a rigorously literal interpretation. It is necessary to consider precisely what Mendelssohn says here in the light of his earlier remarks about historical truths. To what truths is he referring? Who narrates them? What confirms his credibility?

To answer these questions we must first consider the recipients of the revelation, paying particular attention to the state of their knowledge in the period prior to its occurrence. Before the revelation, it is clear, none of the people present at Sinai knew from direct observation that God had made a covenant with their forefathers. All of them did know that they had been rescued from Egypt in an unheard-of fashion, but they did not *know* that God was responsible for their deliverance. The miracles they had hitherto witnessed, as Mendelssohn often reiterated, had proved nothing. And last, the people did not yet know why they had been assembled at the mountain. Now, however, God deemed it necessary that the people know all of these things. Accordingly, he conveyed three kinds of historical truths to them: those concerning the remote past, those concerning the recent past and those concerning the present moment. In the remote past God had made a covenant with their ancestors. Recently, he had delivered them from Egyptian bondage; and presently, he was giving them a law. Of the truth of all these things the people acquire sure knowledge because they are reported to them by a narrator whose credibility is absolutely beyond doubt—God.

With this, Mendelssohn has explained to us how the Israelites redeemed from Egypt obtained knowledge of certain historical truths. He has not, however, established what seemed to have been his primary contention; that is, that the revelation at Sinai is itself a "matter of history." He has not shown that later generations, who have not witnessed the revelation directly, nevertheless have sufficient reason to believe that it actually occurred.

Does he address this fundamental issue at all in *Jerusalem*? To do so, he would have to demonstrate not only that the Israelites were unimpeachable witnesses but also that the text of the Torah is perfectly credible. Surprisingly, he does not repeat in *Jerusalem* the argument of the *Counterreflections* that the biblical account of events at Sinai is incontestable because it is uncontradicted by any other testimony and because it is universally accepted. Even more surprisingly, he does not proceed to argue that the Torah is a book whose divine authorship is beyond doubt. One or another of these arguments would seem to be necessary to strengthen his case. For with respect to the crucial events described in the Torah we are, after all, people "who live at another time." Because we can no longer rely on our senses to convince us of the historical truth of the revelation at Sinai, we must have recourse to the testimony contained in a book—the Torah. The validity of that testimony depends entirely on the authority and credibility of its author. Who is that?

The best indication we receive in *Jerusalem* of Mendelssohn's answer to this question is found in a passage occurring shortly after the discussion of historical truths, in which he refers to the Torah as "the divine book that we have received through Moses."[23] In the end, his entire defense of the historicity of the Sinaitic revelation rests on this premise. Curiously enough, he makes no argument in support of it.[24]

Mendelssohn's Flawed Proof of the Historicity of Revelation

Living long after the end of the Middle Ages and writing for an audience decidedly removed from a medieval outlook, Mendelssohn, in his defense of the historicity of the Sinaitic revelation, resorted entirely to arguments that had their origins in the works of medieval authors. Such arguments, he must have known, may have been good enough to use in a dispute with the likes of Lavater and Bonnet, but they were patently insufficient to respond to criticisms of the kind voiced by Spinoza. They were, in fact, the very arguments which Spinoza had rejected in the course of formulating his own views.

The most striking thing, in fact, about Mendelssohn's discussions of the historicity of revelation is that in none of them does he show any unmistakable signs of having taken heed of the objections raised by Spinoza or any of the other thinkers we examined in the previous chapter. Defending the historicity of the Sinaitic revelation at the end of the eighteenth century, when skepticism regarding the biblical narrative had already made serious headway, Mendelssohn behaves as if he were still living in the fourteenth century, when no one dared to express such doubts. He acts as if no one ever had, and no one ever could, question the authority of the prophets, the testimony of the ancient Israelites, the authentically ancient character of the pentateuchal narrative, and so forth. One understands easily enough why he might conduct himself in this fashion in his Hebrew writings, but how could he, in his German writings, blithely ignore some of the most important developments in recent cultural history? How could he neglect to deal in *Jerusalem*, in particular, with the publications of his own close friend, Lessing, which had so recently caused such a great commotion throughout Germany?

We would be forced to ask these questions even if Mendelssohn had done nothing other than reiterate in a comprehensive manner the medieval Jewish arguments in defense of the historicity of revelation. But he did not do so. As we have seen, his principal treatment of this question, in *Jerusalem*, is curiously disjointed. Because, as Mendelssohn stated, "in historical matters, the authority and credibility of the narrator constitute the only evidence," one would expect to find in *Jerusalem* as full an account as possible of the origin and history of the Pentateuch, which contains the narrative upon which the truth of Judaism depends.[25] We find, however, not a thorough discussion of the matter, but only some rather cryptic ruminations that seem peculiarly incapable of resolving the main issue at hand. With regard to the central, underlying question of the Pentateuch's origins, we find only a reference, in passing, to the fact that it was revealed through Moses. The omission of any argument in defense of this crucial contention is, in view of Mendelssohn's overall purposes, a glaring one.

If Mendelssohn failed to grapple with the writings of Spinoza and his spiritual descendants, it may very well have been because he was all too aware of the difficulties such a discussion might involve. Spinoza, as we have seen, and later others, including Reimarus, had introduced serious questions with regard to the qualifications of the ancient Israelites as witnesses of major historical occurrences and had marshalled a considerable amount of evidence and argumentation against the traditional Jewish understanding of how the Pentateuch came into being. Mendelssohn could conceivably have risen to the challenge and disputed what these men had written—but could he refute them? It is difficult to see, for instance, how he could have made a case for the veracity of the rabbinic tradition of Mosaic authorship that would have totally refuted Spinoza and, for his enlightened readership, placed the credibility of the pentateuchal narrative beyond all doubt. It is especially difficult to imagine how he could have attempted to make such an argument in the immediate aftermath of the controversy generated by Lessing's publication of the "Wolffenbüttel Fragments." In the end, it seems, Mendelssohn preferred not to face these and other such difficulties and decided instead to pretend that they did not exist.

Spinoza and his followers, down through Reimarus, repeatedly demonstrated their unwillingness to accept at face value the Israelite prophets' claim to have been in direct communication with God. They contended—or at least insinuated—that the prophets were either the victims of their own imaginations or mendacious schemers. To these characterizations Mendelssohn makes no direct response whatsoever. He simply observes, without emphasizing the fact, that revelation is, in essence, a miraculous event. To those, like Spinoza, who deny the possibility of miracles, this is, of course, no explanation at all. But it may be similarly unconvincing even to those who accept, in principle, the idea that God can perform such miracles as revelation, but still require, if they are to be persuaded to acknowledge their occurrence, a more detailed explanation of what they are.

With regard to the question of the historicity of the Sinaitic revelation, on the other hand, Mendelssohn has a considerable amount to say—but it is not enough to constitute a convincing defense of his position. For the most part, he merely rehashes timeworn medieval arguments, arguments that he knew could be of no use against serious modern adversaries of revealed religion. But he does not merely employ this outmoded form of argumentation. In his most important treatment of revelation, in *Jerusalem*, he strangely mangles it. When we look closely at what he says, it is impossible to understand how it could possibly have been meant to prove, in the face of powerful contemporary opposition, what it seems to have been meant to prove. Something is conspicuously missing.

Doctrines of Judaism

From Spinoza to Lessing, the critics of the Old Testament repeatedly characterized it as a collection of books that fell far short of propounding the fundamental truths of the universal or natural religion. They attempted to demonstrate its authors' insufficient understanding of divine goodness and providence and, above all, their ignorance of what some of them characterized as the absolutely indispensable doctrine of the immortality of the soul. The Jews, some critics argued, had acquired a genuine religion only *after* the compilation of the Bible, as a result of their exposure to the superior wisdom of other peoples, including the Greeks and the Persians. They then proceeded to read their new knowledge back into the texts they held sacred.

This assessment of the Old Testament and the Jewish religion conflicts in every respect with *all* contemporary Jewish conceptions of them. For all Jews, in the eighteenth century, the Bible was the source of the most profound religious truths, which were either articulated clearly in its text or had been—or indeed could still be—extrapolated from it through the application of the correct hermeneutical techniques. It recounted the actions of the Lord and Preserver of the universe, and among other things, it undoubtedly contained numerous passages that alluded to the existence of a life after death.[26]

It would seem, therefore, that a Jewish response to the Spinozist critique would be most likely to take the form of a defense of the Old Testament and consist of a demonstration of the depths of the wisdom contained within its books. Such a defense could draw on earlier Jewish tradition as well as on the writings of modern, Christian defenders of the Old Testament. For some time, however, no European Jew attempted anything of the kind.

Moses Mendelssohn was the first major Jewish thinker to seek to come to terms with the problems resulting from the Spinozist critique of Judaism. To Mendelssohn, an ardent defender of natural religion *and* a professing Jew, the attempt to drive a wedge between natural religion and the Old Testament was doubly unacceptable. He combated it in two different ways, employing both traditional and unprecedented sorts of arguments. Although it has attracted relatively little attention, he did make something of an effort, as one would only have expected, to show that the teachings of the Old Testament were identical to those of reason. Much better known, on the other hand, is his altogether different contention that the Old Testament *presupposes* but does not teach the truths of natural religion, that Judaism is consequently not a revealed religion at all but a revealed legislation.

Our task in the following section will be to examine Mendelssohn's two rather disparate ways of dealing with the question of the relationship between the Old Testament and the truths of natural religion. We will first examine his unsystematic, scattered, but nonetheless highly significant comments concerning various revealed doctrines. We will then investigate his contradictory—and highly dubious—explanation of Judaism as being devoid of religious doctrines. Finally, we will attempt to explain, in the light of the circumstances under which he was writing, Mendelssohn's peculiarly ambivalent approach to this fundamental question.

The Revealed Doctrines of Judaism

In the course of his dispute with Lavater Mendelssohn formulated his first general statement with regard to the doctrinal content of Judaism. The Jewish religion, he states in an important passage of the *Counterreflections*, is in essence entirely rational. Its basic teachings are ideas discoverable by unassisted human reason. It has only three fundamental principles (*Hauptgrundsätze*): (1) God, (2) providence, and (3) lawgiving.[27] These principles, it is important to note, are described by Mendelssohn as being accessible through human reason *as well as* through the revealed texts of Judaism. The highly salutary doctrine of the immortality of the soul, for instance, which falls under the general rubric of providence,

> is one of our articles of faith, the basis of our religion. The books of the Old Testament, the book of Job, which is at least as old as the books of Moses, the Psalms of David, all the prophets, all of our Talmudic books are full of this doctrine, and an immense number of customs and ceremonies practiced by us are aimed at incessantly reminding us of this truth.[28]

In affirming the rationality of the fundamental principles of Judaism, Mendelssohn was not necessarily implying that *all* of the doctrines contained in his religion's revealed texts were within reach of unassisted human reason. He left open the possibility that some aspects of these fundamental doctrines or some teachings of lesser significance, *not* indispensable to an individual's salvation, might be learned only through revelation. As we shall soon observe, he had occasion to refer to more than one such doctrine.[29]

Mendelssohn's most comprehensive treatment of a revealed doctrine is found in his Hebrew commentary on the book of Ecclesiastes (published in 1769 or 1770).[30] For Mendelssohn, as for the rest of Jewish tradition, Ecclesiastes was a book written by King Solomon and also an inspired book, a book written under the influence of the holy spirit [*be-ruah ha-kodesh*]. And, as he wrote in the introduction to his commentary, "There is no doubt but that the man who speaks in prophecy or under the influence of the holy spirit utters no word without a special intention."[31] Mendelssohn proceeded, accordingly, to interpret the book "in a manner that agrees with the literal sense of Scripture."[32] As we would expect, his interpretation shows Solomon's teaching on providence and immortality to be fully consistent with the teachings of reason.

According to Solomon, Mendelssohn writes, the strongest argument in favor of the immortality of the soul is derived from the consideration of the nature of human life on earth. He sees that here below the wicked prosper and the righteous suffer. This

> is complete proof of the immortality of the soul after death. For no one would be so stubborn as to deny that the Judge of the world is a God of faithfulness and without evil. And if he did not do justice there by justifying the righteous and incriminating the wicked, there would be no way to avoid attributing evil and oppression to him, heaven forbid.[33]

Mendelssohn made reference not only in his commentary on Ecclesiastes but in other writings as well to biblical teachings concerning the afterlife. In a brief piece entitled "Thoughts on Jewish Prayers, Especially on the 'Alenu Prayer," written in 1777 at the behest of the Jewish community of Königsberg, he discussed Psalm 49 in the following terms: "this psalm is one of the most important doctrinal psalms, one in which the doctrine of a future life, of the resurrection of the dead, and the reward and punishment of the good and the evil in a future state are clearly mentioned in order to comfort the oppressed and to induce sinners to better themselves."[34] Here Mendelssohn showed that Scripture taught not only the doctrines of a future life and future retribution, which are accessible to unassisted reason and indispensable to salvation, but the doctrine of resurrection, which is, it seems, neither of these things.

In his notes on his correspondence with Thomas Abbt, published in 1782, Mendelssohn observed that revelation is not designed to satisfy men's curiosity with regard to the precise nature of their posthumous condition, but it can nevertheless calm, soothe and console them. "Strengthened at last through its consolations," he declares, "the psalmist can sing, with complete confidence in the dispensation of the infinitely good Father and in complete submission to him . . ." Mendelssohn then proceeded to quote the concluding verses of Psalm 73, which reflect such confidence and submission.[35]

This is a passage Altmann considered to be quite strange. "One wonders," he wrote, "what kind of revelation he had in mind, seeing that he confined revelation to the Law. His reference is apparently to Scriptural confirmations of rational belief in man's immortality. In his view, the Scriptures do contain allusions to this particular truth."[36] Altmann was clearly puzzled by the evident contradiction between what is written here and the denial in *Jerusalem* that revelation disclosed anything apart from religious legislation. In what seems to be a rather halfhearted attempt at harmonization, he assumed that Mendelssohn was referring here to the psalmist's reliance on earlier biblical "allusions" to but one specific doctrine. If, however, we consider Mendelssohn's comments not in the light of his later statements but in the context of his earlier works, where he makes even more explicit reference to the doctrines contained in Scripture, they will not appear to be at all strange or in need of explanation.

Returning to the *Counterreflections*, we find clear reference to yet another revealed religious doctrine, that of the coming of the messiah. "We still await," Mendelssohn stated, "a future messiah, who will have the mission of restoring our nation, and freeing it from all political oppression . . ." With his arrival, all the nations will unite in the worship of the one, true God. This is a matter on which "all the prophets of the Old Testament agree." In the absence of any suggestion on Mendelssohn's part that this is a matter that can also be known through reason alone, we must conclude that the messianic idea was, in his opinion, an aspect of divine providence known only through revelation. It is evidently also a doctrine that is far from being indispensable to salvation.[37]

What is no doubt the most important example of a revealed religious doctrine appears in *Jerusalem*, the very book in which Mendelssohn states for the first time and in the most comprehensive manner his antidoctrinal position. The passage in question is found near the end of the book. Following his "surmise" concerning the emergence of idolatry and the purpose of the Jewish ceremonial law (which we will examine in a subsequent section of this chapter), Mendelssohn repeats his earlier observation that the pagan religions had a better understanding of the power of the Deity than of his goodness. "You cannot find," he maintains, in all its theology, in all the poems and other testimonies of earlier times, any trace of its having attributed love and mercy toward the children of man to any of its deities."[38] This is as true of the most enlightened of the pagans, the Greeks, as it is of any of the others. Mendelssohn quotes approvingly the testimony of a contemporary historian that

> To the Athenians as well as to the rest of the Greeks, all gods appeared to be so malicious that they imagined an extraordinary or longlasting good fortune would draw upon itself the anger and disfavor of the gods and would be upset by their devices. Moreover, they considered these very same gods to be so irritable that they regarded all cases of misfortune as divine punishments inflicted upon them not because of a general depravity of morals, nor on account of individual great crimes, but because of trivial and, for the most part, involuntary cases of negligence in the performance of certain rites and ceremonies.

To this Mendelssohn himself adds the observation that in "Homer himself, the thought had not yet been kindled that the gods forgive out of love, and that without benevolence they would not be happy in their heavenly abode."[39]

The ancient Israelites, too, prior to their receipt of the Torah, seem to have lacked a proper understanding of God's mercy. After describing the low level of knowledge of the Deity in earlier times, Mendelssohn recounts how God used the occasion of the Israelites' rebellion in the wilderness, "in order to acquaint the human race with so important a doctrine," as that of divine mercy.

Mendelssohn briefly paraphrases the conversation that took place between God and Moses after Moses had reascended the mountain, which is reported in Exodus 33. Moses asks God to show him his glory. He is told that he will be able to see the divine Presence only from behind. As God's Presence passes before him, Moses hears a voice proclaim: "The Lord (who is, was, and will be) eternal being, all-powerful, all-merciful and all-gracious; long-suffering, of great lovingkindness, who preserveth his *lovingkindness, even to the thousandth generation; who forgiveth transgression, sin and rebellion, yet alloweth nothing to go unpunished.*[40] To whom does this voice belong? Mendelssohn does not hesitate to ascribe it to the Eternal himself. This is very striking. Here, in *Jerusalem*, the work in which, as we shall see, Mendelssohn argued most forcefully against the possibility of any divinely revealed doctrines and, in particular, against the possiblity that anything concerning religious truths could be learned from a heavenly voice, he openly recounts how God, with his own voice, taught Moses of his mercy and "how the doctrine of God's mercy was on this important occasion first made known to the nation through Moses."[41]

Mendelssohn does more than show that revelation was the source of the Israelites' knowledge of divine mercy; he proceeds to explicate the biblical verses quoted previously. With the assistance of rabbinic commentators, he seeks to show that God's words propound a particular concept of the nature of his mercy, one that is in accordance with what is taught by reason. "It is true," Mendelssohn observes, that "the Eternal says that He *will allow nothing to go unpunished . . .*" But if these words, "are not to cancel completely what was said before, they lead directly to the great thought which our rabbis discovered in them—that *this, too, is a quality of divine love, that for man nothing is allowed to go entirely unpunished.*"[42] Revelation teaches, in other words, that divine punishments are corrective, inflicted by God in a loving fashion for a man's own good. And this is the teaching of reason as well. As soon, Mendelssohn writes, as a given punishment, "is no longer indispensable for a man's repentance [lit. change of mind], I am, without revelation, as certain that my Father will remit the punishment as I am certain of my own existence."[43]

In *Jerusalem*, then, as in his earlier writings, Mendelssohn continued his attempts to demonstrate the reasonableness of the doctrines revealed in Scripture. He did so on at least one occasion in his later writings as well. In section 49 of *Sache Gottes*, which was composed in 1784, he presented an interpretation of certain verses of Genesis in such a way as to show that they explicitly suggest a teaching of reason; that is, "the doctrine that since all parts of creation are perfect, the whole of creation is absolutely perfect." Mendelssohn begins his exegesis by noting that the Hebrew language has no special word for expressing the superlative. One of the ways in which it indicates it is by adding the word *me'od* to an adjective. Thus, adding *me'od* to the word *tov* [good] is a way of saying "the best." Mendelssohn next points out that at the end of the description of each of the first five days of creation, "which deal only with individual parts of creation," it is written that God saw that what he had created was good. At the end of the sixth day, however, when the creation of the world was completed, Scripture says: "God saw all that he had made, and he saw that it was the best [*tov me'od*]." In other words, the parts of creation, considered independently, were always good. The world as a whole, however, was the most perfect that was possible.[44] Scripture, therefore, teaches the same thing as reason.

It should be clear by now that Mendelssohn, contrary to what is generally believed, discussed with some frequency the revealed doctrines of the Jewish religion. He did not, to be sure, write a great deal on this subject. His occasional treatments of revealed religious doctrines raise, in fact, many more questions than they answer. How, for instance, does one identify such doctrines? And exactly how many are there? There is, however, no point in attempting to answer these questions. Mendelssohn does not tell us enough for it to be possible to do so. Not only does he not provide us with the information necessary to answer these questions, but he eventually begins to take a different tack altogether.

Mendelssohn's Repudiation of Revealed Religion

Only in *Jerusalem*, his principal apologetic work, does Mendelssohn finally present the famous concept of Judaism that deviates so sharply from the pattern established by earlier theological rationalists and, as we have just seen, from his own rather frequent statements conforming to the basic tendencies of that earlier tradition. In this book and in some of his subsequent writings, he emphasizes not the correspondence between the teachings of reason and revealed doctrines but the fundamental difference between reason's proper domain and that of revelation. As if he had never sought to elucidate the meaning of any revealed doctrine, he now maintains that "Judaism boasts of no *exclusive* revelation of eternal truths that are indispensable to salvation, of no revealed religion in the sense in which that term is usually understood."[45] Judaism, he says, consists not of a revealed religion but of revealed legislation which merely presupposes the fundamental truths of natural religion.

In *Jerusalem* Mendelssohn reaffirms his belief that God, in his goodness, has made the indispensable truths of natural religion accessible to all people through the use of their reason alone. The principles of God's existence, providence and immortality, he states, "did not have to be given by direct revelation or made known through *word* and *script*, which are intelligible only *here* and *now*." God "has revealed them to all rational creatures through *things* and *concepts* and inscribed them in the soul with a script that is legible and comprehensible at all times and places."[46]

What is new in *Jerusalem* is the assertion that it was not only unnecessary but also impossible for God to reveal the truths of religion. The voice heard at Sinai, Mendelssohn observed in one of the most famous passages of the book, did not proclaim the "universal religion of mankind." It could not have done so,

> for who was to be convinced of these eternal doctrines of salvation by the voice of thunder and the sound of trumpets? Surely not the unthinking, brutelike man, whose own reflections had not yet led him to the existence of an invisible being that governs the visible. The miraculous voice would not have instilled any concepts in him and, therefore, would not have convinced him. Still less [would it have convinced] the sophist whose ears are buzzing with so many doubts and ruminations that he can no longer hear the voice of common sense. He demands *rational proofs*, not miracles.

A revelation, therefore, could not possibly acquaint its recipients with the "idea of a *unique, eternal* Deity that rules the entire universe according to its unlimited will, and discerns men's most secret thoughts in order to reward their deeds according to their merits, if not here, then in the hereafter."

These truths, which are "indispensable to human felicity," must have been known to the Israelites prior to the revelation at Sinai, because it would otherwise have been impossible for them to learn from the revelation itself anything they had not already known beforehand. "All this was presupposed; it was, perhaps, taught, explained, and placed beyond all doubt by human reasoning (*menschliche Gründe*) during the days of preparation."[47] The cryptic phrase "human reasoning" is here left unexplained. In *To Lessing's Friends*, however, Mendelssohn elucidates this point somewhat more clearly. The rational convictions presupposed by Judaism do not, he says, consist of the kind of metaphysical argumentation found in philosophical textbooks, of demonstrations capable of withstanding the subtlest doubts. They are "the utterances and judgments of a plain, sound understanding, which looks things right in the eye and calmly considers them."[48]

In addition to being at variance with much of what he says

elsewhere, and even with some of what he says in *Jerusalem* itself, this presentation of Judaism as constituting in no sense a revealed religion proves to be quite problematic. Despite appearances, Mendelssohn does not really explain in a satisfactory manner *why*, in terms of his own philosophy, revelation need not or cannot impart religious truths. Nor does he make a convincing argument that the Israelite refugees from Egypt must already have possessed some kind of rational knowledge of the existence of God to become the the recipients of a revealed legislation.

Mendelssohn's belief that the essential truths of religion are readily accessible to all men at all times is deeply rooted in his natural theology, in his understanding of the goodness of God. Knowledge of God, providence, and immortality is, he maintains, a necessary prerequisite of continued human progress toward happiness. It is therefore, in his opinion, a requirement of divine wisdom and goodness that all men, even the most primitive, have access, even without the benefit of direct revelation, to these particular truths.

This alone might seem to render the revelation of religious truths entirely superfluous. However, the ready availability of these truths does not guarantee that everyone will always remain in firm possession of them. Already in the *Counterreflections* Mendelssohn observed that, in reality, by the time of the lawgiving at Sinai most peoples had fallen victim to false notions of God and his rule.[49] In *Jerusalem* he proceeded to develop an elaborate explanation (which we will examine in greater detail in a later section of this chapter) of how, in the pre-Sinaitic period, the original simplicity of natural religion was replaced by twisted and distorted forms of religion. "Men, animals, plants, the most hideous and despicable things in nature," he explained, came to be regarded as deities. Idolatry debased human nature to the point where men worshipped God through the sacrifice of their fellow men. As a consequence, "one had reason to wonder whether godlessness itself, as it were, might not be less ungodly than such a religion."[50]

There have been, therefore, times when the revelation of fundamental truths would have been anything but superfluous, periods when humankind was in dire need of assistance. True, he also maintained that, "as often as it was useful," that is, evidently, at such times when the truths of religion were insufficiently known, God made nonmiraculous assistance available. "Providence caused wise men to arise in every nation on earth, and granted them the gift of looking with a clearer eye into themselves as well as all around them to contemplate God's works and communicate their knowledge to others."⁵¹ But Mendelssohn also made it clear that those wise men are not always heeded. In the worst of times, he wrote, "philosophers sometimes dared to oppose the universal depravity and to purify and enlighten concepts. . . . But in vain!"⁵² It was, according to Mendelssohn, to remedy some of the consequences of this human inability to hold fast to religious truths that the revelation whose occurrence he does acknowledge, that is, the revelation of a Law to Israel, took place.⁴³ But, we must ask, if such divine measures may on occasion be necessary, how can it be said that the revelation of religious truths themselves would never be of any use?

Thomas Wizenmann, in his *Critical Investigation of the Results of Jacobi's and Mendelssohn's Philosophy by a Volunteer*, makes a similar point. As we saw in Chapter 2, Wizenmann's chief aim in this volume is to evaluate Mendelssohn's turn toward a "philosophy of common sense." Much less well-known, if not entirely forgotten, are his criticisms in the final pages of his essay of Mendelssohn's treatment of revelation. As an opponent of natural religion, utterly convinced that revelation was the only means to obtain genuine knowledge of God, Wizenmann clearly could not be expected to appreciate Mendelssohn's new concept of Judaism.⁵⁴ His predisposition to reject Mendelssohn's views does not, however, invalidate his views.

Wizenmann concentrates, as we did earlier, on the passage in *Jerusalem* where Mendelssohn first characterizes paganism's deficient understanding of God's goodness and then describes how he instructed Moses with regard to "so important a doctrine," as that of divine mercy. He quotes this passage in its entirety and then marvels, in an unmistakably sarcastic tone, at the blatant contradictions between what Mendelssohn states here and the teachings contained elsewhere in *Jerusalem*. So, he says, there were times when the Athenians, the wisest of the Greeks, failed to understand that gods are independent beings? So they held the gods to be unjust? So it was necessary for them, if they were bold enough, to hate, fear, and curse Providence? After a few more such questions come the clinchers:

> And the sun of the *universal religion of mankind*, which sheds its light in every direction, did not come to *Athens*? It was not inscribed in the souls of *these* rational creatures? The means of attaining felicity, as generously dispensed as bread and water, did not become available there? It was only Moses who made known to the human race the text, legible in all places

190 • Moses Mendelssohn and the Enlightenment

and at all times, of a worthy, and therefore a good and merciful Deity?

In Wizenmann's eyes, it seems, it is not necessary to do anything more than point to the palpable incompatibility of what Mendelssohn says here about the religious ignorance of the most enlightened of the pagans and the views he expresses elsewhere concerning the religious knowledge possessed by all the peoples of the earth. He concludes his consideration of this matter with nothing more than an admonition: "Let this contradiction be an example to you, you defenders of a universal religion of mankind abstracted from nature! If a master in Israel makes such blunders, what will the exercises of his disciples and imitators look like?"⁵⁵

Mendelssohn, of course, did not deny the occurrence of any revelation of religious truths solely because it would have been unnecessary for God to resort to such a means of communicating such knowledge. He also argued that such a revelation would have been futile. Even if a revelation of religious truths were to take place, "who was to be convinced of these eternal doctrines of salvation by the voice of thunder and the sound of trumpets?" Such a voice could neither instruct the ignorant nor convince the skeptical. It would serve no purpose at all, unless its hearers were already in possession of the indispensable principles of natural religion.

According to Julius Guttman, what Mendelssohn says here "turns out to be a development of one of Spinoza's thoughts."⁵⁶ He compares the view expressed by Mendelssohn in the passage to which we have repeatedly referred with the following passage from the *Theologico-Political Treatise* pertaining to the voice that proclaimed the Ten Commandments to the Israelites assembled at Mt. Sinai:

It seems hardly reasonable to assume that a created thing, depending on God in the same way all other created things do, would be able to express or explain God's essence or existence de facto or verbally by applying God's words to himself, declaring in the first person, "I am the Lord, your God" etc. . . . I fail to see how such a verbal assertion, "I am God," by a creature whose relationship to God is not different from that of any other created thing, and which is not part of the divine essence, can satisfy the desire of people who previously knew nothing of God except His name and who wished to commune with Him in order to be assured of His existence.⁵⁷

Guttman sees further evidence of the connection between Spinoza and Mendelssohn in other passages, where Spinoza derides the notion that one must believe in God's attributes even though one does not understand them, ridicules believers' obedient mouthing of what to them are unintelligible and meaningless formulas and stresses that the only way in which one can come to comprehend invisible things—such as the existence and attributes of God—is through logical proofs.

Guttman is undoubtedly correct to regard Mendelssohn's remarks on this matter as having been influenced by the aforementioned passage from the *Theologico-Political Treatise* concerning the voice heard at Sinai. But it is important to remember, as Guttman notes, that Spinoza's intention in this passage differs from that of Mendelssohn.[58] Spinoza was not arguing that a divine voice could teach nothing with regard to eternal truths; he was seeking to show that a *created* voice, which did not belong to God but was only indirectly caused by God, could, for that very reason, teach nothing certain about the divine or, indeed, about what the Deity desired of men.[59] Such a voice would have no more power to convince than a voice emanating from a beast. From this he concluded (with obvious disingenuousness) that the voice heard at Sinai must have been God's own voice.[60] He raised no doubts—in this context, that is—concerning the convincing power of such a truly divine voice.

For Mendelssohn, the voice heard at Sinai was "a miraculous voice."[61] Precisely what he meant by this is, as Altmann has observed, something that he never explained.[62] But whatever he meant by it, whether he had in mind a created voice or something else, he expressed no doubts concerning its ability to bear witness to its own divine origin. Unlike Spinoza, therefore, he had no logical reason to question its reliability.

Spinoza's doubts concern, of course, as Guttman points out, not only the possibility of deriving knowledge of things divine from a created voice but also the possibility of acquiring any such knowledge by any other means than through logical proofs. But these doubts did not prevent Spinoza himself from affirming that the Old Testament supplies such knowledge of God as is necessary to inspire obedience. Mendelssohn, according to Guttman, following "the cogent inner logic of Spinoza's thesis," went beyond Spinoza himself when he denied the possibility of *any* revealed religious teachings.[63]

Alexander Altmann also sees Mendelssohn as being indebted to Spinoza on this point, but he understands Mendelssohn's position primarily as a consequence of his proceding from a Leibnizian point of departure. A revelation of salvational truths, wrote Altmann, in a restatement of the Leibnizian view, is "impossible because eternal verities (which alone lead to ultimate felicity) simply cannot be revealed in a supernatural way. They have to be understood, and understanding something to be eternally true is inseparable from seeing its inner necessity." Accepting this as his premise, Mendelssohn comes to the conclusion "that the miraculous voice . . . was incapable of conveying truth about God to one who had not previously formed a rational view of the Supreme Being."[64]

Guttman believes that Mendelssohn was following Spinoza's lead and in fact going beyond him; Altmann sees him as following both Spinoza and Leibniz. Nevertheless, these two scholars are in complete agreement with regard to the nature of the conclusion at which Mendelssohn arrived: there can be no knowledge of God that is not solidly grounded in rational proofs. It is abundantly clear, however, that Mendelssohn actually thought otherwise. Far from believing that such proofs were the only means by which men could obtain a useful grasp of religious truths, he did not even believe, as we have seen, that the Israelites present at Sinai were acquainted with such proofs. Their knowledge of God prior to the occurrence of the revelation, was, he supposed, of a much simpler, commonsensical kind. It was, in a sense, rational, but it was not philosophical.

In *Jerusalem*, Mendelssohn describes the typical primitive man, a man who "still knows but little of the difference between direct and indirect causality." Even he, according to Mendelssohn, "hears and sees instead the all-vivifying power of the Deity everywhere—in every sunrise, in every rain that falls, in every flower that blossoms and in every lamb that grazes in the meadow and rejoices in its own existence." Even though this "mode of conceiving things has in it something defective," "it leads directly to the recognition of an invisible, omnipotent being to whom we owe all the good which we enjoy."[65] If there is, evidently, one less than flawless, indeed "defective" way of acquiring knowledge of religious truths that can still suffice to direct men toward perfection and felicity, why cannot there be another, one in which God participates more directly? Why is Mendelssohn therefore unable to acknowledge the possibility of the revelation of religious doctrines?

Thomas Wizenmann has, again, raised rather similar objections to Mendelssohn's contention that it is through reason alone that men can obtain knowledge of God. His statements with regard to this matter are closely tied to a reconsideration of the situation at Sinai, as depicted by Mendelssohn. "Why," he asks, "can a divine lawgiving not take place without a *prior* knowledge of God *on the basis of reason?*" Would the Israelites otherwise not have believed in this lawgiver, who directly revealed himself from heaven? "And was the appearance of the ruler of the elements at Sinai, was the voice of thunder which the people could not bear, not proof enough of his existence, his overwhelming power, his authenticity and his authority?" Wizenmann, at this point, pays no heed to Mendelssohn's contention that miracles in themselves, no matter how grand, can never constitute proof of anything whatsoever, since they might be the product of trickery. Even though he does not take this into consideration, however, his argument is not without its strengths. For he can point immediately to the way in which Mendelssohn has contradicted himself. "If the *mercifulness* of Jehovah can be taught through deed and revelation—why not also his existence in general, his lawgiving power, etc.?"[66]

Wizenmann, then, draws two separate conclusions from Mendelssohn's account of God's self-explanatory revelation to Moses. First of all, as we saw earlier, it indicates to him the baselessness of Mendelssohn's claim that the pagans had sufficient knowledge of religious truth even without having been the recipients of any divine revelation. And now it serves to vitiate Mendelssohn's general claim that knowledge of God can be conveyed only through rational means. If the miraculous voice of God can teach one thing, he concludes, it can teach everything.

Altmann has identified a third aspect of Mendelssohn's rejection of the revelation of religious doctrines. "A revelation of this kind is not only unnecessary and not only impossible," he writes, but

> is also unbefitting the justice and goodness of God. For is it not an act of preferential treatment meted out to a specific group of people, addressing it in its particular language at a particular time and place? It being supposed that the revelation is to show man the way to eternal felicity, does it make sense to believe that God's equal love for all men should be so oblivious of itself as to single out one special object of love? What is to become of those nations who never heard of that revelation? Are they condemned to miss eternal felicity?[67]

Altmann's rhetorical questions accurately paraphrase Mendelssohn's objections to the idea of any direct and *exclusive* revelation of indispensable religious truths. It would theoretically have been possible, however, for Mendelssohn to have acknowledged a special revelation that merely reiterated religious truths *otherwise know-able* through unassisted human reason. Such a revelation would in no way remove people who remained ignorant of its occurrence or who rejected it from the ranks of those eligible for eternal felicity. Regardless of whatever took place beyond their ken, they would still possess the ability to obtain essential religious knowledge through the use of their own fully adequate natural faculties.

It would, to be sure, seem to be rather unfair of God to disclose directly to one people what others were compelled to discover through their own efforts. But to accept, for the moment, Altmann's own argument, Mendelssohn's theory regarding the purpose of the admittedly revealed law is likewise at variance with his "professed egalitarianism" and is consequently open to the same sort of objection.[68] If, therefore, Mendelssohn could accept the idea of God giving the Israelites a law especially useful in maintaining a firmer grip on the essential truths of natural religion, there is no apparent reason why he could not also have acknowledged the existence of a special—though not exclusive—revelation of those truths.

A close examination of Mendelssohn's argument against the necessity or the possibility of revealed religious doctrines shows that it is, in many respects, deeply problematic. When we consider his description of the worst moments in the religious history of humankind, we see that the revelation of religious truths would by no means always have been unnecessary. And when we examine his explanation of the futility of such a revelation, we see that in the end he does not demonstrate convincingly why, in terms of his own thought, a divine intervention of this kind could not have been efficacious, if only in limited ways. Nor, as we have just seen, would such a revelation necessarily have been insuperably at odds with his egalitarian views. Finally, and most important, it should be evident from our previous discussion that despite his denial of the existence of revealed religious doctrines, Mendelssohn repeatedly discussed such doctrines and continued to explicate the texts disclosing them *even in Jerusalem itself.*

The Polemical Purpose of Mendelssohn's Repudiation of Revealed Religion

Mendelssohn, it seems clear, did not really believe that Judaism was devoid of revealed doctrines. On several important occasions, however, and indeed in crucial passages of his principal work on Judaism, it suited his purposes to deny their existence. What, we must ask, were these purposes?

By defining Judaism as an utterly nondoctrinal religion, Mendelssohn may have been seeking to spare himself a task that he might have had to undertake if he had continued to adhere to the position outlined in his *Counterreflections*. He may have chosen to relieve himself, in this manner, of the responsibility of squaring the results of his own natural theology with the teachings of Judaism. As we noted at the beginning of the previous chapter, this would not have been an inordinately difficult task. Still, the match between what he considered to be the teachings of reason and those of classical Judaism was not complete. There is a certain tension between Mendelssohn's philosophical understanding of human immortality and traditional Jewish conceptions of the afterlife. Judaism taught that there would be, in the end of days, a resurrection of the dead, and insisted that the Torah had already disclosed that it would occur; qua philosopher, Mendelssohn had nothing to say about the restoration of the departed to corporeal existence. Traditional Jewish literature identified categories of sinners who were destined to be destroyed or eternally damned; Mendelssohn, on the other hand, maintained that all human beings, without exception, were ultimately headed for some measure of salvation.

Had Mendelssohn consistently maintained that the teachings of reason and the teachings of Judaism were identical, had he sought to reconcile all facets of his own doctrine on immortality with that of rabbinic Judaism, he would undoubtedly have faced some daunting exegetical chores. It was, in all likelihood, as Noah Rosenbloom has recently pointed out, his awareness of these difficulties that had deterred him from carrying out his original plan of basing his teaching on immortality "on the utterances of the rabbis of blessed memory as found in the haggadic portions of the Talmud and in the Midrashim . . ." In a letter to Naphtali Hertz Wessely, Mendelssohn accounts for his failure to write such a work by referring to various obstacles that prevented him from carrying out his intention, including the difficulty of writing in Hebrew.[69] Rosenbloom, however, finds this explanation unsatisfactory. What really deflected Mendelssohn from his original plan, he writes, was the realization that a Hebrew rendition of Mendelssohn's *Phaedon* would not have been well received by "Jewish traditionalists familiar with the views of the Rabbis and the exponents of the main currents of medieval Jewish thought." His "egalitarian view of immortality of the soul in the hereafter (ʿolam habba) could also have involved him in an acrimonious conflict with his coreligionists had *Phaedon* appeared in Hebrew."[70]

If a desire to avoid conflicts of this kind deterred Mendelssohn from attempting to present his teaching on immortality in a specifically Jewish context, similar considerations may also have played a part in his decision to define Judaism as being not a revealed religion but a revealed legislation resting on the doctrines of natural religion. By claiming that Judaism had no distinctive doctrines of its own, he could eliminate any need to reconcile his own views with the statements of the rabbis. He could leave unresolved the discrepancy between his concept of immortality and that of the rabbis and, for that matter, avoid registering any other disagreements regarding doctrinal matters he may have had with traditional Jewish authorities.

Although this may have been Mendelssohn's aim, it seems, on the whole, that when he formulated his new definition of Judaism in *Jerusalem* he was reacting more to developments within the Gentile world than to what his Jewish critics might say. And when we bear in mind that he wrote *Jerusalem* in the early 1780s, the developments most likely to have led to the new turn in Mendelssohn's thought comes immediately into view: Lessing's publication of the "Wolffenbüttel Fragments" and the ensuing controversy. We have already had reason to suggest that these events had a certain impact on the way in which Mendelssohn presented his argument in *Jerusalem* in defense of the historical accuracy of the pentateuchal narrative. There is even more justification for believing that they played a part in determining his approach, in this book and subsequently, to the question of the place of doctrines in Judaism.

The extent to which Mendelssohn was influenced by the Fragments has not gone entirely unnoticed. In his article on "Mendelssohn's *Jerusalem* and Spinoza's *Theologico-Political Treatise*" Julius Guttman at one point calls attention to the way in which one of Mendelssohn's arguments in *Jerusalem* echoes the words of Reimarus.[71] More significant, Leo Strauss has observed that in his *Jerusalem*, "composed after his acquaintance with the Fragmentist, Mendelssohn gives voice to a much more decisive critique of revelation-based religion."[72] But neither Guttman nor Strauss pursued this matter any further.

The major problems with which Reimarus confronted Mendelssohn stem from his contention, in the fourth of the fragments published by Lessing, "that the books of the Old Testament were not written in order to reveal a religion." As we have seen, he there reiterated, with unprecedented ardor and comprehensiveness, the argument of Spinoza that the Old Testament knew only of terrestrial rewards and punishments. Indeed, he went beyond Spinoza and, following in the footsteps of Morgan and Voltaire, he explicitly denigrated the Old Testament on account of its lack of a doctrine of immortality. For this reason, the religion of the Old Testament was, in his opinion, a mean and base one. Judaism ceased to be so only at a much later date, when the Pharisees learned from other peoples of the soul's immortality and forcibly read their new ideas back into their holy books. Lessing himself, as we have seen, in his "counterassertions," voiced his agreement with Reimarus's characterization of the Old Testament's contents, even though he did not exactly share Reimarus's low estimation of the Old Testament's value.

The arguments of Reimarus and Lessing received an enormous amount of attention in the years immediately preceding the publication of *Jerusalem*. In the course of the *Fragmentenstreit* the "Spinozist" position consequently became far better known than ever before throughout Germany. This created great and inescapable difficulties for Mendelssohn. To continue to maintain in the aftermath of the controversy, as he had in the *Counterreflections*, that the teachings of Judaism are accessible through human reason *as well as* through its revealed texts, he would have to come to terms, in some fashion, with the contrary and rather formidable arguments that we reviewed at length in Chapter 5. For if, in *Jerusalem*, Mendelssohn had continued to argue that the teachings contained in the revealed texts of Judaism were simply the same as those of natural religion, it was all too likely that some troublesome opponent, inspired by Reimarus and Lessing, would have responded with a public challenge to prove, step by step, what he had merely asserted. He might have called upon Mendelssohn to prove what Spinoza, Reimarus and others had so often denied, that the Old Testament taught that the human soul was immortal and that human beings face the prospect of posthumous reward or punishment. Or he might have demanded that he demonstrate in detail that the teachings of the Old Testament were in all respects completely in accord with the philosophical views articulated in such works as his *Phaedon*.

Rather than court such risks and face objections with which it would have been so difficult to grapple, Mendelssohn apparently decided to abandon the argument that the fundamental doctrines of the Old Testament were the same as those of natural religion and to claim, instead, that the revelation granted to the Israelites simply *presupposed* the people's prior knowledge of those truths. It was evident, he asserted, that people who were not already acquainted with the "truths indispensable to human felicity" could not have derived any benefit from God's communication with them.

To hear God, they had to know of him. Because they evidently did hear God, one must assume that they possessed such knowledge. The fundamental principles of religion were, Mendelssohn conjectures, "perhaps, taught, explained, and placed beyond all doubt by human reasoning during the days of preparation" prior to the great divine manifestation at Sinai.[73]

Divine revelation, Mendelssohn now asserted, presupposed the truths of natural religion and taught nothing other than the necessity of one people's obedience to a God-given law as well as the specific stipulations of that law. One could therefore not contrast it with natural religion and find it wanting, as Reimarus had done. By denying that the Old Testament contained any doctrines at all, Mendelssohn relieved himself of any responsibility for defending its specific doctrines or explaining its evident failure to include explicit mention of all of the indispensable doctrines of natural religion. This new interpretation of Judaism could serve, therefore, as a means of avoiding the theological disputes that were, as we know, so deeply disagreeable to him.

If we have perhaps succeeded in showing what Mendelssohn had to gain from his new approach to the question of the nature of Judaism, we still face the problem of explaining how he could so blatantly contradict himself by continuing to present discussions of the contents of Judaism's revealed doctrines. How, above all, could he include in *Jerusalem* itself such an extensive treatment of the way in which Exodus 33 first imparted knowledge of the principle of divine mercy to the Israelites and, indeed, despite the complete rationality of this principle, to all of humankind? Would he not have foreseen the dangers posed by this passage to the entire strategy that I am imputing to him?

In answer to these questions I can suggest only the possibility that Mendelssohn sought to have, so to speak, the best of both worlds. He may have wanted to obtain the advantages of his new stance, which denied that revelation contained any religious doctrines whatsoever, without sacrificing all of the advantages of his older approach, which stressed the identity of the teachings of reason with those of revelation. If this seems to have been too improbably audacious an ambition, it is necessary only to observe that it was one that was, in fact, crowned with success. Even those who have questioned the validity of his characterization of Judaism as something completely other than a revealed religion have failed to observe the extent to which Mendelssohn himself treated it as a revealed religion. Scholars who have noticed one or another of the passages in which he discussed the revealed doctrines of Judaism have treated them as puzzling aberrations. And for 200 years, to the best of my knowledge, the most glaring contradiction in his argument, the one we have seen in the text of *Jerusalem* itself, appears to have been overlooked by everyone, with the sole exception of Mendelssohn's nearly forgotten eighteenth-century critic, Thomas Wizenmann.

Moral Questions

As we noted in Chapter 5, Spinoza took Maimonides to task for insisting that Gentiles had to accept the authority of the Bible to become eligible for salvation. Treating the medieval philosopher as an authoritative representative of his religion's position on this matter, he went on to criticize Judaism in general for failing to recognize the intrinsic value of moral conduct, whatever its underlying motivations. Although Spinoza, in all likelihood, did not intend to direct this charge exclusively or even chiefly against Judaism, it was nevertheless one to which Mendelssohn felt compelled to respond.

For all of his disdain for the superstitious and ignorant Israelites, Spinoza generally refrained from assailing their moral character and the moral qualities of their religion. In the writings of subsequent critics, however, such accusations multiplied. Inspired, in part, by classical Greek and Roman anti-Jewish writings and in part by the work of Pierre Bayle, they characterized Judaism as a deeply immoral religion. The Jewish God, they claimed, conducted himself in a manner irreconcilable with high moral standards and demanded improper behavior from his worshippers, especially through his promulgation of an immoral set of laws. The Bible itself recounted the corrupt behavior of the Jews and, indeed, often indicated its approval of it. A religion so thoroughly enmeshed in immorality, the critics concluded, plainly evinced its own discreditable origins.

It was probably Voltaire, in Mendelssohn's lifetime, who gave the greatest currency to charges of this kind. But Reimarus, in the parts of his *Apologie* that Lessing chose not to see published, certainly rivalled him in the harshness of his criticisms, especially when he accused such figures as Abraham, Moses, and David of seeming "to deviate from the rules of virtue and, indeed, [from] the law of nature and of the nations" and of being guilty of "deceit, craftiness, and cruelty."[74] This denigration of Judaism was a phenomenon with which Mendelssohn was no doubt familiar. He had read the pertinent published works and had had the opportunity to peruse the entire, unpublished manuscript of Reimarus's *Apologie*. And, as we have seen, one of his own friends, August Hennings, had reiterated many of the accusations of immorality in a private communication in 1782.

How did Mendelssohn deal with all of this? As we shall see, he replied at length to only one of the many charges leveled against Judaism. He sought to refute what Spinoza had said in condemnation of Judaism's attitude toward virtuous but faithless non-Jews by showing how Judaism expected nothing more of non-Jews than that their behavior correspond to the law of nature. To the moral objections of the other critics, however, he offered little in the way of a response.

The Salvation of the Gentiles

Mendelssohn dealt with the issues raised by Spinoza's citation of Maimonides in the course of his controversy with Lavater. Greatly irked by the Swiss theologian's conversionist zeal, Mendelssohn proceeded both to deplore it and to contrast it with the spirit of his own religion, which made no unjust demands on the faith of those who are not numbered among its practitioners. Maimonides's divergent opinion constituted, of course, an obstacle on Mendelssohn's apologetical path, one that he could not ignore— probably because of the publicity it had received from Spinoza. Without mentioning the name of his archenemy, he sought to mitigate the significance of his argument.

It is true, Mendelssohn admits, that Maimonides points to a requirement not only of good conduct but also of a certain measure of faith on the part of Gentiles. He insists that on this matter, however, he spoke only for himself, not for the Jewish religion, most of whose authoritative spokesmen were in disagreement with him. Mendelssohn then proceeds to outline the full teaching of Judaism with respect to the salvation of Gentiles:

> All of our rabbis unanimously teach that the written and oral laws, of which our revealed religion consists, are binding only on our nation. Moses gave *us* a law, it is an *inheritance for the community of Jacob.* All other peoples of the earth, we believe, are instructed by God to hold fast to the law of nature and to the religion of the patriarchs. Those who live their lives according to the laws of this religion of nature and rea-

son are called *the virtuous men of other nations*, and these are the children of eternal blessedness.

In a footnote to his remark concerning "the law of nature" and "the religion of the patriarchs," Mendelssohn describes the rabbinic concept of the Noahide laws. He observes that the seven commandments incumbent on the Noahides embrace approximately the essential provisions of natural law (*ungefähr die wesentlichen Gesetze des Naturrechts in sich fassen*) and then proceeds to enumerate them, citing tractate *Avodah Zarah* of the Babylonian Talmud and Maimonides's *Mishneh Torah* as his sources. He lists the prohibitions against idolatry, blasphemy, bloodshed, sexual sins, theft, eating the limbs of a living animal, and the injunction to establish courts of justice.[75]

Mendelssohn's assertions concerning the Noahide laws are very much open to doubt. For one thing, it is not correct to imply, as he does, that all of the rabbis identified the righteous among the nations (*hasidei 'ummot ha-'olam*) with those Gentiles who simply lived in accordance with these laws. This was an equation made not in the Talmud but only later, by Maimonides. For the rabbis, adherence to the laws of Noah qualified a Gentile (living under Jewish jurisdiction) for life in *this* world, not the next one. The righteous among the nations were Gentiles who, in some unspecified way, went beyond mere adherence to the Noahide laws.[76]

More important, Mendelssohn's identification of the Noahide laws with the laws of nature is not entirely warranted by his rabbinic sources and is, as Marvin Fox has pointed out, deeply problematic. On the basis of this identification Fox assumes that these seven commandments are, presumably, in Mendelssohn's opinion, "the basic rules of an autonomous rational ethic, the very same rules which he had asserted in his prize-essay could be demonstrated with the rigor of a geometric proof. Whoever observes these is one of the *hasidei 'oomot ha-'olam* and is assured of salvation." But it is necessary to ask, Fox writes,

> just what sense can be made out of the claim that the Noahide laws are rationally demonstrable. Even if we grant to Mendelssohn his claimed "law of nature," namely, that we ought always to seek to make ourselves and others as perfect as possible, we cannot see how it would lead us to the seven Noahide commandments. What for example, is the relationship between human perfection and not eating a limb torn from a living animal? Or, how do we move from the principle

of seeking human perfection to the rule that homosexual unions are forbidden on pain of death, or that sexual relationships with one's sister are similarly forbidden on pain of the same penalty?[77]

Fox finally observes that, "If the Noahide commandments are examples of what Mendelssohn considers to be rationally demonstrated moral rules, he completely fails to show how he arrives at the conclusion that they are, in fact, rationally demonstrable."[78]

Fox, it seems, has pressed this point too far. Mendelssohn, after all, does not immediately identify the Noahide laws in their entirety with the law of nature. To do so would indeed be absurd. What he says is that the Noahide laws "embrace approximately the essential laws of natural law." In saying this he does not deny but rather seems tacitly to admit that they also include certain provisions that go beyond the strictures of natural law, beyond what men could know by themselves without divine guidance. But if he recognizes this fact, he does not directly discuss its full implications. The actual rabbinic doctrine, as he apparently understood it, holds that Gentiles must do something other than live in accordance with natural law if they are to be "children of eternal blessedness." It differs, then, at least in some respects, from what reason teaches.

This in itself need not pose any special problem for Mendelssohn. The Jews, too, after all, must observe certain commandments inaccessible to reason alone in order to attain felicity. If the covenant with the Noahides had taken place as publicly and as miraculously as the lawgiving at Sinai, and if the Gentiles could be expected to have in their possession reliable reports of such an occurrence, there would be nothing objectionable in the rabbinic doctrine. But, as Mendelssohn was well aware, this was not the case. The whole matter of the Noahide laws, as he himself notes in a well-known letter to Rabbi Jacob Emden, is not made explicit in the Torah at all but known only through Jewish tradition or by means of a kind of exegesis known only to the Jews. How, then, could the Gentiles be expected to know anything about their duties?[79] Because, therefore, as Mendelssohn tacitly acknowledged, the Noahide laws did not correspond fully to the law of nature and because, as he himself argued, it could not be reasonably assumed that the nations of the world had access to them, the rabbinic doctrine concerning the Noahide laws was something less than completely rational.

Mendelssohn, to be sure, does not explicitly underline the difference between what reason teaches and what the rabbis taught, but neither does he seek to conceal it (in his letter to Lavater, after all, he lists all of the commandments incumbent on the sons of Noah, including those that were manifestly not rationally demonstrable moral rules). What he seeks to do is overcome it. We can see how he attempts to do so if we turn once again to the pertinent passage of his letter to Lavater.

After reiterating that the written and oral laws of Judaism are meant for the Jews alone, Mendelssohn first states that "all other peoples of the earth, we believe, are instructed by God to hold fast to *the law of nature and to the religion of the patriarchs*" [my emphasis]. This, it seems, is tantamount to an admission that, according to the rabbinic belief, the Gentiles are obligated to do more than live in accordance with the law of nature if they are to merit places in the world to come. They must also live in obedience to the religion of the patriarchs, which apparently includes those provisions of the Noahide laws that are not identical with the law of nature and that Mendelssohn listed in the note appended to this sentence. In the very next sentence of the letter, however, we detect a subtle shift. Here Mendelssohn observed that, "Those who live their lives according to the laws of this *religion of nature and reason* [my emphasis] are called *the virtuous men of other nations*," and so forth. The law of nature and the religion of the patriarchs have been transformed into the religion of nature and reason. The difference between what the rabbis teach and what reason teaches has suddenly and quietly evaporated.

Without misrepresenting the content of the rabbinic doctrine concerning the Noahides, Mendelssohn sought, in his letter to Lavater, to correct it, to neutralize its nonrational element. Those provisions of the Noahide laws accessible only through revelation he mentioned only in a footnote. Then, through a deft verbal maneuver, he attempted to identify the religion of the patriarchs, as the rabbis understood it, with the religion of nature and reason.

By the time Mendelssohn wrote *Jerusalem*, more than a decade later, this subtly modified, more completely rationalistic version of the rabbinic doctrine had become, for him, firmly established as the teaching of "true Judaism." "According to the concepts of true Judaism," he there maintains, "all the inhabitants of the earth are destined to felicity; and the means of attaining it are as widespread as mankind itself, as charitably dispensed as the means of warding off hunger and other natural needs."[80] Judaism's doctrine concerning the salvation of the Gentiles, he now says, corresponds exactly to the teaching of reason that salvation is available to all men, whether or not they are familiar with the details of some of the decidedly nonrational laws of Noah. What Mendelssohn did here was, in effect, to take a rabbinic doctrine that agreed, to a considerable extent, with what he considered to be the teachings of reason and bring it, by means of his own assertions, the rest of the way into accord with them.

The Moral Critique of the Old Testament

Apart from making the argument we have just examined, Mendelssohn, in his published writings, betrays no great concern with contemporary moral critiques of the Old Testament. Apparently, he does not believe that they pose any major threat to his religion. He does not deign to answer, for instance, Voltaire's slanderous charge that the Old Testament endorsed human sacrifice. Nor does he seek to rehabilitate any of the biblical heroes and prophets who had been subjected to such widespread mockery. The situation is not greatly different with regard to his unpublished writings. For the most part, his correspondence is devoid of any reference to these issues. We do not know whether he ever responded to the Voltairean letter he received from Hennings, which we examined in Chapter 5. It is, in the end, only in his correspondence with Lessing that we find some interesting remarks pertaining to the matter at hand.

Lessing, as we have already noted, placed the entire manuscript of Reimarus's *Apologie* at Mendelssohn's disposal. This manuscript, as we have already observed, was replete with mockery, reminiscent of Voltaire, of the prophets and the heroes of the Old Testament. In a letter dated November 29, 1770, Mendelssohn let Lessing know something of what he thought of it. The author, he wrote,

> was unfair. He is as much biased against certain characters as other people are [biased] in their favor. He traces everything to malicious, cruel, and misanthropic designs, without taking into consideration that even the leader of a band of robbers must be presumed to combine at least some good intentions with his malicious designs. If everything [in the biblical stories] is to have happened in a human way, we have to take the people as they actually were in those times, as acting in accordance with the then prevailing exceedingly limited notions about the law of nations, universal justice, and love of the human race. Viewed from this angle, things will appear in a light totally different from the one in which your Unnamed

conceives them. . . . If one wants to consider man as man and to judge him in accordance with the morals, habits, and the culture of his time and in comparison with his contemporaries, one ought to have no prejudice and one should not, out of disgust with prejudice, permit oneself to be misled into unfairness. One ought to know the limitations of man's capacities and not indulge in phantoms that make us dizzy in the head. All the same, the manuscript is very important in every respect . . .[81]

Here Mendelssohn rises to the defense of the biblical heroes, but he does so without making any real effort to exculpate them. He only asks that they be judged fairly, in terms of the standards prevailing in their own time, which were admittedly far below those of the contemporary world.

What is most striking about this letter is the way in which it seems to presuppose a positive view of humankind's moral progress to which Mendelssohn does not otherwise appear to have adhered. Mendelssohn is, on the contrary, well-known for having considered "the measure of human morality (virtue-vice; happiness-misery)" to have remained "more or less static in all periods."[82] This is the gist of one of the most famous passages in *Jerusalem*, a passage in which he disputed the validity of Lessing's account in *The Education of the Human Race* of humankind's moral progress.[83] Mendelssohn can by no means be accused of blatant self-contradiction for stating one thing in a letter in 1770 and something very much at viriance with it in a book written more than a decade later, but it is nonetheless interesting to observe this discrepancy.

Even more significant than this is the great gap between the views expressed by Mendelssohn in his letter to Lessing and the traditional attitude toward the biblical figures in question, an attitude one might have expected Mendelssohn to share. It is, indeed, difficult to imagine how anyone who truly regarded the Pentateuch as a divine book could ever have spoken so condescendingly of Abraham, Jacob, and Moses. Lessing himself appears to have been somewhat taken aback by Mendelssohn's remarks. He could agree that historical conditions had to be taken into account in the evaluation of the moral conduct of ordinary men. "But are patriarchs and prophets," he wrote, "people to whom we must condescend?" They should rather be the most sublime models of virtue. If one finds that they do not live up to such standards, one should speak of them with all of the contempt that they would earn in our own better, more enlightened times.

"The reason why such procedure by our Unnamed startled

you," Lessing wrote to Mendelssohn, "must be entirely due to the fact that you were never obligated to view those blameworthy actions in the light of divinity in which we are supposed to regard them." What Lessing probably meant to say, according to Altmann, is that unlike Jews, "who looked upon the heroes of the Old Testament as mere human beings whose moral frailties might be excused or somehow explained, Christians had been taught to see them as 'types' prefiguring Christ. Hence latter-day scholars were bound to be much more severe in judging their actions."[84]

According to Altmann, Lessing is suggesting that Mendelssohn's equanimity in the face of Reimarus's attacks on the biblical heroes is in harmony with the traditional Jewish approach to them, an approach rooted in an awareness of their human fallibility. Whether or not this is what Lessing meant to say, it cannot really serve as an adequate explanation for Mendelssohn's position. Mendelssohn was apparently undisturbed by derogatory characterizations of the greatest figures of the Jewish past that would no doubt have appalled, say, Jacob Emden, or indeed any other contemporary representative of traditional Judaism who might have dared to familiarize himself with them. Such people would most probably have been equally appalled to learn of the mild response to Reimarus articulated by Mendelssohn in his letter to Lessing, a response that found no echo in any of his published writings.

When Spinoza took Maimonides to task for insisting that Gentiles had to accept the authority of the Bible to become eligible for salvation, his real target was most probably not Judaism but Christianity, which taught that there was no salvation outside of the church. Whatever Spinoza's underlying aims may have been, however, Mendelssohn took what he said to be an accusation against the Jewish religion and treated it as such. He sought to defend Judaism against these charges by referring to the doctrine of the Noahide laws. Although helpful, this doctrine did not exactly prove what Mendelssohn wanted it to prove. Mendelssohn had to stretch the sources somewhat, to interpret them in the spirit of the Enlightenment, to be able to assert that Judaism stipulated that Gentiles can obtain salvation if they simply live their lives in accordance with the laws of the "religion of nature and reason."

With regard to other contemporary assaults on the moral character of the Old Testament and the Jewish religion Mendelssohn had surprisingly little to say. In response to the attacks of Voltaire, Reimarus, and others on biblical prophets and heroes he never sought to publish anything. Only in his correspondence with

Lessing do we find him commenting on these crucial matters. And what he says there is not at all what one might expect. Instead of offering a spirited defense of the biblical figures against Reimarus's ridicule, he laments his failure to "take the people as they actually were in those times, as acting in accordance with the then prevailing exceedingly limited notions about the law of nations, universal justice, and love of the human race." Mendelssohn, it appears, would have been content with a treatment of the biblical figures that was much less than reverential, provided only that it made suitable allowances for the conditions under which they lived and the primitive ideas they held.

Revealed Legislation

We have seen how Spinoza and subsequent thinkers characterized the law of the Pentateuch as nothing more than a burdensome regimen instituted by Moses to render the Jews more easily governable. And we have taken note of Spinoza's argument that the law should now, following the disappearance of the Israelite polity, be judged to be utterly defunct. We must next consider how Mendelssohn, in response to this assessment of Jewish law, sought to demonstrate that it (1) had true religious value and (2) was still in force.

In addition to having to explain the law's ultimate significance and its enduring validity, Mendelssohn had to face certain difficulties connected with its obligatory character. After having gone on record as a proponent of virtually absolute religious liberty, he faced, as we have seen, a public challenge to explain how he could possibly square such a liberal outlook with his acceptance of the theocratic legislation contained in the Old Testament. In this section we must examine Mendelssohn's response to this challenge.

The Law and Collective Felicity

Mendelssohn had no difficulty acknowledging that the Law outlined in the Pentateuch consisted, in part, of political legislation. He was, needless to say, as aware as anyone else that it included provisions for the regulation of innumerable aspects of the life of the ancient Jewish state, including its administration, armed forces, civil law, and so on. In his defense of the law, however, he pays remarkably little attention to its more public dimensions. As Arnold Eisen has pointed out, "collective felicity," as one of the pur-

poses of the law, "is mentioned in *Jerusalem* in only two parenthetical references." Eisen correctly understands this relative
unconcern with the relationship between the law and the well-being of the entire community in terms of the circumstances prevailing at the end of the eighteenth century. "Unlike Maimonides," he
notes, Mendelssohn "could not expect Jews to take on the burden of
observance in the context of integral communities endowed with
the ability to coerce observance if it was not otherwise forthcom-
ing." This accounts for "the decidedly individualist thrust of Mendelssohn's rationale for the commandments, as opposed to Maimonides' emphasis on the welfare of both 'soul' and 'body'—the
latter signifying societal welfare."[85] It would be more accurate, as
we shall seek to show in the next chapter, to say that Mendelssohn
did not *want* to see the preservation of "integral communities endowed with the ability to coerce observance" than that he could not
expect to see such a development, but Eisen is otherwise on the
mark.

Mendelssohn's "Surmise"

Although not ignoring altogether the political character of the
Mosaic law, Mendelssohn concentrates, in *Jerusalem*, in his famous theory concerning "the purpose of the ceremonial law in Judaism," almost exclusively on its nonpolitical dimension, on the
way in which it benefits the souls of those who live in accordance
with it. The most important thing to observe concerning the theory
in question is that it is, by Mendelssohn's own admission, a very
tentative one. It is merely a "surmise" (*Vermuthung*). To understand this surmise better, it would perhaps be advisable, before
examining it in detail, to attempt to reconstruct the reflections that
led up to it. How, in other words, was Mendelssohn predisposed to
understand the significance of the ceremonial law? What kinds of
interpretations of its meaning was he already inclined, at the outset of his inquiry, to reject? It is quite clear that Mendelssohn could
not have entertained for a moment the notion that God might have
ordained the commandments in an arbitrary, nonpurposive manner. And because he believed that God stood in no need of receiving
anything whatsoever from human beings, the purpose of the commandments could be related only to the welfare of their recipients.
They had somehow to contribute to something more than their
temporal well-being, to their religious enlightenment. On the other
hand, they could not be *too* important. It would contradict a vital
tenet of Mendelssohn's natural theology to maintain that God in

any way employed them to afford the Jews access to indispensable religious knowledge otherwise unavailable to those who had not received them. It was necessary for him to argue, therefore, that the commandments bore some relation to the knowledge of religious truths but that they did not serve as an exclusive path to attaining it. And that is the essence of his surmise.

The theory Mendelssohn tentatively develops in *Jerusalem* to account for the purpose of the commandments in a manner consistent with the requirements of his natural theology consists of two basic parts: (1) an account of the emergence of idolatry, and (2) an explanation of the benefits derived from performing the commandments. The first part consists mostly of a reconstruction of the pre-Sinaitic history of humankind. It seeks to demonstrate how the earliest peoples fell victim to idolatry as a result of their employment of hieroglyphic script. The second part develops a hypothesis concerning the way in which the ceremonial law protects the Jews against succumbing to the attractions of idol worship and reinforces their grasp of fundamental religious truths.

Mendelssohn first attempted to outline the early stages of humankind's religious history in the *Counterreflections*. He there wrote that God has enabled even the wildest and the crudest of peoples to obtain "concepts and moral certainty of the truths of natural religion which are indispensable to their felicity." Most members of those peoples, however, must rely for their enlightenment not on their own powers but on the instruction of exceptional individuals whose independent reflections have led them to the truths that they then transmit to others.

Mendelssohn does not, to be sure, portray these early discoverers of the truth as philosophers; he sees them as men who "may, so to speak, have felt the proofs inwardly, without being able to communicate them." As they began to reflect on nature in general and the situation of man in particular, they became aware of difficulties that could be resolved only through "the belief in a higher, entirely beneficent power, in providence, in a future life, and in the immortality of the soul." At the outset, the discoverers themselves had only an unclear and confused comprehension of these principles, and they had difficulty giving a coherent account of them. How, then, could they transmit them to the unsophisticated multitude who were still incapable of absorbing philosophical knowledge? "The experience of most people teaches that this initially took place by means of prejudices. The common people are convinced through superstitions of very important truths, without which they cannot be happy in social life." Allowing essential truths to be based on prejudices may not seem to befit the Supreme Wisdom, but it evidently did so, since this, as experience teaches, is what actually took place among the greater part of humankind.[86]

In *Jerusalem*, Mendelssohn portrays the religious situation of primitive people in a somewhat different light than he does in the *Counterreflections*. Even the simplest of men, he says, is initially in no need of instruction from others. Such a man "still knows but little of the difference between direct and indirect causality." Consequently, "he hears and sees instead the all-vivifying power of the Deity everywhere—in every sunrise, in every rain that falls, in every flower that blossoms and in every lamb that grazes in the meadow and rejoices in its own existence." Even though this "mode of conceiving things has in it something defective," "it leads directly to the recognition of an invisible, omnipotent being to whom we owe all the good which we enjoy."[87] We see, then, that the insights Mendelssohn attributed in the *Counterreflections* to the early teachers of humankind, who then mixed them with superstitious ideas and taught them to others, are presented in *Jerusalem* as being within the unassisted reach of even the simplest of men. In spite of this difference, however, the emphasis is on the same basic point: the fundamental truths are in one way or another accessible to everyone.

There are further differences between the account of the history of religion in the *Counterreflections* and that in *Jerusalem*. In the *Counterreflections*, after describing the condition of relative ignorance in which the peoples of the earth initially find themselves, Mendelssohn goes on to say that they do not remain in that state forever. "As a people," he writes, "becomes more and more refined and enlightened, rational arguments take the place of prejudices." A people may even rise to a level where, in the end, it can sustain all of the religious truths indispensable to the felicity of humankind by rational knowledge alone.[88] At variance with this evolutionist view, as Julius Guttman has observed, is a remark Mendelssohn makes later in the *Counterreflections*.[89] Instead of noting the religious progress made by humankind, Mendelssohn there observes that by the time of the lawgiving at Sinai most peoples had abandoned the simplicity of the earliest religion and fallen victim to false notions of God and his rule.[90] Anticipating what he was later to explain at considerably greater length in *Jerusalem*, Mendelssohn described the ceremonial law of the Jews as being designed to provide them with a means of remembering the sacred truths of natural religion. In *Jerusalem* Mendelssohn abandons altogether the evolutionist view of religion propounded in the earlier pages of the *Counterreflections* and describes in much greater detail than he did in the later passage the steady corruption of human religion prior to the lawgiving at Sinai. In the course of time, he explains, the simplicity of natural religion was replaced by twisted and distorted forms of religion, in which "Men, animals, plants, the most hideous and despicable things in nature," were regarded as deities. Idolatry debased human nature to the point where men worshipped God through the sacrifice of their fellow men. As a consequence, "one had reason to wonder whether godlessness itself, as it were, might not be less ungodly than such a religion." [91]

To account for this corruption of religion, Mendelssohn resorts to a theory that, in Altmann's opinion, is "the least substantiated of all theories he ever advanced." [92] The primary cause of the religious deterioration of humankind was, according to this theory, "an innocent thing, a mere mode of writing," that is, hieroglyphic script. [93] Men initially employed hieroglyphic signs, derived from the images of animals, to symbolize the deity. Eventually, however, they fell victim to their own misunderstanding and the manipulations of unscrupulous priestly hypocrites, they they came to regard these signs themselves as being deities. [94]

Mendelssohn's argument in defense of this theory is purely conjectural and is, as Arnold Eisen has stated, "a painfully weak one." For one thing, as Eisen himself has noted, "Canaan, Greece, and Rome—the idolatrous cultures of most concern to Jewish tradition—all had alphabets," not hieroglyphic scripts. [95] Furthermore, as Altmann has commented, "even if one conceded his point that men tend to take the sign or image for the thing itself, the question of why the worship of animals should have developed via the corruptive influence of hieroglyphic writing, and not more directly, would remain." Mendelssohn's only reason for putting this theory forward, Altmann ultimately concludes, "was to contrast the image worship of paganism and the imageless ceremonial acts of Judaism, the perilous hieroglyphic and the safe living script of Jewish ceremony." [96]

In response to the emergence and prevalence of idolatry, according to Mendelssohn, God ordained the ceremonial law of the Pentateuch. Through its eschewal of all imagery, this law avoids the hazards presented by hieroglyphic script. Its main purpose, however, is not prophylactic but positive, to connect useful truths with actions and practices. It does so because "man's actions are transitory; there is nothing lasting, nothing enduring about them that, like hieroglyphic script, could lead to idolatry through abuse or misunderstanding." But it is not, of course, simply because they have nothing to do with hieroglyphics that the actions commanded by God possess religious value. It is chiefly because their performance involves people in spiritually meaningful interaction with others. Obedience to the few written laws and the more numerous unwritten laws creates an environment rich in religious significance. Mendelssohn describes this environment as follows:

> In everything a youth saw being done, in all public as well as private dealings, on all gates and on all doorposts, in whatever he turned his eyes or ears to, he found occasion for inquiring and reflecting, occasion to follow an older and wiser man at his every step, to observe his minutest actions and doings with childlike attentiveness and to imitate them with childlike docility, to inquire after the spirit and the purpose of those doings and to seek the instruction which his master considered him capable of absorbing and prepared to receive.[97]

Mendelssohn declares toward the conclusion of *Jerusalem*, in his summary of his conception of Judaism, that the ceremonial laws "guide the inquiring intelligence to divine truths, partly to eternal and partly to historical truths" upon which the Jews' religion is founded. They link "action with contemplation, life with theory."[98]

God gave the commandments only to Israel, but he did not do so, according to Mendelssohn, for its sake alone. Israel was to be a priestly nation, a nation that "through its laws, actions, vicissitudes, and changes was continually to call attention to sound and unadulterated ideas of God and his attributes. It was incessantly to teach, to proclaim, and to endeavor to preserve these ideas among the nations, by means of its mere existence, as it were."[99] Mendelssohn believed, then, after his own fashion, in the election of Israel.

Recent Approaches to Mendelssohn's "Surmise"

Over the years, this rather sketchy treatment of the purpose of the commandments has received relatively little scholarly attention. Most analysts of Mendelssohn's thought have treated it as if it were entirely self-explanatory. Even Altmann, who exhaustively analyzed virtually everything Mendelssohn had to say with regard to Judaism, did not subject it to careful analysis. He appears to have considered it a very simple theory, one that merely views the commandments as "constant reminders of universal truths of reason or of the particular historical experiences of the Jewish people in which divine providence had manifested itself."[100] Recently, however, two scholars have sought to clarify more precisely the sense in which Mendelssohn understood the commandments to serve as such reminders.

According to Michael Morgan, Mendelssohn conceived of the connection between the ritual commandments and eternal truths as "a relation of *association*." At Sinai God "fixed the association of *these acts* with *these truths* when He established this particular round of conduct for the Jewish people." As a result, during the period of "pristine Judaism" the Jews came "to associate a specific set of ceremonial practices" with "a specific set of beliefs or doctrines or truths." The relation of association was, in essence, "very much like what holds in people's minds between Sherlock Holmes and his hat and pipe. To be sure, just as a perceived object that stimulates recollection may be alike or similar to the recalled object, one being a copy of the other, so it *may* be that, to Mendelssohn, the ceremonial acts as a 'living script' were somehow *like* the truths with which they were associated."[101]

Dismissing Morgan's approach as too simplistic, Arnold Eisen has presented a thoughtful new interpretation of Mendelssohn's theory concerning the relationship between the commandments and religious truths. According to Eisen, this theory must be understood in the light of various statements Mendelssohn makes in the first part of *Jerusalem*, where he is dealing not with the ceremonial law of the Pentateuch but with the question of whether it is ever justifiable to impose religious oaths. Interestingly enough, this is a subject Mendelssohn discusses at much greater length, and with much more passion, than the positive purpose of the ritual commandments. He is firmly opposed, for a number of reasons, to requiring people under any circumstances to take oaths regarding their religious convictions.

Not the least of these reasons is the one that draws Eisen's attention; that is, his argument concerning the very limited capacity of language to represent clearly the concepts of men's "internal sense" and serve as a vehicle for communicating them. The perceptions of this internal sense are in themselves, Mendelssohn says, quite elusive, and it is extremely difficult to capture them in words. Furthermore, different men, at different times and places, and even at the very same time and place, attach different meanings to the same external signs and words. It is, in short, difficult for a man to say what he means, and even more difficult for him to transmit his meaning to others. In view of this, it is obviously futile to force any man to swear that he accepts the truth of any particular religious proposition. Apart from everything else, those who are doing the enforcement can never really know, even if they get their way, exactly what it is they have succeeded in extracting from the person who has yielded to their compulsion.

What Mendelssohn says here concerning the limitations of language is apparently echoed later in *Jerusalem*, in a passage cited by Eisen. Following his principal remarks concerning the nature of revelation, and prior to his discussion of the emergence of idolatry, he makes a comment in reference to the place doctrines occupied in "ancient, original Judaism." They "were not connected," he writes,

> to words or written characters which always remain the same, for all men and all times, amid all the revolutions of language, morals, manners, and conditions, words and characters which invariably present the same rigid forms, into which we cannot force our concepts without disfiguring them. They were entrusted to living, spiritual instruction, which can keep pace with all changes of time and circumstances, and can be varied and fashioned according to a pupil's needs, ability, and power of comprehension.[102]

On the strength of this observation, Eisen quite plausibly links what Mendelssohn says about language in the context of his treatment of religious oaths with his surmise concerning the purpose of the ritual commandments. Mendelssohn's argument, he maintains, is that God has commanded actions and not the mere recitation of permanently fixed formulas because the former are of much greater efficacy in assisting different kinds of people, living under different circumstances, to gain access to religious truths.

Eisen concludes from what Mendelssohn says about the elusiveness of religious truths that he believed them to be extremely resistant to precise definition. Unlike Maimonides, who believed that the commandments "served as symbols or reminders of truths which he could and did state propositionally," Mendelssohn believed that "God could not and did not reveal truths in words, at Sinai or anywhere else." He saw the ceremonies not as actions that guide people directly to the truth but as providing an occasion for its coming within range of their intuitive grasp.

> That being the case, there could not be one single meaning to a commandment, let alone one single correct meaning. The

meaning lay in what those who practiced it grasped, with the help of their communities and teachers, from the set of behaviors mandated by the Torah. These meanings would presumably fall within a certain range defined (and limited) by the very principles Maimonides had put forward as essential for all to know: God's existence, unity, and power.

Eisen denies most emphatically that Mendelssohn would have held that a particular commandment could "be said to lead to a particular truth or have a single meaning attributed to it." He was "pluralist to the core."

He was also, according to Eisen, a great equalizer. Although he acknowledged the existence of "differing levels of understanding, Mendelssohn leveled the difference between masses and elite." He was convinced "that even the greatest of minds cannot know all that much about God." The little than can be known "can in principle be grasped by almost everyone . . ."[103]

Piecing together arguments found in different sections of *Jerusalem*, Eisen has ingeniously constructed a coherent interpretation of Mendelssohn's theory concerning the commandments, one that also has a remarkably modern ring to it. There are, however, a number of problems with this portrait of Mendelssohn as a pluralist and a leveler. To begin with, Eisen's interpretation focuses exclusively on only one of the two functions Mendelssohn assigns to the ceremonial laws. He neglects to weigh the significance of Mendelssohn's claim that these laws concern historical truths as well as religious truths. Second, Eisen does not consider the context in which Mendelssohn gives voice, in *Jerusalem*, to skepticism regarding the attainability of theological knowledge and also seems to overstate the extent to which he does so. And, more important, even if he correctly assesses the views expressed by Mendelssohn in this book, he fails completely to consider them in the light of the very different views he states elsewhere, in his writings on natural theology. Finally, it seems that he goes somewhat too far in his portrayal of Mendelssohn as a systematic leveler of the differences among men.

Eisen's entire interpretation is designed to relate Mendelssohn's understanding of the function of the commandments to his conception of the elusiveness of ideas about God and his attributes. In summing up the purpose of the commandments, however, Mendelssohn states very clearly that they guide people's minds "partly to eternal and partly to *historical* [my emphasis] truths." He never indicates that truths of the latter sort are difficult to express or communicate to others. On the contrary, in words that now have a very unmodern ring to them, Mendelssohn describes historical reports as narratives that establish facts.[104] At least with regard to historical truths, therefore, Mendelssohn must have perceived the commandments as ordaining actions that reinforced people's recollection of very specific, quite clearly expressible, and fixed ideas.

Eisen is certainly correct to conclude that Mendelssohn's statements in the first part of *Jerusalem* evince a considerable degree of skepticism with regard to the expressibility and communicability of theological ideas. But what he says here ought to be seen, perhaps, in the context of the general intention of the passage in question. Mendelssohn is, after all, attempting to marshall arguments against the imposition of religious oaths. This is a matter concerning which he apparently had very strong feelings and about which he permitted himself to wax very rhetorical. It is conceivable, therefore, that he is, at least in part, exaggerating the difficulties involved in expressing and communicating theological ideas to strengthen his argument against the continuation of a practice he regarded as an impermissible and harmful violation of a person's liberty.

But even if Mendelssohn's comments in Section I of *Jerusalem* are devoid of any exaggeration, neither they nor any of his remarks elsewhere in the book should be understood as denying the possibility of stating truths about God in propositional form. All these statements really do is point to the difficulties involved in doing so. To say that "much confusion and indistinctness are bound to remain in the signification of words" is not necessarily to say that all theological statements will always be very imprecise. Mendelssohn's extensive writings on natural theology amply indicate that he believed, in fact, in the possibility of clear and distinct restatement of the fundamental truths of natural religion.

As we saw in Chapter 3, Mendelssohn experienced, with the passage of the years, growing doubts concerning the *demonstrability* of the tenets of natural theology. What he does not seem to have doubted in the same way, however, was their *expressibility*. In his writings on natural theology, from the *Treatise on Evidence* to the *Sache Gottes*, he elaborated very specific ideas concerning such matters as God's wisdom, goodness, and providence, and the immortality of the human soul. With a great deal of confidence in the correctness of his own views, he criticized what he regarded as the mistaken concepts propounded by others. One need only consider, for example, his discussion of providence in *Morning Hours*. There he refers disparagingly, on the one hand, to the "popular system" that recognizes the hand of God only in miraculous events and, on the other hand, to the once regnant "philosophical prejudice" according to which "the supreme Cause acts" for the most part "only in accordance with general laws." He contrasts these erroneous understandings of divine providence with the insights of Shaftesbury and Leibniz, which represent, in his opinion, "the highest triumph of human wisdom." According to these men, the intentions of God find expression in the operations of nature and reach "down to the smallest change and individual occurrences among lifeless as well as among living things."[105] Here, as in many other passages, Mendelssohn shows himself to be anything but "pluralist to the core."

Finally, although, compared to Maimonides, Mendelssohn is not an elitist, neither does he do away completely with the distinction between the knowledgeable few and what he sometimes designates as "the common heap." The former possess "purified concepts" of God and his attributes; the knowledge possessed by the latter consists of a mixture of truth and prejudice. All people are equal not in respect to their grasp of the truth but only to the extent that all are alike capable of acquiring the rather minimal knowledge necessary for further progress along the path to perfection and felicity.

On the basis of too little textual evidence, then, and without giving adequate consideration to conflicting evidence found in works other than *Jerusalem*, Eisen has constructed a somewhat dubious account of Mendelssohn's position. In fact, Mendelssohn was not so much of a pluralist and an antielitist as to believe that all attempts to articulate theological positions are necessarily tenuous and that there exist a number of them that are of roughly equal validity. He believed in the existence of intellectually accessible eternal truths, however difficult he may have thought it was to understand them. He need not, therefore, have believed that the commandments, on account of the elusive character of religious truths, could have guided only those who performed them to the general "range" of eternal truths. And he certainly must have conceived of some of the commandments as being directly aimed at the evocation of the memory of very specific historical facts.

A small modification would, however, render Eisen's interpretation more acceptable. One could argue that, in Mendelssohn's understanding, the precise details of the eternal truths were, if not absolutely inexpressible, at any rate difficult to grasp. He may consequently have believed that a clear revelational disclosure of them might have been understood by the philosophical few but misconstrued by the "common heap" and that for that reason God chose to command actions that would merely provide occasions for truth to come within people's intuitive reach. The wise and the unwise would then cut their own paths (or have paths cut for them) through the appropriate "range." The wise would make their way to the truth, the unwise to a tolerable approximation of it.

Eisen's dismissal of Morgan's interpretation as too simplistic seems somewhat overhasty. His own interpretation is, I hope to have shown, difficult to accept as it stands but nonetheless quite suggestive. In the end, however, it is probably not possible to determine for sure whether Mendelssohn conceived the commandments to point, insofar as eternal and not historical truths are concerned, to quite specific ideas or merely to bring people within the general range of loosely defined doctrines. Mendelssohn's discussion of this topic in *Jerusalem* is by no means extensive and may lend itself easily to diverse if highly speculative interpretations.

Mendelssohn's "Egalitarianism"

The great brevity of Mendelssohn's discussion of the positive purposes of the commandments suggests that his intentions in treating this subject were rather limited. It does not seem that he was striving to formulate, for coming generations of Jews, a new rationale for continuing to perform the commandments. He was simply seeking to deflect earlier criticisms of the law as being devoid of religious significance—without ascribing to it so much importance that its revelation to only one people would cast doubt on divine justice. The very nebulousness of his presentation could advance this purpose by leaving uncertain, and therefore unassailable, the precise but evidently limited relationship between the commandments and religious truths.

Nevertheless, Mendelssohn does not seem to have attained the dual goal we have ascribed to him. A number of scholars have voiced the opinion that his surmise regarding the purpose of the ceremonial laws is not in accord with his account of God's justice. In the opinion of Julius Guttman, when Mendelssohn "assigns the possession of a preventive against paganism to only one people," he still faces the same difficulty as those who believe in the special revelation of religious truths. If "a religious meaning is ascribed to revelation at all, it is inevitable that revelation must raise its recipient to a higher religious level." Therefore "the meaning of the divine plan for mankind's history can no longer be seen in the undifferentiated sameness of all peoples and ages." The contradiction is not resolved, according to Guttman, by Mendelssohn's notion of Israel's priestly vocation to serve as an example for other peoples.[106]

Altmann sees this problem in a similar light. "Mendelssohn's emphasis on Divine impartiality," he writes, "which obviates any revelation of salvational truths to a particular people, ill accords with his equally emphatic belief in the Election of Israel. Even granting that the Jewish people is elected for arduous duty rather than for special privileges, the very fact that it is given a special mission does not go well with Mendelssohn's professed egalitarianism." The problem is aggravated by Mendelssohn's acknowledgment that the law has as its purpose the felicity of the nation as well as that of each of its individual members. This implies that God has given the Jews access to "a particular kind of felicity not shared by others."[107]

In fact, what Mendelssohn says about the purpose of revelation is fully compatible with his understanding of God's justice. Divine justice, he believed, requires only that all men have independent access to the salvific truths; it does not require that they have *equal* access. Nor does it require that all benefits conferred on one people be conferred upon all others, any more than it requires that all benefits conferred on one individual be conferred upon all others. The Jews' receipt of a special revelation that directly assists only them in no way alters the fact that all of the other nations still have ample capacity and means to arrive at the essential truths of religion on their own, not to speak of the opportunity now accorded them to be drawn back to these truths through observation of the chosen people's way of life.

In this respect, however, this entire theory of the emergence of idolatry and the purpose of the ceremonial law really does seem to be inconsistent with Mendelssohn's basic orientation: it points to the necessity of revelation. Mendelssohn often affirms, in a manner quite reminiscent of the radical Deists, that humankind does not stand in need of any revelation to maintain its grasp of religious truths. His history of religion, however, shows otherwise. It demonstrates that human beings, left on their own, may eventually fail to make use of their God-given capacities to arrive at religious truth and may consequently find themselves in need of providential rescue.[108]

An Important Letter to Naphtali Herz Homberg (1783)

Before leaving the general subject of Mendelssohn's understanding of the significance of the ritual law, we should take note of his observations pertaining to this matter in a well-known letter to a disciple in whom he took a particularly warm interest, Naphtali Herz Homberg.[109] Special attention must be paid to this letter because, as Kenneth Hart Green has observed, Mendelssohn's letters to Homberg "are apparently a very precious source, for they are among the few occasions in which Mendelssohn revealed, in writing, his deepest concerns and opinions."[110]

In a response to *Jerusalem* that is no longer extant, Homberg appears to have expressed the belief that the ritual commandments no longer served the purpose ascribed to them in *Jerusalem*. Mendelssohn, in his reply, did not disagree with him. He argued, instead, that even if they had lost their significance as a kind of symbolic speech, the commandments had not for that reason ceased to be necessary. As long as polytheism, anthropomorphism, and "religious usurpation" (*religiöse Usurpation*) still held sway over the world, he asserted, they would have to be preserved. "As long as these vexatious offenders of reason are banded together, all genuine theists must also unite in some manner, lest the others trample us underfoot."[111]

Here Mendelssohn placed a considerable amount of emphasis on the way in which, in the words of Michael Morgan, "the role of the ceremonial law is like a unifying bond, keeping the Jewish people together and alive."[112] It is nevertheless something of an overstatement to say, as Eisen does, that he argued that "the importance of the commandments, in a word, was sociological."[113] What Mendelssohn said to Homberg was not that the commandments ought to be retained, if only because they helped to keep the Jewish people together. If this was indeed all that was currently being accomplished by their performance, he indicated, it was not a situation with which one should rest content. Under present circumstances, he wrote, "Our efforts must be devoted to eliminating abuses, and to infusing the ceremonies with a genuine and authentic meaning."[114]

In *Jerusalem*, Mendelssohn explained how the very act of observing the commandments guides men's minds to the truth. Here we find him acknowledging that the commandments do not necessarily fulfill this purpose. They are subject to abuse and have been abused—but the situation is not irremediable. Men who are already in possession of the truth, men like himself and his correspondent, can eliminate the abuses and restore the commandments to their original significance. Far from serving automatically as matchless guides to the truth, therefore, the commandments can achieve their proper purpose only if people already acquainted with the truth make the effort to reinfuse them with meaning. The discrepancy between what Mendelssohn says in *Jerusalem* and what he says in his letter to Naphtali Herz Homberg is evidently a rather considerable one and is most intriguing. Unfortunately, the letter's treatment of this subject is even sketchier than the one found in *Jerusalem*.

The Enduring Authority of the Law

In opposition to Spinoza and others who claimed that the law of Moses was exclusively designed to regulate the affairs of a specific, defunct commonwealth and is therefore entirely obsolete, Mendelssohn had but one simple thing to say. The law, he maintained, is eternally binding. It may, in theory, be subject to change, but only "if it pleases the Supreme Lawgiver to make known to us His will on this matter, to make it known in as clear a voice, in as public a manner, and as far beyond all doubt and ambiguity as He did when He gave the law itself." Until that happens, "no sophistry of ours can free us from the strict obedience we owe to the law . . ." Some of the laws, such as those concerning sacrifices, are currently inoperative. "But personal commandments, duties imposed upon a son of Israel, without regard to the Temple service and landed property in Palestine, must, as far as we can see, be observed strictly according to the law" until God clearly decrees otherwise.

Mendelssohn acknowledges that these commandments may constitute something of a burden (*Last*), but only to the same extent that participation in civil life also requires the bearing of a certain burden. Since the dissolution of "the Mosaic constitution," the burden of the law has undoubtedly become greater, if only because the Jews now have to deal with situations in which state and religion are no longer identical and may even be opposed to one another. Consequently, they must sometimes confront situations in which the state in which they live makes demands which conflict with those of their religion. Under such circumstances, what are they to do? Curiously enough, Mendelssohn borrows the words of Jesus to counsel his people: "Render unto Caesear that which is Caesar's and unto God what is God's." For the sake of his contemporaries, he paraphrases this advice: "Adapt yourselves to the morals and the constitution of the land to which you have been removed; but hold fast to the religion of your fathers too. Bear both burdens as well as you can!"[115]

Although derived from a Christian source, this teaching is essentially in accord, as Altmann has observed, with the position of rabbinic Judaism on this matter.[116] Unlike the rabbis, however, Mendelssohn was actively engaged in an effort to tear down the barriers separating Jews from Gentiles. He wanted to bring to an end the semiautonomous existence of the Jewish communities, fully to integrate the Jews into the citizenries of the lands in which they lived. All of this could only have the consequence, as he himself was surely aware, of placing them in positions to which they were unaccustomed and multiplying the difficulties involved in bearing "both burdens." In the world that Mendelssohn envisioned and struggled to bring into being, it would undoubtedly become much harder for a Jew to remain a Jew.

The Response to Mörschel and Cranz

In Chapter 5, we briefly outlined the critical response to Mendelssohn's Preface to Manasseh ben Israel's *Vindiciae Judeorum* on the part of the author of *The Searching After Light and Right*, August Friedrich Cranz, and a certain Mr. Mörschel. Cranz challenged Mendelssohn to explain how he could adhere to beliefs like those expressed in the Preface and still remain a Jew. How, he asked, could the principle of liberty of conscience be reconciled with the Bible's authorization of religious coercion? Mörschel, on the other hand, concluded from Mendelssohn's support of the extension of toleration to naturalists that he was in reality nothing more than a naturalist himself.

By Mendelssohn's own admission, as we have already observed, his principal aim in *Jerusalem* was to respond to these charges, especially the one coming from Cranz. The bulk of the book, it is true, and even most of its second part seem to be concerned primarily with other matters. This should not be taken, however, as a sign that the critics Mendelssohn mentions were of anything less than major concern to him.[117] In this section, we will examine the peculiarly roundabout manner in which he endeavored to deal with the issues raised by these two men.

At the beginning of Section II of *Jerusalem*, Mendelssohn quotes extensively from *The Searching* (omitting, to be sure, any reference to the passage we cited in Chapter 5, where Cranz admonishes him against trying to resolve the issue by distinguishing between past and present Jewish practice).[118] However, in spite of the great significance he attributed to Cranz's basic argument, he does not seek immediately to refute it. Instead, he restates the conclusions drawn by Cranz and Mörschel with regard to what he himself must truly have believed in order to have made the arguments found in his Preface to Manasseh ben Israel's *Vindiciae Ju-*

daeorum. He then focuses his attention on a large variety of other matters. Only at the end of *Jerusalem* does he finally wend his way back to the question he himself acknowledged to be of paramount importance.

Both of Mendelssohn's critics had concluded that the views Mendelssohn had expressed in the Preface marked a definite step away from Judaism. Cranz, for his part, suggested that Mendelssohn was actually drawing closer to Christianity, because he had apparently torn himself loose from "the servitude of iron churchly bonds" and "commenced teaching the liberal system of a more rational worship of God, which constitutes the true character of the Christian religion . . ."[119] Mörschel, as we have just noted, concluded from Mendelssohn's argument that toleration ought to be extended to naturalists that he himself was in reality nothing more than a naturalist.

Mendelssohn deals with these seemingly mutually contradictory suspicions in very different ways. Cranz's conjectures he dismisses by illustrating the fallaciousness of his reasoning with a simple question. If the author of *The Searching* believed that Judaism, the ground floor, was without any solid foundation, how could he invite anyone to ascend to Christianity, the equally endangered upper floor?[120] It was surely evident to Mendelssohn, however, that his anonymous interlocutor, who mocked the Old Testament, was not a genuine believer in the truth of the Christian religion. He was clearly asking him, in the words of Ze'ev Levy, "to abandon Judaism and to convert to Christianity not to reinforce the latter creed but to strengthen the followers of Deism."[121] From his point of view, the superiority of Christianity resulted not from the fact that it was true but from its potentially greater degree of hospitality to people who merely paid lip service to revealed religion.

The suspicion voiced by Mörschel, as anyone can see, rests on faulty logic. One need not be a naturalist to argue that the state ought to tolerate the adherents of natural religion or even to speak well of them. Mendelssohn could have made short shrift of Mörschel's accusation by simply stating this. Or, if he wished to be more thorough, he could have reiterated, as he did in his controversy with Lavater, that his religion, Judaism, was binding only on the members of the Jewish people. Non-Jews, as far as it was concerned, had to live only in accordance with natural law and were under no obligation to accept any of the tenets of Judaism. He could, accordingly, without betraying his religion in any way, express sympathy and support for naturalists. In this way Mendelssohn could have disposed of the issue entirely.

Instead of doing this, however, or instead of briefly disposing of this matter in some other way, Mendelssohn uses Mörschel's charge as his point of departure for his entire defense of Judaism. He acknowledges that Mörschel is correct to suppose that he recognizes no eternal truths other than rational ones. He says that he errs, however, in supposing that this is somehow tantamount to a rejection of Judaism. It is to remove this error that Mendelssohn introduces his distinction between revealed religion and revealed legislation. Judaism, he explained, "knows of no revealed religion in the sense in which Christians understand this term." What was revealed to the Israelites were laws and commandments, not doctrinal opinions or saving truths.[122] The religion they possessed— which they had to have possessed, even before the divine legislation was revealed to them—was no different from "the universal religion of mankind"; that is, natural religion. To speak well of naturalists, therefore, is not to show disloyalty to Judaism.

Mendelssohn subsequently proceeds to elaborate the other positions that we have already subjected to detailed examination: his defense of the historicity of the revelation at Sinai, his theory concerning the emergence of idolatry and the purpose of the ceremonial law in Judaism, and so forth. In the course of discussing these matters he makes no further reference to Mörschel's charge or to what Cranz had said about his drawing closer to Christianity. Nor does he allude in any way to the charge that had "cut him to the heart"; that is, Cranz's argument that his advocacy of religious toleration was incompatible with the spirit and the letter of his religion.

Only at the end of *Jerusalem*, after his final summary of the contents of "the Judaism of former times," does Mendelssohn finally introduce a number of considerations apparently related to this all-important issue. He seeks to show, to begin with, that one misunderstands the nature of biblical religion if one characterizes it as an "ecclesiastical law armed with power." He then strives to show that even if the ancient Israelite constitution included punishment for religious offenses, it still did not punish them very severely. He next stresses how wrong it is to assume, as had *The Searching*, that Judaism inflicted punishments for unbelief or incorrect belief. Finally, he observes that the ancient Israelite constitution is in any case defunct now, and Judaism no longer calls for any coercion of its adherents.

Under the ancient Israelite constitution, Mendelssohn maintained, "state and religion were not conjoined, but *one*; not connected but identical . . . God, the Creator and Preserver of the world, was at the same time the King and Regent of this nation."

Hence, "in this nation, civil matters acquired a sacred and religious aspect, and every civil service was at the same time a true service of God."[123] What he seems to be suggesting is that, as Eliezer Schweid has put it, the fusion of state and religion "is possible and justified only when God himself is the sovereign power in the state." But this is, as Schweid has correctly observed, a forced solution and cannot be Mendelssohn's final word on the subject.[124] This new formulation may distinguish the constitutional arrangements prevailing in ancient Israel from, in Cranz's words, an "ecclesiastical law armed with power," but it in no way alters the fact that under these arrangements, whatever they are called, religious offenses are punished in the manner described by *The Searching*. Thus, even if the Mosaic constitution did not constitute an ecclesiastical law armed with power but was a unique regime in which state and religion were identical, not unified, the enforcement of religious behavior in ancient Israel has still not been rendered consistent with the principles espoused by Mendelssohn in the Preface and, for that matter, in Section I of *Jerusalem*.

After tacitly acknowledging that the ancient Israelite constitution did in fact include punishments for what were in a certain sense religious offenses, Mendelssohn takes pains to show that those punishments were, after all, quite mild. "With what superabundant indulgence for human weakness!" were even the perpetrators of capital crimes punished. "Indeed, as the rabbis say, any court competent to deal with capital offenses and concerned for its good name must see to it that in a period of *seventy* years not more than one person is sentenced to death."[125] But, "as Mendelssohn himself knew, this answer could only soften but not eliminate the criticism" to which he was responding.[126] Punishment, however mild, is still punishment.

Immediately after describing the lenient attitude of the rabbis with regard to capital punishment, Mendelssohn argues that his arguments, thus far, have clearly indicated "how little one must be acquainted with the Mosaic law and the constitution of Judaism to believe that according to them *ecclesiastical right* and *ecclesiastical power* are authorized, or that temporal punishments are to be inflicted for unbelief or for erring belief." He then refers explicitly, for the last time, to the *Searcher After Light and Right* and Mr. Mörschel. They are evidently "far removed from the truth when they believe that I have abolished Judaism by my rational arguments against ecclesiastical right and ecclesiastical power."[127] These comments, which are often treated as if they put the finishing touch to Mendelssohn's refutation of his adversaries, do nothing of the kind.

We should note, to begin with, that this aspect of Mendelssohn's response actually deals not with what he had earlier identified as *The Searching*'s most telling criticism but with a dimension of Cranz's position that he had hitherto failed to mention. Cranz had indeed maintained, as we have seen, that the Old Testament aimed at supressing any free expression of religious opinions "in *word* or deed." He had done so, however, only in a passage of *The Searching* that Mendelssohn had neither quoted nor summarized in *Jerusalem*. In the passages that Mendelssohn does cite, his main emphasis was on Judaism's coercion of *deeds*, even where proper convictions were absent. Mendelssohn's identification of Judaism as a religion that does not coerce opinions directly in no way constitutes a response to this point.

Mendelssohn speaks as if his adversaries' chief complaint had been that he "abolished Judaism" by his "rational arguments against ecclesiastical right and ecclesiastical power." But this is to misrepresent their position. For no one is "ecclesiastical right and ecclesiastical power" the central issue. What Cranz had stressed in *The Searching* was the connection, in the Mosaic law, of "coercion and positive punishment with the non-observance of duties related to the worship of God."[128] How, he wishes to know, can Mendelssohn reconcile this coerciveness with his liberal principles? Despite his confident assertions, nothing Mendelssohn has said up to this point constitutes an adequate answer to this question.

The last point Mendelssohn makes in his multifaceted response to the main point of *The Searching* is that the Mosaic constitution is now defunct. "As the rabbis expressly state," he writes,

> with the destruction of the Temple, all corporal and capital punishments and, indeed, even monetary fines, insofar as they are only national, have ceased to be legal. Perfectly in accord with my principles and inexplicable without them! The civil bonds of the nation were dissolved; religious offenses were no longer crimes against the state; and the religion, as religion, knows of no punishment, no other penalty than the one the remorseful sinner *voluntarily* imposes on himself. It knows of no coercion, uses only the staff [called] gentleness, and affects only mind and heart.[129]

Because contemporary Judaism no longer contains any elements of coercion, it is fully in accord with Mendelssohn's own understanding of religion.

There are, however, two problems with this argument. First,

it is based on faulty history. As Altmann rather delicately puts it, "Mendelssohn's assertion that punitive measures by Jewish courts ceased after the loss of political independence does not fully correspond to the facts."[130] In actuality, although judicial autonomy for Jews in the postexilic period was not universal nor was it always without limitations, Jewish courts often had recourse to the, "usual disciplinary measures: the seizure of property, monetary fines, corporal punishment, imprisonment, and, in exceptional cases, the death penalty." In addition, "two other means of coercion were available . . . the *herem* (ban) and the surrender of a Jew to the gentile authorities."[131] Mendelssohn was surely aware of these facts and was no doubt consciously overstating his case.

More important, however, than the historical inaccuracy of Mendelssohn's argument is its theoretical inadequacy. For even if it were true that postexilic Judaism had entirely abandoned all forms of religious coercion, this would not change the fact that the old, original Judaism had indeed condoned the use of force to compel Jews to obey religious law. Cranz had stressed this point. Even if the ecclesiastical statutory law of Judaism, as he put it, was no longer enforced, it is "still there"; that is, it is present in the Bible. In the passage of *The Searching* that we cited earlier, but that Mendelssohn neglected to quote, he had explicitly warned Mendelssohn not to overlook this fact. To respond to his challenge, Mendelssohn, he said, would have to do more than point to the changed character of Judaism. He would have to show that ancient Judaism as well was fully compatible with his principles. In spite of this admonition, however, Mendelssohn took precisely the path that Cranz had warned him not to take and thereby failed to meet *The Searching*'s challenge.

We have it on Mendelssohn's own testimony that he wrote *Jerusalem* primarily as a response to the challenge presented by *The Searching After Light and Right*. As we have seen, his method of answering that challenge was, to say the least, very indirect. Instead of immediately facing up to the full implications of the fact that ancient Judaism granted the admissability of the coercion of men's religious behavior, Mendelssohn first dealt with other, less significant issues raised by *The Searching* and a certain Mr. Mörschel. He then abandoned, for many pages, any attempt to respond to the main issue at hand and turned to the elaboration of some of the central aspects of his concept of Judaism. Finally, toward the end of *Jerusalem*, Mendelssohn came around to addressing his adversary's principal objection. He first sought to show that the Mosaic constitution was not, as Cranz had said it was, "an ecclesiasti-

228 • Moses Mendelssohn and the Enlightenment

cal law armed with power," but a unique sort of entity. But whatever the significance of this distinction may be, it does not mitigate the extent to which ancient Judaism was at odds with Mendelssohn's own liberal principles. In the end, it was only by asserting that later Judaism was altogether voluntary that Mendelssohn could reconcile his philosophy with his religion. But this was not only historically incorrect, it failed to deal with what *The Searching* had identified as a conflict in principle. Thus, at the end of *Jerusalem*, the question still remains: How is it possible to continue to maintain, on the one hand, that a religious act must be voluntary to be meaningful and pleasing to God and, on the other hand, that God once gave the Israelites a constitution that provided for the enforcement of religious deeds?

The plain and simple fact is that Mendelssohn has no satisfactory answer to this question. The circuitous and evasive manner in which he attempts to deal with it bears sufficient testimony to his own awareness of this fact. What he is trying to do here is not to present a decisive refutation of Cranz's penetrating argument but merely to give the appearance of having done so. He is seeking to deflect a disturbing criticism, not to resolve an insoluble theoretical dilemma.

In his defense of the law, Mendelssohn describes it as consisting, in part, of a legislation designed to regulate the affairs of the Jewish state in such a way as to promote the "collective felicity" of its inhabitants. Precisely how it served to do so is a matter he did not strive to explicate. As someone who was doing his part to integrate the Jews into Gentile society, he had no interest in delineating in any detail the positive side of Jewish self-government. What he did wish to explain was the dimension of Jewish law that was to remain in effect even in the absence of Jewish autonomy and that had, over the years, been most frequently dismissed as meaningless and burdensome, the so-called ceremonial law.

Striving not to violate his egalitarian principles, Mendelssohn developed a theory linking the practice of the ceremonial law to the preservation in the minds of the Jews of historical and eternal truths as well as the enhancement of these truths in the eyes of those who had the opportunity to observe the Jews in action. Despite the importance of this subject, Mendelssohn devoted only a very few sentences to the elucidation of the relationship between the commandments themselves and the religious truths to which they are connected. Ultimately, it is probably not possible, on the basis of these sketchy remarks, to determine with any certainty whether he conceived the commandments to point to quite specific eternal truths or merely to bring people within the general range of loosely defined doctrines. His "surmise" seems to have been crafted more to parry certain attacks on the commandments than to answer all questions concerning their religious significance. Contrary to what some scholars have suggested, his theory of the commandments does not, in the end, assign to the Israelites a position in the entire divine scheme of things inconsistent with his professed egalitarianism.

Mendelssohn explains adequately enough his reasons for considering the Mosaic law to be binding on the individual Jew, even if he does not, in his thematic treatment of the subject, address all of the problems that may arise as a result of the Jews' potentially conflicting duties to the law of Moses and to that of the state. What he does not succeed in doing, in the end, is reconciling his own absolute commitment to liberty of conscience and his insistence that God could never desire coerced worship with the undeniable fact that the God of Israel is reported in the Bible to have required just such a form of worship. He tries very hard to disguise this failure, but it stands out unmistakably when the second section of *Jerusalem* is subjected to careful analysis.

Conclusion

The challenges with which certain individual adversaries directly confronted him inspired Mendelssohn to abandon his reticence and undertake a defense of Judaism. In the course of meeting these challenges, he also sought to grapple with a number of other adversaries, men whose critiques of biblical revelation played an increasingly important part in the evolution of Western thought. He did not, to be sure, refer with any frequency to the writings or even the existence of these men, but, as we have seen, he was clearly preoccupied with many of their arguments, whose significance he could not fail to recognize. His writings on Judaism reflect an even greater concern with Spinoza, Reimarus, and Lessing, who wrote dismissively of Judaism, than they do with Lavater and Cranz, who went out of their way to make his life difficult.

In this chapter we have sought to analyze in a systematic fashion Mendelssohn's various responses to all of the criticisms discussed and analyzed in Chapter 5. Having examined, as it were, the entire forest, tree by tree, it is now time for us to step back and attempt to acquire an overview. To what extent, we must ask, did Mendelssohn, in dealing with all of these critics, succeed in accomplishing his primary goal, defending the rationality of the Jewish religion?

Mendelssohn's success, it is clear, was far from complete. His argument in favor of the historicity of the Sinaitic revelation and the veracity of the documents reporting it simply fails to address the doubts and concerns of skeptics, with which he was quite well acquainted. He leaves the most important questions begging for answers. His contrived definition of Judaism as consisting not of revealed doctrines but of revealed legislation is evidently a device for evading any discussion of his religion's distinctive teachings and the degree to which they may or may not be in accordance with reason. His surmise concerning the origin of idolatry and the purpose of the ceremonial law is in some respects unsubstantiated and in others deeply ambiguous. It is only by subtly adjusting rabbinic tradition that he is able to show that Judaism regards Gentiles as eligible for salvation if they simply live in accordance with the law of nature. In response to the abundant attacks in the course of the eighteenth century on the moral character of the Old Testament prophets and heroes Mendelssohn has almost nothing to say. In his attempt to effect a principled reconciliation between his liberal political philosophy and Judaism's theocratic tendencies he clearly falls short of responding in an adequate fashion to what he himself identifies as the principal question posed by his adversary, the author of *The Searching After Light and Right*.

Mendelssohn, in short, either failed to address or went to considerable lengths to evade the most serious intellectual challenges confronting a believing Jew at the end of the eighteenth century. His arguments did not work, and he knew they did not work. It is simply not possible to believe that he thought, for example, that his recapitulation of the medieval argumentation in defense of the historicity of revelation could dispel modern doubts concerning the truth of the biblical narrative, that he had satisfactorily explained the absence from the Old Testament of a doctrine of immortality, or that he had harmoniously reconciled Judaism with the principle of the absolute inviolability of liberty of conscience. One is consequently forced to conclude that the apologetical arguments with which he defended Judaism were intended not so much to establish a solid rational foundation for his religion as to give the appearance of doing so. The case he made for Judaism was in crucial respects more rhetorical than real.

Warding off the attacks of his own opponents and the opponents of Judaism was not, however, Mendelssohn's sole intention. All of his apologetical efforts, it appears, were ultimately designed to play a part in furthering his broader, constructive goals. He had a vision of a better future, one in which the Jews of Europe would constitute a religious minority living in complete harmony with neighboring Gentile majorities in countries where church and state would be completely separate from each other. They would be full participants in their societies, full citizens of their states, and complete collaborators in collective efforts to fulfill the "destiny of man." As an interpreter of Judaism, Mendelssohn was striving, above all, to lay the basis for the implementation of this vision. To achieve his purposes, he was prepared, as we shall argue in the next chapter, to make practical use of apologetical arguments that were, at bottom, theoretically inadequate.

Notes

1. Altmann, "Mendelssohn's Concept of Judaism Reexamined," in *Von der mittelalterlichen zur modernen Aufklärung* p. 245.

2. See Altmann, *Moses Mendelssohn*, pp. 194–263 for a complete account of the Lavater affair.

3. *JubA*, vol. 7, p. 324. Here, Mendelssohn is obviously relying on Maimonides' *Book of Knowledge* I, 8.1.

4. *Jerusalem*, p. 27.

5. Ibid., p. 215.

6. Ibid., p. 90.

7. Saadia Gaon, *The Book of Beliefs and Opinions*, trans. Samuel Rosenblatt (New Haven, Conn.: Yale University Press, 1948), p. 16.

8. Ibid., p. 1

9. Ibid., p. 157.

10. Yehudah Halevi, *Kuzari*, trans. H. Slonimsky (New York: Schocken Books, 1964), vol. 1, p. 84.

11. Ibid., vol. 1, p. 86.

12. Ibid., vol. 1, p. 87.

13. Ibid., vol. 1, p. 4.

14. Ibid., vol. 1, p. 9.

15. Ibid., vol. 1, p. 10.

16. Maimonides, *Book of Knowledge* I, 8.1.

17. *JubA*, vol. 7, p. 324.

18. Ibid., p. 87.

19. Ibid., p. 88.

20. *Jerusalem*, p. 93.

21. Ibid. p. 98.

22. Altmann, *Moses Mendelssohn*, p. 538.

23. *Jerusalem*, p. 99.

24. We find a more detailed statement of this position only in a work Mendelssohn wrote in Hebrew with a conservative Jewish audience in mind, the introduction to his Pentateuch translation and commentary. "Moses our teacher," he stated there, in accordance with rabbinic tradition, "wrote the whole Torah from 'In the beginning' [the first words of Genesis] to 'in the sight of all Israel' [the last words of Deuteronomy]." There was, Mendelssohn admits, some dispute among the rabbis concerning the question of whether Moses actually wrote the last few verses of the Torah, which report his own death. Nevertheless, it is clear to Mendelssohn that Moses wrote these verses as well as the rest of the Torah "*mi-pi ha-ge-vurah.*" *JubA*, vol. 14, p. 212.

25. *Jerusalem*, p. 93.

26. See above all, Mishnah *Sanhedrin*, X.

27. *JubA*, vol. 7, p. 95.

28. Ibid., pp. 101–2.

29. In a letter dated July 22, 1771, to Elkan Herz (*JubA*, vol. 16, pp. 150–51), Mendelssohn spoke of a total correspondence between natural religion and "the principles and fundamental tenets of our religion ('ikkarei ligion and "the principles and fundamental tenets of our religion ('ikkarei ve-yesodei datenu)." Although he denied that Judaism contained anything contrary to reason or suprarational, he did not maintain in this letter that absolutely all of its teachings were accessible to unassisted human reason. See Altmann, *Moses Mendelssohn*, p. 249, for a complete translation of the letter.

30. For a time, at least, Mendelssohn contemplated the composition of similar commentaries expounding the religious doctrines present in the books of Psalms, Proverbs, and Job (see *JubA*, vol. 14, p. 160). But this was a project he never completed.

31. Ibid., p. 149.

32. Ibid., p. 153.

33. Ibid., p. 171. Solomon, in other words, arrived at his understanding of the immortality of the soul through a kind of reasoning that is on the same level as what Mendelssohn describes elsewhere as "the popular moral teaching" (*JubA*, vol. 3, 2, pp. 235–36). He is, to be sure, aware of

another kind of argumentation, but he rejects it. Interpreting Ecc. 3:18, Mendelssohn presents the following paraphrase of its author's position: "However, some people say that an investigation of the nature of the soul alone will bring us to believe in immortality, for God chose man more than any of the other creatures. . . . They say that God selected and chose men from all the other things of the earth to grant them knowledge, understanding and wisdom. But I see that it is not so. . . . That is to say, that men who are deprived of God's supervision, and who are left to themselves alone, are no different from the animals" (*JubA*, vol. 14, p. 171). The teaching with which Solomon is familiar, but that he does not accept, is not clearly identified. It does sound, however, rather suspiciously like the doctrine propounded by Mendelssohn himself in his *Phaedon*, according to which the immortality of the soul can be deduced from an examination of man's nature and a consideration of God's reasons for creating such a being.

Whether or not Mendelssohn intended to suggest that Solomon was unwisely rejecting a teaching similar to his own, it is in any case clear that in his opinion the doctrine of Ecclesiastes was no more sophisticated than that of "the popular moral teaching." But this does not imply, one should hasten to add, that he considered Solomon's inspired teaching to be fit merely for the vulgar. Mendelssohn believed that there was much truth to "the popular moral teaching," and particularly to this aspect of it (*JubA*, vol. 3, 2, p. 237).

34. *JubA*, vol. 10, 1, p. 309. "Ueberhaupt ist dieser Psalm [no. 49] einer der wichtigsten Lehrpsalmen, in welchem der Lehre von dem zukünftigen Leben, von der Auferstehung der Todten und von der Vergeltung des Guten und Bösen in einem zukünftigen Zustande mit deutlichen Worten erwähnt worden, um den Bedrängeten zur Beruhigung und den Sünder zur Besserung zu erwecken." See Altmann, *Moses Mendelssohn*, pp. 307–9, for a discussion of the circumstances under which this piece was written.

35. *JubA*, vol. 6, 1, p. 62: "Für die wahre, umständliche Beschaffenheit unseres künftigen Zustandes haben die Menschen hier weder Sinn noch Begriff. Auch ist es keines Weges die Absicht und die Bestimmung der Offenbarung, unserm Vorwitz hierinn Genüge zu leisten. Sie soll ihn blos stillen, beruhigen, und das Gemüth in die kindliche, harmlose Lage einwiegen, in welecher allein der Mensch seiner Bestimmung treu, und seines Daseyns froh seyn kann. Durch ihre Tröstungen endlich gestärkt, konnte der Psalmist, ganz Zuversicht, ganz Ergebenheit in die Fügung des allgütigen Vaters, nunmehr singen . . ."

36. Altmann, *Von der mittelalterlichen zur modernen Aufklärung*, p. 239.

37. *JubA*, vol. 7, p. 98.

38. *Jerusalem*, p. 121.

39. Ibid., pp. 121–22.

40. Ibid., p. 122.

41. Ibid., p. 125. Altmann offers a plausible explanation for the presence in *Jerusalem* of this discussion of the biblical doctrine of divine mercy. It is meant, he writes, "to offset the reproach of undue harshness which the 'Searcher' had directed against the Mosaic legislation. The Mosaic notion of God that emerges from the story is, by contrast, one of kindness, grace and forgiving" (p. 227). He does not comment, in this instance, on the peculiarity of Mendelssohn's elucidation of a revealed religious doctrine.

42. Ibid., p. 123.

43. Ibid., p. 124.

44. *JubA*, vol. 3, 2, p. 234.

45. *Jerusalem*, p. 97.

46. Ibid., p. 126.

47. Ibid., pp. 97–98.

48. *JubA*, vol. 3, 2, p. 197.

49. *JubA*, vol. 7, p. 98.

50. *Jerusalem*, p. 116.

51. Ibid., pp. 94–95.

52. Ibid., p. 116.

53. Ibid., pp. 107–20.

54. Thomas Wizenmann, *Dic Resultate*, pp. 234ff. See also Hermann Timm, *Gott und die Freiheit*, pp. 241ff; and Frederick Beiser, *The Fate of Reason*, pp. 112–13.

55. Wizenmann, ibid., pp. 210–14.

56. Guttman, "Mendelssohn's *Jerusalem* and Spinoza's *Theologico-Political Treatise*," p. 365.

57. Quoted in ibid., pp. 365–66.

58. Ibid., p. 366.

59. Spinoza's clear target is Maimonides, see *Guide*, vol. 2, p. 33. In "'The Voice of God' in Medieval Jewish Philosophical Exegesis," *Da'at* 16: 29–38 [Hebrew], Howard Kreisel adduces reasons for regarding Maimonides's concept of a "created voice" as an exoteric position.

60. With regard to Spinoza's disingenuousness, see Leo Strauss, *Persecution and the Art of Writing*, pp. 142ff.

61. *Jerusalem*, p. 27.

62. Ibid., p. 215, note to p. 97, line 35.

63. Guttman, "Spinoza's *Theologico-Political Treatise* and Mendelssohn's *Jerusalem*," p. 367.

64. Altmann, *Von der mittelalterlichen zur modernen Aufklärung*, p. 238. Altmann supports his argument by pointing to another passage, in Mendelssohn's correspondence with Abbt (*JubA*, vol. 6, 1, p. 43), where "he goes so far as to say that man is incapable of understanding the language of revelation, assuming there was some form of personal experience of the supernatural. How, for instance, could we obtain some information about the world-to-come, seeing that a revelation would be couched in a language reflecting modes of existence utterly strange to us and speaking in categories unintelligible to our mentality?"

It does not seem, however, that what Mendelssohn says here has any bearing on the capacity of revelation to impart rational truths to humankind. With regard to the precise nature of the afterlife, that is, the kinds of bodies we will have there, the senses and limbs we will then have, he writes to Abbt that, "die Offenbarung selbst kann uns hierüber keinen nähern Unterricht geben: denn sie würde eine Sprache reden, die wir nicht verstehen, Grundideen voraussetzen, die wir nicht haben." In this passage Mendelssohn is speaking not of things that are accessible to us through reason but not through revelation, but rather of things we can understand neither with the aid of our reason nor through revelation. These remarks do not suggest therefore any belief on his part that there are things we can know through reason but not through revelation.

65. *Jerusalem*, p. 95.

66. Wizenmann, *Critical Investigation*, pp. 227–28.

67. Altmann, *Von der mittelalterlichen zur modernen Aufklärung*, p. 239.

68. Ibid, p. 247.

69. See Altmann, *Moses Mendelssohn*, p. 180.

70. Noah Rosenbloom, "Theological Impediments to a Hebrew Version of Mendelssohn's *Phaedon*," *Proceedings for the American Academy of Jewish Research,* 54 (1990): 72–73.

71. Guttman, "Spinoza's *Theologico-Political Treatise* and Mendelssohn's *Jerusalem*," p. 385, n. 36. "The second of the *Wolfenbüttler Fragmente* contains a detailed exposition echoed by several passages in *Jerusalem* . . ." Guttman quotes one of Mendelssohn's statements to the effect that the means of attaining felicity are accessible to all human beings and compares it with Reimarus's statemtent: "God certainly acts differently in matters of the body. He offers through nature in abundance what people and especially children require to live. . . . How, then, can He possibly have placed the means to attain spiritual and eternal life and well-being so far

beyond the reach of man that they are partly unattainable and partly left to chance?"

72. *JubA*, vol. 3, 2, p. lxxxvi.

73. *Jerusalem*, p. 98.

74. Quoted in Altmann, *Moses Mendelssohn*, p. 255.

75. *JubA*, vol. 7, p. 11.

76. Jose Faur, "The Basis for the Authority of the Divine Commandments According to Maimonides," *Tarbiz* 38, no. 1 (1962): 45–47 [Hebrew].

77. Marvin Fox, "Law and Ethics in Modern Jewish Philosophy: The Case of Moses Mendelssohn," *Proceedings of the American Academy for Jewish Religion* 43 (1976): 7.

78. Ibid., p. 9. In *The Image of the Non-Jew in Judaism, An Historical and Constructive Study of the Noahide Laws* (New York: E. Mellen Press, 1983), p. 375, David Novak appears to be grappling with the difficulty to which Fox has called attention. He relates Mendelssohn's treatment of the Noahide laws to his tripartite division of truths into the necessary, the contingent, and the historical. "It is clear that [for Mendelssohn] the Noahide laws only pertain to necessary and contingent truth. Thus, for example, the prohibitions of idolatry and blasphemy certainly presuppose a belief in the existence of God. For Mendelssohn, following Leibniz and Wolff, the existence of God is a metaphysical necessity. Therefore, these two laws would pertain to necessary truth. The rest of the Noahide laws, concerning as they do empirical relations in the created order, pertain to contingent truth, that is, they are required by virtue of the fact that the world is the way it is. None of the Noahide laws pertains to any particular historical events and, therefore, they are all universal and do indeed pertain to either necessary or contingent truth." But even if each of the Noahide laws is at the very least a contingent truth, it is nevertheless the case that those not accessible through reason can be known only through revelation. Novak's observation does not resolve our problem.

79. *JubA*, 19, p. 178.

80. *Jerusalem*, p. 94.

81. Quoted in Altmann, *Moses Mendelssohn*, p. 255.

82. *Jerusalem*, note on p. 213.

83. Ibid., pp. 95–96.

84. Altmann, *Moses Mendelssohn*, p. 256.

85. Arnold Eisen, "Divine Legislation as 'Ceremonial Script': Mendelssohn on the Commandments," *AJS Review* 15, no. 2 (Fall 1990): 259.

86. *JubA*, vol. 7, p. 74.

87. *Jerusalem*, p. 95.

88. Ibid., p. 75.

89. Guttman, "Mendelssohn's *Jerusalem* and Spinoza's *Theologico-Political Treatise*," p. 370. See also Altmann's comments in *Jerusalem*, p. 210.

90. *JubA*, vol. 7, p. 98.

91. *Jerusalem*, p. 116.

92. Altmann, *Moses Mendelssohn*, p. 546.

93. *Jerusalem*, p. 113.

94. Ibid., pp. 108–13.

95. Eisen, "Divine Legislation as 'Ceremonial Script'," pp. 256–57.

96. Altmann, *Moses Mendelssohn*, p. 546.

97. *Jerusalem*, p. 119.

98. Ibid., p. 128.

99. Ibid., p. 118.

100. Ibid., p. 23. See also Altman, "Moses Mendelssohn's Concept of Judaism Re-examined," p. 245, where he states that "one misses in this account of the *ta amey ha-mitzvot* a sense of the truly symbolic that is more than a recall of the already known." Eisen seems to attribute to Altmann the view that Mendelssohn's surmise concerning the commandments was "the least substantiated of all theories he ever advanced." (Eisen, "Divine Legislation as 'Ceremonial Script'," p. 240). But this remark refers only to Mendelssohn's theory concerning the emergence of idolatry, a theory that Eisen himself, as we have already seen, also considers to be "painfully weak."

101. Michael Morgan, "History and Modern Jewish Thought: Spinoza and Mendelssohn on the Ritual Law," *Judaism* 30 (1981): 476.

102. *Jerusalem*, p. 102.

103. Eisen, "Divine Legislation as 'Ceremonial Script': Mendelssohn on the Commandments," pp. 253–55.

104. *Jerusalem*, pp. 91–93, 127.

105. *JubA*, vol. 3, 2, p. 128.

106. Guttman, "Mendelssohn's *Jerusalem* and Spinoza's *Theologico-Political Treatise*," p. 376.

107. Altmann, "Moses Mendelssohn's Concept of Judaism Re-examined," p. 247.

108. See earlier, pp. 188–89, 210–11.

109. See Altmann, *Moses Mendelssohn*, pp. 359–60.

110. Kenneth Hart Green, "Moses Mendelssohn's Opposition to the *Herem*: The First Step Toward Denominationalism?" *Modern Judaism* 12, no. 1 (February 1992): 52. Green is basing himself on Joseph Mendelssohn's letter to Homberg in 1841, in which Joseph remarks that his father "opened his heart to you about many a thing concerning which he kept it closed vis-a-vis others. I still remember this, and letters of yours found among the papers he left, testify to this fact." (See Altmann, *Moses Mendelssohn*, p. 359.

111. Moses Mendelssohn, *Moses Mendelssohn: Selections from his Writings*, trans. and ed. Eva Jospe, with an introduction by Alfred Jospe (New York, 1975), p. 147.

112. Michael Morgan, "History and Modern Jewish Thought: Spinoza and Mendelssohn on the Ritual Law," p. 475.

113. Arnold Eisen, "Divine Legislation as 'Ceremonial Script'," p. 260.

114. Mendelssohn, *Moses Mendelssohn: Selections from His Writings*, p. 147. I have slightly altered the translation here, see the original, *JubA*, vol. 8, p. 134.

115. *Jerusalem*, pp. 133–34. In this context, interestingly enough, Mendelssohn does not reiterate, as he does in the *Phaedon*, that in the mind of God, "all the duties and rights of a moral entity, just like all truths, are in the most perfect harmony." See earlier, p. 59.

116. See *Jerusalem*, p. 234, note to p. 132, lines 29–30.

117. Eisen seems to say precisely this. After briefly discussing Mendelssohn's response to Cranz, Eisen ("Divine Legislation as 'Ceremonial Script'," p. 250) states that "Our concern, however—and, I believe, Mendelssohn's—lies elsewhere." To arrive at this conclusion, I am afraid, is to fall into Mendelssohn's trap.

118. See earlier, p. 000.

119. *Jerusalem*, p. 86.

120. Ibid., p. 87.

121. Ze'ev Levy, "Johann Georg Hamann's Concept of Judaism and Controversy with Mendelssohn's 'Jerusalem'," p. 297.

122. *Jerusalem*, p. 90.

123. Ibid., p. 128. In his characterization of ancient Israel he insistently eschews the use of that term, preferring instead to refer to its regime as the *Mosaic constitution*. Nevertheless, as adamant as Mendelssohn was about rejecting the use of the term *theocracy* to describe the ancient Israelite constitution, he offered no good reason why it should be considered inappropriate. *Theocracy* means, literally, rule by God, and the "Mosaic constitution," by his own description, was a regime in which God

himself was the King and the Regent (*Jerusalem*, p. 128). If anything, Mendelssohn should have protested not the use of the term *theocracy* to describe ancient Israel but the appropriation of the term to describe anything else. That he did not do this is, it seems, the result of his rejection not of the term itself but of its connotations, which were far from positive during the Enlightenment.

124. Eliezer Schweid, *Ha-Yehudi ha-Boded veha-Yahadut* (Tel Aviv, 1974), p. 173 [Hebrew].

125. *Jerusalem*, p. 130.

126. Isaac Heinemann, *Ta'ammei ha-Mitzvot be-Sefrut Yisrael*, (Jerusalem, 1956), Part II, p. 19.

127. *Jerusalem*, p. 130.

128. Ibid., p. 85.

129. Ibid., p. 130.

130. Ibid., p. 232, note to p. 130, lines 24–27.

131. Jacob Katz, *Tradition and Crisis* (New York: Schocken Books, 1961), pp. 98–99.

7
Refashioning Judaism

The late seventeenth and eighteenth centuries witnessed the emergence in Europe of a number of political philosophers who endeavored, through their writings, to bring into existence what they envisioned as a new, more rational, and freer world. Although these thinkers propounded rather different philosophies, they agreed on the need to transcend certain aspects of the European past. Among the things they all wished to alter was the general state of affairs with respect to religion. In a world torn by sectarian animosities, they sought to weaken divisive dogmatisms and broaden religious toleration. In a world in which politics and religion remained inextricably intertwined, they advocated the separation of church and state, a realignment that they believed ought to culminate in the clear subordination of the former to the latter. Their arguments for these changes are among the factors that earn them the right to be numbered among the foremost pioneers of modernization.

These men could not accept the validity of revealed religion, whose premises they rejected, but they were by no means iconoclasts. In the words of Clifford Orwin, they "aimed to break the political-theological deadlock without giving mortal offense to moderate Christians." They therefore presented their new teaching

> not as a rejection but as the perfection of Christianity. They tricked it out as the true interpretation of Scripture, which had eluded the intolerant sects. It was thus that the classics of civility assumed the garb of scriptural commentary, among them Spinoza's *Theological-Political Treatise* and Locke's *Letter on Toleration* and *Reasonableness of Christianity as Delivered in Scripture*.[1]

What thinkers like Spinoza and Locke sought to do within the realm of Christianity set the stage for Mendelssohn's efforts within the Jewish world. Whether Mendelssohn may have been, at bottom, as skeptical as these political philosophers with regard to the truth of revealed religion is a more difficult question to answer than is generally supposed. But his overall political and social aims were definitely akin to theirs, and as we shall see, he was engaged in a similar sort of operation.

Mendelssohn was, of course, neither a Christian like Locke, nor prepared, like Spinoza, to grant practically equal status to the Old and New Testaments. But this did not lessen his need to be just as careful as they were to avoid "giving mortal offense to moderate Christians." And although Locke and Spinoza were, in all likelihood, completely unconcerned as to whether they might be giving offense to Jews, or may even have relished doing so, Mendelssohn obviously had to concern himself with the manner in which his Jewish as well as his Christian readers would react to what he said.

Where Mendelssohn differed most importantly from the philosophers in question was, needless to say, in his presentation of his own theological-political teaching not as the perfection of Christianity but as the perfection or repristination of Judaism. Even if he was working with different cloth, however, he was cutting it to much the same pattern. He was trying to fashion, through biblical interpretation, a Judaism essentially similar to the Judaeo-Christianity of Spinoza or the Christianity of Locke; that is, a Judaism devoid of illiberal doctrines and theocratic tendencies and that would be capable of serving as a civil religion. Just as Spinoza and Locke sought to achieve their aims by "tricking out" their new teachings as true interpretations of Scripture, Mendelssohn pressed various biblical and rabbinic texts into the service of his own reformist program.

To view Mendelssohn's endeavors in the proper perspective, it will therefore be useful for us to examine briefly certain aspects of the theological-political teachings of the two most notable representatives of the liberal tradition to which he belongs, Spinoza and Locke. We have already examined the more radical aspects of Spinoza's theological teaching, those that turn the Bible, in the words of Leo Strauss, into "the target of philosophical criticism." Now we must look at some of the arguments of the second, altogether different type identified by Strauss, those that he bases on the "premise that the Bible is the only document of revelation . . . and that nothing be considered a revealed doctrine that is not borne out by explicit and clear statements in the Bible."[2] We must consider how, feigning piety and employing these arguments, he propounds an interpretation of the Bible supportive of his own political goals.

Locke, a much more cautious writer than Spinoza, never made the Bible his target. But, as we shall see, he utilized its texts, in much the same way as Spinoza, to advance his own, very similar liberal agenda. After this introduction, we will consider the extent to which Mendelssohn followed in the footsteps of both Spinoza and Locke in the development of his theological-political teaching. Finally, we will take note of the way in which one of the greatest representatives of the liberal trends in eighteenth-century political philosophy, Immanuel Kant, understood Mendelssohn's writings on Judaism.

Spinoza

Spinoza was without doubt an unbeliever. He did not accept the existence of a personal God, an extramundane ruler of the universe, much less the God of Israel. As we have already seen, he considered the religion of the Old Testament to be rooted in falsehood and superstition. He held a similar view of the religion of the New Testament.[3] These heretical opinions do not emerge, however, with unequivocal clarity from his writings. Spinoza, like many other unbelieving philosophers of premodern times, knew the perils to which he would be exposing himself by clearly and totally repudiating his society's regnant faith. He consequently chose to "reveal his views while hiding them behind more or less transparent accommodations to the generally accepted opinions."[4]

It was, in part, for such self-protective reasons that he not only masked his most dangerous ideas but also treated the Bible, much of the time, as if it were a genuinely authoritative, divinely revealed text. But it was not solely for his own sake that he did so. "Spinoza was very bold," according to Leo Strauss,

> in so far as he went to the extreme to which he could go as a man who was convinced that religion, i.e., positive religion is indispensable to society, and who took his social duties seriously. He was cautious in so far as he did not state the whole truth clearly and unequivocally but kept his utterances, to the best of his knowledge, within the limits imposed by what he considered the legitimate claims of society.[5]

Spinoza did not feel, however, that a duty to uphold the generally accepted positive religion implies that one must leave it unaltered. In the very same work in which he sought, in a less than completely forthright manner, to undermine the authority of both Testaments in the eyes of his more discerning readers, he described and lent his support not to any existing church but to what he represented as the true teaching of the entire Bible.

"The purpose of the *Treatise*," Strauss has written, "is to show the way toward a liberal society which is based on the recognition of the authority of the Bible, i.e. of the Old Testament taken by itself and of the two Testaments taken together."[6] Spinoza accomplishes this purpose by paring the Bible down to what he claims are its essentials, the only doctrines that it propounds with complete consistency. The "chief aim and object of Scripture," he declares, is to teach obedience to God. And although the various books of the Bible teach countless other, sometimes contradictory things, "we are not bound by Scriptural command to believe anything beyond what is absolutely necessary for fulfilling its main precept."[7]

To fulfill this precept of obedience, it is necessary to accept the fundamental dogmas enumerated by Spinoza in Chapter XIV of the *Treatise*. They include the doctrines of the existence, unity, omnipresence, and sovereignty of God. The fifth dogma holds "that the worship of God consists only in justice and charity, or love towards one's neighbor." The sixth holds that those who obey God by their manner of life are saved. Finally, the seventh dogma maintains that God forgives repentant sinners. These dogmas, taught throughout the Bible, constitute "the Catholic, or universal, religion."[8] They are, as Strauss puts it, essential to "the religion which will be the established religion in the well-ordered republic; belief in these seven dogmas is the only belief necessary and sufficient for salvation. They derive equally from the Old Testament taken by itself and from the New Testament taken by itself."[9] They are nondenominational and can provide the basis for a liberal society.

Spinoza's reading of the Bible is manifestly tendentious. The essential teaching he discovers within the biblical texts is the very teaching he is determined in advance to locate. The method of interpretation by which he arrives at it is one he chose only to have it lead him to the result he desired. Even so, this method does not exactly work in the way that Spinoza wishes to have us believe it works. He purports to identify the chief aim and purpose of the Bible as the transmission of the dogmas that it everywhere teaches, but as Strauss has shown, he himself, in other chapters of the *Treatise*, points to numerous biblical passages that contradict these very dogmas.

In his list of those Biblical teachings which allegedly are presented clearly everywhere in the Bible, Spinoza mentions the dogma that in consequence of God's decree the pious are rewarded and the wicked are punished; but elsewhere he says that, according to Solomon, the same fate meets the just and the unjust, the pure and the impure. He enumerates among the same kind of teachings the dogma that God takes care of all things; it is hard to see how this can be taught in the Bible everywhere clearly if, as Spinoza maintains, the Bible teaches in a number of important passages that God is not omniscient, that he is ignorant of future human actions, and that he takes care only of his chosen people . . .[10]

But these and other contradictions are not meant, it seems, to be evident to Spinoza's less discerning readers.

Spinoza does not really believe, then, that the Bible everywhere and unequivocally taught the fundamental dogmas of the universal religion. Nor, for that matter, does he really consider these dogmas to be true. Some of them are unmistakably at odds with his own metaphysical teaching. But they are, he believes, necessary fictions, as is his contention that they formed the essential core of the Bible. The construction of "a liberal society which is based on the recognition of the authority of the Bible" evidently demanded, on occasion, a certain amount of deliberate misrepresentation of the contents of the Bible.

Spinoza devoted much ingenuity to the extraction from the Bible of the principle, elucidated most fully in Chapter XIV of the *Theologico-Political Treatise*, that "we are not bound by Scriptural command to believe anything beyond what is absolutely necessary for fulfilling its main precept" of obedience to God. In Chapter XIX, he explains what this really means in practice:

> Now it is the function of the sovereign only to decide what is necessary for the public welfare and the safety of the state, and to give orders accordingly; therefore it is also the function of the sovereign only to decide the limits of our duty towards our neighbor—in other words, to determine how we should obey God. . . . Now, no private citizen can know what is good for the state . . . therefore no one can rightly practice piety or obedience to God, unless he obey the sovereign power's commands in all things.[11]

From this it follows that "the true ministers of God's word are those who teach piety to the people in obedience to the authority of the sovereign rulers by whose decree it has been brought into conformity with the public welfare." Ministers of religion who preach otherwise Spinoza classifies as "private citizens" who "seditiously assume the championship of Divine rights" and castigates as people who can only bring ruin upon their states.[12] Spinoza, as Hillel Fradkin has put it, wished to "subordinate religious authority and activity to political authority, and thereby remove religion as a disturbing factor from public life."[13] As we have already observed, in another context, he held that the state retained the right to establish or forbid the espousal of particular religious doctrines or the practice of particular religions.[14] He did not believe, however, that the state ought to attempt to exercise total control over religious life. In his opinion, the separation of church and state and the toleration of all law-abiding sects were policies much more conducive to the establishment of civil peace.

Such was not the practice in ancient Israel, Spinoza maintained. There the people acknowledged God to be the sovereign, and "the laws of the state were called the laws and commandments of God. Thus in the Hebrew state the civil and religious authority, each consisting solely of obedience to God, were one and the same." As a result, "between civil and religious law and right there was no distinction whatever."[15] The sacred precedent of the biblical theocracy constituted something of an obstacle to the development and acceptance of Spinoza's liberal teachings. He therefore had to explain why it was not, in any respect, an appropriate example for anyone to follow.

Furthermore, as Strauss has observed, in Spinoza's opinion

> the establishment of a liberal society required the abrogation of the Mosaic law in so far as it is a particularistic and political law, and especially of the ceremonial laws. . . . It is for this reason that Spinoza is so anxious to prove that Moses' law lost its obligatory power, and that the Jews ceased to be the chosen people with the loss of the Jewish state: the Jews cannot be at the same time the members of two nations and subject to two comprehensive legal codes.[16]

Spinoza, then, wished to free everyone, but especially the Jews, from the residual influence of the example of biblical theocracy. As we have seen, he sought to accomplish his goals, in some measure, through the characterization of the Mosaic law as a purely political law, one that was intended for the Jews alone and has now, in any case, been rendered completely obsolete by the demise of the Jewish state.[17]

Locke

John Locke is best remembered today, it seems, for his *Essay on Human Understanding*, one of the seminal works of modern epistemology, and his second *Treatise on Government*, arguably the most important and influential exposition of social contract theory of all time. But Locke is also the author, among many other things, of the two "classics of civility" referred to by Orwin, his *Letter on Toleration* and *Reasonableness of Christianity as Delivered in Scripture*. In the *Letter*, Locke presents a multifaceted argument in favor of the granting of liberty of conscience to adherents of all religions (though not to atheists, who do not honor "promises, covenants, and oaths, which are the bonds of human society"). He seeks to show that the "toleration of those that differ from others in matters of religion" is required by both the gospels and "the genuine reason of mankind." [18] In the *Reasonableness of Christianity*, Locke attempts to demonstrate both the authenticity of the Christian revelation and the essential rationality of its contents.

"No one who possesses a sympathetic understanding of Locke's political theology," Thomas Pangle has written, "could ever pronounce against him the accusation of atheism." [19] Atheism is one thing; impiety, however, is another. The author we have just quoted as well as several others have convincingly argued that Locke's profession of belief in the rationality of the Christian religion was, at bottom, completely disingenuous, that he in fact covertly rejected the truth of biblical revelation. [20] In much the same manner as Spinoza, they maintain, but with much greater circumspection, he covertly indicated his genuine, heretical views while overtly accommodating himself to generally accepted opinions.

Again, we owe our understanding of Locke's esotericism mainly to Leo Strauss. In accordance with his usual method, Strauss first called attention to the passages in which Locke subtly indicated to his readers that it is sometimes necessary for a wise man to tread cautiously when discussing matters of religion. He then demonstrated how Locke followed his own advice, overtly professing Christianity while hinting at the same time, "between the lines," that he did not really believe what he was saying.

Strauss points, among other things, to the way in which Locke contrasts the conduct of Socrates with that of Plato and other unnamed philosophers. Living among the Greeks, who lacked a true understanding of religion, Socrates, who knew of the existence of one God, "opposed and laughed at their polytheism, and wrong opinions of the deity; and we see how they rewarded him for it." Plato, on the other hand, as well as other, more sober philosophers "were fain, in their outward professions and worship, to go with the herd, and keep to their religion established by law," whatever they may privately have thought of it. Strauss also notes how Locke describes the way in which Jesus conducted himself among the Jews. According to Locke, Jesus acted with "caution" and "reservedness." He spoke obscurely and concealed his true views, "his circumstances being such, that without such a prudent carriage and reservedness, he could not have gone through with the work which he came to do . . ." According to Strauss, Locke's evident preference for Plato's demeanor over that of Socrates and his approving description of Jesus' conduct reflect his own belief that "cautious speech is legitimate if unqualified frankness would hinder a noble work one is trying to achieve or expose one to persecution or endanger the public peace; and legitimate caution is perfectly compatible with going with the herd in one's outward professions or with using ambiguous language or with so involving one's sense that one cannot easily be understood." Locke's descriptions of the Greek philosophers and Jesus are clearly designed, Strauss maintains, to offer his readers an important hint with regard to his own procedure.

Strauss himself takes the hint and seeks to extract Locke's true opinions from beneath his ambiguous and intentionally obfuscatory language. Eyeing suspiciously Locke's proof of Jesus' divine mission, he discovers sufficient grounds for doubting that it ought to be taken at face value. This proof is based on the miracles performed by Jesus and his apostles. Yet, as Strauss points out, Locke elsewhere betrays a very Spinozist attitude to the question of the knowability of miracles, thereby rendering it quite doubtful "whether a demonstrative argument can be based on Locke's notion of miracles."

The miracles on which the Christian religion is based were, according to Locke, "done in all parts so frequently, and before so many witnesses of all sorts, in broad day-light, that . . . the enemies of Christianity have never dared to deny them; no, not Julian himself: who neither wanted skill nor power to inquire into the truth . . ." How, Strauss wonders, can "a most competent contemporary of Hobbes and Spinoza," a man who was, in addition, well aware of the presence of a considerable number of Deists in his own society and was indeed, by his own admission, writing his defense of Christianity with them in mind, possibly have made such a statement? These thinkers' denials of the Christian miracles most certainly should have indicated to Locke the falseness of his assertion and therefore the inadequacy of his proof of the truth of Jesus' mission.[21]

Michael Zuckert has pursued the same line of reasoning, indicating somewhat more clearly than Strauss the conclusion to which it leads. Unlike Strauss, he focuses not on contemporary doubters of the Christian miracles with whom Locke was certainly familiar but on the ancient heretic he mentions in the passage quoted previously. He notes, in addition, Locke's statement that Julian "durst not deny so plain a matter of fact, which being granted, the truth of our Saviour's doctrine unavoidably follows . . ." But, he observes,

> Apart from the fact that Locke strongly overinterprets Julian's comments on the miracles of the Christians as implying an acceptance of their character as authentic miracles, the instance of Julian himself contradicts Locke's point in a way Locke must have meant to convey. Given the fact that Julian was an "enemy of Christianity," and that there were other enemies too, it must be that men could and did in fact deny either "the matter of fact" of the miracles or the "unavoidable" truth of Jesus' doctrine and mission."

What Locke really meant to say, between the lines, was the opposite of what he appeared to be saying: "In summary, the Christian miracles do not, according to Locke, have the evident force and necessity that compels a reasonable man to accept them as validators of the truth of Christianity."[22]

Both Strauss and Zuckert regard Locke as a writer who expounded his heretical views very cautiously, ever mindful of the price he might have to pay for a misstep. Zuckert also draws attention to the extent to which his adherence to Christianity stemmed from his belief in the necessity of religion as a support for morality. Because most people are, according to Locke, incapable of arriving at a rational understanding of moral principles, "they must believe" in a revelation that propounds them.[23] "[H]uman society requires a civil religion, which, in Locke's historical situation, means the endorsement of Christianity."[24]

Although he was prepared to accommodate himself to Christianity, Locke was well aware of its problematic aspects. In the past it had served to promote not peace, harmony, and unity in society, but "schisms, separations, contentions, animosities, quarrels, blood and butchery." As Zuckert observes, Locke traces this "special propensity of Christianity" to "a combination of two qualities that together distinguish it from other religions." One of these is a quality it shares with Judaism, its monotheism; the other is one that distinguishes it from Judaism, its emphasis on doctrine. Belief in the one true God leads to efforts to establish the worship of that God alone. Concern with correct doctrine leads to internecine strife. "What else," therefore, "can be expected among Christians but their tearing, and being torn in pieces, by one another; whilst every sect assumes to itself a power of declaring fundamentals, and severally thus narrow Christianity to their distinct systems?"[25]

Needless to say, Locke does not propose a return to polytheism, but he does endeavor to mitigate the ill-effects of the Christian religion's focus on matters of faith. His principal method of doing so is to counteract "the narrowing of Christianity to distinctive systems" by reducing, as far as possible, the number and significance of obligatory Christian beliefs and defining those beliefs as loosely and inclusively as he possibly could. He develops what Zuckert calls a " 'stripped down' version of Christianity."[26]

Instead of attempting to identify, as Spinoza had, those doctrines taught without contradiction throughout the entire Bible with the fundamental message of the Old and New Testaments, Locke sought to do something roughly similar but—from a Christian standpoint—more defensible. He endeavored to identify the essential content of Christianity with "the sole doctrine pressed and required to be believed in the whole tenor of our Saviour's and his apostles' teaching." On the basis of a detailed survey of the New Testament, he concluded that there was only one doctrine "upon their assent to which, or disbelief of it, men were pronounced believers or unbelievers; and accordingly received into the church of Christ, as members of his body; as far as mere believing could make them so; or else kept out of it." This was the belief that Jesus was the messiah.[27]

Locke does not provide a very specific explanation of the significance of Jesus' messiahship. He understands this article of faith, as Zuckert puts it, "in a sufficiently broad or ill-defined manner that any number of different sects could happily subscribe to it." Among other things, it represents an attempt to bridge the gap between those who affirm the divinity of Jesus and those who do not. "Locke means to overcome the bloody sectarianism of Christendom through bringing men to such a comprehensive formulation of the fundamental article of faith." Together with his *Letter Concerning Toleration*, it "would go very far toward overcoming that thousand-year history of which he speaks."[28]

Christianity, according to Locke, has only one article of faith, but he by no means considers this one doctrine to constitute the entirety of the Christian religion. Something else is frequently the subject of the preachments of Jesus and his disciples and is also required to obtain salvation: repentance. "Repentance is as absolute a condition of the covenant of grace as faith; and as necessary to be performed as that."[29] By repentance Locke understands "an hearty sorrow for our past misdeeds, and a sincere resolution and endeavour, to the utmost of our power, to conform all our actions to the law of God." It does not consist of a momentary act of contrition but "in a sincere obedience to the law of Christ, the remainder of our lives." Two things, then, "faith and repentance, i.e. believing Jesus to be the Messiah, and a good life, are the indispensable conditions of the new covenant, to be performed by all those who would obtain eternal life."[30]

But why not only one thing? Why does Locke not believe in justification by faith alone, a doctrine for which there is abundant precedent within Protestant Christianity? If, after all, he had consistently applied his fundamental principle of interpretation, according to which one must believe only what Jesus and the apostles everywhere required as a condition of admittance into the church, this is the conclusion at which he would have arrived. As Zuckert points out,

> the argument Locke deployed against other articles of faith applies equally well against his own scriptural derivation of works from the preaching of repentance. For example . . . Locke adduces the preaching of the apostles Phillip and Paul (in Acts 8–17) as evidence for his position on the necessary article of faith: in none of these passages, however, did the apostles conjoin the call to repentance with the preaching of Jesus as Messiah.[31]

In the end, what Jesus and the apostles all said is less important for Locke than what civil society requires. The basic method of interpretation of which he makes use in *The Reasonableness of Christianity* serves only to strip Christianity of unnecessary dogmas, but does not supply those doctrines necessary to provide cosmic support for morality. For this purpose, the doctrine of Jesus' messiahship must be supplemented. Locke must violate his own otherwise serviceable principle of interpretation to derive from the New Testament the requisite elements of a civil religion. Christianity must be construed to supply support for the "law of God," which is identical, according to Locke, with "the law of reason, or, as it is called, of nature." And, as Zuckert puts it, "These laws of nature, these 'just measures of right and wrong,' are 'the bonds of society, and of common life, and laudable practices.' Thus the 'works' which God rewards and punishes in the hereafter are precisely those that support or undermine the requirements of civil life."[32]

In his first *Letter Concerning Toleration*, as we noted earlier, Locke argues in favor of liberty of conscience both on the basis of reason and on the basis of the gospels. It will not be necessary, for our purposes, to examine the manner in which he demonstrates the gospels' position on this matter or to discuss, in any more detail than we already have, his other reasons for advocating toleration. The only thing we need to consider, in the present context, is the manner in which he deals with the somewhat inconvenient discrepancy between the content of the Old Testament, whose sanctity he reaffirms, and the views he espouses in the *Letter*.

In the *Letter*, Locke goes so far as to endorse the toleration of idolators. Against such an audacious proposal he anticipates an obvious objection. It may be argued, he acknowledges, "that by the law of Moses idolaters were to be rooted out." This, Locke admits, is indeed true

> by the law of Moses; but that is not obligatory to us Christians. Nobody pretends that every thing, generally, enjoined by the law of Moses, ought to be practised by Christians. But there is nothing more frivolous than that common distinction of moral, judicial, and ceremonial law, which men ordinarily make use of: for no positive law whatsoever can oblige any people but those to whom it is given.

Opposing what was widely taught by various Christian churches in his own day, Locke insisted that no part of the Old Testament legislation should be considered to retain any authority, at least as far as Christians were concerned. Moses gave his law not to them but to the Jews.

Among the Jews, he goes on to observe, there were "those who, being initiated into the Mosaical rites, and made citizens of that commonwealth, did afterwards apostatize from the worship of the God of Israel." In describing the nature of the offense they committed and the punishment to which they were subjected, Locke elucidates his understanding of the character of the ancient Jewish regime. The Jewish idolators, he writes, were proceeded against as traitors and rebels, guilty of no less than high treason; for the commonwealth of the Jews, different in that from all others, was an absolute theocracy: nor was there, or could there be, any difference between that commonwealth and the church, The laws established there concerning the worship of one invisible Deity, were the laws of that people, and a part of their political government, in which God himself was the legislator.

Locke neither favors nor deplores this kind of regime. He states only that

if any one can show me where there is a commonwealth, at this time, constituted upon that foundation, I will acknowledge that the ecclesiastical laws do there unavoidably become a part of the civil; and that the subjects of that government both may, and ought to be, kept in strict conformity with that church, by the civil power. But there is absolutely no such thing, under the Gospel, as a Christian commonwealth.[33]

Theocracy may have been appropriate for the Jews, but the new dispensation has rendered it entirely obsolete. With this argument Locke has disposed of one possible objection against his call for the toleration of idolators. Even more important, he has explained why the Old Testament theocracy is an altogether inappropriate standard for Christians today to employ in the evaluation of the regimes under which they themselves live. But while Locke may have succeeded in consigning the regulations governing the ancient Jewish commonwealth to the remote past, he leaves one very significant question unanswered. As he himself states, "true and saving religion consists in the inward persuasion of the mind, without which nothing can be acceptable to God. And such is the nature of the understanding, that it cannot be compelled to the belief of any thing by outward force."[34] If this is the case, how could God *ever* have wished to established a theocratic government, which made religious observance compulsory, for any people? It is possible to imagine, of course, a number of ways in which Locke might have chosen to respond to this question. But since no "searcher after light and right" ever challenged him to do so, we cannot know what his answer would have been.

Our examination of the writings of Spinoza and Locke shows that both thinkers adopted rather similar means of pursuing similar agendas. Both were unwilling to accept the truth of biblical revelation, yet both thought it advisable, for their own good as well as that of society as a whole, to veil their true opinions and to treat the revealed texts as authoritative sources. Both devised methods of biblical interpretation that enabled them, or at any rate seemed to enable them, to "strip down" the sacred texts, to derive from them only the teachings which they considered useful while discarding or at least attenuating those which they considered disruptive of social harmony.

Spinoza managed to depict the Bible as containing only those very general and simple doctrines "absolutely necessary for fulfilling its main precept" of obedience to God; that is, obedience to the secular authorities. Locke reduced the teaching of the New Testament to one extremely simple theological doctrine and one practical doctrine, "repentance," which amounted, in essence, to the duty "to conform all our actions to the law of God." Except in extreme circumstances, the law of God, as he understood it, dictated obedience to the law of the state.

Both Spinoza and Locke perceived the Old Testament model of theocratic government to constitute something of an obstacle, at least in theory, to their call for the separation of church and state. Both felt the necessity to explain why the Mosaic law could not serve as a precedent for contemporary peoples. They both stated emphatically that it was bound to a specific time and a specific place and that it fell into desuetude when the commonwealth for which it was designed passed from the stage of history.

Mendelssohn

Unlike Spinoza, Mendelssohn was unquestionably a genuine theist. The tenets of "the universal religion" that were for Spinoza not true but merely useful were in Mendelssohn's eyes both true and indispensable. He may, to be sure, have felt toward the end of his life that his own as well as other philosophers' proofs for the existence of God, providence, and immortality were in jeapordy, but he nevertheless continued to show confidence in the resilience of reason, in its capacity to rise to new challenges and silence the objections invented by skeptics. And although it is true that Leo Strauss, as we saw in Chapter 4, doubts the sincerity of Mendelssohn's insistence that belief in immortality is necessary for the support of morality, even he does not call into question the genuineness of Mendelssohn's belief in this fundamental principle of natural religion.[35] There is no reason to doubt, either, that Mendelssohn means what he says when he claims that human happiness, no less than human morality, rests on a knowledge of the fundamental principles of natural religion.

It is less certain that Mendelssohn truly believed in the revealed character of the Old Testament and the truth of the Jewish religion. In fact, some scholars, such as Konrad Feireis, have suggested that he was, at bottom, nothing more than a Deist who feigned adherence to Judaism to retain his influence among his fellow Jews.[36] Although no one who has voiced this opinion has done so, it seems, on the basis of careful study of Mendelssohn's Jewish writings, this is nonetheless a contention that cannot be dismissed out of hand. There are, after all, ample precedents for such conduct, not only among the political philosophers who influenced Mendelssohn's thinking but also among other eighteenth-century writers with whom he had important affinities.

Whatever allegiance Spinoza showed to revealed religion was unmistakably disingenuous. A good case can be made, as we have seen, that Locke was not a believing Christian but simply adapted his teachings to conform to the faith of his countrymen. Many of the English Deists, too, in a similar fashion, employed what David Berman has called "the art of theological lying."[37]

Hermann Samuel Reimarus also belongs in this general category of writers who were less than completely candid with their readers. As we saw in Chapter 5, his unpublished *Apology* contains a monumental attack on the validity and value of biblical revelation. "There was," however, as Charles H. Talbert has put it, "a public and a private Reimarus."[38] The public Reimarus, the author of *The Foremost Truths of Natural Religion*, prudently and successfully posed, as we noted earlier in this study, as someone who believed that natural religion and Christianity complemented one another, that the former was the necessary foundation of the latter. During the *Fragmentenstreit*, it should be noted, no one suspected him of being the "unnamed" author of the excerpts from his *Apology* published by Lessing.

Could there, we must ask, much as there was "a private and a public Reimarus," also have been "a private and a public Mendelssohn"? In other words, might Mörschel's intuitions have been correct after all? One cannot help but feel a sense of trepidation when one poses such questions. In view of Mendelssohn's repeated reiterations of his loyalty to Judaism and his forceful argumentation in its behalf, they may even seem preposterous. But they are not. From what we have seen so far it should be clear that there is room for doubting the sincerity of any eighteenth-century defender of natural religion professing a belief in a particular divine revelation. If we had in our possession only the writings that Reimarus intended to have published, we would not have any reason whatsoever for suspecting that he was in fact what we know him to have been, a Deist prudently assuming the guise of a Christian. The mere existence of someone like Reimarus, whose private and public stances differed so greatly from each other, legitimates the question of whether there might not have been a private Mendelssohn very dissimilar to the public one.

The "public Mendelssohn" is, to be sure, a great deal more outspoken in his defense of Judaism than is the "public Reimarus" with regard to Christianity. As we have already observed, Reimarus, in *The Foremost Truths*, merely characterized natural religion as the foundation of Christianity and endeavored to leave the impression that his defense of the former was partly motivated by his desire to protect the latter.[39] There is, in his published works, no exposition of the truth of Christianity that could be considered comparable to the extended treatment of Judaism that we find in Mendelssohn's writings. Nevertheless, it is still conceivable that the two men were engaged in fundamentally similar enterprises, the difference lying chiefly in the fact that Mendelssohn's "deceptive maneuvre," to borrow Gawlick's phrase, may have been a more thoroughgoing and comprehensive one.

It does not, in the end, require any great leap of the imagination to conceive of Mendelssohn as a naturalist who was merely assuming the guise of a faithful Jew. He makes no secret, after all, of his belief that the essential truths of religion are accessible to all human beings whether or not they have been the recipients of divine revelation. Even if he did not oppose as consistently as is generally thought the idea of revealed religions doctrines, he certainly maintained at all times that revelation had not been and could not be the source of any *indispensable* religious doctrines. One does not need to look beneath the surface, therefore, to find a Mendelssohn who was arguing that revelation was, in effect, of secondary importance.

When Mendelssohn contemplates the prospect of living without knowledge of God, providence and immortality, he conjures up, as we have seen, rather chilling portraits of a bleak and inhospitable universe. One can scarcely doubt the genuineness, at such moments, of his horror, especially when one bears in mind his lifelong endeavors to ward off the doubts that threaten to make such a universe real. Nowhere, on the other hand, does Mendelssohn suggest that he would be similarly bereft of hope if biblical revelation were to be discredited. Nor could one expect him to say such a thing. For even if he were to be persuaded that the Bible was the product of ignorant and superstitious people and recorded no genuine revelation, he would still possess knowledge of the fundamental principles of natural religion that would be sufficient to afford him complete consolation.

In this connection, it is impossible not to think, of course, of the passage in *Jerusalem* where Mendelssohn does reflect on the situation in which he would find himself if his faith in the truth of the Bible were shaken. Toward the beginning of Section II, as we have seen, he recapitulates the argument of *The Searching for Light and Right*. After summarizing the gist of Cranz's position, he says that if his depiction of Judaism were accurate, "I would indeed shamefully retract my propositions and bring reason into captivity under the yoke of—but no! Why should I dissimulate? . . . Were it true that the word of God so manifestly contradicted my reason, the most I could do would be to impose silence upon my reason." Any such effort would, however, undoubtedly prove futile. In the end, Mendelssohn says, "my unrefuted arguments would, nevertheless, reappear in the most secret recesses of my heart, be transformed into disquieting doubts, and the doubts would resolve themselves into childlike prayers, into fervent supplications for illumination."

What we see here is Mendelssohn admitting that he would indeed be disturbed by a threat to Judaism, that it would reduce him to pained confusion—but not that it would plunge him into the utmost despair. For a way out of his predicament, he would turn in prayer to God, the God to whom the Psalmist prayed for illumination, and in whom his own belief would in any event remain unshaken.

Immediately following this passage, it is true, Mendelssohn explicitly discusses the very possibility that we are here considering. He berates Mörschel for implying that he has "the odious intention of overthrowing the religion I profess and of renouncing it surreptitiously, as it were, though not expressly." Indignantly, Mendelssohn states that

> imputative inferences like these ought to be banished forever from the intercourse of learned men. Not everyone who holds a certain opinion is prepared to accept, at the same time, all the consequences flowing from it, even if they are ever so cor-

rectly deduced. Imputations of this kind are hateful and lead only to bitterness and strife, by which truth rarely gains anything.[40]

Mendelssohn's indignation here seems real enough, but it is not entirely unequivocal. Oddly enough, he seems to be blaming Mörschel for drawing unimpeachably logical conclusions from what he himself had elsewhere written. Why, we must wonder, are his words so hateful to Mendelssohn? Is it, perhaps, simply because they were so troublesome, because he would greatly have preferred not to have had to discuss such matters in public?

If Mendelssohn was indeed a covert denier of revelation, he would have had good reason to conceal such an outlook, even better reason, perhaps, than any of the other figures we have mentioned so far. It does not take much imagination to conceive of the immense difficulties he would have created for himself had he declared publicly that he did not believe that a revelation had actually taken place at Sinai. His activities as a modernizer had already rendered his position in the Jewish community somewhat precarious.[41] An open declaration of his rejection of the authority of revelation would no doubt have destroyed it completely and brought about his ostracism or excommunication and would at the same time have left him with nowhere to turn—unless, of course, he had been willing to convert to Christianity. For even in what Jacob Katz has described as the "semineutral society" of late eighteenth century Germany there was still very little room for anyone who belonged to no religious community whatsoever.[42] An admission of heresy would sooner or later have forced Mendelssohn to choose between the misery of social exclusion and the hypocrisy of disingenuous conversion.

Fear of persecution would not have been Mendelssohn's only reason for concealing any heretical views he may have held. Like Spinoza and Locke, he very clearly distinguished between the requirements of free, philosophical inquiry and the requirements of human society. He did not believe that one should always tell everyone the unvarnished truth. On the contrary, as Altmann has observed, the "idea that 'superstition' may have to be tolerated if it serves as a prop to morality . . . runs as a leitmotif through many of his writings."[43]

We have already seen evidence of this in his description in the *Counterreflections* of the way in which the fundamental truths of religion were first disseminated. "The experience of most peoples teaches," he there maintains, "that this initially took place by means of prejudices. The common people are convinced through superstitions of very important truths, without which they cannot be happy in social life."[44] In a preamble to his *Phaedon* Mendelssohn (in stark contrast to Locke) approvingly portrays Socrates as someone who, in his activities as an educator, remained keenly aware of the need "to avoid offending the weaker minds of his fellow citizens, [thereby] causing annoyance and forfeiting the beneficial influence that even the most absurd religion has on the morals of simple minds."[45] Mendelssohn himself admittedly follows Socrates' example in his treatment of Christianity. Though he clearly regards it as a religion deeply imbued with superstition, he strenuously avoids writing anything "against a religion from which so many of my fellow men expect contentment in this life and unlimited felicity thereafter."[46]

What is probably Mendelssohn's clearest statement of the principle underlying these various remarks is found in his brief essay entitled "What Is Enlightenment?" If it is not possible to disseminate certain useful and elevated truths without demolishing the foundations of religion and morality, he writes, "the virtue-loving proponent of enlightenment [*tugendeliebende Aufklärer*] will conduct himself carefully and with caution. He will sooner endure the prejudice than dispel it together with the truth with which it is so inextricably intertwined." This, Mendelssohn claims, is a difficult but not impossible maxim to follow, one that any friend of humankind "must take into consideration even in the most enlightened times."[47]

These rather well-known comments are usually understood to have reference to the earliest peoples, to the Greeks, to Christians, but not to the Jews. It is perfectly conceivable, however, that considerations of this kind governed Mendelssohn's stance toward his own people as well. This is not to suggest that he meant anything other than what he said when he identified Judaism as the most purely monotheistic religion in existence, but only that he may have regarded it, too, as a mixture of religious truths, on the one hand, and prejudice and superstition, on the other. And he may have defined the latter category so broadly as to include the very idea of divine revelation. His public posture of Jewish piety may have been motivated not by a belief in the truth of Judaism but by an interest in his own safety combined with a concern for the spiritual and moral welfare of his fellow Jews (and, in the end, of his fellow Christians as well, for, as Mendelssohn stressed, Christianity stands on Jewish foundations).[48]

Mendelssohn did indicate on occasion his belief that contemporary Judaism was encrusted with much in the way of prejudice and superstition. In his letter to Lavater, for instance, he referred to the "man-made additions and abuses" that now obscured much too greatly the splendor of the Jewish religion. "What friend of the truth," he asked, could boast of having found his religion free of harmful man-made statutes?" He noted subsequently that "we all know this poisoning breath of hypocrisy and superstition." And a little later in the letter he referred disparagingly to the misconceptions of Judaism disseminated by certain people who were acquainted or half-acquainted with rabbinic literature, misconceptions drawn from "old volumes that no rational Jew reads or knows." Nothing he says in this letter can be taken, however, to confirm the hypothesis outlined earlier. The things Mendelssohn condemns here, he makes clear, are later accretions that have nothing to do with "the essential core" of his religion.[49] Still, these comments may be relevant to the question with which we are concerned. They suggest another reason why Mendelssohn might have concealed any doubts he might have had concerning the truth of "the essential core of Judaism." If he expressed such doubts, he would have thoroughly discredited himself among his fellow Jews and immediately have lost the power—a power that mattered greatly to him—to combat the kind of ignorance and superstition within the contemporary Jewish world that he considered to be genuinely harmful. Mendelssohn, in other words, may have held his tongue to continue playing a part in the promotion of the *Haskalah*, the Jewish Enlightenment.

In the light of what we have said up to now, it ought to be acknowledged that it is at least conceivable that Mendelssohn was, at bottom, as Konrad Feireis maintains, a pure Deist who was merely pretending—for what he considered to be good reasons—to be a believing Jew as well. It is one thing, however, to supply him with possible motives for assuming a certain pose, and a rather different matter to prove that he was in fact acting in accordance with these motives. That this is in fact what he was doing is something we simply cannot say with any certainty. The most we can possibly do is to demonstrate similarities between the argumentation of those thinkers who were masquerading as believers in revealed religion and refashioning it for their own purposes and Mendelssohn's own arguments. If he seems to be saying more or less what they were saying, it may be because he secretly believed what they believed.

The first such resemblance to which we can point is that between Locke's and Mendelssohn's proofs for the occurrence of revelation. In substance these proofs are not closely parallel. Locke, it will be recalled, based his proof of the truth of Jesus' mission on the miracles accompanying it; Mendelssohn, in his effort to establish the historicity of the Sinaitic revelation, denied the probative power of miracles (even as he acknowledged that that revelation itself constituted a miracle) and focused on the requirement of reliable testimony. What the two proofs have in common, however, is the manner in which they both represent evasions of the difficulties to which their authors must have realized they were exposed. Both Locke and Mendelssohn seek to validate revelation on the basis of arguments to which Spinoza and his heirs had already dealt severe blows. Locke saddles miracles with a burden that they can no longer bear. Mendelssohn places a similar, unbearably weighty burden on the shoulders of the ancient Israelites and the authors of the biblical books. Both philosophers were undoubtedly aware of the vulnerabilities of their arguments, yet both proceeded—ostensibly, at any rate—as if they were oblivious to them.

As Strauss and Zuckert have shown, Locke's proof of the truth of Jesus' mission contains, just beneath the surface, telltale signs of his awareness of the specious character of what he presents as his own reasoning, which are presumably intended to catch the attention of his more astute readers. There is no firm evidence that Mendelssohn was doing the same thing. Still, as we have seen, his most important and comprehensive argument for the historicity of the Sinaitic revelation, in *Jerusalem*, is a very peculiar one. Read carefully and literally, it does not at all prove what it seems to purport to prove. This is most likely, a sign, as we argued in the previous chapter, of Mendelssohn's awareness of the new vulnerability of the medieval argument to hostile criticism. But it may also reflect something more; that is, a tacit recognition of the validity of the critique of the medieval argument. This is, of course, too weak a hypothesis on which to build, and nothing more will be made of it here.

The truly significant resemblance between the arguments of Mendelssohn and the other philosophers we have been discussing in this chapter is related not to their respective proofs of the truth of revelation but to their reinterpretations of the content of the different revelations with which they are concerned. Similar motives seem to have inspired them to use materials drawn from very different sources to construct fundamentally similar concepts of religion.

As we have seen, both Spinoza and Locke were deeply concerned with the undesirable consequences of religious dogmatism, especially the different manifestations of Christian dogmatism. To diminish these effects, they resorted to similar, highly arbitrary strategies of biblical interpretation. In roughly similar ways they discounted the significance of doctrines that were not reiterated throughout the Bible (or, in Locke's case, throughout the New Testament) and sought to identify true religion (or, in Locke's case, true Christianity) with what they chose to define as the *essential* teaching of revelation. For Spinoza, this boiled down to nothing more than the teaching of obedience to God's dictates; that is, the laws of the state. For Locke, Jesus retained a special—if ill-defined—status, the affirmation of which constituted, in his opinion, the one absolutely indispensable tenet of Christian faith. Apart from this obligatory acceptance of Jesus' messiahship (whatever this was understood to mean), Christianity consisted, for him, of nothing more than the imperative to conduct oneself in accordance with the law of God, which, in practice, usually means the law of the state.

Mendelssohn, like Spinoza and Locke, was highly conscious of the harm perpetrated in the past by zealous propagators of religious dogma and clearly wished to play a part in bringing an end to such evils. His opportunities to do so were, however, rather limited. Unlike Spinoza, he lacked the temerity to attempt to purify Christianity for the Christians. He could hope that the Christians would become less credulous, but he could call upon them only to be more tolerant. Lacking the necessary qualifications to make any pronouncements with regard to the true, essential content of the majority religion, Mendelssohn could do little to affect the course of its development. What he could undertake, however, was a reassessment of the nature of his own religion. He could discount the signficance of its doctrinal component and thereby show that it and therefore its practitioners were in every way worthy of participating in the world the thinkers of the Enlightenment were trying to summon into being.

Mendelssohn might conceivably have achieved these purposes by arguing that Judaism contained no obligatory dogmas but that it did include revealed doctrines. He might have continued to present, as he generally did prior to the composition of *Jerusalem* and as he sometimes did even later, a version of Judaism based on a rationalist interpretation of the doctrines of the Old Testament. We have already seen, however, what kind of difficulties this would have entailed and some of what he had to gain from employing, instead, his new, very dubiously derived and inadequately defended concept of Judaism as "not a revealed religion, but revealed legislation." What we need to observe now is that this new formula was of use in more ways than one. Not only could it help to ward off accusations that Judaism failed to live up to the standards of natural religion or was less than completely rational, but it could also show how averse it was, in spirit, to the kind of religious contentiousness that threatened civil peace.

It was for this reason highly useful for Mendelssohn to be able to maintain, through a subtle modification of the traditional sources, that "according to the concepts of true Judaism, all the inhabitants of the earth are destined to felicity," if only they adhere to the tenets of natural law.[50] The Jews' broad tolerance of their neighbor's creeds strengthened their claim to eligibility for membership in a liberal society. Mendelssohn's claim that Judaism had no compulsory doctrines, indeed no doctrinal content of its own distinct from that of natural religion, drove the same point home. It showed that the Jews were not even inclined to impose specific beliefs on one another.

Mendelssohn's new teaching also enabled him to downplay the significance of the uniquely Jewish belief that raised the greatest doubts in the minds of Gentiles with regard to the Jews' suitability for citizenship in non-Jewish states; that is, the belief in the advent of a messiah who would one day lead them back to their own land. Mendelssohn himself was well aware of the extent to which this doctrine served as an impediment to the Jews' progress. He saw, for instance, how Johann David Michaelis had responded to the plea for the emancipation of the Jews voiced in Dohm's *Concerning the Amelioration of the Civil Status of the Jews* (1781). Michaelis had stated, among other things, that their messianic expectation of a return to Palestine "casts doubt on the full and steadfast loyalty of the Jews to the state and the possibility of their full integration" into it.[51]

In the face of suspicions of this kind, Mendelssohn did not repudiate messianism, as many of the founders of Reform Judaism were later to do, but he did seek to minimize the role it played in Judaism. Directly replying to Michaelis, he insisted that "the hoped-for return to Palestine, which troubles [him] so much, has no influence on our conduct as citizens. This is confirmed by experience wherever Jews are tolerated." It is only natural, he wrote, for people to feel at home where they live. Anyone "who holds contradictory religious opinions reserves them for church and prayer." In addition, the Talmud explicitly forbids us *"even to think"* of returning to Palestine before the occurrence of "the miracles and signs mentioned in the Scripture."[52] Here, in the course of the controversy resulting from the publication of Dohm's work, Mendelssohn escapes the embarrassment of messianism by describing it as a doctrine of merely theoretical significance.[53] A short while later, his denial of the existence of any distinctively Jewish doctrines enabled him to omit the subject altogether from his most comprehensive discussion of Judaism, in *Jerusalem*.[54]

Activated, in part, by a desire to excise from religion those teachings that had in the past been responsible for generating a great deal of turmoil, Spinoza and Locke had proffered interpretations of the Bible that virtually "stripped it down" to such moral doctrines (or to little more than such doctrines) as they considered essential to the maintenance of obedience to the law of the state. Motivated by kindred aims, operating in a similarly tendentious manner, and employing similarly contrived arguments, Mendelssohn in effect stripped things down even further. The Bible, he argued (though without sufficient justification and most inconsistently, as we have seen) revealed no doctrines at all. In spite of his different approach to the Bible, however, the religion with which he is left, his Judaism, consists, like the civil religions of Spinoza and Locke, mainly of the principles of natural religion and rational morality and is similarly supportive of the laws of the state. In addition to these principles it stipulates nothing more than the continuing duty of every Jew to obey the Mosaic law.

In his insistence on the enduring validity of the law Mendelssohn is, of course, very visibly departing from the pattern established by Spinoza and Locke, both of whom regarded it as being entirely obsolete. But this difference is less significant than it may at first appear to be. The law reaffirmed by Mendelssohn does not correspond exactly to the law Spinoza and Locke relegated to the past.

From the point of view of the latter two philosophers, the most important thing about the Mosaic law is its theocratic features. As we have seen, Spinoza characterized the regime of ancient Israel as one in which the people acknowledged God to be the sovereign, in which "the laws of the state were called the laws and commandments of God," and in which "the civil and religious authority, each consisting solely of obedience to God, were one and the same." Locke similarly speaks of the ancient Jewish system of government as a theocracy, in which there could not be "any difference between that commonwealth and the church. The laws established there concerning the worship of one invisible Deity, were the laws of that people, and a part of their political government, in which God himself was the legislator."

Mendelssohn, in his description of the ancient Israelite constitution, eschews the term *theocracy* and replaces it with the *Mosaic constitution,* but he sounds scarcely any different from Spinoza and Locke: "state and religion were not conjoined, but *one*; not connected but identical. . . . God, the Creator and Preserver of the world, was at the same time the King and Regent of this nation." Hence, "in this nation, civil matters acquired a sacred and religious aspect, and every civil service was at the same time a true service of God."[55]

As we have seen, Spinoza and Locke are both eager to consign this kind of theocratic regime to another time and another place. We need not repeat once again Spinoza's views on this matter, but we should remind ourselves of what Locke has to say about it. He forcefully rejects its contemporary pertinency with a rhetorical challenge that he does not expect any of his readers will be able to meet: "if any one can show me where there is a commonwealth, at this time, constituted upon that foundation, I will acknowledge that the ecclesiastical laws do there unavoidably become a part of the civil; and that the subjects of that government both may, and ought to be, kept in strict conformity with that church, by the civil power." Locke is, however, fully confident that "there is absolutely no such thing, under the Gospel, as a Christian commonwealth." Mendelssohn, in emphasizing the unique character of the ancient Israelite regime, makes basically the same point. "This constitution," he writes, "existed only once; call it the *Mosaic constitution,* by its proper name. It has disappeared, and only the Omniscient knows among what people and in what century something similar will again be seen."[56]

There is, of course, a very signficant difference between the views expressed by Locke and those expressed by Mendelssohn. Locke clearly relegates genuine theocracy to a past that Christendom, at least, has forever transcended; Mendelssohn leaves open the possibility that it might someday reappear. With regard to its current absence from the face of the earth they are, however, in complete agreement. And this is of decisive practical importance. Unlike Spinoza and Locke, Mendelssohn upholds the law, but it is a law that is not concerned with the regulation of political and civil matters nor, most important, is it coercive. It should be entirely up to the individual Jew to determine the extent to which he will live up to his obligation to obey it. In stressing these points, Mendelssohn has utterly transformed the law. He has kept it intact, but he has eliminated, so to speak, its "teeth," and thereby rendered it basically harmless, from a political point of view.

In fact, because August Friedrich Cranz contested what he was saying by emphasizing the inherently *involuntary* character of Jewish law, Mendelssohn considered it to be of such urgent importance to respond to his pamphlet. In his answer to *The Searching*, he was prepared to admit what could not be denied, that the Judaism of former times had indeed been in conflict with his understanding of people's right to liberty of conscience, but he insisted that the Jews' loss of their independence had radically altered the situation and succeeded in bringing the Jewish religion into complete conformity with his rational principles. This was, as we have noted, precisely the path Cranz warned him not to take, for the very good reason that it *failed* to solve the contradiction in principle between the Old Testament's authorization of religious coercion *at any time* and Mendelssohn's unqualified affirmation that men ought to possess liberty of conscience *at all times*.

Mendelssohn went to considerable lengths, as we have seen, to disguise this failure, but he does not seem to have been truly perturbed by it. This is because he was less interested in resolving the theoretical question than in warding off his adversary and, even more important, in supplying the basis for his characterization of the duties prescribed by Jewish law as *now* being a matter of concern only to individual Jews, as individuals, and their Maker. To reach this conclusion he was prepared, as we saw in the previous chapter, to play fast and loose with the facts. Mendelssohn was interested above all not in arriving at a coherent reconciliation of the teachings of the Jewish tradition with the teachings of reason, but in forcing contemporary Judaism to fit into a preconceived liberal mold, in expunging, at all costs, its theocratic dimension.

Mendelssohn's original blend of Judaism and liberalism has been treated by most scholars as a sincere effort on his part to combine two different strands of his own identity. Some, however, have seen his endeavors in this area in a different light. In their opinion, Mendelssohn's allegiance to liberalism was not wholehearted but merely tactical or provisional.

Rabbi Mordecai Eliasberg, a late nineteenth-century Orthodox Zionist thinker and activist, was, to the best of my knowledge, the first to argue that, contrary to appearances, Mendelssohn was at heart not a liberal at all. In his opinion, Mendelssohn was perfectly well aware that in calling for the separation of religion and state he was advocating something contrary to the spirit of Jewish law. Why, then, did he take such a position? It was good for the Jews. What Mendelssohn really sought was to end the involvement of Christianity in the life of the European states, an involvement that posed a continual threat to the Jews residing in them. He argued, accordingly, in favor of the separation of church and state, and sought to reinforce his rational arguments with the claim that his own religion, Judaism, opposed the intertwining of state and religion, including all forms of religious coercion. This was not true, but it was useful. There was nothing to be lost by saying it, since, under modern conditions, the Jews were, in any case, clearly destined to lose their internal autonomy.[57]

Rabbi Eliasberg attempts to exculpate Mendelssohn by showing how he was merely making the best of a bad situation. If he denied, against his own better knowledge, the theocratic nature of Judaism, it was only to bolster his argument against state support for Christianity, which constituted a serious menace to contemporary Jews. Mendelssohn's regrettable endorsement of liberal principles should therefore be understood to have been altogether contingent and purely tactical. Eliasberg makes this argument, almost in passing, in a polemical tract, not in the course of a scholarly treatment of Mendelssohn's philosophy. He does not muster abundant support for his interpretation nor does he spell it out in great detail. One can wonder, therefore, what made him so certain that Mendelssohn was only a lukewarm and provisional supporter of the liberal society for which he seems to have displayed a considerable amount of genuine ardor. Nor does he substantiate his opinion that Mendelssohn regarded the advent of such a society as an inevitability to which one must bow.

An Israeli scholar, Ron Sigad, has recently offered an interpretation of Mendelssohn's position that amounts, in effect, to a scholarly defense of Eliasberg's interpretation of Mendelssohn (though there is no reason to presume that he is familiar with Eliasberg's position). According to Sigad, too, Mendelssohn's advocacy of the separation of state and religion was not absolute but merely conditional. He maintains that Mendelssohn believed that when the Jews are in exile, living in less than ideal non-Jewish states, it is in their interest both as men and as Jews to advocate the establishment of barriers between church and state. In the ideal state, however, the one governed by the original Mosaic constitution, that separation is not necessary. Liberty of conscience, in other words, is not something good in itself, but something to be preferred only where Jews are living on foreign soil and are not their own masters. According to Sigad, then, "Mendelssohn's position on the question of the religion-state-Judaism relationship is entirely consistent."[58] There is no contradiction between his advocacy of church-state separation and his defense of the ancient Jewish regime where no such separation existed.

Sigad begins his analysis by pointing to what he regards as

Mendelssohn's fundamental distinction between the ideal and the empirical. In so far as political matters are concerned, Mendelssohn, he says, philosophizes on two separate planes at the same time. On the one hand, he establishes the nature of the good state, the one in which man is able to satisfy all his needs and attain perfection and felicity. On the other hand, in the course of the same discussion, Mendelssohn treats the question of the empirical situation of the existing states in which men are not able to attain those ends. In the good state men are ruled, as Mendelssohn put it, by education alone. On this point there is full cooperation between state and church. Here Sigad quotes Mendelssohn's statements to the effect that it is the task of religion to prove the identity of men's moral and religious duties and to teach them that the service of the state is service of God. In the good state, therefore, "religion, ethics and politics are identical." Thus, "under ideal conditions, on the level of principle alone, there is no difference between religion, on the one hand, and the state and politics on the other. Mendelssohn's basic position on this question is therefore the exact opposite of the one for which he is known and which he preached, i.e. the separation of religion and state."[59] But this holds true only for the ideal state, which Mendelssohn, according to Sigad, identifies with the ancient Jewish constitution. "The *halakhah* establishes the state as an ideal state and also teaches how to live one's daily life within it."[60] In other states the situation is different.

The existing, defective state cannot attain its ends through education alone but must resort to coercive laws. This state is inferior to the ideal state in that it does not guide men toward perfection and felicity but is capable only of providing them with security. Because religion is by its very nature voluntary, "there is an essential difference between the (defective) state and religion."[61] This does not mean, of course, that there is no place for religion in the defective state. On the contrary, it is the inferior character of this state that renders it particularly important for religion to persist within it. This is because, "freedom of opinions and beliefs is in his [Mendelssohn's] opinion the basic principle which is capable of saving the state from a decisive descent into the enslavement of man and the loss of the rationale for social existence." The defective state must therefore make room for all religions. Thus, "Mendelssohn found the way to ensure the right of Judaism to exist in safety. . . . The establishment of human freedom in the state will guarantee the Jew's freedom to preserve his faith without being disturbed."[62]

It is in the interest of all men that freedom of religion be preserved in the defective state, but it is of particular concern to the practitioners of Judaism, a vulnerable minority whose existence outside their own land, "can be guaranteed only by means of the separation of religion and state."[63] Yet in the end Mendelssohn believed, according to Sigad, that what is in the interest of Judaism is for that very reason in the best interest of humankind as a whole. He believed that to be the case because he considered Judaism to be the only true, universal religion, identical in content with the universal principles of morality and devoted to actualizing them in the political realm. In exile, it is true, Judaism does not actually differ in any appreciable respect from the other religions. Still, the preservation of Judaism outside the Land of Israel, "serves as a reminder to Jews and Gentiles alike that redemption is an existing possibility."[64] That is to say, "by virtue of its very existence it holds out the theoretical possibility of a divine politics and a true religion."[65]

Mendelssohn's commitment to the separation of church and state is, then, just a tactic, a step that is necessary only because the superior regime, the halakhic one in which state and religion are fused, is for the moment unattainable. If Sigad is correct in assuming this, we would have an explanation for the apparent contradiction between Mendelssohn's approbation of the Mosaic constitution and his call for the separation of church and state. Only the former is unqualified, whereas the latter is contingent.

Sigad does not, however, bring sufficient evidence to support his radical conclusion. He attempts to contrast what he considers Mendelssohn's picture of the ideal, halakhic regime with the defective regime, in which state and religion are separated. But his presentation of the preferred halakhic state is strangely misconceived. In it, he says, government is by education alone. While this is indeed true of the ideal state to which Mendelssohn briefly alludes in Section I of *Jerusalem*, it is not true of any halakhic state that he attempts to depict anywhere in his writings. The Mosaic constitution, he clearly acknowledges, had recourse to force when it was unable to attain its purposes by education alone. It is, in this sense, less than ideal. For this reason, one is entitled to conclude, along with Altmann, that far from regarding the Mosaic constitution as the best of all possible arrangements, "Mendelssohn quite welcomed the transformation of Judaism from a theocracy of a unique sort into a mere religion, that is to say, into a spiritual entity in which coercive power—a prerogative of the state—can have no legitimate place."[66]

There are other problems with Sigad's analysis, too. He maintains that Mendelssohn favored the separation of church and state in the existing, defective states largely because that was necessary if Judaism were to survive. A religion can, of course, survive (above ground, at least) only if its existence is tolerated. But is its survival also contingent upon its members' enjoying the full freedom and equal rights that Mendelssohn sought for the Jews? The Jews' centuries in exile clearly proved the contrary. In fact, if the survival of Judaism as a reminder of the possibility of a "divine politics" was truly, as Sigad believes, Mendelssohn's primary concern, it would seem more likely that he would have opposed equal rights and integration into Gentile society. The medieval condition of partial Jewish self-government in accordance with the *halakhah* would have better suited his purposes. In fact, however, Mendelssohn did everything he could to bring about the end of such medieval conditions.

Sigad's argument is, on the whole, quite unconvincing. He does not come to terms with the contradiction between Mendelssohn's repudiation of any religious coercion and his acceptance in principle of a plainly coercive Mosaic constitution. Nor does he offer a sufficient explanation of why Mendelssohn would have seen the separation of religion and state as nothing more than a temporarily useful means for the preservation of Judaism. There is no reason to think that for Mendelssohn separation of church and state and the resulting establishment of liberty of conscience represent anything less than an ideal.

Neither Eliasberg nor Sigad has succeeded, then, in proving that Mendelssohn was merely assuming the guise of a liberal to protect the interests of Judaism. It is, in fact, much more reasonable to believe in the genuineness of his liberalism and conclude that he fought for the separation of state and religion because he believed it to be something good in itself. One of the problems he faced, as a liberal professing allegiance to Judaism, was the Old Testament's plain authorization of the enforcement of religious law. He chose to resolve this problem by insisting, without sufficient warrant, that this authorization had lapsed, and Judaism was now utterly noncoercive. Bypassing the theoretical problem underlined by *The Searching After Light and Right*, he forcibly reconciled, *in practice*, his two disparate loyalties.

Mendelssohn may have departed, then, from Spinoza and Locke by continuing to insist on the validity of the Mosaic law. Nevertheless, by rendering obedience to this law, in this day and age, completely voluntary, he succeeded in depoliticizing it or, to put it slightly differently, in showing that it could be made fully compatible with a detheologized politics. He accomplished, in other words, the principal goal of his predecessors without following too closely in their footsteps, without paying a price that would have involved, at the end of the eighteenth century, stepping outside of the Jewish fold.

Spinoza and Locke wished, above all, to derive from scriptural sources a religion confirming people's duty to obey God, which meant, in practice, their duty to obey the civil authorities. For Spinoza, the "universal, Catholic religion" consisted entirely of this precept and the tenets of faith "absolutely necessary for fulfilling" it. To this Locke added but one doctrine, belief in Jesus' messiahship (however understood). Mendelssohn, too, as we saw in Chapter 4, emphasized, without reference to Scripture, that it was the duty and business of religion to teach that service of the state is service of God.[67] In addition to the duty of obedience, in opposition to Spinoza and Locke and in conformity with Jewish tradition, he derived from Scripture the duty, on the part of the Jews, to continue to observe the Mosaic law. He recognized that this might create problems for them, that it might prove difficult, at times, for individuals to reconcile their duty to the state with their duty to obey another law. He therefore gives them the following advice: "Adapt yourselves to the morals and the constitution of the land to which you have been removed; but hold fast to the religion of your fathers too. Bear both burdens as well as you can!"

Unlike the rabbis, who issued similar advice, Mendelssohn, as we noted earlier, was actively engaged in an effort to tear down the barriers separating Jews from Gentiles. He wanted to bring to an end the semiautonomous existence of the Jewish communities, to fully integrate the Jews into the citizenries of the lands in which they lived. All of this could have only the consequence, as he himself was surely aware, of placing the Jews in positions to which they were unaccustomed and in multiplying the difficulties involved in bearing "both burdens." In the world that Mendelssohn envisioned and struggled to bring into being, it would undoubtedly become much harder for a Jew to remain a Jew.

Judging from what he says in *Jerusalem* and his other apologetic writings, this is not a prospect that filled Mendelssohn with alarm. Nowhere does he evince any fears that the breakdown of the old order could lead to a situation in which the Jews might face much greater temptations to desert what he calls the posts assigned to them by Providence. In one important instance he even appears, on the contrary, to be prepared to welcome such a development.

In his response to Dohm, to which we referred earlier, Michaelis objected to his proposals regarding the Jews on account of their messianic doctrines, but also on several other grounds, not the least of which was their purported inability, because of their religion, to perform the duties required of citizens. He focused, in particular, on the question of military service. The power of a state, he wrote, depends "in large part, on the strength of its soldiers. And the Jews will not contribute soldiers to the state as long as they do not change their religious views." In proof of this point, Michaelis cited the Jews' refusal to fight on the sabbath and their adherence to the dietary laws. "As long as they observe the laws about kosher and non-kosher food it will be almost impossible to integrate them into our ranks." And the Jews are too untrustworthy to be placed in special units of their own.[68]

Mendelssohn's reply to Michaelis is of considerable interest. He does not, as one might expect, explain what a boon it would be to any European army to have in its midst Jewish soldiers whose ritual practices continually called their Gentile comrades' attention to "sound and unadulterated ideas of God and his attributes." Instead, he states that "When personal convictions conflict with the laws, it is up to the individual to resolve this problem on his own. If the fatherland is to be defended, everybody who is called upon to do so must comply." The Jewish religion may now make such compliance difficult, but people "usually know how to modify their convictions and to adjust them to their civic duty." All that is really necessary is to avoid emphasizing the significance of the conflict between the two. "In this way, Christians have neglected the doctrines of their founders and have become conquerors, oppressors and slave-traders, and in this way, Jews too could be made fit for military service."[69]

Here, as in *Jerusalem*, Mendelssohn treats the conflict between their civil and religious duties as something with which individual Jews will have to cope independently. But he is also prepared, as he was not in *Jerusalem*, to make prognostications regarding the use to which they would be most likely to put their freedom. It seems, at first, that what he anticipates is that the Jews, faced with the requirement of military service, would make such minor adjustments in their "convictions" as would be necessary to permit them to perform their civic duties. The analogy he draws between what could happen to Judaism and what has happened to Christianity seems as if it might suggest, however, that he has in mind a more radical transformation. What the Christians have done, by his account, is not to modify their religious principles but to *neglect* them, to conduct themselves in a manner entirely opposite to them. Does Mendelssohn really hope and expect that the Jews will do something similar?

Read literally, the final sentence of Mendelssohn's response to Michaelis appears to imply that such is indeed the case. It would be rash, however, to leap to such a conclusion. What seems far more likely is that Mendelssohn on this occasion permitted himself, in a rather uncharacteristic manner, to resort to bitter sarcasm. Perturbed by Michaelis's derisive treatment of the Jews and Judaism throughout his lengthy response to Dohm, he could not refrain from making one brief attempt to pay him back in kind. Nevertheless, Mendelssohn's statement, taken as a whole, still reveals an extraordinary degree of equanimity with regard to the future fate of Judaism. It shows him to have been more concerned, in the end, with the Jews obtaining the opportunity to be equal citizens—whatever its costs—than with ensuring, as far as possible, their punctilious observance of all of the commandments.

It is instructive to compare Mendelssohn's approach to the question of Jewish service in Gentile armies with that of the first modern European Jews who actually found themselves compelled to perform such service, the Jews of the Habsburg Empire. In 1782 their ruler, Joseph II, had begun to grant them new rights, but he also subjected them to new requirements, including, in 1788, the obligation to serve in his army. The earliest eyewitness account of the Jewish reaction to this development stems from Prague. On the day in the spring of 1789, it is reported, when twenty-five young Jews were carted away to be enlisted, the city was in an uproar. Mothers wept for their sons, sisters for their brothers, and newlywed brides for their young husbands. Rabbi Ezekiel Landau, the chief rabbi of the city and one of the leading rabbinical figures in Europe, went out to counsel and console the young men. "It is the will of God and it is the will of the Emperor that you be taken for military service," he told them. "Do your duty, therefore, but do not forget your religion. Do not be ashamed among so many Christians to be Jews." To help them remember and practice their religion while they were away Rabbi Landau supplied each of the recruits with a prayer shawl, a set of phylacteries, and a prayerbook. They cried, and he cried, and so did all the other Jews who were present.[70]

In their attitudes to Jewish military service, as in their positions on many other matters, Mendelssohn and Rabbi Landau were poles apart.[71] One was trying to push the clock forward, the other would have been happy if he could have pushed it back. One welcomed the alteration of the Jews' status and, at the very least, displayed no qualms about the adjustments of their religious practice that it would force them to make, the other regarded the new state of affairs as utterly lamentable. They both professed a commitment to the preservation of Jewish ritual practice, and for this reason it is not difficult to imagine Mendelssohn standing alongside Rabbi Landau among the recruits, handing out prayer shawls and prayerbooks. But it is hard to believe that he would have done so with tears in his eyes.

In his attitude to the question of Jewish military service, Mendelssohn displays a readiness, even an eagerness, to exchange a situation in which the Jews enjoy neither the duties nor the rights of citizenship for one in which they enjoy both, but have to pay for this improvement in their condition by sacrificing some of their freedom to live in accordance with their own law. In fact, with the least amount of foresight he could have seen that his entire program of Jewish integration, if achieved, would necessarily entail many such compromises in all areas of life. Perhaps Mendelssohn saw all of this quite clearly. Perhaps it did not really bother him. Perhaps he was, at bottom, much less orthodox in his approach to the law than he often strives to appear to be.

Kant

One person who had serious doubts about the genuineness of Mendelssohn's orthodoxy was Immanuel Kant. Kant read *Jerusalem* not long after it was written and readily complimented its author on his achievement. "I consider this book," he wrote to him, "the manifesto of a great reform which, though slow in starting and advancing, will affect not only your nation but others too. You have known how to reconcile your religion with such a degree of freedom of conscience as one would not have imagined it to be capable of, and as no other religion can boast of." [72] On a later occasion, in *Religion Within the Limits of Reason Alone*, Kant referred to Mendelssohn's response, in *Jerusalem*, to Cranz's insinuation that the liberal views outlined in his Preface to *Manasseh ben Israel* reflected a tendency to draw closer to Christianity. Mendelssohn, we recall, answered Cranz by pointing to the fallacy implicit in his reasoning. If the author of *The Searching* believed that Judaism, the ground floor, was without any solid foundation, how could he invite anyone to ascend to Christianity, the equally endangered upper floor? [73] Kant described this as a "very ingenious" way of meeting Cranz's challenge. He then offered something other than a literal interpretation of Mendelssohn's remarks:

> His true opinion, however, shines through rather clearly. He means to say: if you yourselves remove Judaism from your own religion . . . we shall consider your proposal. (In fact, all that would then remain would be a purely moral religion, without any admixture of statutes.) By throwing off the yoke of external observances our burden is not made easier in the least if another [burden] is imposed on us instead, namely that of articles of faith concerning a sacred history, which presses a conscientious person much harder.[74]

Kant, then, had some flattering things to say about Mendelssohn's work. But even after reading *Jerusalem*, he did not believe that he was at all sincere in his protestations of unwavering faith in the enduring validity of the Mosaic law. In considering his perhaps startling judgment of Mendelssohn's true views, we must bear in mind the fact that he knew him fairly well. He was, in adddition, beyond any doubt the most philosophically competent of all of Mendelssohn's contemporary readers, and most probably of all the people who have ever read his works. What he says, therefore, cannot be taken lightly, even if it is completely at odds with most subsequent assessments of Mendelssohn's beliefs and aims.

For the most part, however, Kant's comments on Mendelssohn's approach to Judaism have not received the attention they deserve. Even Altmann discusses them only in a rather cursory fashion. He shows some appreciation for the more complimentary remarks in Kant's letter to Mendelssohn, but he is somewhat wary of them as well. "Unless one wants to read between the lines," he observes, "some sarcasm about the hitherto unsuspected degree of Jewish tolerance, Kant was evidently much impressed by Mendelssohn's achievements."[75] Altmann is far more suspicious of Kant's second reference to Mendelssohn's position on Judaism. Kant, he maintains, "read too much" into Mendelssohn's response to Cranz. "Mendelssohn most certainly did not wish to imply that once Christians had divested themselves of Judaism, Jews would join them in a purely moral religion!"[76]

There is, indeed, good reason to take Kant's laudatory remarks concerning *Jerusalem* with a grain of salt. He is clearly not congratulating Mendelssohn for having done what he purports to have done in the book; that is, for having successfully delineated the nature of "true, original Judaism." In none of Kant's numerous subsequent treatments of the Jewish religion is there any trace of evidence that his reading of Mendelssohn taught him to regard ancient Judaism as having been intrinsically broadminded.[77] What he finds admirable in *Jerusalem* is the skill with which Mendelssohn had succeeded in refashioning Judaism, in infusing it with something that, as far as he could see, had hitherto been absent from it: acceptance of the idea of liberty of conscience.

Kant's statement that Mendelssohn was prepared to see the Jews abandon their law, if only the Christians, for their part, would do something roughly equivalent, evoked from Altmann both surprise and indignation. He apparently regarded it as too patently mistaken to require refutation. Nor did he concern himself with trying to determine how Kant could have managed to misunderstand Mendelssohn so completely.

Nathan Rotenstreich is the first scholar, to the best of my knowledge, to attempt to probe the roots of Kant's assessment of Mendelssohn. He, too, deems it to be obviously erroneous, without any basis in Mendelssohn's writings, but he has sought at least to explain how he could possibly have arrived at it. What he proposes is that Kant may perhaps have formed his opinion of Mendelssohn's intentions largely on the basis of what he was told by one of Mendelssohn's friends and associates, David Friedländer.

Friedländer falls under Rotenstreich's suspicion for the simple reason that he was the person who brought Kant his copy of *Jerusalem*. Bearing this in mind, Rotenstreich asks whether it is possible that Friedländer misled Kant, whether "Friedländer's views and reflections seemed to Kant as if they represented those of Mendelssohn himself, and were not a free interpretation, so to speak, or a structure built on the basis of Mendelssohn's own view from Friedländer's vantage point."[78] Rotenstreich then reviews Friedländer's understanding of the current state of Judaism in his famous open letter of 1799 to Dean Wilhelm Abraham Teller, at that time one of the leading figures in German Protestantism.

The basis of Friedländer's argument in this letter is, in Rotenstreich's words, its "opposition of historical inheritance to eternal truths, which are truths of the intellect and of reason."[79] Friedländer regards Judaism and Christianity as religions that embody more or less the same rational principles but which have both, in the course of their development, encumbered these truths with features injurious to the best interests of their practitioners. In the case of Judaism, the problem lies with the law, which both impedes the Jews' spiritual growth and stands in the way of their fulfillment of their duties as citizens. In the case of Christianity, the problem stems from the irrational dogmas of the church. Friedländer, in his letter to Teller, announces the readiness of a number of Berlin Jews to strike a deal capable of giving them the best and enabling them to escape the worst of both worlds. They are prepared, he says, to renounce Judaism and to join the church, provided they can do so without having to affirm the truth of the irrational dogmas of Christianity, in which they do not believe.

In his letter to Teller, as Rotenstreich observes, Friedländer merely refers in passing to Mendelssohn as someone who extricated himself from "the nursery of mysticism" and made himself into a symbol of practical wisdom. Twenty years later, when, as Rotenstreich pointedly remarks, both Mendelssohn and Kant were no longer alive, Friedländer wrote a small volume of reminiscences of Mendelssohn. "In this book," according to Rotenstreich, "he presents as a central theme of his dealings with Mendelssohn the historicalness of Judaism, that is to say, of its position [as a religion] tied to eras, or to an era, of the human process that had already been outdated." One can say, in other words, "that what is propounded in the appeal to Teller for defensive purposes and for the sake of political and social advancement, is here imposed upon Mendelssohn's view—and that once again the conceptual and metaphorical system of the Hebrew language is presented as proof" of the inferior stage of development it represents.[80]

How Friedländer could find support for these views in Mendelssohn's own words is a matter concerning which Rotenstreich is prepared only to conjecture. Mendelssohn, he notes, had a very different and far more harmonious conception of the relationship between history and reason.

> Pointing out the difference between Friedländer and Mendelssohn leads us to think that Friedländer absorbed, if only on a popular level, a different conception of history from that which pervaded Mendelssohn's outlook. For some reason he accepted the idea of progress in the historical process, an idea with which Mendelssohn explicitly takes issue, even in the form in which it was presented by his friend Lessing.[81]

It is, in fact, possible, according to Rotenstreich, that it was from none other than Kant himself that Friedländer acquired such an idea. And it is likewise possible that Friedländer, in turn, exercised a certain influence over Kant. Even as he was echoing views that he may earlier have imbibed from Kant, Friedländer may have said things in the course of his meetings with him in the early

1780s that were "taken by Kant to be characteristic of Mendelssohn himself. For that reason, perhaps, he attributed to Mendelssohn the view with which we began our discussion, i.e., the passage of the historical faiths, including Judaism, beyond the historical realm, to reason itself."[82]

Rotenstreich's conjecture is rather ingenious but ultimately unconvincing. It rests, first of all, on an extremely dubious reading of Friedländer's volume of reminiscences. In this small work, Friedländer does not put into Mendelssohn's mouth all of the views that Rotenstreich claims he attributed to him, and what he does have him say is in no significant respect at variance with what we find in Mendelssohn's own writings. There is, in fact, no evidence that Friedländer ever sought, in his writings, to foist his own views onto Mendelssohn. Neither is there any reason to think that he did so in his conversations with Kant, thereby leading him into error. Kant must have arrived at his conclusions concerning Mendelssohn's true beliefs by some other means.

The Mendelssohn portrayed in Friedländer's reminiscences does indeed speak of the progress of the human race in a manner inconsistent, to some extent, with the views expressed in Mendelssohn's own writings. He says, for instance, "that it has become clear to us, after much examination of the history of mankind, that it consists of the steady development of its spiritual powers and its moral sentiments."[83] He also speaks, in a manner that is not inconsistent with Mendelssohn's expressed views, of the way in which this development is accompanied by a growing capacity to engage in abstract thinking.[84] In his discussion of the Bible, he describes it as a work characteristic of an earlier stage of human development, a time when people expressed their thoughts in sensible images much more readily than in abstract notions. But none of this is meant to diminish the Bible's significance or to suggest that it has somehow become obsolete. Even if the images employed by the ancient Israelites, he says, may sometimes astonish "us Westerners," there is nothing in them that is at all offensive.[85]

Although the Bible may represent a less abstract mode of thought, it nonetheless contains, according to Friedländer's Mendelssohn, ideas of the greatest profundity. This estimation of the Bible is reflected in his discussion of the creation story: "The narrative is artless and elevated, entirely in the spirit of venerable antiquity, suited entirely to mortals' ability to understand. And it contains the greatest truth, so indispensable to mankind: There is one God, and God is the Creator of all that exists—What more does one need to know?"[86] We may have enriched our language and augmented our cosmological knowledge since the time of the composition of this story, but we have not risen to a decisively superior level of understanding. We are still in fundamentally the same situation as the people who knew only what was taught by the biblical narrative.[87]

Apart from his faith in human progress, this is a Mendelssohn we should not have any difficulty in recognizing as a reasonable facsimile of the true one. He sounds very much like the author of the *Sache Gottes* explaining the significance of the biblical creation story or the author of *Jerusalem* admiring the ability of simple, pious souls to grasp the fundamental truths of religion. Although he describes the Jewish religion as originating in an earlier epoch, nothing he says can be construed to imply, in Rotenstreich's words, "the historicalness of Judaism, that is to say, of its position [as a religion] tied to eras, or to an era, of the human process that had already been outdated." Nor is there any basis for Rotenstreich's opinion that what he says about the limitations of the Hebrew language is meant to derogate it.

Friedländer, in short, does not make Mendelssohn say what Rotenstreich says he makes him say. And from what his Mendelssohn (of 1819) does say it is a very long way to the views Kant attributes to Mendelssohn, especially the idea of the dispensability of the Mosaic law. There is, therefore, absolutely no reason to follow Rotenstreich in supposing that Kant might have acquired his concept of Mendelssohn's intentions from his conversations with Friedländer (in the 1780s).

But even if we cannot accept Rotenstreich's solution, we must still concern ourselves with the question he has raised: What, in fact, is it that led Kant to ascribe to Mendelssohn views for which there seems to be so little textual support? Surely it was not the passage from *Jerusalem* that he cites in *Religion Within the Limits of Reason Alone*. No reasonable reader of this comparison of Judaism and Christianity to two stories of the same building could possibly suppose it to mean what Kant takes it to mean, especially in view of its appearance in a book in which Mendelssohn unambiguously acknowledges the enduring validity of the Mosaic law. And Kant was a reasonable man, if ever there was one.

If, in fact, we bear in mind certain aspects of Kant's rationalism, we may come to understand what prompted him to see Mendelssohn in this particular light. The views and practices he attributes to him are, we must note, remarkably similar to his own. Kant was a philosopher who was "able, in theory, to dispose altogether of revealed religion and its sacred documents" and who looked forward to the replacement of the historical forms of religion by a purely rational religion.[88] In practice, however, he assumed the guise of a respectful interpreter of Scripture. He did so, in part, on the basis of his need for "personal security."[89] More important, however, he "used the Bible to reach out to the masses and subvert their longstanding attitudes."[90] As Yirmiahu Yovel has put it, he used "biblical hermeneutics as an agent of moral history." He made frequent references to the Bible, but he did so largely so that he could "pose as sharing the believer's first principles by appealing to the Bible," a practice that would enable him to "turn the former against themselves."

"On this point," according to Yovel, "Kant subscribes to a program initiated by Spinoza, but he gives it a different emphasis." Kant "wishes to exploit his audience's deep-rooted respect for the Bible and divert it to serve his own philosophical interests," but, unlike Spinoza, he "never seeks proofs of any kind in the Bible, nor does he claim that adherence to the original spirit of the Scripture will of itself liberate people from superstition. For him the Bible is only a psychological and educational auxiliary, theoretically to be discarded at the end of the process."[91]

What Yovel describes as the endeavor engaged in by Kant is more or less what Kant seems to have assumed to have been Mendelssohn's mode of procedure. Kant evidently does not take Mendelssohn at face value. When he discusses *Jerusalem* in *Religion Within the Limits of Reason Alone*, he pointedly distinguishes between what Mendelssohn says, on the one hand, and his true opinion (*Seine wahre Meinung*), on the other.[92] Mendelssohn says that the Jews should never change their religion, but what he really means to say, it seems, is something quite different, something that is both subversive of the texts to which he is ostensibly demonstrating his allegiance and more or less in tune with Kant's overall thinking.

As Yovel has shown, Kant stood partly within but also partly outside of the Spinozist tradition, inasmuch as he hopefully anticipated a time when it would no longer be necessary to have recourse to the Bible at all. He seems to have considered Mendelssohn also to have departed, as he had, from any belief that the Bible possessed binding authority and even from the belief, still shared by Spinoza, that it remained and would continue to remain, in a certain sense, indispensable. What led him to believe these things we cannot say for sure.

One could argue, perhaps, that Kant was, without taking his cue from Friedländer, "projecting" his own ideas onto Mendelssohn's writings. Or perhaps he derived his concept of Mendelssohn's "true opinion" from particularly frank private conversations with him. It is most likely, however, that Kant simply suspected that a man who was as thorough a rationalist as he believed Mendelssohn to be could not possibly have been a genuine believer in the validity of biblical revelation and the eternally binding character of the Mosaic law.[93] Read with a skeptical eye, as I have sought to show, Mendelssohn's writings provide ample cause for entertaining at least some such doubts.

Conclusion

Mendelssohn's own statements concerning the problematic relationship between philosophical truth and the welfare of human society entitle us to wonder whether he himself always shared his real convictions with his readers, especially in his treatment of Judaism. They do not help us to distinguish, however, between what he genuinely believed and what he may merely have pretended to believe. Mendelssohn does not warn us that his works are replete with thought-provoking contradictions through which we must make our way to arrive at his true opinions. Nor do his works contain signposts pointing the way to hidden statements implicitly subverting his ostensible positions. Any attempt therefore to locate a "private Mendelssohn" lurking beneath the surface of his writings is necessarily fraught with great difficulties and is probably bound to seem less than fully convincing. But the attempt is nevertheless worthwhile.

It is evident and indeed has long been recognized that Mendelssohn shared with Spinoza and Locke a certain number of liberal political aims. Many scholars have already pointed to the ways in which the latter two philosophers sought to derive from Scripture a "stripped down" biblically based religion, devoid of irrational dogmas and theocratic tendencies that would comport with these aims. The methods they deployed and the results at which they arrived are, as we have sought to demonstrate, strikingly similar to those of Mendelssohn. He seems to have been doing much the same thing they were doing, for much the same reasons.

The principal differences between Mendelssohn and his philosophical predecessors appear to stem from the fact that he concerned himself exclusively with Judaism and clearly wished to propound a teaching that other Jews would find acceptable. Unlike Spinoza and Locke, therefore, Mendelssohn had to affirm the continuing validity of the Mosaic law. In the course of doing so, however, he implemented, against the spirit and the letter of Jewish tradition, a "privatization" of the law. What remains of the law, when he is finished, is in no sense whatever a theocratic legislation but a set of religious ceremonies, which individual Jews ought to be coerced by no human agency to perform. Redefined in this way, the law would no longer be a major impediment to the Jews' complete integration into the polities in the midst of which they found themselves or in any more liberal states to be constituted in the future.

There remains, of course, the possibility that even voluntary obedience to the demands of the law might impede individual Jews' performance of their civic duties. Mendelssohn considers this possibility in *Jerusalem* but does not dwell on it. His advice, in the end, to people who face such problems is simply that they do the best they can to reconcile their conflicting duties. Our suspicions are aroused by the very fact that Mendelssohn is so eager to lead the Jews out of their relative isolation and place them in circumstances in which such conflicts would be bound to multiply. They grow stronger when we reflect on his prognosis with regard to the way in which most Jews would be likely to respond in one specific instance that he considers, their performance of military service. He seems to be able to contemplate their radical adjustment of the requirements of the law with much greater nonchalance than one would expect from a genuinely traditional Jew.

In the light of everything we have seen, Immanuel Kant's remarks about Mendelssohn's attitude to Jewish law seem more plausible than they are generally considered to have been. Kant, in all likelihood, did not base his assessment of Mendelssohn's "true opinion" on his assurances to Michaelis with regard to the probable behavior of Jewish soldiers. Whether as a result of some kind of "projection," his conversations with Mendelssohn, or his reading of his works, he seems to have arrived at the conclusion that Mendelssohn was, like himself, a representative of the (at that time) century-old, Spinoza-initiated program of cloaking liberal political aims with disingenuous and selective appeals to the authority of the Bible. He seems also to have concluded that Mendelssohn, like himself, saw it as the task of religious reformers to create the circumstances under which it would no longer be necessary to have recourse to the Bible, when revealed religion could be utterly transcended and replaced by a purely moral religion uniting all of humankind.

In the end, Kant's analysis of Mendelssohn's procedure is more convincing than his assessment of the aims he was attempting to achieve. There is very good reason to believe that Kant is correct in identifying Mendelssohn as a thinker who was manipulatively seeking to reorient Judaism, to take it down a path it had never before traversed. It does not follow from this, however, that he was prepared to lead it into oblivion if only the Christians would prove willing to do the same with their religion. It is quite possible that Mendelssohn, without really believing that it was truly of divine origin, nevertheless thought that Judaism, suitably transformed, still had a positive role to play. The destiny of Judaism to serve as a repository of true religion is, of course, something that Mendelssohn publicly proclaims, in *Jerusalem* and elsewhere. But it is also something he affirms in private, even in his correspondence with intimate associates such as Naphtali Herz Homberg, to whom, as his son Joseph wrote, "he opened his heart" about "many a thing concerning which he kept it closed vis-a-vis others." In one of his well-known letters to Homberg, in 1783, Mendelssohn, as we have seen, justifies the Jews' perseverance in the observance of their law in terms very much at variance with the teaching he propounds in *Jerusalem*. Instead of stressing their God-given character or their innate significance, he focuses on the way in which they can serve as a bond unifying the Jewish people. As long as polytheism, anthropomorphism, and religious usurpation jointly exercise sway over the world, he maintains, the commandments can still serve a purpose. Although "these vexatious offenders of reason are banded together, all genuine theists must also unite in some manner, lest the others trample us underfoot."[94]

Of the depth of Mendelssohn's commitment to genuine theism there can be no doubt whatsoever. And, whether or not he really believed in the truth of biblical revelation, he certainly believed that Judaism was closer to genuine theism than other existing religions, especially Christianity. In his letter to Homberg, Mendelssohn defends Judaism not as a divinely revealed legislation but as a suitable vessel for the preservation of genuine theism in a world still dominated by highly defective forms of religion. It is entirely conceivable that he recognized the utility of this vessel, and even the necessity of retaining it for ages to come, without truly believing it to be of divine origin. He may, then, have been as dubious of its origins as Kant seems to think that he was, but at the same time much more convinced of its enduring value than Kant considered him to be.

Notes

1. Clifford Orwin, "Civility," *The American Scholar* (Autumn 1991), p. 557.

2. Leo Strauss, *Persecution and the Art of Writing*, p. 193.

3. Strauss, ibid., pp. 171–75.

4. Ibid., p. 179.

5. Ibid., p. 183.

6. Leo Strauss, *Spinoza's Critique of Religion*, trans. E. M. Sinclair (New York: Schocken Books, 1965), p. 20.

7. Spinoza, *Theologico-Political Treatise*, pp. 183–84.

8. Ibid., pp. 186–87.

9. Strauss, *Spinoza's Critique of Religion*, p. 20.

10. Strauss, *Persecution and the Art of Writing*, p. 196.

11. Spinoza, *Theologico-Political Treatise*, p. 250.

12. Ibid., p. 254.

13. Hillel Fradkin, "The 'Separation' of Religion and Politics: The Paradoxes of Spinoza," p. 605.

14. See earlier, p. 115.

15. Spinoza, *Theologico-Political Treatise*, p. 220.

16. Strauss, *Spinoza's Critique of Religion*, p. 20.

17. See earlier, p. 147.

18. *The Works of John Locke* (London: Thomas Tegg, 1823), vol. 6, p. 9.

19. Thomas Pangle, *The Spirit of Modern Republicanism: The Moral Vision of the American Founders and the Philosophy of Locke* (Chicago: University of Chicago Press, 1988), p. 149.

20. Ibid., p. 201.

21. Leo Strauss, *Natural Right and History* (Chicago: University of Chicago Press, 1953), pp. 207–12. This passage has generated a great deal of controversy. A number of scholars of political philosophy have sought to refute Strauss's claims by demonstrating the integrity and coherence of Locke's overtly Christian theologico-political teaching. Some of Strauss's students, and some of the students of his students, have over the years sought to refute these critics and to restate and strengthen Strauss's arguments. In my opinion, the Straussians have successfully proven their point. They have patiently and convincingly dealt with all of their opponents' arguments, whereas their opponents have by and large dismissed their arguments without examining them carefully. The best summaries of this ongoing debate can be found in Michael Zuckert, "Of Wary Physicians and Weary Readers: The Debate on Locke's Way of Writing," *Independent Journal of Philosophy* 2 (1978): 55–66; Pangle, *The Spirit of Modern Republicanism*, pp. 304–6, notes 10 and 11; and Michael S. Rabieh, "The

Reasonableness of Locke, or the Questionableness of Christianity," *The Journal of Politics* 53, no. 4 (November 1991): 933–39.

22. Michael P. Zuckert, "John Locke and the Problem of Civil Religion," in *The Moral Foundations of the American Republic*, ed. Robert H. Horwitz (Charlottesville: University Press of Virginia, 1986), pp. 198–99.

23. Ibid., p. 199.

24. Ibid., p. 201.

25. Ibid., p. 184.

26. Ibid., p. 190.

27. *The Works of John Locke*, vol. 7, p. 102.

28. Zuckert, "John Locke and the Problem of Civil Religion," p. 188.

29. *The Works of John Locke*, vol. 7, p. 103.

30. Ibid., p. 105.

31. Zuckert, "John Locke and the Problem of Civil Religion," p. 192.

32. Ibid., pp. 188–89.

33. *The Works of John Locke*, vol. 6, p. 37.

34. Ibid., p. 11.

35. See earlier, p. 108.

36. See Feiereis, *Die Umprägung der Natürlichen Theologie in Religionsphilosophie*, p. 87. "Damit bekennt sich Mendelssohn unmi verständlich zur Religionsauffassung der Deismus. Das hinderete ihm jedoch in keiner Weise daran, sein ganzes Leben hindurch die jüdischen Zeremonialgesetze aufs strengste zu beobachten. Diese Widersprüchlichkeit dürfte mit der absicht Mendelssohns zu erklären sein, den Geist der Aufklärung auch unter seinen Glaubensgenossen zu verbreiten."

37. See earlier, p. 147.

38. Talbert, *Reimarus: Fragments*, p. 6.

39. See earlier, p. 26.

40. *Jerusalem*, pp. 85–86.

41. See Altmann, *Moses Mendelssohn*, pp. 346–552.

42. Katz, *Out of the Ghetto*, pp. 42ff.

43. Altmann, *Moses Mendelssohn*, p. 158.

44. *JubA*, vol. 7, p. 74.

45. Altmann, *Moses Mendelssohn*, p. 158.

46. *Jerusalem*, p. 89.

47. *JubA*, vol. 7, 1, p. 118.

48. *Jerusalem*, p. 87.

49. *JubA*, vol. 7, pp. 9–10.

50. See earlier, p. 200–4.

51. Johann David Michaelis, quoted in Jehuda Reinharz and Paul Mendes-Flohr, eds., *The Jew in the Modern World*, p. 37.

52. *JubA*, vol. 3, 2, p. 43.

53. Isaac Einstein-Barzilay, makes the following comment concerning these remarks: "Though political in aim and written in the heat of the controversy aroused by Dohm's book, these 'notes' contain Mendelssohn's real attitude to the problem. They are in agreement with his common-sense and almost businesslike approach. . . . The hope of returning to Zion is nothing more than a dream of mystics, nurtured in the soil of hate for the Jew. Were the Christians to make the Jews feel at home, the dream would dissipate altogether. Whatever its strength, it has little or no effect at all on the actual behavior of the Jews, and is reserved to the prayer-book alone. Had Mendelssohn lived for another generation, it is doubtful whether he would still grant this asylum to the Jewish national aspiration . . ." See "Moses Mendelssohn (1729–1786), A Study in Ideas and Attitudes," *Jewish Quarterly Review* 52 (1961): 183–84.

Efraim Shmueli has noted that "only on extremely rare occasions, when compelled by some external pressures, did Mendelssohn proffer any statements about the Messianic idea. His feebly worded statements on the subject raise more questions than they resolve." See *Seven Jewish Cultures: A Reinterpretation of Jewish History and Thought*, trans. Gila Shmueli (Cambridge: Cambridge University Press, 1990), p. 169.

54. He omits any explicit reference to it, at any rate. Altmann has suggested that his enigmatic reference to the year 2240 (p. 59) alludes to the messianic era (see his note on p. 185).

55. *Jerusalem*, p. 128. If anything, Mendelssohn should have protested not the use of the term *theocracy* to describe ancient Israel but the appropriation of the term to describe anything else. That he did not do this is, it seems, the result of his rejection not of the term itself but of its connotations, which were far from positive during the Enlightenment.

56. Ibid., p. 131.

57. Mordecai Eliasberg, *Shvil ha-Zahav*, pp. 23–25.

58. Ron Sigad, "Moshe Mendelssohn—Yahadut, Politikah Elohit u-Medinat Yisrael," *Da'at*, no. 7 (1981): 102 [Hebrew].

59. Ibid, p. 95.

60. Ibid., p. 100.

61. Ibid., p. 96.

62. Ibid., p. 97.

63. Ibid., p. 102.

64. Ibid., p. 100.

65. Ibid., p. 102.

66. Altmann, "Moses Mendelssohn's Concept of Judaism Re-examined," p. 244.

67. Under certain circumstances, to be sure, he believed that religion should withhold its support from the state, but he never indicated that it could ever have the duty to enter into active opposition to it.

68. Johann David Michaelis, quoted in Reinharz and Mendes-Flohr, *The Jew in the Modern World*, p. 38.

69. Ibid., p. 43.

70. *Ha Meassef* (Leipzig, 1789), pp. 252–55. See Simon Dubnov, *History of the Jews*, trans. Moshe Spiegel (Cranbury, N.J.: Thomas Yoseloff, 1971), vol. 4, p. 460.

71. See Altmann, *Moses Mendelssohn*, pp. 381–83, 396–98, 479–89.

72. Ibid., p. 517.

73. *Jerusalem*, p. 87; see earlier, p. 223.

74. Immanuel Kant, *Religion Within the Limits of Reason Alone*, trans. T. M. Greene and H. H. Hudson (New York: Harper and Row, 1960), p. 154. I have slightly altered the translation here (see later, p. 000).

75. Altmann, *Moses Mendelssohn*, p. 517.

76. Ibid., p. 534.

77. See Emil L. Fackenheim, *Encounters Between Judaism and Modern Philosophy* (New York: Basic Books, 1973), pp. 33–77.

78. Nathan Rotenstreich, "Between Historical Truth and Religion of Reason," *Jerusalem Studies in Jewish Thought* 9, Part II (1990): 282 [Hebrew].

79. Ibid., p. 284.

80. Ibid., pp. 284–85.

81. Ibid., p. 285.

82. Ibid., p. 286.

83. David Friedländer, *Moses Mendelssohn: Fragmente von ihm und über ihn; Für Gönner und Freunde* (Berlin, 1819), p. 51.

84. Ibid., p. 52.

85. Ibid., p. 53.

86. Ibid., p. 54.

87. Ibid., p. 60.

88. Yirmiahu Yovel, "Bible Interpretation as Philosophical Praxis: A Study of Spinoza and Kant," *Journal of the History of Philosophy* 11 (1973): 193.

89. Ibid., p. 194.

90. Yirmiahu Yovel, *Kant and the Philosophy of History* (Princeton, N.J.: Princeton University Press, 1980), p. 216.

91. Ibid., pp. 214–15.

92. This is partly obscured in the standard English translation. In this version, the beginning of Kant's footnote reads as follows: "Mendelssohn very ingeniously makes use of this weak spot in the customary presentation of Christianity wholly to reject every demand upon a son of Israel that he change his religion. For, *he says* [my emphasis], since the Jewish faith itself is, according to the avowal of Christians, the substructure upon which the superstructure of Christianity rests, the demand that it be abandoned is equivalent to expecting someone to demolish the ground floor of a house in order to take up his abode in the second story. His real intention is fairly clear. He means to say. . ." In the original, the last complete sentence of the passage just quoted reads as follows: "Seine wahre Meinung aber scheint ziemlich klar durch." He says one thing, *but* his real opinion is another matter. See Immanuel Kant, *Gesammelte Schriften*, vol. 4 (Berlin, 1907), p. 166.

93. As we saw in Chapter 4, Thomas Wizenmann argued that Mendelssohn's reaffirmations of reason's ability to arrive at demonstrations of the existence of God should not be taken at face value. Kant, on the other hand, argued that Mendelssohn meant what he said when insisted on the possibility of a fully rational theistic metaphysics. Clearly, however, he did not believe that Mendelssohn always voiced his true opinion.

94. See earlier, p. 220.

Conclusion

Moses Mendelssohn appeared before the world as both a philosopher of religion and a faithful practitioner of Judaism. As a philosopher of religion in general, he did not strike out in any new directions but followed, for the most part, the path marked out by Leibniz, who was for him the highest philosophical authority. His proofs for the existence of God were essentially the same as those of Leibniz. His understanding of the other fundamental principles of natural religion, divine providence and human immortality, was also, at bottom, Leibnizian.

With regard to these latter two principles, Mendelssohn's position was, as we have seen, very much in tune with the later representatives of the Leibniz-Wolffian school. These thinkers accepted Leibniz's understanding of God's goodness and wisdom and the part destined to be played by rational creatures in the whole divine scheme of things. They refused to follow him, however, in accommodating their rational understanding of God and his purposes to some of Christianity's harsher doctrines. Discarding the belief that most human souls are destined to eternal damnation, they eliminated the dark shadow looming over Leibniz's "best of all possible worlds." They opened the way, consequently, to a concept of divine providence vastly more consoling than that of their teacher.

Mendelssohn took their more optimistic Leibnizian outlook to its logical conclusion. As he saw things, God's goodness mandates progress toward perfection and felicity for all of humankind. This happiness, to be sure, will come to some individuals only after a delay—involving posthumous, corrective punishment—and in limited measure. But it will come to all. Those who truly understand the nature of divine providence should be able to love God with all their hearts.

During his final years, it is true, Mendelssohn lost his confidence in the philosophy that had hitherto provided him with complete assurance of the truth of the principles of natural religion.

But he never lost his faith in these principles. Nor did he ever lose his faith in philosophy per se. He yearned to see his kind of philosophy restored to its former glory, rendered capable once again of proving the truth of the most important principles. But he did not feel that he himself had the strength to accomplish this task. Until providence raised up someone else to do so, he felt, people would have to take their bearings by their common sense, which they could at least count upon to point them in the right direction.

Mendelssohn derived from Leibniz his view of the nature and purpose of human existence as the pursuit of true perfection and felicity. He followed Wolff in seeing man's special destiny as both the will of God and the ordinance of nature. For him, as for Wolff, this law of nature served as the basis of human morality. Upon very similar foundations, however, the two philosophers built rather different edifices. Wolff constructed a moral and political doctrine that culminated in the endorsement of a tutelary state, one that has among its powers the right to govern the religious lives of its citizens. Mendelssohn, on the other hand, developed a contractarian theory establishing that the state has, at most, only a very limited right to concern itself with the religion in which its citizens place their faith. He did so even though he was, if anything, more convinced than Wolff of the indispensable part played by religious belief in supporting people's resolve to live in a correct manner.

In one important respect Mendelssohn's moral philosophy departs from that of Wolff, and this difference appears to explain their divergent ideas concerning the proper relationship between church and state. Unlike Wolff, Mendelssohn considers the enjoyment of liberty to be a vitally important dimension of human happiness. This strong commitment to liberty, it seems, inspires him to envision the formation of a state in which people retain the absolute right to believe and practice whatever religion they please, provided they show due respect for the properly constituted authorities.

The political theory that Mendelssohn deploys in defense of liberty of conscience is, as I believe I have shown, both incomplete and deeply flawed. Mendelssohn does not begin to address many of the most important questions pertaining to church-state relations. He does not convincingly substantiate the existence of a right to liberty of conscience nor is he fully consistent in his protection of it. He does not explain why an inalienable right to possess one's own convictions ought necessarily to lead to an absolute right to *voice* them. Nor does he resign himself, as his principles would seem to require, to the idea that atheists ought to be allowed to run completely wild. In the end, Mendelssohn's political theory seems to be a rather haphazard and makeshift effort to give expression to his commitment to the idea of religious liberty. This commitment evidently derives much if not all of its strength from his desire to see his own coreligionists released from the onerous restrictions under which they were forced to live.

As we have seen, Mendelssohn was able, with little difficulty, to harmonize the doctrines of natural religion with the tenets of Judaism. Reconciling his liberalism with his intrinsically theocratic religion proved, however, to be a much more difficult task. Still more difficult was the defense of Judaism in the face of the comprehensive critiques stemming from the likes of Spinoza, Reimarus, and Lessing.

Ultimately, Mendelssohn fails to grapple with all of these challenges in a consistent and compelling way. His proofs for the historicity of the Sinaitic revelation are either antiquated or strangely incoherent. His redefinition of Judaism as a religion altogether lacking in distinctive teachings of its own seems to be, at bottom, a way of avoiding any discussion of the discrepancy between the doctrines of natural religion and the contents of the Old Testament. In many other respects, too, Mendelssohn fails to deal decisively with the criticisms leveled by Spinoza and his intellectual heirs. And his roundabout response to the *Searching After Light and Right* fails to account, as he himself evidently knew, for the gap between the underlying principles of the Old Testament and his own insistence on the absolutely voluntary character of religious belief and practice.

In the end, Mendelssohn's defense of Judaism was, as we noted earlier, more rhetorical than real. He could not possibly have believed that his arguments had the power to overcome contemporary doubts concerning the truth of biblical revelation or to refute the hostile characterizations of its contents found in the writings of such men as Spinoza, Reimarus, and Lessing. But he could hope that his apologetical efforts would at least enable him to retain his credentials as a loyal Jew.

Mendelssohn needed these credentials to effect within the Jewish world what he considered to be necessary changes. While posing as the restorer of "ancient, original Judaism," he was in fact engaged in an attempt to transform his ancestral religion into something radically new and different. He was seeking to construct a version of Judaism suitable for a time when the Jews would take their places as citizens, alongside their Gentile neighbors, in a fully liberal polity. He was trying to pave the way to a world in which the Jews would be distinguished from their neighbors only by their voluntary practice of ritual observances designed to remind them of the same religious truths in which, it was to be hoped, their neighbors would also have faith and of historical truths that would do little to set them apart from other people. The Jews would continue to profess their own religion, but it would be one that could never be expected to provide the occasion for any civil discord. It would be, in addition, a religion totally devoid of any theocratic tendencies.

Mendelssohn supported his new version of Judaism by referring to the authoritative Jewish texts. Or, to be more precise, he turned to these texts to locate support for his preconceived positions. What Michael S. Rabieh has said of John Locke and his treatment of Christianity could with equal justice, it seems, be said of Mendelssohn and his treatment of the Jewish sources. It "is not a faithful one which informs his reasoning but a manipulative one informed by his reasoning."[1] He knew what he wanted the Bible and Jewish tradition to say, and he did whatever was necessary to make them say it—while seeking, all the time, to make it appear as if they unequivocally said these things without any urging on his part.

Immanuel Kant seems to have believed that he saw quite clearly what Mendelssohn was doing. He regarded him as someone who was approaching his own religious tradition in the same free spirit in which he himself came to terms with Christianity. Kant, however, was probably going too far when he concluded that Mendelssohn was prepared, under the right circumstances, to dispense with Judaism altogether and to welcome the Jews' joining with other peoples in the practice of one entirely rational, purely moral religion. Although it is not inconceivable that this is a result he would have been willing to accept, it seems more likely that Mendelssohn's true vision of the future corresponded to what he wrote in his much-cited letter to Naphtali Herz Homberg. In a world in which ignorance and superstition were still rampant, Judaism, appropriately reinterpreted, would continue to provide a solid framework within which true theists would be able to find a home.

Notes

1. Michael S. Rabieh, "The Reasonableness of Locke, or the Questionableness of Christianity," p. 938.

Bibliography

Medieval and Early Modern Sources

Albo, Joseph. *Book of Principles*. Philadelphia: Jewish Publication Society, 1946.

Crusius, Christian August. *Entwurf der nothwendigen Vernunft-Wahrheiten*. Leipzig, 1766.

Eberhard, Johann August. *Neue Apologie des Sokrates oder Untersuchung der Lehre von der Seligkeit der Heiden*. Berlin and Stettin: F. Nicolai, 1772.

Friedländer, David. *Moses Mendelssohn: Fragmente von ihm und über ihn; Für Gönner und Freunde*. Berlin, 1819.

Ha Meassef. Leipzig, 1789.

Jakob, Ludwig Heinrich. *Prüfung der Mendelssohnschen Morgenstunden oder aller spekulativen Beweise für das Daseyn Gottes*. Leipzig: J. S. Heinsius, 1786.

Jefferson, Thomas. *Notes on the State of Virginia*, ed. William Peden. Chapel Hill: University of North Carolina Press, 1955.

Kant, Immanuel. *Immanuel Kants Werke*, ed. Ernst Cassirer. Berlin: B. Cassirer, 1922.

———. *Religion Within the Limits of Reason Alone*, trans. T. M. Greene and H. H. Hudson. New York: Harper and Row, 1960.

———. *Immanuel Kant's gesammelte Schriften*, ed. Royal Prussian Academy of Sciences. Berlin: Geroge Reimer, 1912.

Leibniz, Gottfried Wilhelm. *Discourse on Metaphysics, Correspondence with Arnauld and Monadology*, trans. George R. Montgomery. La Salle, Ill.: Open Court, 1962.

———. *Essais de Théodicée*, ed. J. Brunschwig. Paris: Garnier-Flammarion, 1969.

———. *Principles of Nature and of Grace, Founded on Reason* in *Leibniz, Philosophical Writings*, trans. Mary Morris. London, 1934.

———. *Theodicy*, trans. E. M. Huggard. London: Routledge & Keegan Paul, 1951.

———. *G. W. Leibniz's Monadology*, ed. Nicholas Rescher. Pittsburgh: University of Pittsburgh Press, 1991.

Lessing, Gotthold Ephraim. *Nathan the Wise, Minna von Barnhelm and Other Plays and Writings*, ed. Peter Denetz. New York: Continuum, 1991.

_____. *G. E. Lessings Werke*, ed. Leopold Zscharnack. New York: Hildsheim, 1970.

Locke, John. *Works of John Locke*. London: Thomas Tegg, 1823.

Maimonides, Moses. *The Code of Maimonides*, trans. Abraham M. Hershman. New Haven, Conn.: Yale University Press, 1949.

_____. *Guide of the Perplexed*, trans. Shlomo Pines. Chicago: University of Chicago Press, 1963.

_____. *A Maimonides Reader*, ed. I. Twersky. New York: Behrman House, 1972.

Mendelssohn, Moses. *Moses Mendelssohns gesammelte Schriften*. Leipzig: G. B. Mendelssohn, 1843–45.

_____. *Moses Mendelssohn Gesammelte Scrhiften Jubiläumsausgabe*, Berlin and Stuttgart-Bad Cannstatt: Friedrich Frommannn Verlag, 1929–1984.

_____. *Jerusalem*, Introduction and Commentary by Alexander Altmann, trans. Allan Arkush. Hanover, N.H. and London: University Press of New England, 1983.

_____. *Moses Mendelssohn: Selections from His Writings*, trans. and ed. Eva Jospe, with an introduction by Alfred Jospe. New York, 1975.

Reimarus, Hermann Samuel. *Die vornehmste Wahrheiten der natürlichen Religion*, ed. Günter Gawlick. Göttingen: Vandenhoeck and Ruprecht, 1985.

_____. *Apologie oder Schutzschrift für die Vernünftigen Verehrer Gottes*. Hamburg: Insel Verlag, 1972.

Saadia Gaon. *The Book of Beliefs and Opinions*, trans. Samuel Rosenblatt. New Haven, Conn.: Yale University Press, 1948.

Spalding, Johann Joachim. *Bestimmung des Menschen* in *Studien zur Geschichte des neueren Protestantismus*, ed. Heinrich Hoffman and Leopole Zscharnack. Giessen: A. Topelmann, 1908.

Spinoza, Benedict. *Theologico-Political Treatise*, trans. R. H. M. Elwes. New York: Dover Publications, 1951.

Talbert, Charles H. *Reimarus: Fragments*, trans. Ralph S. Fraser. Philadelphia: Fortress Press, 1970.

Wizenmann, Thomas. *Die Resultate der Jacobischer und Mendelssohnischer Philosophie von einem Freywilligen*. Leipzig: Göschen, 1786.

Wolff, Christian. *Vernünftige Gedancken von dem Gesellschaftlichen Leben der Menschen und Insonderheit dem Gemeinen Wesen*. Leipzig, 1736.

_____. *Vernüfftige Gedancken von der Menschen Thun und Lassen zu Beförderung ihrer Glückseligkeit*. New York, 1976.

Yehudah Halevi. *Kuzari*, trans. H. Slonimsky. New York: Schocken Books, 1964.

Secondary Sources

Albrecht, Michael. "Moses Mendelssohn: Ein Forschungsbericht, 1965–1980." *Deutsche Vierteljahrs Schrift fur Literaturwissenschaft und Geistesgeschichte* 57 (1983): 64–166.

Allison, Henry. *Lessing and the Enlightenment.* Ann Arbor: University of Michigan Press, 1966.

Altmann, Alexander. "Die Entstehung von Moses Mendelssohns Phädon." *Lessing Yearbook* 1 (1969): 200–34.

———. *Die trostvolle Aufklärung, Studien zur Metaphysik und politschen Theorie Moses Mendelssohns.* Stuttgart-Bad Cannstatt: Friedrich Fromman Verlag, 1982.

———. *Essays in Jewish Intellectual History.* Hanover, N.H., and London: University Press of New England, 1981.

———. *Moses Mendelssohn, A Biographical Study.* University: University of Alabama Press, 1973.

———. *Moses Mendelssohns Frühschriften zur Metaphysik.* Tübingen: J. C. B. Mohr, 1969.

———. *Von der mittelalterlichen zur modernen Aufklärung.* Tübingen: J. C. B. Mohr, 1987.

———. "The Quest for Liberty in Moses Mendelssohn's Political Philosophy." In *Humanität und Dialog: Lessing und Mendelssohn in neuer Sicht*, Beiheft zum Lessing Yearbook, ed. Ehrhard Bahr, Edward P. Harris, and Laurence G. Lyon. New York, 1977.

Arkush, Allan. "The Contribution of Alexander Altmann to the Study of Moses Mendelssohn." *Leo Baeck Year Book* 34 (1989): 415–20.

———. "Voltaire on Judaism and Christianity." *AJS Review*, 18, no. 2 (1993): 223–43.

Bachmann, Hans-Martin. *Die naturrechtliche Staatslehre Christian Wolffs.* Berlin, 1977.

Baeck, Leo. "Does Traditional Judaism Possess Dogmas." In *Studies in Jewish Thought*, ed. Alfred Jospe, pp. 41–54. Detroit: Wayne State Universtiy Press, 1981.

Bamberger, Fritz. "Mendelssohn's Concept of Judaism." In *Studies in Jewish Thought*, ed. Alfred Jospe, pp. 343–61. Detroit: Wayne State Universtiy Press , 1981.

Beck, Lewis White. *Early German Philosophy.* Cambridge, Mass.: Harvard University Press, 1969.

Beiser, Frederick. *The Fate of Reason: German Philosophy from Kant to Fichte.* Cambridge, Mass., and London: Harvard University Press, 1987.

Berman, David. "Deism, Immortality, and the Art of Theological Lying." In *Deism, Masonry, and the Enlightenment, Essays Honoring Alfred Owen Aldridge*, ed. J. A. Leo Lemay. Newark, N.J.: Associated University Presses, 1987.

Bissinger, Anton. "Zur metaphysischen Begründung der Wolffschen Ethik." In *Ch. Wolff, 1679–1754, Interpretationen zu seiner Philosophie und deren Wirkung*, Hamburg, 1983.

———. *Die Struktur der Gotteserkenntnis, Studien zur Philosophie Christian Wolffs.* Bonn: H. Bouvier, 1970.

Brown, Stuart. *Leibniz.* Minneapolis: University of Minnesota Press, 1984.

Cohen, Stuart A. *The Three Crowns: Structures of Communal Politics in*

Early Rabbinic Jewry. Cambridge: Cambridge University Press, 1990.

Cragg, Gerald R. *Reason and Authority in the Eighteenth Century*, London: Cambridge University Press, 1964.

Dubnov, Simon. *History of the Jews*, trans. Moshe Spiegel. Cranbury, N.J.: Thomas Yoseloff, 1971.

Einstein-Barzilay, Isaac. "Moses Mendelssohn (1729–1786), A Study in Ideas and Attitudes." *Jewish Quarterly Review* 52 (1961): 69–93.

Eisen, Arnold. *Galut: Modern Jewish Reflections on Homelessness and Homecoming*. Bloomington: University of Indiana Press, 1986.

Eisen, Arnold, "Divine Legislation as 'Ceremonial Script': Mendelssohn on the Commandments." In *AJS Review* 15, no. 2 (Fall 1990): 239–68.

Eliasberg, Mordecai. *Shvil ha-Zahav*. Warsaw, 1897.

Emmrich, Hanna. *Das Judentum bei Voltaire*. Berlin, 1930.

Fackenheim, Emil L. *Encounters Between Judaism and Modern Philosophy*. New York: Basic Books, 1973.

Faur, Jose. "The Basis for the Authority of the Divine Commandments According to Maimonides." *Tarbiz* 38, no. 1 (1968): 43–53.

Feiereis, Konrad, *Die Umprägung der Natürlichen Theologie in Religionsphilosophie* (Leipzig: St. Benno-Verlag, 1965).

Fox, Marvin. "Law and Ethics in Modern Jewish Philosophy: The Case of Moses Mendelssohn." *Proceedings of the American Academy for Jewish Religion* 43 (1976): 1–14.

Fradkin, Hillel. "The 'Separation' of Religion and Politics: The Paradoxes of Spinoza." *The Review of Politics* (Fall 1988): 603–27.

Gildin, Hilail. "Spinoza and the Political Problem." In *Spinoza, A Collection of Critical Essays*, ed. Marjorie Grene. New York: Anchor Books, 1973.

Graetz, Heinrich. *History of the Jews*, ed. Bella Löwy. Philadelphia: Jewish Publication Society, 1895.

Green, Kenneth Hart. "Moses Mendelssohn's Opposition to the *Herem*: The First Step Toward Denominationalism?" *Modern Judaism* 12, no. 1 (February 1992): 39–60.

Grua, Gaston. *Jurisprudence Universelle et Théodicée selon Leibniz*. Paris: Presses Universitaire de France, 1953.

Guttman, Julius. "Mendelssohn's *Jerusalem* and Spinoza's *Theologico-Political Treatise*." In *Studies in Jewish Thought*, ed. Alfred Jospe, pp. 361–86. Detroit: Wayne State University Press, 1981.

Guttman, Julius. *Philosophies of Judaism*, trans. David W. Silverman. New York, 1963.

Hazard, Paul. *The European Mind (1680–1715)*, trans. J. Lewis May. New York: New American Library, 1963.

Heinemann, Isaac. *Ta'ammei ha-Mitzvot be-Sefrut Yisrael*. Jerusalem, 1956.

Henrich, Dieter. *Der ontologische Gottesbeweis*. Tübingen: J. C. B. Mohr, 1967.

Hick, John. *Evil and the God of Love*. San Francisco: Harper and Row, 1978.

Hinske, Norbert, ed. *"Ich Handle mit Vernunft . . ." Moses Mendelssohn und die europäische Aufklärung*. Hamburg: Meiner, 1981.

Hirsch, Emanuel, *Geschichte der Neuern Evangelischen Theologie*, vol. 4. Munster: Antiquariat T. Stenderhoff, 1964.

Katz, Jacob. *Tradition and Crisis*. New York: Schocken Books, 1961.

―――. *Exclusiveness and Tolerance*. New York: Schocken Books, 1973.

―――. *Out of the Ghetto*. Cambridge, Mass.: Harvard University Press, 1973.

―――. "To Whom Was Mendelssohn Replying in His *Jerusalem*." *Zion* 36, nos. 1–2 (1971).

Klippel, Diethelm. *Politische Freiheit und Freiheitsrechte im deutschen Naturrecht des 18. Jahrhunderts*. Paderborn, 1976.

Kreisel, Howard. " 'The Voice of God' in Medieval Jewish Philosophical Exegesis." *Da'at* 16 (1987): 29–38 [Hebrew].

Kuehn, Manfred. *Scottish Common Sense in Germany, 1768–1800: A Contribution to the History of Critical Philosophy*. Kingston and Montreal: McGill-Queen's University Press, 1987.

Levy, Ze'ev. "Johann Georg Hamann's Concept of Judaism and Controversy with Mendelssohn's 'Jerusalem'." *Leo Baeck Institute Year Book* 29 (1984).

Lovejoy, Arthur O. *The Great Chain of Being*. Cambridge, Mass.: Harvard University Press, 1976.

Manuel, Frank. *The Eighteenth Century Confronts the Gods*. Cambridge, Mass.: Harvard University Press, 1959.

Mendes-Flohr, Paul, and Reinharz, Jehuda. *The Jew in the Modern World*. Oxford and New York: Oxford University Press, 1980.

Meyer, Michael. *The Origins of the Modern Jew*. Detroit: Wayne State University Press, 1967.

Morgan, Michael. "History and Modern Jewish Thought: Spinoza and Mendelssohn on the Ritual Law." *Judaism* 30 (1981): 467–79.

Novak, David. *The Image of the Non-Jew in Judaism, An Historical and Constructive Study of the Noahide Laws*. New York: E. Mellen Press, 1983.

Orwin, Clifford. "Civility." *The American Scholar* (Autumn 1991): 555–568.

Pangle, Thomas. *The Spirit of Modern Republicanism: The Moral Vision of the American Founders and the Philosophy of Locke*. Chicago: University of Chicago Press, 1988.

Rabieh, Michael S. "The Reasonableness of Locke, or the Questionableness of Christianity." *The Journal of Politics* 53, no. 4 (November 1991): 933–39.

Reventlow, Henning Graf. *The Authority of the Bible and the Rise of the Modern World*, trans. John Bowden. Philadelphia: Fortress Press, 1984.

Rohls, Jan. *Theologie und Metaphysik, Der ontologische Gottbeweis und seine Kritiker*. Gütersloh: Gutersloher Verlaghaus G. Mohn, 1987.

Rosenbloom, Noah. "Theological Impediments to a Hebrew Version of Mendelssohn's *Phaedon*." *Proceedings for the Academy of Jewish Research* 54 (1990).

Rotenstreich, Nathan. *Jewish Philosophy in Modern Times*. New York: Holt, Rinehart and Winston, 1968.

_____. "Between Historical Truth and Religion of Reason." *Jerusalem Studies in Jewish Thought* 9, Part II (1990): 275–93.

_____. *Jews and German Philosophy*. New York: Schocken Books, 1984.

Saine, Thomas P. *Von der Kopernikanischen bis zur Französischen Revolution, Die Auseinandersetzung der deutschen Frühaufklärung mit der neuen Zeit*. Berlin: Erich Schmidt, 1987.

Schneider, Hans Joachim. *Moses Mendelssohns Anthropologie und Ästhetik*. Berlin, 1970.

Schneiders, Werner. *Die wahre Aufklärung, Zum Selbstverständnis der deutschen Aufklärung*. Freiburg, 1974.

Schweid, Eliezer. *Ha-Yehudi ha-Boded veha-Yahadut*, Tel Aviv, 1974.

_____. *Toldot he-Hagut haYehudit be-Et haHadashah*. Jerusalem: Hakibbutz Hameuchad and Keter, 1977.

Schweitzer, Albert. *The Quest of the Historical Jesus*, New York: Macmillan, 1948.

Shmueli, Efraim. *Seven Jewish Cultures: A Reinterpretation of Jewish History and Thought*, trans. Gila Shmueli. Cambridge: Cambridge University Press, 1990.

Sigad, Ron. "Moshe Mendelssohn—Yahadut, Politikah Elohit u-Medinat Yisrael." *Da'at*, no.7 (1981): 93–103 [Hebrew].

Sirat, Colette. *A History of Jewish Philosophy in the Middle Ages*. Cambridge: Cambridge University Press, 1985.

Strauss, Leo. *Natural Right and History*. Chicago: University of Chicago Press, 1953.

_____. *On Tyranny*. Ithaca, N.Y.: Cornell University Press, 1963.

_____. *Persecution and the Art of Writing*. Glencoe, Ill.: The Free Press, 1952.

_____. *Spinoza's Critique of Religion*. New York: Schocken Books, 1965.

Sullivan, Robert E. *John Toland and the Deist Controversy*. Cambridge, Mass., and London: Harvard University Press, 1981.

Timm, Hermann. *Gott und die Freiheit*. Frankfurt am Main, 1974.

Torrey, Norman L. *Voltaire and the English Deists*. New Haven, Conn.: Yale University Press, 1963.

Velkley, Richard L. *Freedom and the End of Reason*. Chicago and London: University of Chicago Press, 1989.

Walker, D. P. *The Decline of Hell: Seventeenth-Century Discussions of Eternal Torment*. Chicago: University of Chicago Press, 1964.

Wood, Allen W. *Kant's Rational Theology*. Ithaca, N.Y.: Cornell University Press, 1978.

Yovel, Yirmiahu. "Bible Interpretation as Philosophical Praxis: A Study of Spinoza and Kant." *Journal of the History of Philosophy* 11 (1973): 193.

———. *Kant and the Philosophy of History*. Princeton, N.J.: Princeton University Press, 1980.

Zuckert, Michael. "Of Wary Physicians and Weary Readers: The Debate on Locke's Way of Writing." *Independent Journal of Philosophy* 2 (1978): 55–66.

———. "John Locke and the Problem of Civil Religion." In *The Moral Foundations of the American Republic*, ed. Robert H. Horwitz, pp. 181–203. Charlottesville: University Press of Virginia, 1986.

Index

Talbert, Charles H., 26, 255
Teller, Dean Wilhelm Abraham, 276–277
Theocracy, 147, 238 n. 123, 245–246, 253, 264–265
Timm, Heinrich, 72, 94 n. 25
Tindall, Matthew, 135, 148–149
Toland, John, 135

Velkley, Richard, 71
Voltaire, Francois Marie Arouet de, 7, 135–137, 148–150, 196, 199, 204, 206
Wizenmann, Thomas, 79–86, 89, 91, 92, 96 n. 53, 189–190, 192–193, 288 n. 93

Wolfenbuttel Fragments. *See* Lessing, Gotthold Ephraim; Reimarus, Hermann Samuel
Wolff, ix, xi, xiii, 1, 2, 5, 22, 25–26, 37–38, 46, 71, 105–107, 116, 126, 133, 160, 290; on atheists, 103–104; on providence, 20–21, 99; on perfection, 100–103; on politics, 103–104, 111–112
Wood, Allen W., 44

Yehudah Halevi, 170–174
Yovel Yirmiahu, 280

Zuckert, Michael, 249–252, 261